Tom Stoppard
Plays Five

Tom Stoppard's other work includes *Rosencrantz and Guildenstern Are Dead*, *The Real Inspector Hound*, *Jumpers*, *Travesties*, *Night and Day*, *Every Good Boy Deserves Favour* (with André Previn), *After Magritte*, *Dirty Linen*, *The Real Thing*, *Hapgood*, *Arcadia*, *Indian Ink*, *The Invention of Love*, the trilogy *The Coast of Utopia* and *Rock 'n' Roll*. His radio plays include: *If You're Glad I'll Be Frank*, *Albert's Bridge*, *Where Are They Now?*, *Artist Descending a Staircase*, *The Dog It Was That Died* and *In the Native State*. Work for television includes *Professional Foul* and *Squaring the Circle*. His film credits include *Empire of the Sun*, *Rosencrantz and Guildenstern Are Dead*, which he also directed, *Shakespeare in Love* (with Marc Norman) and *Enigma*.

TOM STOPPARD

Plays Five

Arcadia
The Real Thing
Night and Day
Indian Ink
Hapgood

faber and faber

This collection first published in 1999
by Faber and Faber Limited
Bloomsbury House
74-77 Great Russell Street
London WC1B 3DA

Typeset by Country Setting, Kingsdown, Kent CT14 8ES
Printed in the UK by CPI Bookmarque, Croydon, CR0 4TD

A CIP record for this book is
available from the British Library

ISBN 978-0-571-19751-4

11 13 15 17 19 20 18 16 14 12

Contents

ARCADIA

Characters
in order of appearance

Thomasina Coverly
aged thirteen, later sixteen

Septimus Hodge
her tutor, aged twenty-two, later twenty-five

Jellaby
a butler, middle-aged

Ezra Chater
a poet, aged thirty-one

Richard Noakes
a landscape architect, middle-aged

Lady Croom
middle thirties

Capt. Brice, RN
middle thirties

Hannah Jarvis
an author, late thirties

Chloë Coverly
aged eighteen

Bernard Nightingale
a don, late thirties

Valentine Coverly
aged twenty-five to thirty

Gus Coverly
aged fifteen

Augustus Coverly
aged fifteen

Arcadia was first performed at the Lyttelton Theatre, Royal National Theatre, on 13 April 1993. The cast was as follows:

Thomasina Coverly Emma Fielding
Septimus Hodge Rufus Sewell
Jellaby Allan Mitchell
Ezra Chater Derek Hutchinson
Richard Noakes Sidney Livingstone
Lady Croom Harriet Walter
Captain Brice, RN Graham Sinclair
Hannah Jarvis Felicity Kendal
Chloë Coverly Harriet Harrison
Bernard Nightingale Bill Nighy
Valentine Coverly Samuel West
Gus Coverly, Augustus Coverly Timothy Matthews

Director Trevor Nunn
Designer Mark Thompson
Lighting Paul Pyant
Music Jeremy Sams

Act One

A room on the garden front of a very large country house in Derbyshire in April 1809. Nowadays, the house would be called a stately home. The upstage wall is mainly tall, shapely, uncurtained windows, one or more of which work as doors. Nothing much need be said or seen of the exterior beyond. We come to learn that the house stands in the typical English park of the time. Perhaps we see an indication of this, perhaps only light and air and sky.

The room looks bare despite the large table which occupies the centre of it. The table, the straight-backed chairs and, the only other item of furniture, the architect's stand or reading stand, would all be collectable pieces now but here, on an uncarpeted wood floor, they have no more pretension than a schoolroom, which is indeed the main use of this room at this time. What elegance there is, is architectural, and nothing is impressive but the scale. There is a door in each of the side walls. These are closed, but one of the french windows is open to a bright but sunless morning.

There are two people, each busy with books and paper and pen and ink, separately occupied. The pupil is Thomasina Coverly, aged 13. The tutor is Septimus Hodge, aged 22. Each has an open book. Hers is a slim mathematics primer. His is a handsome thick quarto, brand new, a vanity production, with little tapes to tie when the book is closed. His loose papers, etc, are kept in a stiff-backed portfolio which also ties up with tapes.

Septimus has a tortoise which is sleepy enough to serve as a paperweight.

Elsewhere on the table there is an old-fashioned theodolite and also some other books stacked up.

Thomasina Septimus, what is carnal embrace?

Septimus Carnal embrace is the practice of throwing one's arms around a side of beef.

Thomasina Is that all?

Septimus No . . . a shoulder of mutton, a haunch of venison well hugged, an embrace of grouse . . . *caro, carnis;* feminine; flesh.

Thomasina Is it a sin?

Septimus Not necessarily, my lady, but when carnal embrace is sinful it is a sin of the flesh, QED. We had *caro* in our Gallic Wars – 'The Britons live on milk and meat' – *'lacte et carne vivunt'*. I am sorry that the seed fell on stony ground.

Thomasina That was the sin of Onan, wasn't it, Septimus?

Septimus Yes. He was giving his brother's wife a Latin lesson and she was hardly the wiser after it than before. I thought you were finding a proof for Fermat's last theorem.

Thomasina It is very difficult, Septimus. You will have to show me how.

Septimus If I knew how, there would be no need to ask *you*. Fermat's last theorem has kept people busy for a hundred and fifty years, and I hoped it would keep *you* busy long enough for me to read Mr Chater's poem in praise of love with only the distraction of its own absurdities.

Thomasina Our Mr Chater has written a poem?

Septimus He believes he has written a poem, yes. I can see that there might be more carnality in your algebra than in Mr Chater's 'Couch of Eros'.

Thomasina Oh, it was not my algebra. I heard Jellaby telling cook that Mrs Chater was discovered in carnal embrace in the gazebo.

Septimus (*pause*) Really? With whom, did Jellaby happen to say?

Thomasina considers this with a puzzled frown.

Thomasina What do you mean, with whom?

Septimus With what? Exactly so. The idea is absurd. Where did this story come from?

Thomasina Mr Noakes.

Septimus Mr Noakes!

Thomasina Papa's landskip gardener. He was taking bearings in the garden when he saw – through his spyglass – Mrs Chater in the gazebo in carnal embrace.

Septimus And do you mean to tell me that Mr Noakes told the butler?

Thomasina No. Mr Noakes told Mr Chater. *Jellaby* was told by the groom, who overheard Mr Noakes telling Mr Chater, in the stable yard.

Septimus Mr Chater being engaged in closing the stable door.

Thomasina What do you mean, Septimus?

Septimus So, thus far, the only people who know about this are Mr Noakes the landskip architect, the groom, the butler, the cook and, of course, Mrs Chater's husband, the poet.

Thomasina And Arthur who was cleaning the silver, and the bootboy. And now you.

Septimus Of course. What else did he say?

Thomasina Mr Noakes?

Septimus No, not Mr Noakes. Jellaby. You heard Jellaby telling the cook.

Thomasina Cook hushed him almost as soon as he started. Jellaby did not see that I was being allowed to finish yesterday's upstairs' rabbit pie before I came to my lesson. I think you have not been candid with me, Septimus. A gazebo is not, after all, a meat larder.

Septimus I never said my definition was complete.

Thomasina Is carnal embrace kissing?

Septimus Yes.

Thomasina And throwing one's arms around Mrs Chater?

Septimus Yes. Now, Fermat's last theorem –

Thomasina I thought as much. I hope you are ashamed.

Septimus I, my lady?

Thomasina If *you* do not teach me the true meaning of things, who will?

Septimus Ah. Yes, I am ashamed. Carnal embrace is sexual congress, which is the insertion of the male genital organ into the female genital organ for purposes of procreation and pleasure. Fermat's last theorem, by contrast, asserts that when x, y and z are whole numbers each raised to power of n, the sum of the first two can never equal the third when n is greater than 2.

Pause.

Thomasina Eurghhh!

Septimus Nevertheless, that is the theorem.

Thomasina It is disgusting and incomprehensible. Now when I am grown to practise it myself I shall never do so without thinking of you.

Septimus Thank you very much, my lady. Was Mrs Chater down this morning?

Thomasina No. Tell me more about sexual congress.

Septimus There is nothing more to be said about sexual congress.

Thomasina Is it the same as love?

Septimus Oh no, it is much nicer than that.

One of the side doors leads to the music room. It is the other side door which now opens to admit Jellaby, the butler.

I am teaching, Jellaby.

Jellaby Beg your pardon, Mr Hodge, Mr Chater said it was urgent you receive his letter.

Septimus Oh, very well. (*Septimus takes the letter.*) Thank you. (*And to dismiss Jellaby.*) Thank you.

Jellaby (*holding his ground*) Mr Chater asked me to bring him your answer.

Septimus My answer?

He opens the letter. There is no envelope as such, but there is a 'cover' which, folded and sealed, does the same service. Septimus tosses the cover negligently aside and reads.

Well, my answer is that as is my custom and my duty to his lordship I am engaged until a quarter to twelve in the education of his daughter. When I am done, and if Mr Chater is still there, I will be happy to wait upon him in – (*He checks the letter.*) – in the gunroom.

Jellaby I will tell him so, thank you, sir.

Septimus folds the letter and places it between the pages of 'The Couch of Eros'.

Thomasina What is for dinner, Jellaby?

Jellaby Boiled ham and cabbages, my lady, and a rice pudding.

Thomasina Oh, goody.

Jellaby leaves.

Septimus Well, so much for Mr Noakes. He puts himself forward as a gentleman, a philosopher of the picturesque, a visionary who can move mountains and cause lakes, but in the scheme of the garden he is as the serpent.

Thomasina When you stir your rice pudding, Septimus, the spoonful of jam spreads itself round making red trails like the picture of a meteor in my astronomical atlas. But if you stir backward, the jam will not come together again. Indeed, the pudding does not notice and continues to turn pink just as before. Do you think this is odd?

Septimus No.

Thomasina Well, I do. You cannot stir things apart.

Septimus No more you can, time must needs run backward, and since it will not, we must stir our way onward mixing as we go, disorder out of disorder into disorder until pink is complete, unchanging and unchangeable, and we are done with it for ever. This is known as free will or self-determination.

He picks up the tortoise and moves it a few inches as though it had strayed, on top of some loose papers, and admonishes it.

Sit!

Thomasina Septimus, do you think God is a Newtonian?

Septimus An Etonian? Almost certainly, I'm afraid. We must ask your brother to make it his first enquiry.

Thomasina No, Septimus, a Newtonian. Septimus! Am I the first person to have thought of this?

Septimus No.

Thomasina I have not said yet.

Septimus 'If everything from the furthest planet to the smallest atom of our brain acts according to Newton's law of motion, what becomes of free will?'

Thomasina No.

Septimus God's will.

Thomasina No.

Septimus Sin.

Thomasina (*derisively*) No!

Septimus Very well.

Thomasina If you could stop every atom in its position and direction, and if your mind could comprehend all the actions thus suspended, then if you were really, *really* good at algebra you could write the formula for all the future; and although nobody can be so clever as to do it, the formula must exist just as if one could.

Septimus (*pause*) Yes. (*Pause.*) Yes, as far as I know, you are the first person to have thought of this. (*Pause. With*

13

an effort.) In the margin of his copy of *Arithmetica,*
Fermat wrote that he had discovered a wonderful proof
of his theorem but, the margin being too narrow for his
purpose, did not have room to write it down. The note
was found after his death, and from that day to this –

Thomasina Oh! I see now! The answer is perfectly
obvious.

Septimus This time you may have overreached yourself.

*The door is opened, somewhat violently. Chater
enters.*

Mr Chater! Perhaps my message miscarried. I will be at
liberty at a quarter to twelve, if that is convenient.

Chater It is not convenient, sir. My business will not
wait.

Septimus Then I suppose you have Lord Croom's
opinion that your business is more important than his
daughter's lesson.

Chater I do not, but, if you like, I will ask his lordship
to settle the point.

Septimus (*pause*) My lady, take Fermat into the music
room. There will be an extra spoonful of jam if you find
his proof.

Thomasina There is no proof, Septimus. The thing that
is perfectly obvious is that the note in the margin was a
joke to make you all mad. (*She leaves.*)

Septimus Now, sir, what is this business that cannot
wait?

Chater I think you know it, sir. You have insulted my
wife.

Septimus Insulted her? That would deny my nature, my conduct, and the admiration in which I hold Mrs Chater.

Chater I have heard of your admiration, sir! You insulted my wife in the gazebo yesterday evening!

Septimus You are mistaken. I made love to your wife in the gazebo. She asked me to meet her there, I have her note somewhere, I dare say I could find it for you, and if someone is putting it about that I did not turn up, by God, sir, it is a slander.

Chater You damned lecher! You would drag down a lady's reputation to make a refuge for your cowardice. It will not do! I am calling you out!

Septimus Chater! Chater, Chater, Chater! My dear friend!

Chater You dare to call me that. I demand satisfaction!

Septimus Mrs Chater demanded satisfaction and now you are demanding satisfaction. I cannot spend my time day and night satisfying the demands of the Chater family. As for your wife's reputation, it stands where it ever stood.

Chater You blackguard!

Septimus I assure you. Mrs Chater is charming and spirited, with a pleasing voice and a dainty step, she is the epitome of all the qualities society applauds in her sex – and yet her chief renown is for a readiness that keeps her in a state of tropical humidity as would grow orchids in her drawers in January.

Chater Damn you, Hodge, I will not listen to this! Will you fight or not?

Septimus (*definitively*) Not! There are no more than two or three poets of the first rank now living, and I will not shoot one of them dead over a perpendicular poke in a gazebo with a woman whose reputation could not be adequately defended with a platoon of musketry deployed by rota.

Chater Ha! You say so! Who are the others? In your opinion? – no – no –! – this goes very ill, Hodge. I will not be flattered out of my course. You say so, do you?

Septimus I do. And I would say the same to Milton were he not already dead. Not the part about his wife, of course –

Chater But among the living? Mr Southey?

Septimus Southey I would have shot on sight.

Chater (*shaking his head sadly*) Yes, he has fallen off. I admired 'Thalaba' *quite,* but 'Madoc', (*He chuckles.*) oh dear me! – but we are straying from the business here – you took advantage of Mrs Chater, and if that were not bad enough, it appears every stableboy and scullery maid on the strength –

Septimus Damn me! Have you not listened to a word I said?

Chater I have heard you, sir, and I will not deny I welcome your regard, God knows one is little appreciated if one stands outside the coterie of hacks and placemen who surround Jeffrey and the *Edinburgh* –

Septimus My dear Chater, they judge a poet by the seating plan of Lord Holland's table!

Chater By heaven, you are right! And I would very much like to know the name of the scoundrel who slandered my verse drama 'The Maid of Turkey' in the *Piccadilly Recreation,* too!

Septimus 'The Maid of Turkey'! I have it by my bedside! When I cannot sleep I take up 'The Maid of Turkey' like an old friend!

Chater (*gratified*) There you are! And the scoundrel wrote he would not give it to his dog for dinner were it covered in bread sauce and stuffed with chestnuts. When Mrs Chater read that, she wept, sir, and would not give herself to me for a fortnight – which recalls me to my purpose –

Septimus The new poem, however, will make your name perpetual –

Chater Whether it do or not –

Septimus It is not a question, sir. No coterie can oppose the acclamation of the reading public. 'The Couch of Eros' will take the town.

Chater Is that your estimation?

Septimus It is my intent.

Chater Is it, is it? Well, well! I do not understand you.

Septimus You see I have an early copy – sent to me for review. I say review, but I speak of an extensive appreciation of your gifts and your rightful place in English literature.

Chater Well, I must say. That is certainly . . . You have written it?

Septimus (*crisply*) Not yet.

Chater Ah. And how long does . . .?

Septimus To be done right, it first requires a careful re-reading of your book, of both your books, several readings, together with outlying works for an exhibition of deference or disdain as the case merits. I make notes,

17

of course, I order my thoughts, and finally, when all is ready and I am *calm in my mind* . . .

Chater (*shrewdly*) Did Mrs Chater know of this before she – before you –

Septimus I think she very likely did.

Chater (*triumphantly*) There is nothing that woman would not do for me! Now you have an insight to her character. Yes, by God, she is a wife to me, sir!

Septimus For that alone, I would not make her a widow.

Chater Captain Brice once made the same observation!

Septimus Captain Brice did?

Chater Mr Hodge, allow me to inscribe your copy in happy anticipation. Lady Thomasina's pen will serve us.

Septimus Your connection with Lord and Lady Croom you owe to your fighting her ladyship's brother?

Chater No! It was all nonsense, sir – a canard! But a fortunate mistake, sir. It brought me the patronage of a captain of His Majesty's Navy and the brother of a countess. I do not think Mr Walter Scott can say as much, and here I am, a respected guest at Sidley Park.

Septimus Well, sir, you can say you have received satisfaction.

> *Chater is already inscribing the book, using the pen and ink-pot on the table. Noakes enters through the door used by Chater. He carries rolled-up plans. Chater, inscribing, ignores Noakes. Noakes, on seeing the occupants, panics.*

Noakes Oh!

Septimus Ah, Mr Noakes! – my muddy-mettled rascal! Where's your spyglass?

Noakes I beg your leave – I thought her ladyship – excuse me –

He is beating an embarrassed retreat when he becomes rooted by Chater's voice. Chater reads his inscription in ringing tones.

Chater 'To my friend Septimus Hodge, who stood up and gave his best on behalf of the Author – Ezra Chater, at Sidley Park, Derbyshire, April 10th, 1809.' (*giving the book to Septimus*) There, sir – something to show your grandchildren!

Septimus This is more than I deserve, this is handsome, what do you say, Noakes?

They are interrupted by the appearance, outside the windows, of Lady Croom and Captain Edward Brice, RN. Her first words arrive through the open door.

Lady Croom Oh, no! Not the gazebo!

She enters, followed by Brice who carries a leather-bound sketch book.

Mr Noakes! What is this I hear?

Brice Not only the gazebo, but the boat-house, the Chinese bridge, the shrubbery –

Chater By God, sir! Not possible!

Brice Mr Noakes will have it so.

Septimus Mr Noakes, this is monstrous!

Lady Croom I am glad to hear it from *you*, Mr Hodge.

Thomasina (*opening the door from the music room*) May I return now?

Septimus (*attempting to close the door*) Not just yet –

Lady Croom Yes, let her stay. A lesson in folly is worth two in wisdom.

Brice takes the sketch book to the reading stand, where he lays it open. The sketch book is the work of Mr Noakes, who is obviously an admirer of Humphry Repton's 'Red Books'. The pages, drawn in water-colours, show 'before' and 'after' views of the landscape, and the pages are cunningly cut to allow the latter to be superimposed over portions of the former, though Repton did it the other way round.

Brice Is Sidley Park to be an Englishman's garden or the haunt of Corsican brigands?

Septimus Let us not hyperbolise, sir.

Brice It is rape, sir!

Noakes (*defending himself*) It is the modern style.

Chater (*under the same misapprehension as Septimus*) Regrettable, of course, but so it is.

Thomasina has gone to examine the sketch book.

Lady Croom Mr Chater, you show too much submission. Mr Hodge, I appeal to you.

Septimus Madam, I regret the gazebo, I sincerely regret the gazebo – and the boat-house up to a point – but the Chinese bridge, fantasy! – and the shrubbery I reject with contempt! Mr Chater! – would you take the word of a jumped-up jobbing gardener who sees carnal embrace in every nook and cranny of the landskip!

Thomasina Septimus, they are not speaking of carnal embrace, are you, Mama?

Lady Croom Certainly not. What do you know of carnal embrace?

Thomasina Everything, thanks to Septimus. In my opinion, Mr Noakes's scheme for the garden is perfect. It is a Salvator!

Lady Croom What does she mean?

Noakes (*answering the wrong question*) Salvator Rosa, your ladyship, the painter. He is indeed the very exemplar of the picturesque style.

Brice Hodge, what is this?

Septimus She speaks from innocence not from experience.

Brice You call it innocence? Has he ruined you, child?

   Pause.

Septimus Answer your uncle!

Thomasina (*to Septimus*) How is a ruined child different from a ruined castle?

Septimus On such questions I defer to Mr Noakes.

Noakes (*out of his depth*) A ruined castle is picturesque, certainly.

Septimus That is the main difference. (*to Brice*) I teach the classical authors. If I do not elucidate their meaning, who will?

Brice As her tutor you have a duty to keep her in ignorance.

Lady Croom Do not dabble in paradox, Edward, it puts you in danger of fortuitous wit. Thomasina, wait in your bedroom.

Thomasina (*retiring*) Yes, mama. I did not intend to get you into trouble, Septimus. I am very sorry for it. It is plain that there are some things a girl is allowed to understand, and these include the whole of algebra, but there are others, such as embracing a side of beef, that must be kept from her until she is old enough to have a carcass of her own.

Lady Croom One moment.

Brice What is she talking about?

Lady Croom Meat.

Brice Meat?

Lady Croom Thomasina, you had better remain. Your knowledge of the picturesque obviously exceeds anything the rest of us can offer. Mr Hodge, ignorance should be like an empty vessel waiting to be filled at the well of truth – not a cabinet of vulgar curios. Mr Noakes – now at last it is your turn –

Noakes Thank you, your ladyship –

Lady Croom Your drawing is a very wonderful transformation. I would not have recognized my own garden but for your ingenious book – is it not? – look! Here is the Park as it appears to us now, and here as it might be when Mr Noakes has done with it. Where there is the familiar pastoral refinement of an Englishman's garden, here is an eruption of gloomy forest and towering crag, of ruins where there was never a house, of water dashing against rocks where there was neither spring nor a stone I could not throw the length of a cricket pitch. My hyacinth dell is become a haunt for hobgoblins, my Chinese bridge, which I am assured is superior to the one at Kew, and for all I know at Peking, is usurped by a fallen obelisk overgrown with briars –

Noakes (*bleating*) Lord Little has one very similar –

Lady Croom I cannot relieve Lord Little's misfortunes by adding to my own. Pray, what is this rustic hovel that presumes to superpose itself on my gazebo?

Noakes That is the hermitage, madam.

Lady Croom I am bewildered.

Brice It is all irregular, Mr Noakes.

Noakes It is, sir. Irregularity is one of the chiefest principles of the picturesque style –

Lady Croom But Sidley Park is already a picture, and a most amiable picture too. The slopes are green and gentle. The trees are companionably grouped at intervals that show them to advantage. The rill is a serpentine ribbon unwound from the lake peaceably contained by meadows on which the right amount of sheep are taste-fully arranged – in short, it is nature as God intended, and I can say with the painter, *'Et in Arcadia ego!'* 'Here I am in Arcadia,' Thomasina.

Thomasina Yes, mama, if you would have it so.

Lady Croom Is she correcting my taste or my translation?

Thomasina Neither are beyond correction, mama, but it was your geography caused the doubt.

Lady Croom Something has occurred with the girl since I saw her last, and surely that was yesterday. How old are you this morning?

Thomasina Thirteen years and ten months, mama.

Lady Croom Thirteen years and ten months. She is not due to be pert for six months at the earliest, or to have notions of taste for much longer. Mr Hodge, I hold you accountable. Mr Noakes, back to you –

Noakes Thank you, my –

Lady Croom You have been reading too many novels by Mrs Radcliffe, that is my opinion. This is a garden for *The Castle of Otranto* or *The Mysteries of Udolpho* –

Chater *The Castle of Otranto,* my lady, is by Horace Walpole.

Noakes (*thrilled*) Mr Walpole the gardener?!

Lady Croom Mr Chater, you are a welcome guest at Sidley Park but while you are one, *The Castle of Otranto* was written by whomsoever I say it was, otherwise what is the point of being a guest or having one?

The distant popping of guns heard.

Well, the guns have reached the brow – I will speak to his lordship on the subject, and we will see by and by – (*She stands looking out.*) Ah! – your friend has got down a pigeon, Mr Hodge. (*calls out*) Bravo, sir!

Septimus The pigeon, I am sure, fell to your husband or to your son, your ladyship – my schoolfriend was never a sportsman.

Brice (*looking out*) Yes, to Augustus! – bravo, lad!

Lady Croom (*outside*) Well, come along! Where are my troops?

Brice, Noakes and Chater obediently follow her, Chater making a detour to shake Septimus's hand fervently.

Chater My dear Mr Hodge!

Chater leaves also. The guns are heard again, a little closer.

Thomasina Pop, pop, pop . . . I have grown up in the sound of guns like the child of a siege. Pigeons and rooks in the close season, grouse on the heights from August, and the pheasants to follow – partridge, snipe, woodcock, and teal – pop – pop – pop, and the culling of the herd.

Papa has no need of the recording angel, his life is written in the game book.

Septimus A calendar of slaughter. 'Even in Arcadia, there am I!'

Thomasina Oh, phooey to Death! (*She dips a pen and takes it to the reading stand.*) I will put in a hermit, for what is a hermitage without a hermit? Are you in love with my mother, Septimus?

Septimus You must not be cleverer than your elders. It is not polite.

Thomasina Am I cleverer?

Septimus Yes. Much.

Thomasina Well, I am sorry, Septimus. (*She pauses in her drawing and produces a small envelope from her pocket.*) Mrs Chater came to the music room with a note for you. She said it was of scant importance, and that therefore I should carry it to you with the utmost safety, urgency and discretion. Does carnal embrace addle the brain?

Septimus (*taking the letter*) Invariably. Thank you. That is enough education for today.

Thomasina There. I have made him like the Baptist in the wilderness.

Septimus How picturesque.

Lady Croom is heard calling distantly for Thomasina who runs off into the garden, cheerfully, an uncomplicated girl. Septimus opens Mrs Chater's note. He crumples the envelope and throws it away. He reads the note, folds it and inserts it into the pages of 'The Couch of Eros'.

SCENE TWO

The lights come up on the same room, on the same sort of morning, in the present day, as is instantly clear from the appearance of Hannah Jarvis; and from nothing else.

Something needs to be said about this. The action of the play shuttles back and forth between the early nineteenth century and the present day, always in this same room. Both periods must share the stage of the room, without the additions and subtractions which would normally be expected. The general appearance of the room should offend neither period. In the case of props – books, paper, flowers, etc. – there is no absolute need to remove the evidence of one period to make way for another. However, books, etc., used in both periods should exist in both old and new versions. The landscape outside, we are told, has undergone changes. Again, what we see should neither change nor contradict.

On the above principle, the ink and pens etc., of the first scene can remain. Books and papers associated with Hannah's research, in Scene Two, can have been on the table from the beginning of the play. And so on. During the course of the play the table collects this and that, and where an object from one scene would be an anachronism in another (say a coffee mug) it is simply deemed to have become invisible. By the end of the play the table has collected an inventory of objects.

Hannah is leafing through the pages of Mr Noakes's sketch book. Also to hand, opened and closed, are a number of small volumes like diaries (these turn out to be Lady Croom's 'garden books'). After a few moments, Hannah takes the sketch book to the windows, comparing the view with what has been drawn, and then she replaces the sketch book on the reading stand.

She wears nothing frivolous. Her shoes are suitable for

*the garden, which is where she goes now after picking up
the theodolite from the table. The room is empty for a
few moments.*

*One of the other doors opens to admit Chloë and
Bernard. She is the daughter of the house and is dressed
casually. Bernard, the visitor, wears a suit and a tie. His
tendency is to dress flamboyantly, but he has damped
it down for the occasion, slightly. A peacock-coloured
display handkerchief boils over in his breast pocket.
He carries a capacious leather bag which serves as a
briefcase.*

Chloë Oh! Well, she *was* here . . .

Bernard Ah . . . the french window . . .

Chloë Yes. Hang on.

*Chloë steps out through the garden door and dis-
appears from view. Bernard hangs on. The second
door opens and Valentine looks in.*

Valentine Sod.

*Valentine goes out again, closing the door. Chloë
returns, carrying a pair of rubber boots. She comes in
and sits down and starts exchanging her shoes for the
boots, while she talks.*

Chloë The best thing is, you wait here, save you tramp-
ing around. She spends a good deal of time in the
garden, as you may imagine.

Bernard Yes. Why?

Chloë Well, she's writing a history of the garden, didn't
you know?

Bernard No, I knew she was working on the Croom
papers but . . .

Chloë Well, it's not exactly a history of the garden either.

27

I'll let Hannah explain it. The trench you nearly drove into is all to do with it. I was going to say make yourself comfortable but that's hardly possible, everything's been cleared out, it's en route to the nearest lavatory.

Bernard Everything is?

Chloë No, this room is. They drew the line at chemical 'Ladies''.

Bernard Yes, I see. Did you say Hannah?

Chloë Hannah, yes. Will you be all right? (*She stands up wearing the boots.*) I won't be . . . (*But she has lost him.*) Mr Nightingale?

Bernard (*waking up*) Yes. Thank you. Miss Jarvis is Hannah Jarvis the author?

Chloë Yes. Have you read her book?

Bernard Oh, yes. Yes.

Chloë I bet she's in the hermitage, can't see from here with the marquee . . .

Bernard Are you having a garden party?

Chloë A dance for the district, our annual dressing up and general drunkenness. The wrinklies won't have it in the house, there was a teapot we once had to bag back from Christie's in the nick of time, so anything that can be destroyed, stolen or vomited on has been tactfully removed; tactlessly, I should say – (*She is about to leave.*)

Bernard Um – look – would you tell her – would you mind not mentioning my name just yet?

Chloë Oh. All right.

Bernard (*smiling*) More fun to surprise her. Would you mind?

28

Chloë No. But she's bound to ask . . . Should I give you another name, just for the moment?

Bernard Yes, why not?

Chloë Perhaps another bird, you're not really a Nightingale.

She leaves again. Bernard glances over the books on the table. He puts his briefcase down. There is the distant pop-pop of a shotgun. It takes Bernard vaguely to the window. He looks out. The door he entered by now opens and Gus looks into the room. Bernard turns and sees him.

Bernard Hello.

Gus doesn't speak. He never speaks. Perhaps he cannot speak. He has no composure, and faced with a stranger, he caves in and leaves again. A moment later the other door opens again and Valentine crosses the room, not exactly ignoring Bernard and yet ignoring him.

Valentine Sod, sod, sod, sod, sod, sod . . .

As many times as it takes him to leave by the opposite door, which he closes behind him. Beyond it, he can be heard shouting. Chlo! Chlo! Bernard's discomfort increases. The same door opens and Valentine returns. He looks at Bernard.

Bernard She's in the garden looking for Miss Jarvis.

Valentine Where is everything?

Bernard It's been removed for the, er . . .

Valentine The dance is all in the tent, isn't it?

Bernard Yes, but this is the way to the nearest toilet.

Valentine I need the commode.

Bernard Oh. Can't you use the toilet?

Valentine It's got all the game books in it.

Bernard Ah. The toilet has or the commode has?

Valentine Is anyone looking after you?

Bernard Yes. Thank you. I'm Bernard Nigh – I've come to see Miss Jarvis. I wrote to Lord Croom but unfortunately I never received a reply, so I –

Valentine Did you type it?

Bernard Type it?

Valentine Was your letter typewritten?

Bernard Yes.

Valentine My father never replies to typewritten letters. (*He spots a tortoise which has been half-hidden on the table.*) Oh! Where have you been hiding, Lightning? (*He picks up the tortoise.*)

Bernard So I telephoned yesterday and I think I spoke to you –

Valentine To me? Ah! Yes! Sorry! You're doing a talk about – someone – and you wanted to ask Hannah – something –

Bernard Yes. As it turns out. I'm hoping Miss Jarvis will look kindly on me.

Valentine I doubt it.

Bernard Ah, you know about research?

Valentine I know Hannah.

Bernard Has she been here long?

Valentine Well in possession, I'm afraid. My mother had read her book, you see. Have you?

Bernard No. Yes. Her book. Indeed.

Valentine She's terrifically pleased with herself.

Bernard Well, I dare say if I wrote a bestseller –

Valentine No, for reading it. My mother basically reads gardening books.

Bernard She must be delighted to have Hannah Jarvis writing a book about her garden.

Valentine Actually it's about hermits.

Gus returns through the same door, and turns to leave again.

It's all right, Gus – what do you want? –

But Gus has gone again.

Well . . . I'll take Lightning for his run.

Bernard Actually, we've met before. At Sussex, a couple of years ago, a seminar . . .

Valentine Oh. Was I there?

Bernard Yes. One of my colleagues believed he had found an unattributed short story by D. H. Lawrence, and he analysed it on his home computer, most interesting, perhaps you remember the paper?

Valentine Not really. But I often sit with my eyes closed and it doesn't necessarily mean I'm awake.

Bernard Well, by comparing sentence structures and so forth, this chap showed that there was a ninety per cent chance that the story had indeed been written by the same person as *Women in Love*. To my inexpressible joy, one of your maths mob was able to show that on the same statistical basis there was a ninety per cent chance that Lawrence also wrote the *Just William* books and much of the previous day's *Brighton and Hove Argus*.

Valentine (*pause*) Oh, Brighton. Yes. I was there. (*and looking out*) Oh – here she comes, I'll leave you to talk. By the way, is yours the red Mazda?

Bernard Yes.

Valentine If you want a tip I'd put it out of sight through the stable arch before my father comes in. He won't have anyone in the house with a Japanese car. Are you queer?

Bernard No, actually.

Valentine Well, even so.

Valentine leaves, closing the door. Bernard keeps staring at the closed door. Behind him, Hannah comes to the garden door.

Hannah Mr Peacock?

Bernard looks round vaguely then checks over his shoulder for the missing Peacock, then recovers himself and turns on the Nightingale bonhomie.

Bernard Oh . . . hello! Hello. Miss Jarvis, of course. Such a pleasure. I was thrown for a moment – the photograph doesn't do you justice.

Hannah Photograph? (*Her shoes have got muddy and she is taking them off.*)

Bernard On the book. I'm sorry to have brought you indoors, but Lady Chloë kindly insisted she –

Hannah No matter – you would have muddied your shoes.

Bernard How thoughtful. And how kind of you to spare me a little of your time.

He is overdoing it. She shoots him a glance.

Hannah Are you a journalist?

Bernard (*shocked*) No!

Hannah (*resuming*) I've been in the ha-ha, very squelchy.

Bernard (*unexpectedly*) Ha-*hah!*

Hannah What?

Bernard A theory of mine. Ha-hah, not ha-ha. If you were strolling down the garden and all of a sudden the ground gave way at your feet, you're not going to go 'ha-ha', you're going to jump back and go 'ha-hah!', or more probably, 'Bloody 'ell!'. . . though personally I think old Murray was up the pole on that one – in France, you know, 'ha-ha' is used to denote a strikingly ugly woman, a much more likely bet for something that keeps the cows off the lawn.

This is not going well for Bernard but he seems blithely unaware. Hannah stares at him for a moment.

Hannah Mr Peacock, what can I do for you?

Bernard Well, to begin with, you can call me Bernard, which is my name.

Hannah Thank you.

She goes to the garden door to bang her shoes together and scrape off the worst of the mud.

Bernard The book! – the book is a revelation! To see Caroline Lamb through your eyes is really like seeing her for the first time. I'm ashamed to say I never read her fiction, and how right you are, it's extraordinary stuff – Early Nineteenth is my period as much as anything is.

Hannah You teach?

Bernard Yes. And write, like you, like we all, though I've never done anything which has sold like *Caro*.

Hannah I don't teach.

Bernard No. All the more credit to you. To rehabilitate a forgotten writer, I suppose you could say that's the main reason for an English don.

Hannah Not to teach?

Bernard Good God, no, let the brats sort it out for themselves. Anyway, many congratulations. I expect someone will be bringing out Caroline Lamb's oeuvre now?

Hannah Yes, I expect so.

Bernard How wonderful! Bravo! Simply as a document shedding reflected light on the character of Lord Byron, it's bound to be –

Hannah Bernard. You did say Bernard, didn't you?

Bernard I did.

Hannah I'm putting my shoes on again.

Bernard Oh. You're not going to go out?

Hannah No, I'm going to kick you in the balls.

Bernard Right. Point taken. Ezra Chater.

Hannah Ezra Chater.

Bernard Born Twickenham, Middlesex, 1778, author of two verse narratives, 'The Maid of Turkey', 1808, and 'The Couch of Eros', 1809. Nothing known after 1809, disappears from view.

Hannah I see. And?

Bernard (*reaching for his bag*) There is a Sidley Park connection. (*He produces 'The Couch of Eros' from the bag. He reads the inscription.*) 'To my friend Septimus Hodge, who stood up and gave his best on behalf of the Author – Ezra Chater, at Sidley Park, Derbyshire, April 10th 1809. (*He gives her the book.*) I am in your hands.

Hannah 'The Couch of Eros'. Is it any good?

Bernard Quite surprising.

Hannah You think there's a book in him?

Bernard No, no – a monograph perhaps for the *Journal of English Studies*. There's almost nothing on Chater, not a word in the *DNB*, of course – by that time he'd been completely forgotten.

Hannah Family?

Bernard Zilch. There's only one other Chater in the British Library database.

Hannah Same period?

Bernard Yes, but he wasn't a poet like our Ezra, he was a botanist who described a dwarf dahlia in Martinique and died there after being bitten by a monkey.

Hannah And Ezra Chater?

Bernard He gets two references in the periodical index, one for each book, in both cases a substantial review in the *Piccadilly Recreation,* a thrice weekly folio sheet, but giving no personal details.

Hannah And where was this (*the book*)?

Bernard Private collection. I've got a talk to give next week, in London, and I think Chater is interesting, so anything on him, or this Septimus Hodge, Sidley Park, any leads at all . . . I'd be most grateful.

Pause.

Hannah Well! This is a new experience for me. A grovelling academic.

Bernard Oh, I say.

Hannah Oh, but it is. All the academics who reviewed my book patronized it.

Bernard Surely not.

Hannah Surely yes. The Byron gang unzipped their flies and patronized all over it. Where is it you don't bother to teach, by the way?

Bernard Oh, well, Sussex, actually.

Hannah Sussex. (*She thinks a moment.*) Nightingale. Yes; a thousand words in the *Observer* to see me off the premises with a pat on the bottom. You must know him.

Bernard As I say, I'm in your hands.

Hannah Quite. Say please, then.

Bernard Please.

Hannah Sit down, do.

Bernard Thank you.

He takes a chair. She remains standing. Possibly she smokes; if so, perhaps now. A short cigarette-holder sounds right, too. Or brown-paper cigarillos.

Hannah How did you know I was here?

Bernard Oh, I didn't. I spoke to the son on the phone but he didn't mention you by name and then he forgot to mention me.

Hannah Valentine. He's at Oxford, technically.

Bernard Yes, I met him. Brideshead Regurgitated.

Hannah My fiancé. (*She holds his look.*)

Bernard (*pause*) I'll take a chance. You're lying.

Hannah (*pause*) Well done, Bernard.

Bernard Christ.

Hannah He calls me his fiancée.

Bernard Why?

Hannah It's a joke.

Bernard You turned him down?

Hannah Don't be silly, do I look like the next Countess of –

Bernard No, no – a freebie. The joke that consoles. My tortoise Lightning, my fiancée Hannah.

Hannah Oh. Yes. You have a way with you, Bernard. I'm not sure I like it.

Bernard What's he doing, Valentine?

Hannah He's a postgrad. Biology.

Bernard No, he's a mathematician.

Hannah Well, he's doing grouse.

Bernard Grouse?

Hannah Not actual grouse. Computer grouse.

Bernard Who's the one who doesn't speak?

Hannah Gus.

Bernard What's the matter with him?

Hannah I didn't ask.

37

Bernard And the father sounds like a lot of fun.

Hannah Ah yes.

Bernard And the mother is the gardener. What's going on here?

Hannah What do you mean?

Bernard I nearly took her head off – she was standing in a trench at the time.

Hannah Archaeology. The house had a formal Italian garden until about 1740. Lady Croom is interested in garden history. I sent her my book – it contains, as you know if you've read it – which I'm not assuming, by the way – a rather good description of Caroline's garden at Brocket Hall. I'm here now helping Hermione.

Bernard (*impressed*) Hermione.

Hannah The records are unusually complete and they have never been worked on.

Bernard I'm beginning to admire you.

Hannah Before was bullshit?

Bernard Completely. Your photograph does you justice, I'm not sure the book does.

She considers him. He waits, confident.

Hannah Septimus Hodge was the tutor.

Bernard (*quietly*) Attagirl.

Hannah His pupil was the Croom daughter. There was a son at Eton. Septimus lived in the house: the pay book specifies allowances for wine and candles. So, not quite a guest but rather more than a steward. His letter of self-recommendation is preserved among the papers. I'll dig it out for you. As far as I remember he studied mathematics and natural philosophy at Cambridge. A scientist, therefore, as much as anything.

Bernard I'm impressed. Thank you. And Chater?

Hannah Nothing.

Bernard Oh. Nothing at all?

Hannah I'm afraid not.

Bernard How about the library?

Hannah The catalogue was done in the 1880s. I've been through the lot.

Bernard Books or catalogue?

Hannah Catalogue.

Bernard Ah. Pity.

Hannah I'm sorry.

Bernard What about the letters? No mention?

Hannah I'm afraid not. I've been very thorough in your period because, of course, it's my period too.

Bernard Is it? Actually, I don't quite know what it is you're . . .

Hannah The Sidley hermit.

Bernard Ah. Who's he?

Hannah He's my peg for the nervous breakdown of the Romantic Imagination. I'm doing landscape and literature 1750 to 1834.

Bernard What happened in 1834?

Hannah My hermit died.

Bernard Of course.

Hannah What do you mean, of course?

Bernard Nothing.

Hannah Yes, you do.

Bernard No, no . . . However, Coleridge also died in 1834.

Hannah So he did. What a stroke of luck. (*softening*) Thank you, Bernard. (*She goes to the reading stand and opens Noakes's sketch book.*) Look – there he is.

Bernard goes to look.

Bernard Mmm.

Hannah The only known likeness of the Sidley hermit.

Bernard Very biblical.

Hannah Drawn in by a later hand, of course. The hermitage didn't yet exist when Noakes did the drawings.

Bernard Noakes the painter?

Hannah Landscape gardener. He'd do these books for his clients, as a sort of prospectus. (*She demonstrates.*) Before and after, you see. This is how it all looked until, say, 1810 – smooth, undulating, serpentine – open water, clumps of trees, classical boat-house –

Bernard Lovely. The real England.

Hannah You can stop being silly now, Bernard. English landscape was invented by gardeners imitating foreign painters who were evoking classical authors. The whole thing was brought home in the luggage from the grand tour. Here, look – Capability Brown doing Claude, who was doing Virgil. Arcadia! And here, superimposed by Richard Noakes, untamed nature in the style of Salvator Rosa. It's the Gothic novel expressed in landscape. Everything but vampires. There's an account of my hermit in a letter by your illustrious namesake.

Bernard Florence?

Hannah What?

Bernard No. You go on.

Hannah Thomas Love Peacock.

Bernard Ah yes.

Hannah I found it in an essay on hermits and anchorites published in the *Cornhill Magazine* in the 1860s . . . (*She fishes for the magazine itself among the books on the table, and finds it.*) . . . 1862 . . . Peacock calls him (*She quotes from memory.*) 'Not one of your village simpletons to frighten the ladies, but a savant among idiots, a sage of lunacy.'

Bernard An oxy-moron, so to speak.

Hannah (*busy*) Yes. What?

Bernard Nothing.

Hannah (*having found the place*) Here we are. 'A letter we have seen, written by the author of *Headlong Hall* nearly thirty years ago, tells of a visit to the Earl of Croom's estate, Sidley Park –'

Bernard Was the letter to Thackeray?

Hannah (*brought up short*) I don't know. Does it matter?

Bernard No. Sorry.

But the gaps he leaves for her are false promises – and she is not quick enough. That's how it goes.

Only, Thackeray edited the *Cornhill* until '63 when, as

you know, he died. His father had been with the East
India Company where Peacock, of course, had held the
position of Examiner, so it's quite possible that if the
essay were by Thackeray, the *letter* . . . Sorry. Go on.

Of course, the East India Library in Blackfriars has
most of Peacock's letters, so it would be quite easy to . . .
Sorry. Can I look?

Silently she hands him the Cornhill.

Yes, it's been topped and tailed, of course. It might be
worth . . . Go on. I'm listening . . . (*Leafing through the
essay, he suddenly chuckles.*) Oh yes, it's Thackeray all
right . . . (*He slaps the book shut.*) Unbearable . . . (*He
hands it back to her.*) What were you saying?

Hannah Are you always like this?

Bernard Like what?

Hannah The point is, the Crooms, of course, had the
hermit under their noses for twenty years so hardly
thought him worth remarking. As I'm finding out. The
Peacock letter is still the main source, unfortunately.
When I read this (*the magazine in her hand*) well, it was
one of those moments that tell you what your next book
is going to be. The hermit of Sidley Park was my . . .

Bernard Peg.

Hannah Epiphany.

Bernard Epiphany, that's it.

Hannah The hermit was *placed* in the landscape exactly
as one might place a pottery gnome. And there he lived
out his life as a garden ornament.

Bernard Did he do anything?

Hannah Oh, he was very busy. When he died, the

cottage was stacked solid with paper. Hundreds of pages.
Thousands. Peacock says he was suspected of genius. It
turned out, of course, he was off his head. He'd covered
every sheet with cabalistic proofs that the world was
coming to an end. It's perfect, isn't it? A perfect symbol,
I mean.

Bernard Oh, yes. Of what?

Hannah The whole Romantic sham, Bernard! It's what
happened to the Enlightenment, isn't it? A century of
intellectual rigour turned in on itself. A mind in chaos
suspected of genius. In a setting of cheap thrills and false
emotion. The history of the garden says it all, beautifully.
There's an engraving of Sidley Park in 1730 that makes
you want to weep. Paradise in the age of reason. By
1760 everything had gone – the topiary, pools and
terraces, fountains, an avenue of limes – the whole
sublime geometry was ploughed under by Capability
Brown. The grass went from the doorstep to the horizon
and the best box hedge in Derbyshire was dug up for the
ha-ha so that the fools could pretend they were living in
God's countryside. And then Richard Noakes came in to
bring God up to date. By the time he'd finished it looked
like this (*the sketch book*). The decline from thinking to
feeling, you see.

Bernard (*a judgement*) That's awfully good.

> *Hannah looks at him in case of irony but he is
> professional.*

No, that'll stand up.

Hannah Thank you.

Bernard Personally I like the ha-ha. Do you like hedges?

Hannah I don't like sentimentality.

Bernard Yes, I see. Are you sure? You seem quite sentimental over geometry. But the hermit is very very good. The genius of the place.

Hannah (*pleased*) That's my title!

Bernard Of course.

Hannah (*less pleased*) Of course?

Bernard Of course. Who was he when he wasn't being a symbol?

Hannah I don't know.

Bernard Ah.

Hannah I mean, yet.

Bernard Absolutely. What did they do with all the paper? Does Peacock say?

Hannah Made a bonfire.

Bernard Ah, well.

Hannah I've still got Lady Croom's garden books to go through.

Bernard Account books or journals?

Hannah A bit of both. They're gappy but they span the period.

Bernard Really? Have you come across Byron at all? As a matter of interest.

Hannah A first edition of 'Childe Harold' in the library, and *English Bards, I* think.

Bernard Inscribed?

Hannah No.

Bernard And he doesn't pop up in the letters at all?

44

Hannah Why should he? The Crooms don't pop up in his.

Bernard (*casually*) That's true, of course. But Newstead isn't so far away. Would you mind terribly if I poked about a bit? Only in the papers you've done with, of course.

Hannah twigs something.

Hannah Are you looking into Byron or Chater?

Chloë enters in stockinged feet through one of the side doors, laden with an armful of generally similar leather-covered ledgers. She detours to collect her shoes.

Chloë Sorry – just cutting through – there's tea in the pantry if you don't mind mugs –

Bernard How kind.

Chloë Hannah will show you.

Bernard Let me help you.

Chloë No, it's all right –

Bernard opens the opposite door for her.

Thank you – I've been saving Val's game books. Thanks.

Bernard closes the door.

Bernard Sweet girl.

Hannah Mmm.

Bernard Oh, really?

Hannah Oh really what?

Chloë's door opens again and she puts her head round it.

Chloë Meant to say, don't worry if father makes remarks about your car, Mr Nightingale, he's got a thing

45

about – (*and the Nightingale now being out of the bag*) ooh – ah, how was the surprise? – not yet, eh? Oh, well – sorry – tea, anyway – so sorry if I –

Embarrassed, she leaves again, closing the door. Pause.

Hannah You absolute shit. (*She heads off to leave.*)

Bernard The thing is, there's a Byron connection too.

Hannah stops and faces him.

Hannah I don't care.

Bernard You should. The Byron gang are going to get their dicks caught in their zip.

Hannah (*pause*) Oh really?

Bernard If we collaborate.

Hannah On what?

Bernard Sit down, I'll tell you.

Hannah I'll stand for the moment.

Bernard This copy of 'The Couch of Eros' belonged to Lord Byron.

Hannah It belonged to Septimus Hodge.

Bernard Originally, yes. But it was in Byron's library which was sold to pay his debts when he left England for good in 1816. The sales catalogue is in the British Library. 'Eros' was lot 74A and was bought by the book-seller and publisher John Nightingale of Opera Court, Pall Mall . . . whose name survives in the firm of Nightingale and Matlock, the present Nightingale being my cousin.

He pauses. Hannah hesitates and then sits down at the table.

I'll just give you the headlines. 1939, stock removed to Nightingale country house in Kent. 1945, stock returned to bookshop. Meanwhile, overlooked box of early nineteenth-century books languish in country house cellar until house sold to make way for the Channel Tunnel rail-link. 'Eros' discovered with sales slip from 1816 attached – photocopy available for inspection.

He brings this from his bag and gives it to Hannah who inspects it.

Hannah All right. It was in Byron's library.

Bernard A number of passages have been underlined.

Hannah picks up the book and leafs through it.

All of them, and only them – no, no, look at me, not at the book – all the underlined passages, word for word, were used as quotations in the review of 'The Couch of Eros' in the *Piccadilly Recreation* of April 30th 1809. The reviewer begins by drawing attention to his previous notice in the same periodical of 'The Maid of Turkey'.

Hannah The reviewer is obviously Hodge. 'My friend Septimus Hodge who stood up and gave his best on behalf of the Author.'

Bernard That's the point. The *Piccadilly* ridiculed both books.

Hannah (*pause*) Do the reviews read like Byron?

Bernard (*producing two photocopies from his case*) They read a damn sight more like Byron than Byron's review of Wordsworth the previous year.

Hannah glances over the photocopies.

Hannah I see. Well, congratulations. Possibly. Two previously unknown book reviews by the young Byron. Is that it?

Bernard No. Because of the tapes, three documents survived undisturbed in the book. (*He has been carefully opening a package produced from his bag. He has the originals. He holds them carefully one by one.*) 'Sir – we have a matter to settle. I wait on you in the gun room. E. Chater, Esq.'

'My husband has sent to town for pistols. Deny what cannot be proven – for Charity's sake – I keep my room this day.' Unsigned.

'Sidley Park, April 11th 1809. Sir – I call you a liar, a lecher, a slanderer in the press and a thief of my honour. I wait upon your arrangements for giving me satisfaction as a man and a poet. E. Chater, Esq.'

Pause.

Hannah Superb. But inconclusive. The book had seven years to find its way into Byron's possession. It doesn't connect Byron with Chater, or with Sidley Park. Or with Hodge for that matter. Furthermore, there isn't a hint in Byron's letters and this kind of scrape is the last thing he would have kept quiet about.

Bernard *Scrape?*

Hannah He would have made a comic turn out of it.

Bernard Comic turn, fiddlesticks! (*He pauses for effect.*) He killed Chater!

Hannah (*a raspberry*) Oh, really!

Bernard Chater was thirty-one years old. The author of two books. Nothing more is heard from him after 'Eros'. He disappears completely after April 1809. And Byron – Byron had just published his satire, *English Bards and Scotch Reviewers*, in March. He was just getting a name. Yet he sailed for Lisbon as soon as he could find a ship, and stayed abroad for two years.

Hannah, *this is fame*. Somewhere in the Croom papers there will be *something* –

Hannah There isn't, I've looked.

Bernard But you were looking for something else! It's not going to jump out at you like 'Lord Byron remarked wittily at breakfast!'

Hannah Nevertheless his presence would be unlikely to have gone unremarked. But there is nothing to suggest that Byron was here, and I don't believe he ever was.

Bernard All right, but let me have a look.

Hannah You'll queer my pitch.

Bernard Dear girl, I know how to handle myself –

Hannah And don't call me dear girl. If I find anything on Byron, or Chater, or Hodge, I'll pass it on. Nightingale, Sussex.

Pause. She stands up.

Bernard Thank you. I'm sorry about that business with my name.

Hannah Don't mention it . . .

Bernard What was Hodge's college, by the way?

Hannah Trinity.

Bernard Trinity?

Hannah Yes. (*She hesitates.*) Yes. Byron's old college.

Bernard How old was Hodge?

Hannah I'd have to look it up but a year or two older than Byron. Twenty-two . . .

Bernard Contemporaries at Trinity?

Hannah (*wearily*) Yes, Bernard, and no doubt they were both in the cricket eleven when Harrow played Eton at Lords!

Bernard approaches her and stands close to her.

Bernard (*evenly*) Do you mean that Septimus Hodge was at school with Byron?

Hannah (*falters slightly*) Yes . . . he must have been . . . as a matter of fact.

Bernard Well, you silly cow.

With a large gesture of pure happiness, Bernard throws his arms around Hannah and gives her a great smacking kiss on the cheek. Chloë enters to witness the end of this.

Chloë Oh – erm . . . I thought I'd bring it to you. (*She is carrying a small tray with two mugs on it.*)

Bernard I have to go and see about my car.

Hannah Going to hide it?

Bernard Hide it? I'm going to sell it! Is there a pub I can put up at in the village? (*He turns back to them as he is about to leave through the garden.*) Aren't you glad I'm here? (*He leaves.*)

Chloë He said he knew you.

Hannah He couldn't have.

Chloë No, perhaps not. He said he wanted to be a surprise, but I suppose that's different. I thought there was a lot of sexual energy there, didn't you?

Hannah What?

Chloë Bouncy on his feet, you see, a sure sign. Should I invite him for you?

Hannah To what? No.

Chloë You can invite him – that's better. He can come as your partner.

Hannah Stop it. Thank you for the tea.

Chloë If you don't want him, I'll have him. Is he married?

Hannah I haven't the slightest idea. Aren't you supposed to have a pony?

Chloë I'm just trying to fix you up, Hannah.

Hannah Believe me, it gets less important.

Chloë I mean for the dancing. He can come as Beau Brummell.

Hannah I don't want to dress up and I don't want a dancing partner, least of all Mr Nightingale. I don't dance.

Chloë Don't be such a prune. You were kissing him, anyway.

Hannah He was kissing me, and only out of general enthusiasm.

Chloë Well, don't say I didn't give you first chance. My genius brother will be much relieved. He's in love with you, I suppose you know.

Hannah (*angry*) That's a joke!

Chloë It's not a joke to him.

Hannah Of course it is – not even a joke – how can you be so ridiculous?

Gus enters from the garden, in his customary silent awkwardness.

Chloë Hello, Gus, what have you got?

Gus has an apple, just picked, with a leaf or two still attached. He offers the apple to Hannah.

Hannah (*surprised*) Oh! . . . Thank you!

Chloë (*leaving*) Told you. (*She closes the door on herself.*)

Hannah Thank you. Oh dear.

SCENE THREE

The schoolroom. The next morning. Present are: Thomasina, Septimus, Jellaby. We have seen this composition before: Thomasina at her place at the table; Septimus reading a letter which has just arrived; Jellaby waiting, having just delivered the letter.
'The Couch of Eros' is in front of Septimus, open, together with sheets of paper on which he has been writing. His portfolio is on the table. Plautus the tortoise is the paperweight. There is also an apple on the table now, the same apple from all appearances.

Septimus (*with his eyes on the letter*) Why have you stopped?

Thomasina is studying a sheet of paper, a 'Latin unseen' lesson. She is having some difficulty.

Thomasina *Solio insessa . . . in igne . . .* seated on a throne . . . in the fire . . . and also on a ship . . . *sedebat regina . . .* sat the queen . . .

Septimus There is no reply, Jellaby. Thank you. (*He folds the letter up and places it between the leaves of 'The Couch of Eros'.*)

Jellaby I will say so, sir.

Thomasina . . . the wind smelling sweetly . . . *purpureis velis* . . . by, with or from purple sails –

Septimus (*to Jellaby*) I will have something for the post, if you would be so kind.

Jellaby (*leaving*) Yes, sir.

Thomasina . . . was like as to – something – by, with or from lovers – oh, Septimus! – *musica tibiarum imperabat* . . . music of pipes commanded . . .

Septimus 'Ruled' is better.

Thomasina . . . the silver oars – exciting the ocean – as if – as if – amorous –

Septimus That is very good. (*He picks up the apple. He picks off the twig and leaves, placing these on the table. With a pocket knife he cuts a slice of apple, and while he eats it, cuts another slice which he offers to Plautus.*)

Thomasina *Regina reclinabat* . . . the queen – was reclining – *praeter descriptionem* – indescribably – in a golden tent . . . like Venus and yet more –

Septimus Try to put some poetry into it.

Thomasina How can I if there is none in the Latin?

Septimus Oh, a critic!

Thomasina Is it Queen Dido?

Septimus No.

Thomasina Who is the poet?

Septimus Known to you.

Thomasina Known to me?

Septimus Not a Roman.

Thomasina Mr Chater?

Septimus Your translation is quite like Chater. (*He picks up his pen and continues with his own writing.*)

Thomasina I know who it is, it is your friend Byron.

Septimus Lord Byron, if you please.

Thomasina Mama is in love with Lord Byron.

Septimus (*absorbed*) Yes. Nonsense.

Thomasina It is not nonsense. I saw them together in the gazebo.

> *Septimus's pen stops moving, he raises his eyes to her at last.*

Lord Byron was reading to her from his satire, and mama was laughing, with her head in her best position.

Septimus She did not understand the satire, and was showing politeness to a guest.

Thomasina She is vexed with papa for his determination to alter the park, but that alone cannot account for her politeness to a guest. She came downstairs hours before her custom. Lord Byron was amusing at breakfast. He paid you a tribute, Septimus.

Septimus Did he?

Thomasina He said you were a witty fellow, and he had almost by heart an article you wrote about – well, I forget what, but it concerned a book called 'The Maid of Turkey' and how you would not give it to your dog for dinner.

Septimus Ah. Mr Chater was at breakfast, of course.

Thomasina He was, not like certain lazybones.

Septimus He does not have Latin to set and mathematics to correct. (*He takes Thomasina's lesson book from underneath Plautus and tosses it down the table to her.*)

Thomasina Correct? What was incorrect in it? (*She looks into the book.*) Alpha minus? Pooh! What is the minus for?

Septimus For doing more than was asked.

Thomasina You did not like my discovery?

Septimus A fancy is not a discovery.

Thomasina A gibe is not a rebuttal.

> *Septimus finishes what he is writing. He folds the pages into a letter. He has sealing wax and the means to melt it. He seals the letter and writes on the cover. Meanwhile –*

You are churlish with me because mama is paying attention to your friend. Well, let them elope, they cannot turn back the advancement of knowledge. I think it is an excellent discovery. Each week I plot your equations dot for dot, xs against ys in all manner of algebraical relation, and every week they draw themselves as commonplace geometry, as if the world of forms were nothing but arcs and angles. God's truth, Septimus, if there is an equation for a curve like a bell, there must be an equation for one like a bluebell, and if a bluebell, why not a rose? Do we believe nature is written in numbers?

Septimus We do.

Thomasina Then why do your equations only describe the shapes of manufacture?

Septimus I do not know.

Thomasina Armed thus, God could only make a cabinet.

Septimus He has mastery of equations which lead into infinities where we cannot follow.

Thomasina What a faint-heart! We must work outward from the middle of the maze. We will start with something simple. (*She picks up the apple leaf.*) I will plot this leaf and deduce its equation. You will be famous for being my tutor when Lord Byron is dead and forgotten.

> *Septimus completes the business with his letter. He puts the letter in his pocket.*

Septimus (*firmly*) Back to Cleopatra.

Thomasina Is it Cleopatra? – I hate Cleopatra!

Septimus You hate her? Why?

Thomasina Everything is turned to love with her. New love, absent love, lost love – I never knew a heroine that makes such noodles of our sex. It only needs a Roman general to drop anchor outside the window and away goes the empire like a christening mug into a pawn shop. If Queen Elizabeth had been a Ptolemy history would have been quite different – we would be admiring the pyramids of Rome and the great Sphinx of Verona.

Septimus God save us.

Thomasina But instead, the Egyptian noodle made carnal embrace with the enemy who burned the great library of Alexandria without so much as a fine for all that is overdue. Oh, Septimus! – can you bear it? All the lost plays of the Athenians! Two hundred at least by Aeschylus, Sophocles, Euripides – thousands of poems – Aristotle's own library brought to Egypt by the noodle's ancestors! How can we sleep for grief?

Septimus By counting our stock. Seven plays from Aeschylus, seven from Sophocles, *nineteen* from Euripides, my lady! You should no more grieve for the rest than for a buckle lost from your first shoe, or for your lesson book which will be lost when you are old. We shed as we pick up, like travellers who must carry everything in their arms, and what we let fall will be picked up by those behind. The procession is very long and life is very short. We die on the march. But there is nothing outside the march so nothing can be lost to it. The missing plays of Sophocles will turn up piece by piece, or be written again in another language. Ancient cures for diseases will reveal themselves once more. Mathematical discoveries glimpsed and lost to view will have their time again. You do not suppose, my lady, that if all of Archimedes had been hiding in the great library of Alexandria, we would be at a loss for a corkscrew? I have no doubt that the improved steam-driven heat-engine which puts Mr Noakes into an ecstasy that he and it and the modern age should all coincide, was described on papyrus. Steam and brass were not invented in Glasgow. Now, where are we? Let me see if I can attempt a free translation for you. At Harrow I was better at this than Lord Byron. (*He takes the piece of paper from her and scrutinizes it, testing one or two Latin phrases speculatively before committing himself.*) Yes – 'The barge she sat in, like a burnished throne . . . burned on the water . . . the – something – the poop was beaten gold, purple the sails, and – what's this? – oh yes, – so perfumed that –'

Thomasina (*catching on and furious*) Cheat!

Septimus (*imperturbably*) – 'the winds were lovesick with them. . .'

Thomasina Cheat!

Septimus '. . . the oars were silver which to the tune of flutes kept stroke . . .'

Thomasina (*jumping to her feet*) Cheat! Cheat! Cheat!

Septimus (*as though it were too easy to make the effort worthwhile*) '. . . and made the water which they beat to follow faster, as *amorous* of their strokes. For her own person, it beggared all description – she did lie in her pavilion –'

Thomasina, in tears of rage, is hurrying out through the garden.

Thomasina I hope you die!

She nearly bumps into Brice who is entering. She runs out of sight. Brice enters.

Brice Good God, man, what have you told her?

Septimus Told her? Told her what?

Brice Hodge!

Septimus looks outside the door, slightly contrite about Thomasina, and sees that Chater is skulking out of view.

Septimus Chater! My dear fellow! Don't hang back – come in, sir!

Chater allows himself to be drawn sheepishly into the room, where Brice stands on his dignity.

Chater Captain Brice does me the honour – I mean to say, sir, whatever you have to say to me, sir, address yourself to Captain Brice.

Septimus How unusual. (*to Brice*) Your wife did not appear yesterday, sir. I trust she is not sick?

Brice My wife? I have no wife. What the devil do you mean, sir?

58

Septimus makes to reply, but hesitates, puzzled. He turns back to Chater.

Septimus I do not understand the scheme, Chater. Whom do I address when I want to speak to Captain Brice?

Brice Oh, slippery, Hodge – slippery!

Septimus (*to Chater*) By the way, Chater – (*He interrupts himself and turns back to Brice, and continues as before.*) – by the way, Chater, I have amazing news to tell you. Someone has taken to writing wild and whirling letters in your name. I received one not half an hour ago.

Brice (*angrily*) Mr Hodge! Look to your honour, sir! If you cannot attend to me without this foolery, nominate your second who might settle the business as between gentlemen. No doubt your friend Byron would do you the service.

Septimus gives up the game.

Septimus Oh yes, he would do me the service. (*His mood changes, he turns to Chater.*) Sir – I repent your injury. You are an honest fellow with no more malice in you than poetry.

Chater (*happily*) Ah well! – that is more like the thing! (*overtaken by doubt*) Is he apologizing?

Brice There is still the injury to his conjugal property, Mrs Chater's –

Chater Tush, sir!

Brice As you will – her tush. Nevertheless –

But they are interrupted by Lady Croom, also entering from the garden.

Lady Croom Oh – excellently found! Mr Chater, this will please you very much. Lord Byron begs a copy of your new book. He dies to read it and intends to include your name in the second edition of his *English Bards and Scotch Reviewers*.

Chater *English Bards and Scotch Reviewers,* your ladyship, is a doggerel aimed at Lord Byron's seniors and betters. If he intends to include me, he intends to insult me.

Lady Croom Well, of course he does, Mr Chater. Would you rather be thought not worth insulting? You should be proud to be in the company of Rogers and Moore and Wordsworth – ah! 'The Couch of Eros!' (*For she has spotted Septimus's copy of the book on the table.*)

Septimus That is my copy, madam.

Lady Croom So much the better – what are a friend's books for if not to be borrowed?

> *Note: 'The Couch of Eros' now contains the three letters, and it must do so without advertising the fact. This is why the volume has been described as a substantial quarto.*

Mr Hodge, you must speak to your friend and put him out of his affectation of pretending to quit us. I will not have it. He says he is determined on the Malta packet sailing out of Falmouth! His head is full of Lisbon and Lesbos, and his portmanteau of pistols, and I have told him it is not to be thought of. The whole of Europe is in a Napoleonic fit, all the best ruins will be closed, the roads entirely occupied with the movement of armies, the lodgings turned to billets and the fashion for godless republicanism not yet arrived at its natural reversion. He says his aim is poetry. One does not aim at poetry with pistols. At poets, perhaps. I charge you to take command of his pistols, Mr Hodge! He is not safe with them. His lameness, he confessed to me, is entirely the result of his habit from boyhood of shooting himself in the foot. What is that *noise?*

> *The noise is a badly played piano in the next room. It has been going on for some time since Thomasina left.*

Septimus The new Broadwood pianoforte, madam. Our music lessons are at an early stage.

Lady Croom Well, restrict your lessons to the *piano* side of the instrument and let her loose on the *forte* when she has learned something. (*Holding the book, she sails out back into the garden.*)

Brice Now! If that was not God speaking through Lady Croom, he never spoke through anyone!

Chater (*awed*) Take command of Lord Byron's pistols!

Brice You hear Mr Chater, sir – how will you answer him?

> *Septimus has been watching Lady Croom's progress up the garden. He turns back.*

Septimus By killing him. I am tired of him.

Chater (*startled*) Eh?

Brice (*pleased*) Ah!

Septimus Oh, damn your soul, Chater! Ovid would have stayed a lawyer and Virgil a farmer if they had known the bathos to which love would descend in your sportive satyrs and noodle nymphs! I am at your service with a half-ounce ball in your brain. May it satisfy you – behind the boat-house at daybreak – shall we say five o'clock? My compliments to Mrs Chater – have no fear for her, she will not want for protection while Captain Brice has a guinea in his pocket, he told her so himself.

Brice You lie, sir!

Septimus No, sir. Mrs Chater, perhaps.

Brice You lie, or you will answer to me!

Septimus (*wearily*) Oh, very well – I can fit you in at five minutes after five. And then it's off to the Malta packet out of Falmouth. You two will be dead, my penurious schoolfriend will remain to tutor Lady Thomasina, and I trust everybody including Lady Croom will be satisfied! (*He slams the door behind him.*)

Brice He is all bluster and bladder. Rest assured, Chater, I will let the air out of him.

> Brice leaves by the other door. Chater's assurance lasts only a moment. When he spots the flaw . . .

Chater Oh! But . . . (*He hurries out after Brice.*)

SCENE FOUR

Hannah and Valentine. She is reading aloud. He is listening. Lightning, the tortoise, is on the table and is not readily distinguishable from Plautus. In front of Valentine is Septimus's portfolio, recognizably so but naturally somewhat jaded. It is open. Principally associated with the portfolio (although it may contain sheets of blank paper also) are three items: a slim maths primer; a sheet of drawing paper on which there is a scrawled diagram and some mathematical notations, arrow marks, etc.; and Thomasina's mathematics lesson book, i.e. the one she writes in, which Valentine is leafing through as he listens to Hannah reading from the primer.

Hannah 'I, Thomasina Coverly, have found a truly

wonderful method whereby all the forms of nature must give up their numerical secrets and draw themselves through number alone. This margin being too mean for my purpose, the reader must look elsewhere for the New Geometry of Irregular Forms discovered by Thomasina Coverly.'

Pause. She hands Valentine the text book. Valentine looks at what she has been reading. From the next room, a piano is heard, beginning to play quietly, unintrusively, improvisationally.

Does it mean anything?

Valentine I don't know. I don't know what it means, except mathematically.

Hannah I meant mathematically.

Valentine (*now with the lesson book again*) It's an iterated algorithm.

Hannah What's that?

Valentine Well, it's . . . Jesus . . . it's an algorithm that's been . . . iterated. How'm I supposed to . . .? (*He makes an effort.*) The left-hand pages are graphs of what the numbers are doing on the right-hand pages. But all on different scales. Each graph is a small section of the previous one, blown up. Like you'd blow up a detail of a photograph, and then a detail of the detail, and so on, forever. Or in her case, till she ran out of pages.

Hannah Is it difficult?

Valentine The maths isn't difficult. It's what you did at school. You have some x-and-y equation. Any value for x gives you a value for y. So you put a dot where it's right for both x and y. Then you take the next value for x which gives you another value for y, and when you've

63

done that a few times you join up the dots and that's your graph of whatever the equation is.

Hannah And is that what she's doing?

Valentine No. Not exactly. Not at all. What she's doing is, every time she works out a value for *y*, she's using *that* as her next value for *x*. And so on. Like a feedback. She's feeding the solution back into the equation, and then solving it again. Iteration, you see.

Hannah And that's surprising, is it?

Valentine Well, it is a bit. It's the technique I'm using on my grouse numbers, and it hasn't been around for much longer than, well, call it twenty years.

Pause.

Hannah Why would she be doing it?

Valentine I have no idea. (*Pause.*) I thought you were doing the hermit.

Hannah I am. I still am. But Bernard, damn him . . . Thomasina's tutor turns out to have interesting connections. Bernard is going through the library like a bloodhound. The portfolio was in a cupboard.

Valentine There's a lot of stuff around. Gus loves going through it. No old masters or anything . . .

Hannah The maths primer she was using belonged to him – the tutor; he wrote his name in it.

Valentine (*reading*) 'Septimus Hodge.'

Hannah Why were these things saved, do you think?

Valentine Why should there be a reason?

Hannah And the diagram, what's it of?

64

Valentine How would I know?

Hannah Why are you cross?

Valentine I'm not cross. (*Pause.*) When your Thomasina was doing maths it had been the same maths for a couple of thousand years. Classical. And for a century after Thomasina. Then maths left the real world behind, just like modern art, really. Nature was classical, maths was suddenly Picassos. But now nature is having the last laugh. The freaky stuff is turning out to be the mathematics of the natural world.

Hannah This feedback thing?

Valentine For example.

Hannah Well, could Thomasina have –

Valentine (*snaps*) No, of course she bloody couldn't!

Hannah All right, you're not cross. What did you mean you were doing the same thing she was doing? (*Pause.*) What *are* you doing?

Valentine Actually I'm doing it from the other end. She started with an equation and turned it into a graph. I've got a graph – real data – and I'm trying to find the equation which would give you the graph if you used it the way she's used hers. Iterated it.

Hannah What for?

Valentine It's how you look at population changes in biology. Goldfish in a pond, say. This year there are x goldfish. Next year there'll be y goldfish. Some get born, some get eaten by herons, whatever. Nature manipulates the x and turns it into y. Then y goldfish is your starting population for the following year. Just like Thomasina. Your value for y becomes your next value for x. The question is: what is being done to x? What is the manipulation? Whatever it is, it can be written down as mathematics. It's called an algorithm.

Hannah It can't be the same every year.

Valentine The details change, you can't keep tabs on everything, it's not nature in a box. But it isn't necessary to know the details. When they are all put together, it turns out the population is obeying a mathematical rule.

Hannah The goldfish are?

Valentine Yes. No. The numbers. It's not about the behaviour of fish. It's about the behaviour of numbers. This thing works for any phenomenon which eats its own numbers – measles epidemics, rainfall averages, cotton prices, it's a natural phenomenon in itself. Spooky.

Hannah Does it work for grouse?

Valentine I don't know yet. I mean, it does undoubtedly, but it's hard to show. There's more noise with grouse.

Hannah Noise?

Valentine Distortions. Interference. Real data is messy. There's a thousand acres of moorland that had grouse on it, always did till about 1930. But nobody counted the grouse. They shot them. So you count the grouse they shot. But burning the heather interferes, it improves the food supply. A good year for foxes interferes the other way, they eat the chicks. And then there's the weather. It's all very, very noisy out there. Very hard to spot the tune. Like a piano in the next room, it's playing your song, but unfortunately it's out of whack, some of the strings are missing, and the pianist is tone deaf and drunk – I mean, the *noise*! Impossible!

Hannah What do you do?

Valentine You start guessing what the tune might be. You try to pick it out of the noise. You try this, you try that, you start to get something – it's half-baked but you start putting in notes which are missing or not quite the right notes . . . and bit by bit . . . (*He starts to dumdi-da to the tune of 'Happy Birthday'*.) Dumdi-dum-dum, dear Val-en-tine, dumdidum-dum to you – the lost algorithm!

Hannah (*soberly*) Yes, I see. And then what?

Valentine I publish.

Hannah Of course. Sorry. Jolly good.

Valentine That's the theory. Grouse are bastards compared to goldfish.

Hannah Why did you choose them?

Valentine The game books. My true inheritance. Two hundred years of real data on a plate.

Hannah Somebody wrote down everything that's shot?

Valentine Well, that's what a game book is. I'm only using from 1870, when butts and beaters came in.

Hannah You mean the game books go back to Thomasina's time?

Valentine Oh yes. Further. (*and then getting ahead of her thought*) No – really. I promise you. I *promise* you. Not a schoolgirl living in a country house in Derbyshire in eighteen-something!

Hannah Well, what was she doing?

Valentine She was just playing with the numbers. The truth is, she wasn't doing anything.

Hannah She must have been doing something.

Valentine Doodling. Nothing she understood.

67

TOM STOPPARD

Hannah A monkey at a typewriter?

Valentine Yes. Well, a piano.

Hannah picks up the algebra book and reads from it.

Hannah '. . . a method whereby all the forms of nature must give up their numerical secrets and draw themselves through number alone.' This feedback, is it a way of making pictures of forms in nature? Just tell me if it is or it isn't.

Valentine (*irritated*) To *me* it is. Pictures of turbulence – growth – change – creation – it's not a way of drawing an elephant, for God's sake!

Hannah I'm sorry. (*She picks up an apple leaf from the table. She is timid about pushing the point.*) So you couldn't make a picture of this leaf by iterating a whatsit?

Valentine (*off-hand*) Oh yes, you could do that.

Hannah (*furiously*) Well, tell me! Honestly, I could kill you!

Valentine If you knew the algorithm and fed it back say ten thousand times, each time there'd be a dot somewhere on the screen. You'd never know where to expect the next dot. But gradually you'd start to see this shape, because every dot will be inside the shape of this leaf. It wouldn't *be* a leaf, it would be a mathematical object. But yes. The unpredictable and the predetermined unfold together to make everything the way it is. It's how nature creates itself, on every scale, the snowflake and the snowstorm. It makes me so happy. To be at the beginning again, knowing almost nothing. People were talking about the end of physics. Relativity and quantum looked as if they were going to clean out the whole problem between them. A theory of everything. But they

68

only explained the very big and the very small. The universe, the elementary particles. The ordinary-sized stuff which is our lives, the things people write poetry about – clouds – daffodils – waterfalls – and what happens in a cup of coffee when the cream goes in – these things are full of mystery, as mysterious to us as the heavens were to the Greeks. We're better at predicting events at the edge of the galaxy or inside the nucleus of an atom than whether it'll rain on auntie's garden party three Sundays from now. Because the problem turns out to be different. We can't even predict the next drip from a dripping tap when it gets irregular. Each drip sets up the conditions for the next, the smallest variation blows prediction apart, and the weather is unpredictable the same way, will always be unpredictable. When you push the numbers through the computer you can see it on the screen. The future is disorder. A door like this has cracked open five or six times since we got up on our hind legs. It's the best possible time to be alive, when almost everything you thought you knew is wrong.

Pause.

Hannah The weather is fairly predictable in the Sahara.

Valentine The scale is different but the graph goes up and down the same way. Six thousand years in the Sahara looks like six months in Manchester, I bet you.

Hannah How much?

Valentine Everything you have to lose.

Hannah (*pause*) No.

Valentine Quite right. That's why there was corn in Egypt.

Hiatus. The piano is heard again.

Hannah What is he playing?

Valentine I don't know. He makes it up.

Hannah Chloë called him 'genius'.

Valentine It's what my mother calls him – only *she* means it. Last year some expert had her digging in the wrong place for months to find something or other – the foundations of Capability Brown's boat-house – and Gus put her right first go.

Hannah Did he ever speak?

Valentine Oh yes. Until he was five. You've never asked about him. You get high marks here for good breeding.

Hannah Yes, I know. I've always been given credit for my unconcern.

Bernard enters in high excitement and triumph.

Bernard *English Bards and Scotch Reviewers.* A pencilled superscription. Listen and kiss my cycle-clips! (*He is carrying the book. He reads from it.*)

'O harbinger of Sleep, who missed the press
And hoped his drone might thus escape redress!
The wretched Chater, bard of Eros' Couch,
For his narcotic let my pencil vouch!'

You see, you *have to turn over every page.*

Hannah Is it his handwriting?

Bernard Oh, come *on.*

Hannah Obviously not.

Bernard Christ, what do you want?

Hannah Proof.

Valentine Quite right. Who are you talking about?

Bernard Proof? *Proof?* You'd have to be there, you silly bitch!

Valentine (*mildly*) I say, you're speaking of my fiancée.

Hannah Especially when I have a present for you. Guess what I found. (*producing the present for Bernard*) Lady Croom writing from London to her husband. Her brother, Captain Brice, married a Mrs Chater. In other words, one might assume, a widow.

Bernard looks at the letter.

Bernard I *said* he was dead. What year? 1810! Oh my God, 1810! Well *done,* Hannah! Are you going to tell me it's a different Mrs Chater?

Hannah Oh no. It's her all right. Note her Christian name.

Bernard Charity. Charity . . . 'Deny what cannot be proven for Charity's sake!'

Hannah Don't kiss me!

Valentine She won't let anyone kiss her.

Bernard You see! They wrote – they scribbled – they put it on paper. It was their employment. Their diversion. Paper is what they had. And there'll be more. There is always more. We can find it!

Hannah Such passion. First Valentine, now you. It's moving.

Bernard The aristocratic friend of the tutor – under the same roof as the poor sod whose book he savaged – the first thing he does is seduce Chater's wife. All is discovered. There is a duel. Chater dead, Byron fled! P.S. guess what?, the widow married her ladyship's brother! Do you honestly think no one wrote a word? How could they not! It dropped from sight but we will write it again!

71

Hannah You can, Bernard. I'm not going to take any credit, I haven't done anything.

The same thought has clearly occurred to Bernard. He becomes instantly po-faced.

Bernard Well, that's – very fair – generous –

Hannah Prudent. Chater could have died of anything, anywhere.

The po-face is forgotten.

Bernard But he fought a duel with Byron!

Hannah You haven't established it was fought. You haven't established it was Byron. For God's sake, Bernard, you haven't established Byron was even here!

Bernard I'll tell you your problem. No guts.

Hannah Really?

Bernard By which I mean a visceral belief in yourself. Gut instinct. The part of you which doesn't reason. The certainty for which there is no back-reference. Because time is reversed. Tock, tick goes the universe and then recovers itself, but it was enough, you were in there and you bloody *know*.

Valentine Are you talking about Lord Byron, the poet?

Bernard No, you fucking idiot, we're talking about Lord Byron the chartered accountant.

Valentine (*unoffended*) Oh well, *he* was here all right, the poet.

Silence.

Hannah How do you know?

Valentine He's in the game book. I think he shot a hare. I read through the whole lot once when I had mumps – some quite interesting people –

Hannah Where's the book?

Valentine It's not one I'm using – too early, of course –

Hannah 1809.

Valentine They've always been in the commode. Ask Chloë.

Hannah looks to Bernard. Bernard has been silent because he has been incapable of speech. He seems to have gone into a trance, in which only his mouth tries to work. Hannah steps over to him and gives him a demure kiss on the cheek. It works. Bernard lurches out into the garden and can be heard croaking for 'Chloë . . . Chloë!'

Valentine My mother's lent him her bicycle. Lending one's bicycle is a form of safe sex, possibly the safest there is. My mother is in a flutter about Bernard, and he's no fool. He gave her a first edition of Horace Walpole, and now she's lent him her bicycle. (*He gathers up the three items [the primer, the lesson book and the diagram] and puts them into the portfolio.*) Can I keep these for a while?

Hannah Yes, of course.

The piano stops. Gus enters hesitantly from the music room.

Valentine (*to Gus*) Yes, finished . . . coming now. (*to Hannah*) I'm trying to work out the diagram.

Gus nods and smiles, at Hannah too, but she is preoccupied.

Hannah What I don't understand is . . . why nobody did this feedback thing before – it's not like relativity, you don't have to be Einstein.

Valentine You couldn't see to look before. The electronic calculator was what the telescope was for Galileo.

Hannah Calculator?

Valentine There wasn't enough time before. There weren't enough *pencils*! (*He flourishes Thomasina's lesson book.*) This took her I don't know how many days and she hasn't scratched the paintwork. Now she'd only have to press a button, the same button over and over. Iteration. A few minutes. And what I've done in a couple of months, with only a *pencil* the calculations would take me the rest of my life to do again – thousands of pages – tens of thousands! And so boring!

Hannah Do you mean –?

She stops because Gus is plucking Valentine's sleeve.

Do you mean –?

Valentine All right, Gus, I'm coming.

Hannah Do you mean that was the only problem? Enough time? And paper? And the boredom?

Valentine We're going to get out the dressing-up box.

Hannah (*driven to raising her voice*) *Val! Is* that what you're saying?

Valentine (*surprised by her. Mildly*) No, I'm saying you'd have to have a reason for doing it.

Gus runs out of the room, upset.

(*Apologetically*) He hates people shouting.

Hannah I'm sorry.

74

Valentine starts to follow Gus.

But anything else?

Valentine Well, the other thing is, you'd have to be insane.

Valentine leaves.
    Hannah stays thoughtful. After a moment, she turns to the table and picks up the Cornhill Magazine. *She looks into it briefly, then closes it, and leaves the room, taking the magazine with her.*
    The empty room.
    The light changes to early morning. From a long way off, there is a pistol shot. A moment later there is the cry of dozens of crows disturbed from the unseen trees.

Act Two

SCENE FIVE

*Bernard is pacing around, reading aloud from a hand-
ful of typed sheets. Valentine, Chloë and Gus are his
audience. Gus sits somewhat apart, perhaps less
attentive. Valentine has his tortoise and is eating a
sandwich from which he extracts shreds of lettuce to
offer the tortoise.*

Bernard 'Did it happen? Could it happen?

'Undoubtedly it could. Only three years earlier the
Irish poet Tom Moore appeared on the field of combat
to avenge a review by Jeffrey of the *Edinburgh*. These
affairs were seldom fatal and sometimes farcical but,
potentially, the duellist stood in respect to the law no
differently from a murderer. As for the murderee, a
minor poet like Ezra Chater could go to his death in a
Derbyshire glade as unmissed and unremembered as his
contemporary and namesake, the minor botanist who
died in the forests of the West Indies, lost to history like
the monkey that bit him. On April 16th 1809, a few
days after he left Sidley Park, Byron wrote to his solicitor
John Hanson: "If the consequences of my leaving England
were ten times as ruinous as you describe, I have no
alternative; there are circumstances which render it
absolutely indispensable, and quit the country I must
immediately." To which, the editor's note in the Collected
Letters reads as follows: "What Byron's urgent reasons
for leaving England were at this time has never been
revealed." The letter was written from the family seat,
Newstead Abbey, Nottinghamshire. A long day's ride
to the north-west lay Sidley Park, the estate of the

Coverlys – a far grander family, raised by Charles II to the Earldom of Croom . . .'

Hannah enters briskly, a piece of paper in her hand.

Hannah Bernard . . .! Val . . .

Bernard Do you mind?

Hannah puts her piece of paper down in front of Valentine.

Chloë (*angrily*) *Hannah*!

Hannah What?

Chloë She's so *rude*!

Hannah (*taken aback*) What? Am I?

Valentine Bernard's reading us his lecture.

Hannah Yes, I know. (*then recollecting herself*) Yes – yes – that *was* rude. I'm sorry, Bernard.

Valentine (*with the piece of paper*) What is this?

Hannah (*to Bernard*) Spot on – the India Office Library. (*to Valentine*) Peacock's letter in holograph, I got a copy sent –

Chloë *Hannah*! Shut up!

Hannah (*sitting down*) Yes, sorry.

Bernard It's all right, I'll read it to myself.

Chloë No.

Hannah reaches for the Peacock letter and takes it back.

Hannah Go on, Bernard. Have I missed anything? Sorry.

Bernard stares at her balefully but then continues to read.

Bernard 'The Byrons of Newstead in 1809 comprised an eccentric widow and her undistinguished son, the "lame brat", who until the age of ten when he came into the title, had been carted about the country from lodging to lodging by his vulgar hectoring monster of a mother –'

Hannah's hand has gone up.

– *overruled* – 'and who four months past his twenty-first birthday was master of nothing but his debts and his genius. Between the Byrons and the Coverlys there was no social equality and none to be expected. The connection, undisclosed to posterity until now, was with Septimus Hodge, Byron's friend at Harrow and Trinity College –'

Hannah's hand goes up again.

– sustained – (*He makes an instant correction with a silver pencil.*) 'Byron's contemporary at Harrow and Trinity College, and now tutor in residence to the Croom daughter, Thomasina Coverly. Byron's letters tell us where he was on April 8th and on April 12th. He was at Newstead. But on the 10th he was at Sidley Park, as attested by the game book preserved there: "April 10th 1809 – forenoon. High cloud, dry, and sun between times, wind south-easterly. Self – Augustus – Lord Byron. Fourteen pigeon, one hare (Lord B.)." But, as we know now, the drama of life and death at Sidley Park was not about pigeons but about sex and literature.'

Valentine Unless you were the pigeon.

Bernard I don't have to do this. I'm paying you a compliment.

Chloë Ignore him, Bernard – go on, get to the duel.

Bernard Hannah's not even paying attention.

Hannah Yes I am, it's all going in. I often work with the radio on.

Bernard Oh thanks!

Hannah Is there much more?

Chloë *Hannah*!

Hannah No, it's fascinating. I just wondered how much more there was. I need to ask Valentine about this (*letter*) – sorry, Bernard, go on, this will keep.

Valentine Yes – sorry, Bernard.

Chloë Please, Bernard!

Bernard Where was I?

Valentine Pigeons.

Chloë Sex.

Hannah Literature.

Bernard Life and death. Right. 'Nothing could be more eloquent of that than the three documents I have quoted: the terse demand to settle a matter in private; the desperate scribble of "my husband has sent for pistols" and on April 11th, the gauntlet thrown down by the aggrieved and cuckolded author Ezra Chater. The covers have not survived. What is certain is that all three letters were in Byron's possession when his books were sold in 1816 – preserved in the pages of 'The Couch of Eros' which seven years earlier at Sidley Park Byron had borrowed from Septimus Hodge.'

Hannah Borrowed?

Bernard I will be taking questions at the end. Constructive comments will be welcome. Which is indeed my reason for trying out in the provinces before my London opening under the auspices of the Byron Society prior to publication. By the way, Valentine, do you want a credit? – 'the game book recently discovered by.'?

Valentine It was never lost, Bernard.

Bernard 'As recently pointed out by.' I don't normally like giving credit where it's due, but with scholarly articles as with divorce, there is a certain cachet in citing a member of the aristocracy. I'll pop it in ad lib for the lecture, and give you a mention in the press release. How's that?

Valentine Very kind.

Hannah Press release? What happened to the *Journal of English Studies?*

Bernard That comes later with the apparatus, and in the recognized tone – very dry, very modest, absolutely gloat-free, and yet unmistakably 'Eat your heart out, you dozy bastards'. But first, it's 'Media Don, book early to avoid disappointment'. Where was I?

Valentine Game book.

Chloë Eros.

Hannah Borrowed.

Bernard Right. '– borrowed from Septimus Hodge. Is it conceivable that the letters were already in the book when Byron borrowed it?'

Valentine Yes.

Chloë Shut up, Val.

Valentine Well, it's conceivable.

Bernard 'Is it *likely* that Hodge would have lent Byron the book without first removing the three private letters?'

Valentine Look, sorry – I only meant, Byron could have borrowed the book without asking.

Hannah That's true.

Bernard Then why wouldn't Hodge get them back?

Hannah I don't know, I wasn't there.

Bernard That's right, you bloody weren't.

Chloë Go on, Bernard.

Bernard 'It is the third document, the challenge itself, that convinces. Chater "as a man and a poet", points the finger at his "slanderer in the press". Neither as a man nor a poet did Ezra Chater cut such a figure as to be habitually slandered or even mentioned in the press. It is surely indisputable that the slander was the review of 'The Maid of Turkey' in the *Piccadilly Recreation*. Did Septimus Hodge have any connection with the London periodicals? No. Did Byron? Yes! He had reviewed Wordsworth two years earlier, he was to review Spencer two years later. And do we have any clue as to Byron's opinion of Chater the poet? Yes! Who but Byron could have written the four lines pencilled into Lady Croom's copy of *English Bards and Scotch Reviewers'* –

Hannah Almost anybody.

Bernard Darling –

Hannah Don't call me darling.

Bernard Dickhead, then, is it likely that the man Chater calls his friend Septimus Hodge is the same man who screwed his wife and kicked the shit out of his last book?

Hannah Put it like that, almost certain.

Chloë (*earnestly*) You've been deeply wounded in the past, haven't you, Hannah?

Hannah Nothing compared to listening to this. Why is there nothing in Byron's letters about the *Piccadilly* reviews?

Bernard Exactly. Because he killed the author.

Hannah But the first one, 'The Maid of Turkey', was the year before. Was he clairvoyant?

Chloë Letters get lost.

Bernard Thank you! Exactly! There is a platonic letter which confirms everything – lost but ineradicable, like radio voices rippling through the universe for all eternity. 'My dear Hodge – here I am in Albania and you're the only person in the whole world who knows why. Poor C! I never wished him any harm – except in the *Piccadilly,* of course – it was the woman who bade me eat, dear Hodge! – what a tragic business, but thank God it ended well for poetry. Yours ever, B. –
   PS. Burn this.'

Valentine How did Chater find out the reviewer was Byron?

Bernard (*irritated*) I don't know, I wasn't there, was I? (*Pause. To Hannah*) You wish to say something?

Hannah Moi?

Chloë I know. Byron told Mrs Chater in bed. Next day he dumped her so she grassed on him, and pleaded date rape.

Bernard (*fastidiously*) Date rape? What do you mean, date rape?

Hannah April the tenth.

Bernard cracks. Everything becomes loud and overlapped as Bernard threatens to walk out and is cajoled into continuing.

Bernard Right! – forget it!

Hannah Sorry –

Bernard No – I've had nothing but sarcasm and childish interruptions –

Valentine What did I do?

Bernard No credit for probably the most sensational literary discovery of the century –

Chloë I think you're jolly unfair – they're jealous, Bernard –

Hannah I won't say another word –

Valentine Yes, go on, Bernard – we promise.

Bernard (*finally*) Well, only if you stop *feeding tortoises*!

Valentine Well, it's his lunch time.

Bernard And on condition that I am afforded the common courtesy of a scholar among scholars –

Hannah Absolutely mum till you're finished –

Bernard After which, any comments are to be couched in terms of accepted academic –

Hannah Dignity – you're right, Bernard.

Bernard – respect.

Hannah Respect. Absolutely. The language of scholars. Count on it.

Having made a great show of putting his pages away, Bernard reassembles them and finds his place, glancing suspiciously at the other three for signs of levity.

Bernard Last paragraph. 'Without question, Ezra Chater issued a challenge to *somebody*. If a duel was fought in the dawn mist of Sidley Park in April 1809, his opponent, on the evidence, was a critic with a gift for ridicule and a taste for seduction. Do we need to look far? Without

83

question, Mrs Chater was a widow by 1810. If we seek
the occasion of Ezra Chater's early and unrecorded
death, do we need to look far? Without question, Lord
Byron, in the very season of his emergence as a literary
figure, quit the country in a cloud of panic and mystery,
and stayed abroad for two years at a time when
Continental travel was unusual and dangerous. If we
seek his reason – *do we need to look far?*'

*No mean performer, he is pleased with the effect of
his peroration. There is a significant silence.*

Hannah Bollocks.

Chloë Well, I think it's true.

Hannah You've left out everything which doesn't fit.
Byron had been banging on for months about leaving
England – there's a letter in February –

Bernard But he didn't go, did he?

Hannah And then he didn't sail until the beginning of
July!

Bernard Everything moved more slowly then. Time was
different. He was two weeks in Falmouth waiting for
wind or something –

Hannah Bernard, I don't know why I'm bothering –
you're arrogant, greedy and reckless. You've gone from
a glint in your eye to a sure thing in a hop, skip and a
jump. You deserve what you get and I think you're mad.
But I can't help myself, you're like some exasperating
child pedalling its tricycle towards the edge of a cliff, and
I have to do something. So listen to me. If Byron killed
Chater in a duel I'm Marie of Romania. You'll end up
with so much *fame* you won't leave the house without a
paper bag over your head.

Valentine Actually, Bernard, as a scientist, your theory is incomplete.

Bernard But I'm not a scientist.

Valentine (*patiently*) No, *as a scientist* –

Bernard (*beginning to shout*) I have yet to hear a proper argument.

Hannah Nobody would kill a man and then pan his book. I mean, not in that order. So he must have borrowed the book, written the review, *posted* it, seduced Mrs Chater, fought a duel and departed, all in the space of two or three days. Who would do that?

Bernard Byron.

Hannah It's hopeless.

Bernard You've never understood him, as you've shown in your novelette.

Hannah In my what?

Bernard Oh, sorry – did you think it was a work of historical revisionism? Byron the spoilt child promoted beyond his gifts by the spirit of the age! And Caroline the closet intellectual shafted by a male society!

Valentine I read that somewhere –

Hannah It's his review.

Bernard And bloody well said, too!

Things are turning a little ugly and Bernard seems in a mood to push them that way.

You got them backwards, darling. Caroline was Romantic waffle on wheels with no talent, and Byron was an eighteenth-century Rationalist touched by genius. And he killed Chater.

Hannah (*pause*) If it's not too late to change my mind, I'd like you to go ahead.

Bernard I intend to. Look to the mote in your own eye! – you even had the wrong bloke on the dust-jacket!

Hannah Dust-jacket?

Valentine What about my computer model? Aren't you going to mention it?

Bernard It's inconclusive.

Valentine (*to Hannah*) The *Piccadilly* reviews aren't a very good fit with Byron's other reviews, you see.

Hannah (*to Bernard*) What do you mean, the wrong bloke?

Bernard (*ignoring her*) The other reviews aren't a very good fit for each other, are they?

Valentine No, but differently. The parameters –

Bernard (*jeering*) Parameters! You can't stick Byron's head in your laptop! Genius isn't like your average grouse.

Valentine (*casually*) Well, it's all trivial anyway.

Bernard What is?

Valentine Who wrote what when . . .

Bernard Trivial?

Valentine Personalities.

Bernard I'm sorry – did you say trivial?

Valentine It's a technical term.

Bernard Not where I come from, it isn't.

Valentine The questions you're asking don't matter, you see. It's like arguing who got there first with the calculus.

The English say Newton, the Germans say Leibnitz. But it doesn't *matter*. Personalities. What matters is the calculus. Scientific progress. Knowledge.

Bernard Really? Why?

Valentine Why what?

Bernard Why does scientific progress matter more than personalities?

Valentine Is he serious?

Hannah No, he's trivial. Bernard –

Valentine (*interrupting, to Bernard*) Do yourself a favour, you're on a loser.

Bernard Oh, you're going to zap me with penicillin and pesticides. Spare me that and I'll spare you the bomb and aerosols. But don't confuse progress with perfectibility. A great poet is always timely. A great philosopher is an urgent need. There's no rush for Isaac Newton. We were quite happy with Aristotle's cosmos. Personally, I preferred it. Fifty-five crystal spheres geared to God's crankshaft is my idea of a satisfying universe. I can't think of anything more trivial than the speed of light. Quarks, quasars – big bangs, black holes – who gives a shit? How did you people con us out of all that status? All that money? And why are you so pleased with yourselves?

Chloë Are you against penicillin, Bernard?

Bernard Don't feed the animals. (*back to Valentine*) I'd push the lot of you over a cliff myself. Except the one in the wheelchair, I think I'd lose the sympathy vote before people had time to think it through.

Hannah (*loudly*) What the hell do you mean, the dust-jacket?

Bernard (*ignoring her*) If knowledge isn't self-knowledge it isn't doing much, mate. Is the universe expanding? Is it contracting? Is it standing on one leg and singing 'When Father Painted the Parlour'? Leave me out. I can expand my universe without you. 'She walks in beauty, like the night of cloudless climes and starry skies, and all that's best of dark and bright meet in her aspect and her eyes.' There you are, he wrote it after coming home from a party. (*with offensive politeness*) What is it that you're doing with grouse, Valentine, I'd love to know?

Valentine stands up and it is suddenly apparent that he is shaking and close to tears.

Valentine (*to Chloë*) He's not against penicillin, and he knows I'm not against poetry. (*to Bernard*) I've given up on the grouse.

Hannah You haven't, Valentine!

Valentine (*leaving*) I can't do it.

Hannah *Why?*

Valentine Too much noise. There's just too much *bloody noise*!

On which, Valentine leaves the room. Chloë, upset and in tears, jumps up and briefly pummels Bernard ineffectually with her fists.

Chloë You bastard, Bernard!

She follows Valentine out and is followed at a run by Gus. Pause.

Hannah Well, I think that's everybody. *You* can leave now, give Lightning a kick on your way out.

Bernard Yes, I'm sorry about that. It's no fun when it's not among pros, is it?

Hannah No.

Bernard Oh, well . . . (*He begins to put his lecture sheets away in his briefcase, and is thus reminded . . .*) Do you want to know about your book jacket? 'Lord Byron and Caroline Lamb at the Royal Academy'? Ink study by Henry Fuseli?

Hannah What about it?

Bernard It's not them.

Hannah (*she explodes*) Who says!?

Bernard brings the Byron Society Journal *from his briefcase.*

Bernard This Fuseli expert in the *Byron Society Journal*. They sent me the latest . . . as a distinguished guest speaker.

Hannah But of course it's them! Everyone knows –

Bernard Popular tradition only. (*He is finding the place in the journal.*) Here we are. 'No earlier than 1820'. He's analysed it. (*Offers it to her.*) Read at your leisure.

Hannah (*she sounds like Bernard jeering*) Analysed it?

Bernard Charming sketch, of course, but Byron was in Italy . . .

Hannah But, Bernard – I *know* it's them.

Bernard How?

Hannah How? It just *is*. 'Analysed it', my big toe!

Bernard Language!

Hannah He's wrong.

Bernard Oh, gut instinct, you mean?

Hannah (*flatly*) He's wrong.

Bernard snaps shut his briefcase.

Bernard Well, it's all trivial, isn't it? Why don't you come?

Hannah Where?

Bernard With me.

Hannah To London? What for?

Bernard What for.

Hannah Oh, your lecture.

Bernard No, no, bugger that. Sex.

Hannah Oh . . . No. Thanks . . . (*then, protesting*) Bernard!

Bernard You should try it. It's very underrated.

Hannah Nothing against it.

Bernard Yes, you have. You should let yourself go a bit. You might have written a better book. Or at any rate the right book.

Hannah Sex and literature. Literature and sex. Your conversation, left to itself, doesn't have many places to go. Like two marbles rolling around a pudding basin. One of them is always sex.

Bernard Ah well, yes. Men all over.

Hannah No doubt. Einstein – relativity and sex. Chippendale – sex and furniture. Galileo – 'Did the earth move?' What the hell is it with you people? Chaps sometimes wanted to marry me, and I don't know a worse bargain. Available sex against not being allowed to fart in bed. What do you mean the right book?

Bernard It takes a romantic to make a heroine of Caroline Lamb. You were cut out for Byron.

Pause.

Hannah So, cheerio.

Bernard Oh, I'm coming back for the dance, you know. Chloë asked me.

Hannah She meant well, but I don't dance.

Bernard No, no – I'm going with her.

Hannah Oh, I see. I don't, actually.

Bernard I'm her date. Sub rosa. Don't tell Mother.

Hannah She doesn't want her mother to know?

Bernard No – *I* don't want her mother to know. This is my first experience of the landed aristocracy. I tell you, I'm boggle-eyed.

Hannah Bernard! – you haven't seduced that girl?

Bernard Seduced her? Every time I turned round she was up a library ladder. In the end I gave in. That reminds me – I spotted something between her legs that made me think of you. (*He instantly receives a sharp stinging slap on the face but manages to remain completely unperturbed by it. He is already producing from his pocket a small book. His voice has hardly hesitated.*) *The Peaks Traveller and Gazetteer* – James Godolphin 1832 – unillustrated, I'm afraid. (*He has opened the book to a marked place.*) 'Sidley Park in Derbyshire, property of the Earl of Croom . . .'

Hannah (*numbly*) The world is going to hell in a hand-cart.

Bernard 'Five hundred acres including forty of lake – the Park by Brown and Noakes has pleasing features in the horrid style – viaduct, grotto, etc – a hermitage occupied by a lunatic since twenty years without discourse or companion save for a pet tortoise, Plautus by name, which he suffers children to touch on request.' (*He holds out the book for her.*) A tortoise. They must be a feature.

After a moment Hannah takes the book.

Hannah Thank you.

Valentine comes to the door.

Valentine The station taxi is at the front . . .

Bernard Yes . . . thanks . . . Oh – did Peacock come up trumps?

Hannah For some.

Bernard Hermit's name and cv? (*He picks up and glances at the Peacock letter.*) 'My dear Thackeray . . .' God, I'm good. (*He puts the letter down.*) Well, wish me luck – (*vaguely to Valentine*) Sorry about . . . you know . . . (*and to Hannah*) and about your . . .

Valentine Piss off, Bernard.

Bernard Right. (*He goes.*)

Hannah Don't let Bernard get to you. It's only performance art, you know. Rhetoric. They used to teach it in ancient times, like PT. It's not about being right, they had philosophy for that. Rhetoric was their chat show. Bernard's indignation is a sort of aerobics for when he gets on television.

Valentine I don't care to be rubbished by the dustbin man. (*He has been looking at the letter.*) The what of the lunatic?

Hannah reclaims the letter and reads it for him.

Hannah 'The testament of the lunatic serves as a caution against French fashion . . . for it was Frenchified mathematick that brought him to the melancholy certitude of a world without light or life . . . as a wooden stove that must consume itself until ash and stove are as one, and heat is gone from the earth.'

Valentine (*amused, surprised*) Huh!

Hannah 'He died aged two score years and seven, hoary as Job and meagre as a cabbage-stalk, the proof of his prediction even yet unyielding to his labours for the restitution of hope through good English algebra.'

Valentine That's it?

Hannah (*nods*) Is there anything in it?

Valentine In what? We are all doomed? (*casually*) Oh yes, sure – it's called the second law of thermodynamics.

Hannah Was it known about?

Valentine By poets and lunatics from time immemorial.

Hannah Seriously.

Valentine No.

Hannah Is it anything to do with . . . you know, Thomasina's discovery?

Valentine She didn't discover anything.

Hannah Her lesson book.

Valentine No.

Hannah A coincidence, then?

Valentine What is?

93

Hannah (*reading*) 'He died aged two score years and seven.' That was in 1834. So he was born in 1787. So was the tutor. He says so in his letter to Lord Croom when he recommended himself for the job: 'Date of birth – 1787.' The hermit was born in the same year as Septimus Hodge.

Valentine (*pause*) Did Bernard bite you in the leg?

Hannah Don't you see? I thought my hermit was a perfect symbol. An idiot in the landscape. But this is better. The Age of Enlightenment banished into the Romantic wilderness! The genius of Sidley Park living on in a hermit's hut!

Valentine You don't *know* that.

Hannah Oh, but I do. I do. Somewhere there will be *something* . . . if only I can find it.

SCENE SIX

The room is empty.

A reprise: early morning – a distant pistol shot – the sound of the crows.

Jellaby enters the dawn-dark room with a lamp. He goes to the windows and looks out. He sees something. He returns to put the lamp on the table, and then opens one of the french windows and steps outside.

Jellaby (*outside*) Mr Hodge!

Septimus comes in, followed by Jellaby, who closes the garden door. Septimus is wearing a greatcoat.

Septimus Thank you, Jellaby. I was expecting to be locked out. What time is it?

Jellaby Half past five.

94

Septimus That is what I have. Well! – what a bracing experience! (*He produces two pistols from inside his coat and places them on the table.*) The dawn, you know. Unexpectedly lively. Fishes, birds, frogs . . . rabbits . . . (*He produces a dead rabbit from inside his coat.*) and very beautiful. If only it did not occur so early in the day. I have brought Lady Thomasina a rabbit. Will you take it?

Jellaby It's dead.

Septimus Yes. Lady Thomasina loves a rabbit pie.

Jellaby takes the rabbit without enthusiasm. There is a little blood on it.

Jellaby You were missed, Mr Hodge.

Septimus I decided to sleep last night in the boat-house. Did I see a carriage leaving the Park?

Jellaby Captain Brice's carriage, with Mr and Mrs Chater also.

Septimus Gone?!

Jellaby Yes, sir. And Lord Byron's horse was brought round at four o'clock.

Septimus Lord Byron too!

Jellaby Yes, sir. The house has been up and hopping.

Septimus But I have his rabbit pistols! What am I to do with his rabbit pistols?

Jellaby You were looked for in your room.

Septimus By whom?

Jellaby By her ladyship.

Septimus In my room?

95

Jellaby I will tell her ladyship you are returned. (*He starts to leave.*)

Septimus Jellaby! Did Lord Byron leave a book for me?

Jellaby A book?

Septimus He had the loan of a book from me.

Jellaby His lordship left nothing in his room, sir, not a coin.

Septimus Oh. Well, I'm sure he would have left a coin if he'd had one. Jellaby – here is a half-guinea for you.

Jellaby Thank you very much, sir.

Septimus What has occurred?

Jellaby The servants are told nothing, sir.

Septimus Come, come, does a half-guinea buy nothing any more?

Jellaby (*sighs*) Her ladyship encountered Mrs Chater during the night.

Septimus Where?

Jellaby On the threshold of Lord Byron's room.

Septimus Ah. Which one was leaving and which entering?

Jellaby Mrs Chater was leaving Lord Byron's room.

Septimus And where was Mr Chater?

Jellaby Mr Chater and Captain Brice were drinking cherry brandy. They had the footman to keep the fire up until three o'clock. There was a loud altercation upstairs, and –

Lady Croom enters the room.

96

Lady Croom Well, Mr Hodge.

Septimus My lady.

Lady Croom All this to shoot a hare?

Septimus A rabbit.

She gives him one of her looks.

No, indeed, a hare, though very rabbit-like –

Jellaby is about to leave.

Lady Croom My infusion.

Jellaby Yes, my lady.

He leaves. Lady Croom is carrying two letters. We have not seen them before. Each has an envelope which has been opened. She flings them on the table.

Lady Croom How dare you!

Septimus I cannot be called to account for what was written in private and read without regard to propriety.

Lady Croom Addressed to me!

Septimus Left in my room, in the event of my death –

Lady Croom Pah! – what earthly use is a love letter from beyond the grave?

Septimus As much, surely, as from this side of it. The second letter, however, was not addressed to your ladyship.

Lady Croom I have a mother's right to open a letter addressed by you to my daughter, whether in the event of your life, your death, or your imbecility. What do you mean by writing to her of rice pudding when she has just suffered the shock of violent death in our midst?

97

Septimus Whose death?

Lady Croom Yours, you wretch!

Septimus Yes, I see.

Lady Croom I do not know which is the madder of your ravings. One envelope full of rice pudding, the other of the most insolent familiarities regarding several parts of my body, but have no doubt which is the more intolerable to me.

Septimus Which?

Lady Croom Oh, aren't we saucy when our bags are packed! Your friend has gone before you, and I have despatched the harlot Chater and her husband – and also my brother for bringing them here. Such is the sentence, you see, for choosing unwisely in your acquaintance. Banishment. Lord Byron is a rake and a hypocrite, and the sooner he sails for the Levant the sooner he will find society congenial to his character.

Septimus It has been a night of reckoning.

Lady Croom Indeed I wish it had passed uneventfully with you and Mr Chater shooting each other with the decorum due to a civilized house. You have no secrets left, Mr Hodge. They spilled out between shrieks and oaths and tears. It is fortunate that a lifetime's devotion to the sporting gun has halved my husband's hearing to the ear he sleeps on.

Septimus I'm afraid I have no knowledge of what has occurred.

Lady Croom Your trollop was discovered in Lord Byron's room.

Septimus Ah. Discovered by Mr Chater?

Lady Croom Who else?

Septimus I am very sorry, madam, for having used your kindness to bring my unworthy friend to your notice. He will have to give an account of himself to me, you may be sure.

Before Lady Croom can respond to this threat, Jellaby enters the room with her 'infusion'. This is quite an elaborate affair: a pewter tray on small feet on which there is a kettle suspended over a spirit lamp. There is a cup and saucer and the silver 'basket' containing the dry leaves for the tea. Jellaby places the tray on the table and is about to offer further assistance with it.

Lady Croom I will do it.

Jellaby Yes, my lady. (*to Septimus*) Lord Byron left a letter for you with the valet, sir.

Septimus Thank you.

Septimus takes the letter off the tray. Jellaby prepares to leave. Lady Croom eyes the letter.

Lady Croom When did he do so?

Jellaby As he was leaving, your ladyship.

Jellaby leaves. Septimus puts the letter into his pocket.

Septimus Allow me.

Since she does not object, he pours a cup of tea for her. She accepts it.

Lady Croom I do not know if it is proper for you to receive a letter written in my house from someone not welcome in it.

Septimus Very improper, I agree. Lord Byron's want of delicacy is a grief to his friends, among whom I no

99

longer count myself. I will not read his letter until I have followed him through the gates.

She considers that for a moment.

Lady Croom That may excuse the reading but not the writing.

Septimus Your ladyship should have lived in the Athens of Pericles! The philosophers would have fought the sculptors for your idle hour!

Lady Croom (*protesting*) Oh, really! . . . (*protesting less*) Oh really . . .

Septimus has taken Byron's letter from his pocket and is now setting fire to a corner of it using the little flame from the spirit lamp.

Oh . . . really . . .

The paper blazes in Septimus's hand and he drops it and lets it burn out on the metal tray.

Septimus Now there's a thing – a letter from Lord Byron never to be read by a living soul. I will take my leave, madam, at the time of your desiring it.

Lady Croom To the Indies?

Septimus The Indies! Why?

Lady Croom To follow the Chater, of course. She did not tell you?

Septimus She did not exchange half-a-dozen words with me.

Lady Croom I expect she did not like to waste the time. The Chater sails with Captain Brice.

Septimus Ah. As a member of the crew?

Lady Croom No, as wife to Mr Chater, plant-gatherer to my brother's expedition.

Septimus I knew he was no poet. I did not know it was botany under the false colours.

Lady Croom He is no more a botanist. My brother paid fifty pounds to have him published, and he will pay a hundred and fifty to have Mr Chater picking flowers in the Indies for a year while the wife plays mistress of the Captain's quarters. Captain Brice has fixed his passion on Mrs Chater, and to take her on voyage he has not scrupled to deceive the Admiralty, the Linnean Society and Sir Joseph Banks, botanist to His Majesty at Kew.

Septimus Her passion is not as fixed as his.

Lady Croom It is a defect of God's humour that he directs our hearts everywhere but to those who have a right to them.

Septimus Indeed, madam. (*Pause.*) But is Mr Chater deceived?

Lady Croom He insists on it, and finds the proof of his wife's virtue in his eagerness to defend it. Captain Brice is *not* deceived but cannot help himself. He would die for her.

Septimus I think, my lady, he would have Mr Chater die for her.

Lady Croom Indeed, I never knew a woman worth the duel, or the other way about. Your letter to me goes very ill with your conduct to Mrs Chater, Mr Hodge. I have had experience of being betrayed before the ink is dry, but to be betrayed before the pen is even dipped, and with the village noticeboard, what am I to think of such a performance?

Septimus My lady, I was alone with my thoughts in the gazebo, when Mrs Chater ran me to ground, and I being in such a passion, in an agony of unrelieved desire –

Lady Croom Oh . . .!

Septimus – I thought in my madness that the Chater with her skirts over her head would give me the momentary illusion of the happiness to which I dared not put a face.

Pause.

Lady Croom I do not know when I have received a more unusual compliment, Mr Hodge. I hope I am more than a match for Mrs Chater with her head in a bucket. Does she wear drawers?

Septimus She does.

Lady Croom Yes, I have heard that drawers are being worn now. It is unnatural for women to be got up like jockeys. I cannot approve. (*She turns with a whirl of skirts and moves to leave.*) I know nothing of Pericles or the Athenian philosophers. I can spare them an hour, in my sitting room when I have bathed. Seven o'clock. Bring a book.

She goes out. Septimus picks up the two letters, the ones he wrote, and starts to burn them in the flame of the spirit lamp.

SCENE SEVEN

Valentine and Chloë are at the table. Gus is in the room.
  Chloë is reading from two Saturday newspapers. She is wearing workaday period clothes, a Regency dress, no hat.

Valentine is pecking at a portable computer. He is wearing unkempt Regency clothes, too.

The clothes have evidently come from a large wicker laundry hamper, from which Gus is producing more clothes to try on himself. He finds a Regency coat and starts putting it on.

The objects on the table now include two geometrical solids, pyramid and cone, about twenty inches high, of the type used in a drawing lesson; and a pot of dwarf dahlias (which do not look like modern dahlias).

Chloë 'Even in Arcadia – Sex, Literature and Death at Sidley Park'. Picture of Byron.

Valentine Not of Bernard?

Chloë 'Byron Fought Fatal Duel, Says Don'. . . Valentine, do you think I'm the first person to think of this?

Valentine No.

Chloë I haven't said yet. The future is all programmed like a computer – that's a proper theory, isn't it?

Valentine The deterministic universe, yes.

Chloë Right. Because everything including us is just a lot of atoms bouncing off each other like billiard balls.

Valentine Yes. There was someone, forget his name, 1820s, who pointed out that from Newton's laws you could predict everything to come – I mean, you'd need a computer as big as the universe but the formula would exist.

Chloë But it doesn't work, does it?

Valentine No. It turns out the maths is different.

Chloë No, it's all because of sex.

Valentine Really?

Chloë That's what I think. The universe is deterministic all right, just like Newton said, I mean it's trying to be, but the only thing going wrong is people fancying people who aren't supposed to be in that part of the plan.

Valentine Ah. The attraction that Newton left out. All the way back to the apple in the garden. Yes. (*Pause.*) Yes, I think you're the first person to think of this.

Hannah enters, carrying a tabloid paper, and a mug of tea.

Hannah Have you seen this? 'Bonking Byron Shot Poet'.

Chloë (*pleased*) Let's see.

Hannah gives her the paper, smiles at Gus.

Valentine He's done awfully well, hasn't he? How did they all know?

Hannah Don't be ridiculous. (*to Chloë*) Your father wants it back.

Chloë All right.

Hannah What a fool.

Chloë Jealous. I think it's brilliant. (*She gets up to go. To Gus*) Yes, that's perfect, but not with trainers. Come on, I'll lend you a pair of flatties, they'll look period on you –

Hannah Hello, Gus. You all look so romantic.

Gus following Chloë out, hesitates, smiles at her.

Chloë (*pointedly*) Are you coming?

She holds the door for Gus and follows him out, leaving a sense of her disapproval behind her.

Hannah The important thing is not to give two monkeys for what young people think about you. (*She goes to look at the other newspapers.*)

Valentine (*anxiously*) You don't think she's getting a thing about Bernard, do you?

Hannah I wouldn't worry about Chloë, she's old enough to vote on her back. 'Byron Fought Fatal Duel, Says Don'. Or rather – (*sceptically*) 'Says Don!'

Valentine It may all prove to be true.

Hannah It can't prove to be true, it can only not prove to be false yet.

Valentine (*pleased*) Just like science.

Hannah If Bernard can stay ahead of getting the rug pulled till he's dead, he'll be a success.

Valentine *Just* like science . . . The ultimate fear is of posterity . . .

Hannah Personally I don't think it'll take that long.

Valentine . . . and then there's the afterlife. An afterlife would be a mixed blessing. 'Ah – Bernard Nightingale, I don't believe you know Lord Byron.' It must be heaven up there.

Hannah You can't believe in an afterlife, Valentine.

Valentine Oh, you're going to disappoint me at last.

Hannah Am I? Why?

Valentine Science and religion.

Hannah No, no, been there, done that, boring.

Valentine Oh, Hannah. Fiancée. Have pity. Can't we have a trial marriage and I'll call it off in the morning?

Hannah (*amused*) I don't know when I've received a more unusual proposal.

Valentine (*interested*) Have you had many?

Hannah That would be telling.

Valentine Well, why not? Your classical reserve is only a mannerism; and neurotic.

Hannah Do you want the room?

Valentine You get nothing if you give nothing.

Hannah I ask nothing.

Valentine No, stay.

> *Valentine resumes work at his computer. Hannah establishes herself among her references at 'her' end of the table. She has a stack of pocket-sized volumes, Lady Croom's 'garden books'.*

Hannah What are you doing? Valentine?

Valentine The set of points on a complex plane made by –

Hannah Is it the grouse?

Valentine Oh, the grouse. The damned grouse.

Hannah You mustn't give up.

Valentine Why? Didn't you agree with Bernard?

Hannah Oh, that. It's *all* trivial – your grouse, my hermit, Bernard's Byron. Comparing what we're looking for misses the point. It's wanting to know that makes us matter. Otherwise we're going out the way we came in. That's why you can't believe in the afterlife, Valentine. Believe in the after, by all means, but not the life. Believe in God, the soul, the spirit, the infinite, believe in angels if you like, but not in the great celestial get-together for an exchange of views. If the answers are in the back of the book I can wait, but what a drag. Better to struggle on knowing that failure is final. (*She looks over Valentine's shoulder at the computer screen. Reacting*) Oh!, but . . . how beautiful!

Valentine The Coverly set.

Hannah The Coverly set! My goodness, Valentine!

Valentine Lend me a finger. (*He takes her finger and presses one of the computer keys several times.*) See? In an ocean of ashes, islands of order. Patterns making themselves out of nothing. I can't show you how deep it goes. Each picture is a detail of the previous one, blown up. And so on. For ever. Pretty nice, eh?

Hannah Is it important?

Valentine Interesting. Publishable.

Hannah Well done!

Valentine Not me. It's Thomasina's. I just pushed her equations through the computer a few million times further than she managed to do with her pencil.

From the old portfolio he takes Thomasina's lesson book and gives it to Hannah. The piano starts to be heard.

You can have it back now.

Hannah What does it mean?

Valentine Not what you'd like it to.

Hannah Why not?

Valentine Well, for one thing, she'd be famous.

Hannah No, she wouldn't. She was dead before she had time to be famous . . .

Valentine She died?

Hannah . . . burned to death.

Valentine (*realizing*) Oh . . . the girl who died in the fire!

Hannah The night before her seventeenth birthday. You can see where the dormer doesn't match. That was her bedroom under the roof. There's a memorial in the Park.

Valentine (*irritated*) I know – it's my house.

Valentine turns his attention back to his computer. Hannah goes back to her chair. She looks through the lesson book.

Hannah Val, Septimus was her tutor – he and Thomasina would have –

Valentine You do yours.

Pause. Two researchers.
Lord Augustus, fifteen years old, wearing clothes of 1812, bursts in through the non-music room door. He is laughing. He dives under the table. He is chased into the room by Thomasina, aged sixteen and furious. She spots Augustus immediately.

Thomasina You swore! You crossed your heart!

Augustus scampers out from under the table and Thomasina chases him around it.

Augustus I'll tell mama! I'll tell mama!

Thomasina You beast!

She catches Augustus as Septimus enters from the other door, carrying a book, a decanter and a glass, and his portfolio.

Septimus Hush! What is this? My lord! Order, order!

Thomasina and Augustus separate.

I am obliged.

Septimus goes to his place at the table. He pours himself a glass of wine.

Augustus Well, good day to you, Mr Hodge!

He is smirking about something. Thomasina dutifully picks up a drawing book and settles down to draw the geometrical solids. Septimus opens his portfolio.

Septimus Will you join us this morning, Lord Augustus? We have our drawing lesson.

Augustus I am a master of it at Eton, Mr Hodge, but we only draw naked women.

Septimus You may work from memory.

Thomasina Disgusting!

Septimus We will have silence now, if you please.

From the portfolio Septimus takes Thomasina's lesson book and tosses it to her; returning homework. She snatches it and opens it.

Thomasina No marks?! Did you not like my rabbit equation?

Septimus I saw no resemblance to a rabbit.

Thomasina It eats its own progeny.

Septimus (*pause*) I did not see that.

He extends his hand for the lesson book. She returns it to him.

Thomasina I have not room to extend it.

Septimus and Hannah turn the pages doubled by time. Augustus indolently starts to draw the models.

Hannah Do you mean the world is saved after all?

Valentine No, it's still doomed. But if this is how it started, perhaps it's how the next one will come.

Hannah From good English algebra?

Septimus It will go to infinity or zero, or nonsense.

Thomasina No, if you set apart the minus roots they square back to sense.

Septimus turns the pages. Thomasina starts drawing the models.
   Hannah closes the lesson book and turns her attention to her stack of 'garden books'.

Valentine Listen – you know your tea's getting cold.

Hannah I like it cold.

Valentine *(ignoring that)* I'm telling you something. Your tea gets cold by itself, it doesn't get hot by itself. Do you think that's odd?

Hannah No.

Valentine Well, it is odd. Heat goes to cold. It's a one-way street. Your tea will end up at room temperature. What's happening to your tea is happening to everything everywhere. The sun and the stars. It'll take a while but we're all going to end up at room temperature. When your hermit set up shop nobody understood this. But let's say you're right, in 18-whatever nobody knew more about heat than this scribbling nutter living in a hovel in Derbyshire.

Hannah He was at Cambridge – a scientist.

Valentine Say he was. I'm not arguing. And the girl was his pupil, she had a genius for her tutor.

Hannah Or the other way round.

Valentine Anything you like. But not *this*! Whatever he thought he was doing to save the world with good English algebra it wasn't this!

Hannah Why? Because they didn't have calculators?

Valentine No. Yes. Because there's an order things can't happen in. You can't open a door till there's a house.

Hannah I thought that's what genius was.

Valentine Only for lunatics and poets.

Pause.

Hannah
'I had a dream which was not all a dream.
The bright sun was extinguished, and the stars
Did wander darkling in the eternal space,
Rayless, and pathless, and the icy earth
Swung blind and blackening in the moonless air . . .'

Valentine Your own?

Hannah Byron.

Pause. Two researchers again.

Thomasina Septimus, do you think that I will marry Lord Byron?

Augustus Who is he?

Thomasina He is the author of 'Childe Harold's Pilgrimage', the most poetical and pathetic and bravest hero of any book I ever read before, and the most modern and the handsomest, for Harold is Lord Byron himself to those who know him, like myself and Septimus. Well, Septimus?

Septimus (*absorbed*) No.

Then he puts her lesson book away into the portfolio and picks up his own book to read.

Thomasina Why not?

Septimus For one thing, he is not aware of your existence.

Thomasina We exchanged many significant glances when he was at Sidley Park. I do wonder that he has been home almost a year from his adventures and has not written to me once.

Septimus It is indeed improbable, my lady.

Augustus Lord Byron?! – he claimed my hare, although my shot was the earlier! He said I missed by a hare's breadth. His conversation was very facetious. But I think Lord Byron will not marry you, Thom, for he was only lame and not blind.

Septimus Peace! Peace until a quarter to twelve. It is intolerable for a tutor to have his thoughts interrupted by his pupils.

Augustus You are not *my* tutor, sir. I am visiting your lesson by my free will.

Septimus If you are so determined, my lord.

Thomasina laughs at that, the joke is for her. Augustus, not included, becomes angry.

Augustus Your peace is nothing to me, sir. You do not rule over me.

Thomasina (*admonishing*) Augustus!

Septimus I do not rule here, my lord. I inspire by reverence for learning and the exaltation of knowledge whereby man may approach God. There will be a shilling for the best cone and pyramid drawn in silence by a quarter to twelve *at the earliest*.

Augustus You will not buy my silence for a shilling, sir. What I know to tell is worth much more than that.

And throwing down his drawing book and pencil, he leaves the room on his dignity, closing the door sharply. Pause. Septimus looks enquiringly at Thomasina.

Thomasina I told him you kissed me. But he will not tell.

Septimus When did I kiss you?

Thomasina What! Yesterday!

Septimus Where?

Thomasina On the lips!

Septimus In which county?

Thomasina In the hermitage, Septimus!

Septimus On the lips in the hermitage! That? That was not a shilling kiss! I would not give sixpence to have it back. I had almost forgot it already.

Thomasina Oh, cruel! Have you forgotten our compact?

Septimus God save me! Our compact?

Thomasina To teach me to waltz! Sealed with a kiss, and a second kiss due when I can dance like mama!

Septimus Ah yes. Indeed. We were all waltzing like mice in London.

Thomasina I must waltz, Septimus! I will be despised if I do not waltz! It is the most fashionable and gayest and boldest invention conceivable – started in Germany!

Septimus Let them have the waltz, they cannot have the calculus.

Thomasina Mama has brought from town a whole book of waltzes for the Broadwood, to play with Count Zelinsky.

Septimus I need not be told what I cannot but suffer. Count Zelinsky banging on the Broadwood without relief has me reading in waltz time.

Thomasina Oh, stuff! What is your book?

Septimus A prize essay of the Scientific Academy in Paris. The author deserves your indulgence, my lady, for you are his prophet.

Thomasina I? What does he write about? The waltz?

Septimus Yes. He demonstrates the equation of the propagation of heat in a solid body. But in doing so he has discovered heresy – a natural contradiction of Sir Isaac Newton.

Thomasina Oh! – he contradicts determinism?

Septimus No! . . . Well, perhaps. He shows that the atoms do not go according to Newton.

Her interest has switched in the mercurial way characteristic of her – she has crossed to take the book.

Thomasina Let me see – oh! In French?

Septimus Yes. Paris is the capital of France.

Thomasina Show me where to read.

He takes the book back from her and finds the page for her. Meanwhile, the piano music from the next room has doubled its notes and its emotion.

Thomasina Four-handed now! Mama is in love with the Count.

Septimus He is a Count in Poland. In Derbyshire he is a piano tuner.

She has taken the book and is already immersed in it. The piano music becomes rapidly more passionate, and then breaks off suddenly in mid-phrase. There is an expressive silence next door which makes Septimus raise his eyes. It does not register with Thomasina. The silence allows us to hear the distant regular thump of the steam engine which is to be a topic. A few moments later Lady Croom enters from the music room, seeming surprised and slightly flustered to find the schoolroom occupied. She collects herself, closing the door behind her. And remains watching, aimless and discreet, as though not wanting to interrupt the lesson. Septimus has stood, and she nods him back into his chair.

Chloë, in Regency dress, enters from the door opposite the music room. She takes in Valentine and Hannah but crosses without pausing to the music room door.

Chloë Oh! – where's Gus?

Valentine Dunno.

Chloë goes into the music room.

Lady Croom (*annoyed*) Oh! – Mr Noakes's engine!

She goes to the garden door and steps outside. Chloë re-enters.

Chloë Damn.

Lady Croom (*calls out*) Mr Noakes!

Valentine He was there not long ago . . .

Lady Croom Halloo!

Chloë Well, he has to be in the photograph – is he dressed?

Hannah Is Bernard back?

Chloë No – he's late!

The piano is heard again, under the noise of the steam engine. Lady Croom steps back into the room.
Chloë steps outside the garden door. Shouts.

Gus!

Lady Croom I wonder you can teach against such a disturbance and I am sorry for it, Mr Hodge.

Chloë comes back inside.

Valentine (*getting up*) Stop ordering everybody about.

Lady Croom It is an unendurable noise.

Valentine The photographer will wait.

But, grumbling, he follows Chloë out of the door she came in by, and closes the door behind them. Hannah remains absorbed. In the silence, the rhythmic thump can be heard again.

Lady Croom The ceaseless dull overbearing monotony of it! It will drive me distracted. I may have to return to town to escape it.

Septimus Your ladyship could remain in the country and let Count Zelinsky return to town where you would not hear him.

Lady Croom I mean Mr Noakes's engine! (*semi-aside to Septimus*) Would you sulk? I will not have my daughter study sulking.

Thomasina (*not listening*) What, mama?

*Thomasina remains lost in her book. Lady Croom
returns to close the garden door and the noise of the
steam engine subsides.*
    *Hannah closes one of the 'garden books', and opens
the next. She is making occasional notes.*
    The piano ceases.

Lady Croom (*to Thomasina*) What are we learning
today? (*Pause.*) Well, not manners.

Septimus We are drawing today.

*Lady Croom negligently examines what Thomasina
had started to draw.*

Lady Croom Geometry. I approve of geometry.

Septimus Your ladyship's approval is my constant object.

Lady Croom Well, do not despair of it. (*Returning to
the window impatiently.*) Where is 'Culpability' Noakes?
(*She looks out and is annoyed.*) Oh! – he has gone for
his hat so that he may remove it.

*She returns to the table and touches the bowl of
dahlias.*
    *Hannah sits back in her chair, caught by what she is
reading.*

For the widow's dowry of dahlias I can almost forgive
my brother's marriage. We must be thankful the monkey
bit the husband. If it had bit the wife the monkey would
be dead and we would not be first in the kingdom to
show a dahlia.

Hannah, still reading the garden book, stands up.

I sent one potted to Chatsworth. The Duchess was most
satisfactorily put out by it when I called at Devonshire
House. Your friend was there lording it as a poet.

Hannah leaves through the door, following Valentine and Chloë.

Meanwhile, Thomasina thumps the book down on the table.

Thomasina Well! Just as I said! Newton's machine which would knock our atoms from cradle to grave by the laws of motion is incomplete! Determinism leaves the road at every corner, as I knew all along, and the cause is very likely hidden in this gentleman's observation.

Lady Croom Of what?

Thomasina The action of bodies in heat.

Lady Croom Is this geometry?

Thomasina This? No, I despise geometry! (*Touching the dahlias she adds, almost to herself:*) The Chater would overthrow the Newtonian system in a weekend.

Septimus Geometry, Hobbes assures us in the *Leviathan*, is the only science God has been pleased to bestow on mankind.

Lady Croom And what does he mean by it?

Septimus Mr Hobbes or God?

Lady Croom I am sure I do not know what either means by it.

Thomasina Oh, pooh to Hobbes! Mountains are not pyramids and trees are not cones. God must love gunnery and architecture if Euclid is his only geometry. There is another geometry which I am engaged in discovering by trial and error, am I not, Septimus?

Septimus Trial and error perfectly describes your enthusiasm, my lady.

Lady Croom How old are you today?

Thomasina Sixteen years and eleven months, mama, and three weeks.

Lady Croom Sixteen years and eleven months. We must have you married before you are educated beyond eligibility.

Thomasina I am going to marry Lord Byron.

Lady Croom Are you? He did not have the manners to mention it.

Thomasina You have spoken to him?!

Lady Croom Certainly not.

Thomasina Where did you see him?

Lady Croom (*with some bitterness*) Everywhere.

Thomasina Did you, Septimus?

Septimus At the Royal Academy where I had the honour to accompany your mother and Count Zelinsky.

Thomasina What was Lord Byron doing?

Lady Croom Posing.

Septimus (*tactfully*) He was being sketched during his visit . . . by the Professor of Painting . . . Mr Fuseli.

Lady Croom There was more posing *at* the pictures than *in* them. His companion likewise reversed the custom of the Academy that the ladies viewing wear more than the ladies viewed – well, enough! Let him be hanged there for a Lamb. I have enough with Mr Noakes, who is to a garden what a bull is to a china shop.

This as Noakes enters.

Thomasina The Emperor of Irregularity! (*She settles down to drawing the diagram which is to be the third item in the surviving portfolio.*)

Lady Croom Mr Noakes!

Noakes Your ladyship –

Lady Croom What have you done to me!

Noakes Everything is satisfactory, I assure you. A little behind, to be sure, but my dam will be repaired within the month –

Lady Croom (*banging the table*) Hush!

In the silence, the steam engine thumps in the distance.

Can you hear, Mr Noakes?

Noakes (*pleased and proud*) The Improved Newcomen steam pump – the only one in England!

Lady Croom That is what I object to. If everybody had his own I would bear my portion of the agony without complaint. But to have been singled out by the only Improved Newcomen steam pump in England, this is hard, sir, this is not to be borne.

Noakes Your lady –

Lady Croom And for what? My lake is drained to a ditch for no purpose I can understand, unless it be that snipe and curlew have deserted three counties so that they may be shot in our swamp. What you painted as forest is a mean plantation, your greenery is mud, your waterfall is wet mud, and your mount is an opencast mine for the mud that was lacking in the dell. (*pointing through the window*) What is that cowshed?

Noakes The hermitage, my lady?

Lady Croom It is a cowshed.

Noakes Madam, it is, I assure you, a very habitable cottage, properly founded and drained, two rooms and a closet under a slate roof and a stone chimney –

Lady Croom And who is to live in it?

Noakes Why, the hermit.

Lady Croom Where is he?

Noakes Madam?

Lady Croom You surely do not supply a hermitage without a hermit?

Noakes Indeed, madam –

Lady Croom Come, come, Mr Noakes. If I am promised a fountain I expect it to come with water. What hermits do you have?

Noakes I have no hermits, my lady.

Lady Croom Not one? I am speechless.

Noakes I am sure a hermit can be found. One could advertise.

Lady Croom Advertise?

Noakes In the newspapers.

Lady Croom But surely a hermit who takes a news-paper is not a hermit in whom one can have complete confidence.

Noakes I do not know what to suggest, my lady.

Septimus Is there room for a piano?

Noakes (*baffled*) A piano?

Lady Croom We are intruding here – this will not do, Mr Hodge. Evidently, nothing is being learned. (*to Noakes*) Come along, sir!

Thomasina Mr Noakes – bad news from Paris!

Noakes Is it the Emperor Napoleon?

Thomasina No. (*She tears the page off her drawing block, with her 'diagram' on it.*) It concerns your heat engine. Improve it as you will, you can never get out of it what you put in. It repays eleven pence in the shilling at most. The penny is for this author's thoughts.

She gives the diagram to Septimus who looks at it.

Noakes (*baffled again*) Thank you, my lady. (*He goes out into the garden.*)

Lady Croom (*to Septimus*) Do you understand her?

Septimus No.

Lady Croom Then this business is over. I was married at seventeen. *Ce soir il faut qu'on parle français, je te demande,* Thomasina, as a courtesy to the Count. Wear your green velvet, please, I will send Briggs to do your hair. Sixteen and eleven months . . .! (*She follows Noakes out of view.*)

Thomasina Lord Byron was with a lady?

Septimus Yes.

Thomasina Huh!

Now Septimus retrieves his book from Thomasina. He turns the pages, and also continues to study Thomasina's diagram. He strokes the tortoise absently as he reads. Thomasina takes up pencil and paper and starts to draw Septimus with Plautus.

Septimus Why does it mean Mr Noakes's engine pays eleven pence in the shilling? Where does he say it?

Thomasina Nowhere. I noticed it by the way. I cannot remember now.

Septimus Nor is he interested by determinism –

Thomasina Oh . . . yes. Newton's equations go forwards and backwards, they do not care which way. But the heat equation cares very much, it goes only one way. That is the reason Mr Noakes's engine cannot give the power to drive Mr Noakes's engine.

Septimus Everybody knows that.

Thomasina Yes. Septimus, they know it about engines!

Septimus (*pause. He looks at his watch.*) A quarter to twelve. For your essay this week, explicate your diagram.

Thomasina I cannot. I do not know the mathematics.

Septimus Without mathematics, then.

Thomasina has continued to draw. She tears the top page from her drawing pad and gives it to Septimus.

Thomasina There. I have made a drawing of you and Plautus.

Septimus (*looking at it*) Excellent likeness. Not so good of me.

Thomasina laughs, and leaves the room. Augustus appears at the garden door. His manner cautious and diffident. Septimus does not notice him for a moment. Septimus gathers his papers together.

Augustus Sir . . .

Septimus My lord . . .?

Augustus I gave you offence, sir, and I am sorry for it.

Septimus I took none, my lord, but you are kind to mention it.

Augustus I would like to ask you a question, Mr Hodge. (*Pause.*) You have an elder brother, I dare say, being a Septimus?

Septimus Yes, my lord. He lives in London. He is the editor of a newspaper, the *Piccadilly Recreation*. (*Pause.*) Was that your question?

Augustus, evidently embarrassed about something, picks up the drawing of Septimus.

Augustus No. Oh . . . it is you? . . . I would like to keep it.

Septimus inclines his head in assent.

There are things a fellow cannot ask his friends. Carnal things. My sister has told me . . . my sister believes such things as I cannot, I assure you, bring myself to repeat.

Septimus You must not repeat them, then. The walk between here and dinner will suffice to put us straight, if we stroll by the garden. It is an easy business. And then I must rely on you to correct your sister's state of ignorance.

A commotion is heard outside – Bernard's loud voice in a sort of agony.

Bernard (*outside the door*) Oh no – no – no – oh, bloody hell! –

Augustus Thank you, Mr Hodge, I will.

Taking the drawing with him, Augustus allows himself to be shown out through the garden door, and Septimus follows him.

Bernard enters the room, through the door Hannah left by. Valentine comes in with him, leaving the door open and they are followed by Hannah who is holding the 'garden book'.

Bernard Oh, no – no –

Hannah I'm sorry, Bernard.

Bernard Fucked by a dahlia! Do you think? Is it open and shut? Am I fucked? What does it really amount to? When all's said and done? Am I fucked? What do you think, Valentine? Tell me the truth.

Valentine You're fucked.

Bernard Oh God! Does it mean that?

Hannah Yes, Bernard, it does.

Bernard I'm not sure. Show me where it says. I want to see it. No – read it – no, wait . . . (*He sits at the table. He prepares to listen as though listening were an oriental art.*) Right.

Hannah (*reading*) 'October 1st, 1810. Today under the direction of Mr Noakes, a parterre was dug on the south lawn and will be a handsome show next year, a consolation for the picturesque catastrophe of the second and third distances. The dahlia having propagated under glass with no ill effect from the sea voyage, is named by Captain Brice 'Charity' for his bride, though the honour properly belongs to the husband who exchanged beds with my dahlia, and an English summer for everlasting night in the Indies.'

Pause.

Bernard Well it's so round the houses, isn't it? Who's to say what it means?

Hannah (*patiently*) It means that Ezra Chater of the Sidley Park connection is the same Chater who described a dwarf dahlia in Martinique in 1810 and died there, of a monkey bite.

Bernard (*wildly*) Ezra wasn't a botanist! He was a poet!

Hannah He was not much of either, but he was both.

Valentine It's not a disaster.

Bernard Of course it's a disaster! I was on 'The Breakfast Hour'!

Valentine It doesn't mean Byron didn't fight a duel, it only means Chater wasn't killed in it.

Bernard Oh, pull yourself together! – do you think I'd have been on 'The Breakfast Hour' if Byron had *missed*!

Hannah Calm down, Bernard. Valentine's right.

Bernard (*grasping at straws*) Do you think so? You mean the *Piccadilly* reviews? Yes, two completely unknown Byron essays – and my discovery of the lines he added to 'English Bards'. That counts for something.

Hannah (*tactfully*) Very possible – persuasive, indeed.

Bernard Oh, bugger persuasive! I've proved Byron was here and as far as I'm concerned he wrote those lines as sure as he shot that hare. If only I hadn't somehow . . . made it all about *killing Chater*. Why didn't you stop me?! It's bound to get out, you know – I mean this – this *gloss* on my discovery – I mean how long do you think it'll be before some botanical pedant blows the whistle on me?

Hannah The day after tomorrow. A letter in *The Times*.

Bernard You wouldn't.

Hannah It's a dirty job but somebody –

Bernard Darling. Sorry. Hannah –

Hannah – and, after all, it is my discovery.

Bernard Hannah.

Hannah Bernard.

Bernard Hannah.

Hannah Oh, shut up. It'll be very short, very dry, absolutely gloat-free. Would you rather it were one of your friends?

Bernard (*fervently*) Oh God, no!

Hannah And then in your letter to *The Times* –

Bernard Mine?

Hannah Well, of course. Dignified congratulations to a colleague, in the language of scholars, I trust.

Bernard Oh, eat shit, you mean?

Hannah Think of it as a breakthrough in dahlia studies.

Chloë hurries in from the garden.

Chloë Why aren't you coming?! – Bernard! And you're not dressed! How long have you been back?

Bernard looks at her and then at Valentine and realizes for the first time that Valentine is unusually dressed.

Bernard Why are you wearing those clothes?

Chloë Do be quick! (*She is already digging into the basket and producing odd garments for Bernard.*) Just put anything on. We're all being photographed. Except Hannah.

Hannah I'll come and watch.

Valentine and Chloë help Bernard into a decorative coat and fix a lace collar round his neck.

Chloë (*to Hannah*) Mummy says have you got the theodolite?

Valentine What are you supposed to be, Chloë? Bo-Peep?

Chloë Jane Austen!

Valentine Of course.

Hannah (*to Chloë*) Oh – it's in the hermitage! Sorry.

Bernard I thought it wasn't till this evening. What photograph?

Chloë The local paper of course – they always come before we start. We want a good crowd of us – Gus looks gorgeous –

Bernard (*aghast*) The newspaper!

He grabs something like a bishop's mitre from the basket and pulls it down completely over his face.

(*Muffled*) I'm ready!

And he staggers out with Valentine and Chloë, followed by Hannah.

A light change to evening. The paper lanterns outside begin to glow. Piano music from the next room.

Septimus enters with an oil lamp. He carries Thomasina's algebra primer, and also her essay on loose sheets. He settles down to read at the table. It is nearly dark outside, despite the lanterns.

Thomasina enters, in a nightgown and barefoot, holding a candlestick. Her manner is secretive and excited.

Septimus My lady! What is it?

Thomasina Septimus! Shush! (*She closes the door quietly.*) Now is our chance!

Septimus For what, dear God?

She blows out the candle and puts the candlestick on the table.

Thomasina Do not act the innocent! Tomorrow I will be seventeen! (*She kisses Septimus full on the mouth.*) There!

Septimus Dear Christ!

Thomasina Now you must show me, you are paid in advance.

Septimus (*understanding*) Oh!

Thomasina The Count plays for us, it is God-given! I cannot be seventeen and not waltz.

Septimus But your mother –

Thomasina While she swoons, we can dance. The house is all abed. I heard the Broadwood. Oh, Septimus, teach me now!

Septimus Hush! I cannot now!

Thomasina Indeed you can, and I am come barefoot so mind my toes.

Septimus I cannot because it is not a waltz.

Thomasina It is not?

Septimus No, it is too slow for waltzing.

Thomasina Oh! Then we will wait for him to play quickly.

Septimus My lady –

Thomasina Mr Hodge! (*She takes a chair next to him and looks at his work.*) Are you reading my essay? Why do you work here so late?

Septimus To save my candles.

Thomasina You have my old primer.

Septimus It is mine again. You should not have written in it.

She takes it, looks at the open page.

Thomasina It was a joke.

Septimus It will make me mad as you promised. Sit over there. You will have us in disgrace.

Thomasina gets up and goes to the furthest chair.

Thomasina If mama comes I will tell her we only met to kiss, not to waltz.

Septimus Silence or bed.

Thomasina Silence!

Septimus pours himself some more wine. He continues to read her essay.
The music changes to party music from the marquee. And there are fireworks – small against the sky, distant flares of light like exploding meteors.
Hannah enters. She has dressed for the party. The difference is not, however, dramatic. She closes the door and crosses to leave by the garden door. But as she gets there, Valentine is entering. He has a glass of wine in his hand.

Hannah Oh . . .

But Valentine merely brushes past her, intent on something, and half-drunk.

Valentine (*to her*) Got it!

He goes straight to the table and roots about in what is now a considerable mess of papers, books and objects. Hannah turns back, puzzled by his manner. He finds what he has been looking for – the 'diagram'.
Meanwhile, Septimus reading Thomasina's essay, also studies the diagram.
Septimus and Valentine study the diagram doubled by time.

It's heat.

Hannah Are you tight, Val?

Valentine It's a diagram of heat exchange.

Septimus So, we are all doomed!

Thomasina (*cheerfully*) Yes.

Valentine Like a steam engine, you see –

Hannah fills Septimus's glass from the same decanter, and sips from it.

She didn't have the maths, not remotely. She saw what things meant, way ahead, like seeing a picture.

Septimus This is not science. This is story-telling.

Thomasina Is it a waltz now?

Septimus No.

The music is still modern.

Valentine Like a film.

Hannah What did she see?

Valentine That you can't run the film backwards. Heat was the first thing which didn't work that way. Not like Newton. A film of a pendulum, or a ball falling through the air – backwards, it looks the same.

Hannah The ball would be going the wrong way.

Valentine You'd have to know that. But with heat – friction – a ball breaking a window –

Hannah Yes.

Valentine It won't work backwards.

Hannah Who thought it did?

Valentine She saw why. You can put back the bits of glass but you can't collect up the heat of the smash. It's gone.

Septimus So the Improved Newtonian Universe must cease and grow cold. Dear me.

Valentine The heat goes into the mix. (*He gestures to indicate the air in the room, in the universe.*)

Thomasina Yes, we must hurry if we are going to dance.

Valentine And everything is mixing the same way, all the time, irreversibly . . .

Septimus Oh, we have time, I think.

Valentine . . . till there's no time left. That's what time means.

Septimus When we have found all the mysteries and lost all the meaning, we will be alone, on an empty shore.

Thomasina Then we will dance. Is this a waltz?

Septimus It will serve. (*He stands up.*)

Thomasina (*jumping up*) Goody!

Septimus takes her in his arms carefully and the waltz lesson, to the music from the marquee, begins.
    Bernard, in unconvincing Regency dress, enters carrying a bottle.

Bernard Don't mind me, I left my jacket . . . (*He heads for the area of the wicker basket.*)

Valentine Are you leaving?

Bernard is stripping off his period coat. He is wearing his own trousers, tucked into knee socks and his own shirt.

Bernard Yes, I'm afraid so.

Hannah What's up, Bernard?

Bernard Nothing I can go into –

Valentine Should I go?

Bernard No, *I'm* going!

Valentine and Hannah watch Bernard struggling into his jacket and adjusting his clothes.
    Septimus, holding Thomasina, kisses her on the mouth. The waltz lesson pauses. She looks at him. He kisses her again, in earnest. She puts her arms round him.

Thomasina Septimus . . .

Septimus hushes her. They start to dance again, with the slight awkwardness of a lesson.
    Chloë bursts in from the garden.

Chloë I'll kill her! I'll *kill* her!

Bernard Oh dear.

Valentine What the hell is it, Chloë?

Chloë (*venomously*) Mummy!

Bernard (*to* Valentine) Your mother caught us in that cottage.

Chloë She snooped!

Bernard I don't think so. She was rescuing a theodolite.

Chloë I'll come with you, Bernard.

Bernard No, you bloody won't.

Chloë Don't you want me to?

Bernard Of course not. What for? (*to* Valentine) I'm sorry.

Chloë (*in furious tears*) What are you saying sorry to *him* for?

Bernard Sorry to you too. Sorry one and all. Sorry, Hannah – sorry, Hermione – sorry, Byron – sorry, sorry, sorry, now can I go?

Chloë stands stiffly, tearfully.

Chloë Well . . .

Thomasina and Septimus dance.

Hannah What a bastard you are, Bernard.

Chloë rounds on her.

Chloë And you mind your own business! What do you know about anything?

Hannah Nothing.

Chloë (*to* Bernard) It *was* worth it, though, wasn't it?

Bernard It was wonderful.

Chloë goes out, through the garden door, towards the party.

Hannah (*an echo*) Nothing.

Valentine Well, you shit. I'd drive you but I'm a bit sloshed.

Valentine follows Chloë out and can be heard outside calling 'Chlo! Chlo!'

Bernard A scrape.

Hannah Oh . . . (*She gives up.*) Bernard!

Bernard I look forward to *The Genius of the Place*. I hope you find your hermit. I think out front is the safest.

He opens the door cautiously and looks out.

Hannah Actually, I've got a good idea who he was, but I can't prove it.

Bernard (*with a carefree expansive gesture*) Publish!

He goes out closing the door.
Septimus and Thomasina are now waltzing freely. She is delighted with herself.

Thomasina Am I waltzing?

Septimus Yes, my lady.

He gives her a final twirl, bringing them to the table where he bows to her. He lights her candlestick.
Hannah goes to sit at the table, playing truant from the party. She pours herself more wine. The table contains the geometrical solids, the computer, decanter, glasses, tea mug, Hannah's research books, Septimus's books, the two portfolios, Thomasina's candlestick, the oil lamp, the dahlia, the Sunday papers . . .
Gus appears in the doorway. It takes a moment to realize that he is not Lord Augustus; perhaps not until Hannah sees him.

Septimus Take your essay, I have given it an alpha in blind faith. Be careful with the flame.

Thomasina I will wait for you to come.

Septimus I cannot.

Thomasina You may.

Septimus I may not.

Thomasina You must.

Septimus I will not.

She puts the candlestick and the essay on the table.

Thomasina Then I will not go. Once more, for my birthday.

Septimus and Thomasina start to waltz together. Gus comes forward, startling Hannah.

Hannah Oh! – you made me jump.

Gus looks resplendent. He is carrying an old and somewhat tattered stiff-backed folio fastened with a tape tied in a bow. He comes to Hannah and thrusts this present at her.

Oh . . .

She lays the folio down on the table and starts to open it. It consists only of two boards hinged, containing Thomasina's drawing.

'Septimus holding Plautus'. (*to Gus*) I was looking for that. Thank you.

Gus nods several times. Then, rather awkwardly, he bows to her. A Regency bow, an invitation to dance.

Oh, dear, I don't really . . .

*After a moment's hesitation, she gets up and they hold
each other, keeping a decorous distance between them,
and start to dance, rather awkwardly.*

*Septimus and Thomasina continue to dance,
fluently, to the piano.*

End.

THE REAL THING

For Miriam

Characters

Max 40-ish
Charlotte 35-ish
Henry 40-ish
Annie 30-ish
Billy 22-ish
Debbie 17
Brodie 25

The Real Thing was first performed on 16 November 1982 at the Strand Theatre, London, with the following cast:

Max Jeremy Clyde
Charlotte Polly Adams
Henry Roger Rees
Annie Felicity Kendal
Billy Michael Thomas
Debbie Susanna Hamilton
Brodie Ian Oliver

Directed by Peter Wood
Lighting by William Bundy
Designed by Carl Toms
Presented by Michael Codron

Act One

SCENE ONE

Max and Charlotte.
   Max doesn't have to be physically impressive, but you wouldn't want him for an enemy. Charlotte doesn't have to be especially attractive, but you instantly want her for a friend.
   Living-room. Architect's drawing board, perhaps. A partly open door leads to an unseen hall and an unseen front door. One or two other doors to other rooms.
   Max is alone, sitting in a comfortable chair, with a glass of wine and an open bottle to hand. He is using a pack of playing cards to build a pyramidical, tiered viaduct on the coffee table in front of him. He is about to add a pair of playing cards (leaning against each other to hold each other up), and the pyramid is going well. Beyond the door to the hall, the front door is heard being opened with a key. The light from there changes as the unseen front door is opened.
   Max does not react to the opening of the door, which is more behind him than in front of him.

Max Don't slam –

   The front door slams, not violently. The viaduct of cards collapses.

(*Superfluously, philosophically*) . . . the door.

   Charlotte, in the hall, wearing a topcoat, looks round the door just long enough to say two words and disappears again.

Charlotte It's me.

Max leaves the cards where they have fallen. He takes a drink from the glass. He doesn't look up at all.
 Charlotte, without the topcoat, comes back into the room carrying a small suitcase and a plastic duty-free airport bag. She puts the case down and comes up behind Max's chair and kisses the top of his head.

Charlotte Hello.

Max Hello, lover.

Charlotte That's nice. You used to call me lover. (*She drops the airport bag on his lap and returns towards the suitcase.*)

Max Oh, it's you. I thought it was my lover. (*He doesn't look at his present. He puts the bag on the floor by his chair.*) Where is it you've been?

The question surprises her. She is deflected from picking up her suitcase – presumably to take it into the bedroom – and the case remains where it is.

Charlotte Well, Switzerland, of course. Weren't you listening?

Max finally looks at her.

Max You look well. Done you good.

Charlotte What, since yesterday?

Max Well, something has. How's Ba'l?

Charlotte Who?

Max affects to puzzle very briefly over her answer.

Max I meant Ba'l.
 Do you say 'Basel'?
 I say Ba'l.

Charlotte Oh . . . yes. I say Basel.

Max (*lilts*) '*Let's* call the whole thing *off* . . .'

Charlotte studies him briefly, quizzically.

Charlotte Fancy a drink? (*She notes the glass, the bottle and his behaviour. Pointedly, but affectionately*) Another drink?

He smiles at her, empties his glass and holds it up for her. She takes the glass, finds a second glass, pours wine into both glasses and gives Max his own glass.

Max How's old Basel, then? Keeping fit?

Charlotte Are you a tiny bit sloshed?

Max Certainly.

Charlotte I didn't go to Basel.

Max is discreetly but definitely interested by that.

Max No? Where did you go, then?

Charlotte Geneva.

Max is surprised. He cackles.

Max Geneva! (*He drinks from his glass.*) How's old Geneva, then? Franc doing well?

Charlotte Who?

He affects surprise.

Max The Swiss franc. Is it doing well?

Charlotte Are you all right?

Max Absolutely.

Charlotte How have you got on?

Max Not bad. My best was eleven pairs on the bottom row, but I ran out of cards.

Charlotte What about the thing you were working on? . . . What is it?

Max An hotel.

Charlotte Yes. You were two elevators short.

Max I've cracked it.

Charlotte Good.

Max I'm turning the whole place on its side and making it a bungalow. I still have a problem with the rooftop pool. As far as I can see, all the water is going to fall into the shallow end. How's the lake, by the way?

Charlotte What lake?

He affects surprise.

Max Lake Geneva. You haven't been to Virginia Water, have you? Lake Geneva. It is at Geneva? It must be. They wouldn't call it Lake Geneva if it was at Ba'l or Basel. They'd call it Lake Ba'l or Basel. You know the Swiss. Utterly reliable. And they've done it without going digital, that's what I admire so much. They know it's all a snare and a delusion. I can remember digitals when they first came out. You had to give your wrist a vigorous shake like bringing down a thermometer, and the only place you could buy one was Tokyo. But it looked all over for the fifteen-jewelled movement. Men ran through the market place shouting, 'The cog is dead.' But still the Swiss didn't panic. In fact, they made a few digitals themselves, as a feint to draw the Japanese further into the mire, and got on with numbering the bank accounts. And now you see how the Japs are desperately putting hands on their digital watches. It's yodelling in the dark. They can yodel till the cows come home. The days of the digitals are numbered.

The metaphor is built into them like a self-destruct mechanism. Mark my words, I was right about the skate-board, I was right about *nouvelle cuisine,* and I'll be proved right about the digital watch. Digitals have got no class, you see. They're science and technology. Makes nonsense of a decent pair of cufflinks, as the Swiss are the first to understand. Good sale?

Charlotte stares at him.

Charlotte What?

He affects surprise.

Max Good sale. Was the sale good? The sale in Geneva, how was it? Did it go well in Geneva, the sale?

Charlotte What's the matter?

Max I'm showing an interest in your work. I thought you liked me showing an interest in your work. *My* showing. Save the gerund and screw the whale. Yes, I'm sure you do. I remember how cross you got when I said to someone, 'My wife works for Sotheby's or Christie's, I forget which.' You misjudged me, as it happens. You thought I was being smart at your expense. In fact, I had forgotten. How's old Christie, by the way? (*Strikes his forehead.*) There I go. How's old Sothers, by the way? Happy with the Geneva sale, I trust?

Charlotte puts her glass down and moves to stand facing him.

Charlotte (*to call a halt*) All right.

Max Just all right? Well, that's the bloody Swiss for you. Conservative, you see. The Japs could show them a thing or two. They'd have a whaling fleet in Lake Geneva by now. How's the skiing, by the way? Plenty of snow?

Charlotte Stop it – stop it – *stop it.*
  What have I done?

Max You forgot your passport.

Charlotte I did what?

Max You went to Switzerland without your passport.

Charlotte What makes you think that?

Max I found it in your recipe drawer.

Charlotte (*quietly*) Jesus God.

Max Quite.

  *Charlotte moves away and looks at him with some
  curiosity.*

Charlotte What were you looking for?

Max Your passport.

Charlotte It's about the last place I would have looked.

Max It was.

Charlotte Why were you looking for it?

Max I didn't know it was going to be your passport.
If you see what I mean.

Charlotte I think I do. You go through my things when
I'm away? (*Pause. Puzzled*) Why?

Max I liked it when I found nothing. You should have
just put it in your handbag. We'd still be an ideal couple.
So to speak.

Charlotte Wouldn't you have checked to see if it had
been stamped?

Max That's a very good point. I notice that you never
went to Amsterdam when you went to Amsterdam.

I must say I take my hat off to you, coming home with Rembrandt place mats for your mother. It's those little touches that lift adultery out of the moral arena and make it a matter of style.

Charlotte I wouldn't go on, if I were you.

Max Rembrandt place mats! I wonder who's got the originals. Some Arab, is it? 'Put the Rembrandts round, Abdul, and tell the kids to wash their hands, it's shoulder of goat.'

Charlotte It's like when we were burgled. The same violation. Worse.

Max I'm not a burglar. I'm your husband.

Charlotte As I said. Worse.

Max Well, I'm sorry.
I think I just apologized for finding out that you've deceived me.
Yes, I did.
How does she do it?

She moves away, to leave the room.

Are you going somewhere?

Charlotte I'm going to bed.

Max Aren't you going to tell me who it is?

Charlotte Who what is?

Max Your lover, lover.

Charlotte Which lover?

Max I assumed there'd only be the one.

Charlotte Did you?

Max Well, do you see them separately or both together?
Sorry, that's not fair.
Well, tell you what, nod your head if it's separately.

She looks at him.

Heavens. If you have an opening free, I'm not doing
much at the moment. Or is the position taken?
It is only two, is it?
Nod your head.

She looks at him.

Golly, you are a dark horse. How do they all three get
away at the same time? Do they work together, like the
Marx Brothers?
I'm not upsetting you, I hope?

Charlotte You underestimate me.

Max (*interested*) Do I? A string quartet, you mean? That
sort of thing? (*He ponders for a moment.*) What does the
fourth one do?

She raises her hand.

Got it. Plays by himself.
You can slap me if you like. I won't slap you back.
I abhor cliché. It's one of the things that has kept me
faithful.

*Charlotte returns to the hall and reappears wearing
her topcoat.*

Charlotte If you don't mind, I think I will go out after
all. (*She moves to close the door behind her.*)

Max You've forgotten your suitcase.

*Pause. She comes back and picks up the suitcase. She
takes the case to the door.*

Charlotte I'm sorry if you've had a bad time. But you've done everything wrong. There's a right thing to say if you can think what it is.

She waits a moment while Max thinks.

Max Is it anyone I know?

Charlotte You aren't anyone I know.

She goes out, closing the door, and then the front door is heard opening and closing.
  Max remains seated. After a moment he reaches down for the airport bag, puts it back on his lap and looks inside it. He starts to laugh. He withdraws from the bag a miniature Alp in a glass bowl. He gives the bowl a shake and creates a snowstorm within it. Then the snowstorm envelops the stage.
  Music – a pop record – makes a bridge into the next scene.

SCENE TWO

Henry, Charlotte, Max and Annie.
  Henry is amiable but can take care of himself. Charlotte is less amiable and can take even better care of herself. Max is nice, seldom assertive, conciliatory. Annie is very much like the woman whom Charlotte has ceased to be.
  A living-room. A record player and shelves of records. Sunday newspapers.
  The music is coming from the record player.
  Henry, with several record sleeves around him, is searching for a particular piece of music.
  There are doors to hall, kitchen, bedroom. Charlotte enters barefoot, wearing Henry's dressing-gown which is too big for her. She is unkempt from sleep and seems generally disordered. Henry looks up briefly.

Henry Hello.

Charlotte moves forward without answering, sits down and looks around in a hopeless way.

Charlotte Oh, God.

Henry I thought you'd rather lie in. Do you want some coffee?

Charlotte I don't know. (*possibly referring to the litter of record sleeves, wanly*) What a mess.

Henry Don't worry . . . don't worry . . . (*He continues to search among the records.*)

Charlotte I think I'll just stay in bed.

Henry Actually, I phoned Max.

Charlotte What? Why?

Henry He was on my conscience. He's coming round.

Charlotte (*quite strongly*) I don't want to see *him*.

Henry Sorry.

Charlotte Honestly, Henry.

Henry Hang on – I think I've found it.

He removes the pop record, which might have come to its natural end by now, from the record player and puts a different record on. Meanwhile –

Charlotte Are you still doing your list?

Henry Mmm.

Charlotte Have you got a favourite book?

Henry *Finnegans Wake.*

Charlotte Have you read it?

Henry Don't be difficult. (*He lowers the arm on to the record and listens to a few bars of alpine Strauss – or sub-Strauss. Then he lifts the arm again.*) No . . . No . . . Damnation. (*He starts to put the record away.*) Do you remember when we were in some place like Bournemouth or Deauville, and there was an open-air dance floor right outside our window?

Charlotte No.

Henry Yes you do, I was writing my Sartre play, and there was this bloody orchestra which kept coming back to the same tune every twenty minutes, so I started shouting out of the window and the hotel manager –

Charlotte That was Zermatt. (*scornfully*) *Bournemouth.*

Henry Well, what was it?

Charlotte What was what?

Henry What was the tune called? It sounded like Strauss or somebody.

Charlotte How does it go?

Henry I don't know, do I?

Charlotte Who were you with in Bournemouth?

Henry Don't mess about. I'm supposed to give them my eight records tomorrow, and so far I've got five and *Finnegans Wake*.

Charlotte Well, if you don't know what it's called and you can't remember how it goes, why in Christ's name do you want it on your desert island?

Henry It's not supposed to be eight records you love and adore.

Charlotte Yes, it is.

Henry It is not. It's supposed to be eight records you associate with turning-points in your life.

Charlotte Well, I'm a turning-point in your life, and when you took me to Zermatt your favourite record was the Ronettes doing 'Da Doo Ron Ron'.

Henry The Crystals. (*scornfully*) The Ronettes.

Charlotte gets up and during the following searches, successfully, for a record, which she ends up putting on the machine.

Charlotte You're going about this the wrong way. Just pick your eight all-time greats and then remember what you were doing at the time. What's wrong with that?

Henry I'm supposed to be one of your intellectual playwrights. I'm going to look a total prick, aren't I, announcing that while I was telling Jean-Paul Sartre and the post-war French existentialists where they had got it wrong, I was spending the whole time listening to the Crystals singing 'Da Doo Ron Ron'. Look, ages ago, Debbie put on one of those classical but not too classical records – she must have been about ten or eleven, it was before she dyed her hair – and I said to you, 'That's that bloody tune they were driving me mad with when I was trying to write "Jean-Paul is up the Wall" in that hotel in Deauville all those years ago.' Or Zermatt. Maybe *she'll* remember.

Charlotte Where is she?

Charlotte has placed the record on the machine, which now starts to play the Skater's Waltz.

Henry Riding stables. That's it! (*triumphant and pleased, examining the record sleeve*) Skater's Waltz! How did you know?

Charlotte They don't have open-air dance floors in the Alps in mid-winter. They have skating rinks. Now you've got six.

Henry Oh, I can't use that. It's so banal.

The doorbell rings. Henry goes to take the record off the machine.

That's Max. Do you want to let him in?

Charlotte No. Say I'm not here.

Henry He knows perfectly well you're here. Where else would you be? I'll say you don't want to see him because you've seen quite enough of him. How's that?

Charlotte (*giving up*) Oh, I'll get dressed.

She goes out the way she came in, towards the bedroom. Henry goes out through another door into the hall. His voice and Max's voice are heard, and the two men come in immediately afterwards.

Henry Hello, Max. Come in.

Max Hello, Henry.

Henry (*entering*) It's been some time.

Max enters unassertively.

Max Well, you've rather been keeping out of the way, haven't you?

Henry Yes. I'm sorry, Max. (*indicating the bedroom*) Charlotte's not here. How are you?

Max I'm all right.

Henry Good.

Max And you?

Henry I'm all right.

Max Good.

Henry Well, we all seem to be all right.

Max Is Charlotte all right?

Henry I don't think she's terribly happy. Well, is it coffee or open a bottle?

Max Bottle, I should think.

Henry Hang on, then.

Henry goes out through the door to the kitchen.
Max turns aside and looks at a paper without interest.
Charlotte enters from the bedroom, having dressed
without trying hard. She regards Max, who then
notices her.

Max Hello, darling.

Charlotte Don't I get a day off?

Max (*apologetically*) Henry phoned . . .

Charlotte (*more kindly*) It's all right, Max.

Henry enters busily from the kitchen, carrying an
open champagne bottle and a jug of orange juice.
Wine glasses are available in the living-room. Henry
puts himself in charge of arranging the drinks.

Henry Hello, Charlotte. I was just telling Max you weren't here. So nice to see you, Max. What are you doing with yourself?

Max Is he joking?

Henry I mean apart from that. Actors are so sensitive. They feel neglected if one isn't constantly checking up on them.

Max I was just telling Henry off for keeping out of the way.

Charlotte You'd keep out of the way if you'd written it. (*to Henry*) If that orange juice is for me, you can forget it.

Henry No, no – buck's fizz all round. I feel reckless, extravagant, famous, in love, and I'm next week's castaway on *Desert Island Discs*.

Max Are you really?

Henry Head over heels.
   How was last night, by the way? (*He hands Max and Charlotte their glasses.*)

Charlotte Hopeless. I had to fake it again.

Henry Very witty woman, my present wife. Actually, I was talking about my play.

Charlotte Actually, so was I. I've decided it's a mistake appearing in Henry's play.

Max Not for me, it isn't.

Charlotte Well, of course not for you, you idiot, you're not his wife.

Max Oh, I see what you mean.

Charlotte Max sees what I mean. All those people out front thinking, that's why she got the job. You're right, Max.

Max I never said anything!

Charlotte And also thinking that I'm *her* . . . coming in with my little suitcase and my duty-free bag – 'It's me!' – ooh, it's her! – so that's what they're like at home – he's scintillating and she's scintillated.

Henry starts to speak.

Look out, he's going to scintillate.

Henry How was it really? – last night.

Charlotte Not good. The stalls had a deserted look, about two-thirds, I should think. (*with false innocence*) Oh, sorry, darling, is that what you meant?

Max (*disapproving*) Honestly, Charlotte. It was all right, Henry, *really*. All the laughs were in place, for a Saturday night anyway, and I had someone who came round afterwards who said the reconciliation scene was extremely moving. Actually, that reminds me. They *did* say – I mean, it's a tiny thing but I thought I'd pass it on because I do feel rather the same way . . . I mean all that stuff about the Japanese and digital watches – they suddenly have no idea what I'm talking about, you see, and I thought if we could just try it one night without –

Henry halts him, like a traffic policeman.

Henry Excuse me, Max. (*Henry turns to Charlotte.*) Two-thirds empty or two-thirds full?

Charlotte laughs brazenly.

Charlotte Hard luck, Max. (*She toasts.*) Well, here's to closing night. To the collapse of *House of Cards*.

Max (*shocked*) Charlotte!

Charlotte Well, you try playing the feed one night instead of acting Henry after a buck's fizz and two rewrites. All *his* laughs are in place all right. So's my groan. Groan, groan, they all go when they find out. Oh, *groan,* so she hasn't got a lover at all, eh? And they lose interest in me totally. I'm a victim of Henry's fantasy – a quiet, faithful bird with an interesting job, and a recipe drawer, and a stiff upper lip, and two semi-stiff lower ones all trembling for him – 'I'm sorry if you've had a bad time . . . There's a right thing to say now . . .'

Max Jesus, Charlotte –

Charlotte (*quite genially*) Oh, shut up, Max. If he'd given her a lover instead of a temporary passport, we'd be in a play. But he could no more do that than he could architect a hotel. Sorry, *an* hotel.

Henry It's a little early in the day for all this.

Charlotte No, darling, it's a little late.

Henry She's good, you know, she's awfully good. She gets it from me.

Charlotte Oh, yes, without you I'd be like one of your women. 'Fancy a drink?' 'Let me get you a drink.' 'Care for a drink?' That's Henry's idea of women's parts. Drinks and feeds. That's the public parts. There's a feed, Henry.

Henry You know, this desert island thing has a lot to be said for it.

Charlotte You'd go mad, darling.

Henry I was thinking of you, darling. You could have one of my plays as your book.

Charlotte I'll have the one with the largest number of pages.

Max interposes his body, as it were.

Max Er, where's young Deborah today?

Charlotte Who?

Max Debbie.

Charlotte (*baffled*) Debbie?

Max Your daughter.

Charlotte Daughter? Daughter? Must be some mistake. No place for children. Smart talk, that's the thing. Children are so unsmart. Before you know where you are, the chat is all about the price of sandals. Henry couldn't do that. He doesn't like research.

Henry True.

Charlotte Can't have a lot of kids complicating the clean exit with suitcase.

Max (*to Charlotte*) Lots of people don't have children, in real life. Me and Annie . . .

Henry Oh, don't – I told her once that lots of women were only good for fetching drinks, and she became quite unreasonable.

Blithely, knowing what he is doing, Henry holds his empty glass towards Charlotte.

Is there any more of that?

Max glances at Charlotte and hastily tries to defuse the bomb.

Max Let me . . .

Max takes Henry's glass and fills it from the bottle and the jug.

Charlotte Lots of *men* are only good for fetching drinks – why don't you write about *them*?

Max hands the glass back to Henry.

Henry (*smiling up at Max*) Terribly pleased you could come round.

Charlotte Oh, yes, you owe him a drink. I'm the victim of his fantasy, and you're quids in on it. What an ego trip! Having all the words to come back with just as you need them. That's the difference between plays and real life – thinking time, time to get your bottle back. 'Must say, I take my hat off to you, coming home with Rembrandt place mats for your mother.' You don't really think that if Henry caught me out with a lover, he'd sit around being witty about place mats? Like hell he would. He'd come apart like a pick-a-sticks. His sentence structure would go to pot, closely followed by his sphincter. You know that, don't you, Henry? Henry? No answer. Are you there, Henry? Say something witty.

Henry turns his head to her.

Henry Is it anyone I know?

Max (*starting to rise*) Well, look, thanks for the drink –

Charlotte Oh, sit down, Max, for God's sake, or he'll think it's you.

Max subsides unhappily.

Henry Just kidding, Max. Badinage. You know, *dialogue*.

The doorbell rings.

See what I mean?

Max Annie said she'd come round if her committee finished early. She's on this Justice for Brodie Committee . . . you know . . . (*Pause.*) I'll go, should I?

Henry I'll go.

Max No, stay where you are, I'll see if it's her. (*He goes out to the front door.*)

Charlotte Thanks very much. Anyone else coming?

Henry Just give them a Twiglet. They won't stay.

Charlotte What did you phone him for in the first place?

Henry Well, I only have to write it once. He has to show up every night. I had a conscience.

Charlotte Do you have a conscience about me too?

Henry Absolutely. You can have a Twiglet.

Charlotte Well, don't ask her about Brodie.

Henry Right.

Charlotte If she starts on about scapegoats and cover-ups, she'll get a Twiglet up her nostril.

Henry Right.

Charlotte (*enthusiastically*) Darling! It's been ages!

Annie has entered, followed by Max. Annie is carrying a carrier bag loaded with greengrocery.

Annie Hello, Charlotte. This is jolly nice of you.

Max We can only stay a minute.

Annie How are you, Henry?

Henry Fine.

Max Annie's stewarding at the protest meeting this afternoon, so we can't –

Henry Oh, do shut up. Don't take any notice of Max. I made him nervous.

Annie What did you do to him?

Henry Nothing at all. I asked him if he was having an affair with Charlotte, and he was offended.

Annie Was he?

Henry Apparently not. Been shopping?

Annie Not exactly. I saw a place open on my way back and . . . Anyway, you might as well take it as an offering.

Charlotte (*taking the bag from her and investigating it*) Darling, there was absolutely no need to bring . . . mushrooms?

Annie Yes.

Charlotte (*not quite behaving well*) And a turnip . . .

Annie (*getting unhappy*) And carrots . . . Oh, dear, it must look as if –

Henry Where's the meat?

Charlotte Shut up.

Annie I wish I'd brought flowers now.

Charlotte This is much nicer.

Henry So original. I'll get a vase.

Annie It's supposed to be crudités.

Henry Crudités! Perfect title for a pornographic revue.

Charlotte I'll make a dip.

Max We're not staying to eat, for heaven's sake.

Henry Just a quick dip.

Annie Would you like *me* to?

Charlotte No, no. I know where everything is.

Henry Yes, Charlotte will provide dips for the crudity. She knows where everything is.

> *Charlotte takes charge of the vegetables. Henry gets a fourth glass.*

Sit down, have some buck's fizz. I feel reckless, extravagant, famous, and I'm next week's castaway on *Desert Island Discs*. You can be my luxury if you like.

Annie I'm not sure I'm one you can afford.

Max What are your eight records?

Henry This is the problem. I hate music.

Charlotte He likes pop music.

Henry You don't have to repeat everything I say.

Max I don't understand the problem.

Charlotte The problem is he's a snob without being an inverted snob. He's *ashamed* of liking pop music. (*She takes the vegetables out into the kitchen, closing the door.*)

Henry This is true. The trouble is I don't like the pop music which it's all right to like. You can have a bit of Pink Floyd shoved in between your symphonies and your Dame Janet Baker – that shows a refreshing breadth of taste or at least a refreshing candour – but *I* like Wayne Fontana and the Mindbenders doing 'Um Um Um Um Um Um'.

Max Doing what?

Henry That's the title. (*He demonstrates it.*) 'Um-Um-Um-Um-Um-Um'. I like Neil Sedaka. Do you remember 'Oh, Carol'?

Max For God's sake.

Henry (*cheerfully*) Yes, I'm not very up to date. I like Herman's Hermits, and the Hollies, and the Everly Brothers, and Brenda Lee, and the Supremes . . . I don't mean everything they did. I don't like *artists*. I like singles.

Max This is sheer pretension.

Henry (*insistently*) No. It *moves* me, the way people are supposed to be moved by *real* music. I was taken once to Covent Garden to hear a woman called Callas in a sort of foreign musical with no dancing which people were donating kidneys to get tickets for. The idea was that I would be cured of my strange disability. As though the place were a kind of Lourdes, except that instead of the front steps being littered with wooden legs, it would be tin ears. My illness at the time took the form of believing that the Righteous Brothers' recording of 'You've Lost that Lovin' Feelin'' on the London label was possibly the most haunting, the most deeply moving noise ever produced by the human spirit, and this female vocalist person was going to set me right.

Max No good?

Henry Not even close. That woman would have had a job getting into the top thirty if she was *hyped*.

Max You preferred the Brothers.

Henry I did. Do you think there's something wrong with me?

Max Yes. I'd say you were a moron.

Henry What can I do?

Max There's nothing you can do.

Henry I mean about *Desert Island Discs*.

Annie You know damned well what you should do.

Henry Cancel?

Max Actually, I remember it. (*He sings, badly.*) 'You've lost that lovin' feeling . . .'

Henry That's an idea – aversion therapy.

Max (*sings*) '. . . that lovin' feeling . . . You've lost that lovin' feeling . . .'

Henry I think it's working.

Max (*sings*)
    '. . . it's gorn, gorn, gorn . . . oh – oh – oh – yeah . . .'

Henry (*happily*) God, it's *rubbish*! You've cracked it. Now do 'Oh Carol'.

Max I don't know that one.

Henry I'll play it for you.

Max I think I'll go and help Charlotte.

Annie I should go.

Max No. I thought of it first.

   Charlotte enters, carrying a bowl.

Charlotte One dip.

Max I was coming to help.

Charlotte All right, you can chop.

Max Fine. Chop . . .

   Max goes out into the kitchen. Charlotte places the bowl and is about to follow Max out. Henry dips his finger into the bowl and tastes the dip.

Henry It needs something.

Charlotte I beg your pardon?

Henry It needs something. A bit of interest. Garlic? Lemon juice? I don't know.

Charlotte (*coldly*) Perhaps you should employ a cook.

Henry Surely that would be excessive – a cook who spends all her time emptying jars of mayonnaise and adding lemon juice? What would we do with the surplus?

Charlotte Presumably put it on stage with the rest of your stuff.

Charlotte goes out into the kitchen, closing the door. Pause.

Henry Are you all right?

Annie nods.

Annie Are you all right?

Henry nods.

Touch me.

Henry shakes his head.

Touch me.

Henry No.

Annie Come on, touch me.
Help yourself.
Touch me anywhere you like.

Henry No.

Annie Touch me.

Henry No.

Annie Coward.

Henry I love you anyway.

Annie Yes, say that.

Henry I love you.

169

Annie Go on.

Henry I love you.

Annie That's it.

Henry I love you.

Annie Touch me then. They'll come in or they won't. Take a chance. Kiss me.

Henry For Christ's sake.

Annie Quick one on the carpet then.

Henry You're crackers.

Annie I'm not interested in your mind.

Henry Yes, you are.

Annie No, I'm not, I lied to you.

Pause. Henry smiles at her.

I hate Sunday.

Henry Thought I'd cheer you up with an obscene phone call, but Max got to it first, so I improvised.

Annie I might have come round anyway. 'Hello, Henry, Charlotte, just passing, long time no see.'

Henry That would have been pushing it.

Annie I'm in a mood to push it. Let's go while they're chopping turnips.

Henry You *are* crackers.

Annie We'll go, and then it will be done. Max will suffer. Charlotte will make you suffer and get custody. You'll see Debbie on Sundays, and in three years she'll be at university not giving a damn either way.

Henry It's not just Debbie.

Annie No, you want to give it time –

Henry Yes –

Annie . . . time to go wrong, change, spoil. Then you'll know it wasn't the real thing.

Henry I don't steal other men's wives.

Annie *Sod* you.

Henry You know what I mean.

Annie Yes, you mean you love me but you don't want it to get around. Me and the Righteous Brothers. Well, sod you.

The kitchen door is flung open and Max enters rather dramatically, bleeding from a cut finger.

Max Don't panic! Have you got a hankie?

Annie Max?

Annie and Henry respond appropriately, each searching for a handkerchief. Henry produces one first, a clean white one, from his pocket.

Henry Here –

Max Thanks. No, let me –

Annie Let me see.

Max It's all right, it's not as bad as it looks. (*to Henry.*) Typical of your bloody kitchen – all champagne and no elastoplast.

Annie Poor love, just hold the cut for a while.

Max I think I'll put it back under the tap. (*He moves towards the kitchen.*)

Henry Sorry about this, Max. She tried to do it to me once.

Max leaves, leaving the door open. Henry and Annie's conversation is in no way furtive but pitched to acknowledge the open door.

Annie I'm sorry.

Henry No, I'm sorry.

Annie It's all right. Anything's all right.

Henry moves forward and kisses her lightly.

Henry It'll get better.

Annie How?

Henry Maybe we'll get found out.

Annie Better to tell them. Whoever comes in first, eh? If it's Max, I'll tell him. If it's Charlotte, you start.
All right?
It's easy. Like Butch Cassidy and the Sundance Kid jumping off the cliff.
It's only a couple of marriages and a child.
All right?

Charlotte enters from the kitchen, carrying a tray of chopped-up vegetables.

(*To Henry*) All right?

This is bold as brass and, consequently, safe as houses: in this way Annie and Henry continue to speak quite privately to each other in the interstices of the general conversation, under or over the respective preoccupations of Charlotte and Max.

Charlotte Did Max tell you? It's red cabbage. I've taken him off the knives. He's making another dip. He says it's

Hawaiian. It's supposed to be served in an empty
pineapple. We haven't got a pineapple. He's going to
serve it in an empty tin of pineapple chunks. I do envy
you being married to a man with a sense of humour.
Henry thinks he has a sense of humour, but what he has
is a joke reflex. Eh, Henry? His mind is racing. Pineapple,
pineapple . . . Come on, darling.

Henry (*to Annie*) No. Sorry.

Annie It's all right.

Charlotte (*busy with cutlery*) Is Debbie expecting lunch?

Henry (*to Annie*) No.

Charlotte What?

Henry No. She wants to stay out.

Annie drinks what remains in her glass.

Annie Where is Debbie?

Henry Riding school. Drink?

Henry takes her empty glass out of her hand.

Annie Love you.

Charlotte She used to eat like a horse, till she had one.

Henry refills Annie's glass.

Henry I'm picking her up this afternoon. (*He returns
Annie's glass.*) Buck's fizz all right?

Charlotte Picking her up?

Annie I don't care.

*Max enters with the Hawaiian dip in the pineapple
tin.*

Max Here we are.

Annie Anything's all right.

Max It's Hawaiian.

Henry You're a lovely feller.

Charlotte Well done, Max.

Annie So are you. (*She meets Max, dips her finger into the tin and tastes the dip.*)

Max I hope I've got it right. What do you think?

In his other hand Max has Henry's somewhat blood-stained handkerchief, which he now offers back.

(*To Henry*) Thanks. What should I do with it?

Henry (*taking it*) It's OK, I'll take it. (*He puts the handkerchief in his pocket.*)

Annie (*to Max*) Not bad. (*to Charlotte*) May I?

Charlotte Feel free.

Annie Hang on a sec. (*She takes the tin from Max and leaves the room with it, going to the kitchen.*)

Charlotte (*to Henry*) You're over-protective. She could walk it in half an hour.

Max Who, what?

Charlotte Debbie.

Henry By the time she finished mucking out, whatever they call it . . .

Charlotte Grooming the mount, mounting the groom . . .

Henry (*unamused*) Hilarious.

Max *I* wouldn't let her walk. Someone got murdered on the common not long ago. Mustn't put temptation in the way.

174

Charlotte Debbie wouldn't murder anyone. She'd just duff them up a little bit. I can't make her out at all.

Annie re-enters with the dip.

Some people have daughters who love ponies.

Passing Henry, Annie casually puts her finger in his mouth, without pausing.

Annie What do you think?

Charlotte Some people have daughters who go punk. We've got one who goes riding on Barnes Common looking like the Last of the Mohicans.

Henry Crackers.

Annie delivers the dip to Charlotte.

Charlotte (*to Annie*) Is yours a case of sperm count or twisted tubes? Or is it that you just can't stand the little buggers?

Max Charlotte!

Henry What business is that of yours?

Charlotte He's in love with his, you know.

Annie Isn't that supposed to be normal?

Charlotte No, dear, normal is the other way round.

Henry I say, Annie, what's this Brodie Committee all about? Charlotte was asking.

Max You know, Private Brodie.

Annie It's all right.

Max Annie knows him.

Annie I don't know him.

Max Tell them about meeting him on the train.

Annie Yes. I met him on a train.

Pause. But Henry, exhibiting avid interest, disobliges her.

Henry Yes?

Annie (*laughs uncomfortably*) I seem to have told this story before.

Henry But we haven't seen you for ages.

Max Annie was travelling up to London from our cottage, weren't you?

Henry *Were* you?

Annie Yes.

Henry (*fascinated*) You have a cottage in . . .?

Annie Norfolk.

Henry Norfolk! What, up in the hills there?

Annie (*testily*) *What* hills? Norfolk is absolutely – (*She brings herself up short.*)

Charlotte Oh, very funny. Stop it, Henry.

Henry I have no idea what you are talking about. So, you were coming up to London from your flat in Norfolk – *cottage* – and you met this Private Brodie on the train.

Annie Yes.

Max It was quite remarkable. Brodie was on his way to the anti-missiles demonstration, just like Annie.

Henry *Really?*

Annie Yes.

Henry How did you know? Was he wearing a 'Missiles Out' badge on his uniform?

Annie He wasn't in uniform.

Max The guts of it, the sheer moral courage. An ordinary soldier using his weekend pass to demonstrate against their bloody missiles.

Henry *Their? I* thought they were ours.

Max No, they're American.

Henry Oh, yes – *their* . . .

Max Pure moral conscience, you see – I mean, he didn't have our motivation.

Henry *Our?*

Max Mine and Annie's.

Henry appears not to understand.

Owning property in Little Barmouth.

Henry Yes, of course. Private Brodie didn't own a week-end cottage in Little Barmouth, you mean.

Max No, he's a Scots lad. He was stationed at the camp down the road. He was practically guarding the base where these rockets are making Little Barmouth into a sitting duck for the Russian counter-attack, should it ever come to that.

Henry (*to Annie*) I see what you mean.

Annie Do you?

Henry Well, yes. Little Barmouth isn't going to declare war on Russia, so why should Little Barmouth be wiped out in a war not of Little Barmouth's making?

Max Quite.

Charlotte Shut up, Henry.

Max Is he being like that?

Charlotte Yes, he's being like that.

Max I don't see what he's got to be like that about.

Henry (*capitulating enthusiastically*) Absolutely! So you met this Private Brodie on the train, and Brodie said, 'I see you're going to the demo down Whitehall.' Right?

Annie No. He recognized me from my children's serial. He used to watch *Rosie of the Royal Infirmary* when he was a kid.

Max How *about* that? It seems like the day before yesterday Annie was doing *Rosie of the Royal Infirmary.* He's *still* a kid.

Annie Yes. Twenty-one.

Max He's a child.

Henry He kicked two policemen inside out, didn't he?

Max Piss off.
(*To Charlotte*) If you want to know what it's all about, you should come to the meeting.

Charlotte I know I should, but I like to keep my Sundays free. For entertaining friends, I mean. Fortunately, there are people like Annie to make up for people like me.

Henry Perhaps I'll go.

Charlotte No, you're people like me. You tell him, Annie.

Annie You're picking up Debbie from riding school.

Charlotte When Henry comes across a phrase like 'the caring society' he scrunches up the *Guardian* and draws his knees up into his chest.

Henry That's merely professional fastidiousness. Yes, come to that, I think I'll join the Justice for Brodie Committee. I should have thought of that before.

Charlotte They don't want dilettantes. You have to be properly motivated, like Annie.

Henry I don't see that my motivation matters a damn. Least of all to Brodie. He just wants to get out of jail. What does he care if we're motivated by the wrong reasons.

Max Like what?

Henry Like the desire to be taken for properly motivated members of the caring society. One of us is probably kicking his father, a policeman. Another is worried that his image is getting a bit too right-of-centre. Another is in love with a committee member and wishes to gain her approbation . . .

Charlotte Which one are you?

Henry You think I'm kidding, but I'm not. Public postures have the configuration of private derangement.

Max Who said that?

Henry I did, you fool.

Max I mean first.

Henry Oh, first. (*to Annie*) Take him off to your meeting, I'm sick of him.

Annie He's not coming.

Henry (*savouring it*) You are not going to the meeting?

Max No, actually. Not that I wouldn't, but it would mean letting down my squash partner.

Henry Squash partner? An interesting moral dilemma. I wonder what Saint Augustine would have done?

Max I don't think Saint Augustine had a squash partner.

Henry I know that. Nobody would play with him. Even so. I put myself in his place. I balance a pineapple chunk on my carrot. I ponder. On the one hand, Max's squash partner. Decent chap but not a deprivation of the first magnitude. And on the other hand, Brodie, an out-and-out thug, an arsonist, vandalizer of a national shrine, *but* mouldering in jail for years to come owing, *perhaps*, to society's inability to comprehend a man divided against himself, a pacifist hooligan.

Max I don't condone vandalism, however idealistic. I just –

Henry Yes, well, as acts of vandalism go, starting a fire on the Cenotaph using the wreath to the Unknown Soldier as kindling scores very low on discretion. I assumed he was trying to be provocative.

Max Of course he was, you idiot. But he got hammered by an emotional backlash.

Henry No, no, you *can't* –

Max Yes, he bloody was!

Henry I mean 'hammer' and 'backlash'. You can't *do it*!

Max Oh, for Christ's sake. This is your house, and I'm drinking your wine, but if you don't mind me saying so, Henry –

Henry *My* saying, Max.

Max Right. (*He puts down his glass definitively and stands up.*) Come on, Annie.
There's something wrong with you.
You've got something missing. You may have all the answers, but having all the answers is not what life's about.

Henry I'm sorry, but it actually *hurts*.

Max Brodie may be no intellectual, like you, but he did march for a cause, and now he's got six years for a stupid piece of bravado and a punch-up, and he'd have been forgotten in a week if it wasn't for Annie. That's what life's about – messy bits of good and bad luck, and people caring and not necessarily having all the answers. Who the hell are you to patronize Annie? She's worth ten of you.

Henry I know that.

Max I'm sorry, Charlotte.

Charlotte Well done, Henry.

Max leaves towards the front door. Charlotte, with a glance at Henry, rolling her eyes in rebuke, follows him out of the room. Annie stands up. For the rest of the scene she is moving, hardly looking at Henry, perhaps fetching her handbag.

Henry It was just so I could look at you without it looking funny.

Annie What time are you going for Debbie?

Henry Four o'clock. Why?

Annie Three o'clock. Look for my car.

Henry What about Brodie?

Annie Let him rot.

Annie leaves, closing the door. Pop music: Herman's Hermits, 'I'm Into Something Good'.

SCENE THREE

Max and Annie.
A living-room.
*Max is alone, listening to a small radio, from which
Herman's Hermits continue to be heard, at an adjusted
level. The disposition of furniture and doors makes the
scene immediately reminiscent of the beginning of Scene 1.
The front door, offstage, is heard being opened with a
key. The door closes. Annie, wearing a topcoat, appears
briefly round the door to the hall. She is in a hurry.*

Annie Have you got it on? (*She disappears and reappears
without the coat.*) How much have I missed?

Max Five or ten minutes.

Annie Damn. If I'd had the car, I'd have caught the
beginning.

Max Where have you been?

Annie You know where I've been. Rehearsing.

*The music ends and is followed by Henry being
interviewed on* Desert Island Discs, *but the radio
dialogue, during the few moments before Max turns
the sound down, is meaningless under the stage
dialogue.*

Max How's Julie?

Annie Who?

Max Julie. Miss Julie. Strindberg's Miss Julie. Miss Julie
by August Strindberg, how is she?

Annie Are you all right?

Max This probably –

Annie Shush up.

Max This probably isn't anything, but –

Annie *Max,* can I *listen?*

Max turns the radio sound right down.

What's up? Are you cross?

Max This probably isn't anything, but I found this in the car, between the front seats. (*He shows her a soiled and blood-stained white handkerchief.*)

Annie What is it?

Max Henry's handkerchief.

Annie Well, give it back to him. (*She reaches for it.*) Here, I'll wash it and you can give it to Charlotte at the theatre.

Max I did give it back to him.
When was he in the car?

Pause

It was a clean handkerchief, apart from my blood.
Have you got a cold?
It looks filthy. It's dried filthy.
You're filthy.
You filthy cow.
You rotten filthy –

He starts to cry, barely audible, immobile. Annie waits. He recovers his voice.

It's not true, is it?

Annie Yes.

Max Oh, God. (*He starts up.*) Why did you?

Annie I'm awfully sorry, Max –

Max (*interrupting, suddenly pulled together*) All right.
It happened. All right. It didn't mean anything.

Annie I'm awfully sorry, Max, but I love him.

Max Oh, no.

Annie Yes.

Max Oh, *no*. You don't.

Annie Yes, I do. And he loves me. That's that, isn't it?
I'm sorry it's awful. But it's better really. All that lying.

Max (*breaking up again*) Oh, Christ, Annie, stop it.
I love you. Please don't –

Annie Come on, please – it doesn't have to be like this.

Max How long for? And *him* – oh, *God*.

> *He kicks the radio savagely. The radio has gone into*
> *music again – the Righteous Brothers singing 'You've*
> *Lost That Lovin' Feelin'' – and Max's kick has the*
> *effect of turning up the volume rather loud. He flings*
> *himself upon Annie in something like an assault which*
> *turns immediately into an embrace. Annie does no*
> *more than suffer the embrace, looking over Max's*
> *shoulder, her face blank.*

SCENE FOUR

Henry and Annie.
> *Living-room. Obviously temporary and makeshift*
> *quarters, divided left and right by a clothes rail, making*
> *two areas, 'his' and 'hers'. Henry is alone, writing at*
> *a desk.*
> *The disposition of door and furniture makes the scene*
> *immediately reminiscent of Scene Two. On the floor are*

a number of cardboard boxes containing files, papers,
letters, scripts, bills . . . The pillage of a filing system.
There is also a couch. The Sunday newspapers and a
bound script are on or near the couch.
    A radio plays pop music quietly while Henry writes.
Annie enters from the bedroom door, barefoot and
wearing Henry's robe, which is too big for her. Henry,
in mid-sentence, looks up briefly and looks down again.

Annie I'm not here. Promise.

> *She goes to the couch and carefully opens a newspaper.*
> *Henry continues to write. Annie glances towards him*
> *once or twice. He takes no notice. She stands up and*
> *goes behind his chair, looking over his shoulder as he*
> *works. He takes no notice. She goes round the desk*
> *and stands in front of him. He takes no notice. She*
> *flashes open the robe for his benefit. He takes no*
> *notice. She moves round behind him again and looks*
> *over his shoulder. He turns and grabs her with great*
> *suddenness, causing her to scream and laugh. The*
> *assault turns into a standing embrace.*

Henry You're a bloody nuisance.

Annie Sorry, sorry, sorry. I'll be good. I'll sit and learn
my script.

Henry No, you won't.

Annie I'll go in the other room.

Henry This room will do.

Annie No, you've got to do my play.

Henry I can't write it. Let me off.

Annie No, you promised. It's my gift.

Henry All right. Stay and talk a minute. (*He turns off* *the radio.*) Raw material, then I'll do this page, then I'll rape you, then I'll do the page again, then I'll – Oh (*happily*), are you all right?

Annie nods.

Annie Yeah. Are you all right?

He nods.

(*Gleefully, self-reproachful*) Isn't it awful? Max is so unhappy while I feel so . . . *thrilled*. His misery just seems . . . not in very good taste. Am I awful? He leaves letters for me at rehearsal, you know, and gets me to come to the phone by pretending to be my agent and people. He loves me, and he wants to punish me with his pain, but I can't come up with the proper guilt. I'm sort of irritated by it. It's so *tiring* and so *uninteresting*. You never write about that, you lot.

Henry What?

Annie Gallons of ink and miles of typewriter ribbon expended on the misery of the unrequited lover; not a word about the utter tedium of the unrequiting. It's a very interesting . . .

Henry Lacuna?

Annie What? No, I mean it's a very interesting sort of . . .

Henry Prejudice?

Annie It's a very interesting . . . thing.

Henry Yes, thing.

Annie No, I mean it shows – never mind – I've lost it now.

Henry How are you this morning?

Annie One behind. Where were you?

Henry You were flat out.

Annie Your own fault. When I take a Mog, I'm on the downhill slope. You should have come to bed when you said.

Henry (*indicating his desk*) It wasn't where I could leave it. I would have gone to sleep depressed.

Annie Well, I thought, the honeymoon is over. Fifteen days and fuckless to bye-byes.

Henry No, actually, I managed.

Annie You did not.

Henry Yes, I did. You were totally zonked. Only your reflexes were working.

Annie Liar.

Henry Honestly.

Annie Why didn't you wake me?

Henry I thought I'd try it without you talking.
Look, I'm not doing any good, why don't we –?

Annie You rotter. Just for that I'm going to learn my script.

Henry I'll read in for you.

She glowers at him but finds a page in the script and hands the script to him.

Annie You didn't really, did you?

Henry Yes.

She 'reads' without inflection.

Annie 'Très gentil, Monsieur Jean, très gentil!'

Henry (*reading*) 'Vous voulez plaisanter, madame!'

Annie '*Et vous voulez parler français?* Where did you pick that up?'

Henry 'In Switzerland. I worked as a waiter in one of the best hotels in Lucerne.'

Annie 'You're quite the gentleman in that coat . . . *charmant.*' You rotter.

Henry 'You flatter me, Miss Julie.'

Annie 'Flatter? I flatter?'

Henry 'I'd like to accept the compliment, but modesty forbids. And, of course, my modesty entails your insincerity. Hence, you flatter me.'

Annie 'Where did you learn to talk like that? Do you spend a lot of time at the theatre?'

Henry 'Oh yes. I get about, you know.'

Annie Oh, Hen. Are you all right?

Henry Not really. I can't do mine. I don't know how to write love. I try to write it properly, and it just comes out embarrassing. It's either childish or it's rude. And the rude bits are absolutely juvenile. I can't use any of it. My credibility is already hanging by a thread after *Desert Island Discs.* Anyway, I'm too prudish. Perhaps I should write it completely artificial. Blank verse. Poetic imagery. Not so much of the 'Will you still love me when my tits are droopy?' 'Of course I will, darling, it's your bum I'm mad for', and more of the 'By my troth, thy beauty makest the moon hide her radiance', do you think?

Annie Not really, no.

Henry No. Not really. I don't know. Loving and being loved is unliterary. It's happiness expressed in banality and lust. It makes me nervous to see three-quarters of a page and no *writing* on it. I mean, I *talk* better than this.

Annie You'll have to learn to do sub-text. My Strindberg is steaming with lust, but there is nothing rude on the page. We just talk round it. Then he sort of bites my finger and I do the heavy breathing and he gives me a quick feel, kisses me on the neck . . .

Henry Who does?

Annie Gerald. It's all very exciting.

Henry laughs, immoderately, and Annie continues coldly.

Or amusing, of course.

Henry We'll do that bit . . . you breathe, I'll feel . . .

She pushes him away.

Annie Go away. You'll just get moody afterwards.

Henry When was I ever moody?

Annie Whenever you get seduced from your work.

Henry You mean the other afternoon?

Annie What other afternoon? No, I don't mean *seduced*, for God's sake. Can't you think about anything else?

Henry Certainly. Like what?

Annie I mean 'seduced', like when you're seduced by someone on the television.

Henry I've never been seduced on the television.

Annie You were seduced by Miranda Jessop on the television.

Henry Professional duty.

Annie If she hadn't been in it, you wouldn't have watched that play if they'd come round and done it for you on your carpet.

Henry Exactly. I had a postcard from her agent, would I be sure to watch her this week in *Trotsky Playhouse* or whatever they call it.

Annie You only looked up when she stripped off. Think I can't see through you? That's why I took my Mog. Sod you, I thought, feel free.

Henry You're daft. I've got to watch her if she's going to do my telly. It's just good manners.

Annie *Her* tits are droopy already.

Henry I'm supposed to have an opinion, you see.

Annie I think she's bloody overrated, as a matter of fact.

Henry I have to agree. I wouldn't give them more than six out of ten.

She clouts him with her script.

Four.

She clouts him again.

Three.

Annie You think you're so bloody funny.

Henry What's up with you? I hardly know the woman.

Annie You'll like her. She wears leopard-skin pants.

Henry How do you know?

Annie I shared a dressing-room with her.

Henry I don't suppose she wears them all the time.

Annie I'm bloody sure she doesn't.

Henry 'By my troth thy beauty makest the moon –'
Annie Oh, shut up.

Henry What are you jealous about?

Annie I'm not jealous.

Henry All right, what are you cross about?

Annie I'm not cross. Do your work.

She makes a show of concentrating on her script.
Henry makes a show of resuming work. Pause.

Henry I'm sorry.

Annie What for?

Henry I don't know. I'll have to be going out to pick up Debbie. I don't want to go if we're not friends. Will you come, then?

Annie No. It was a mistake last time. It spoils it for her, being nervous.

Henry She wasn't nervous.

Annie Not her. You.

Pause.

Henry Well, I'll be back around two.

Annie I won't be here.

Pause.

Henry (*remembering*) Oh, yes. Is it today you're going prison visiting? You're being very – um – faithful to Brodie.

Annie That surprises you, does it?

Henry I only mean that you haven't got much time for good causes. You haven't got a weekend cottage either.

Annie You think I'm more like you.

191

Henry Yes.

Annie It's just that I happen to know him.

Henry You don't know him. You met him on a train.

Annie Well, he's the only political prisoner I've ever met on a train. He's lucky.

Henry Political?

Annie It was a political act which got him jumped on by the police in the first place so it's . . .

Henry A priori?

Annie No, it's –

Henry De facto?

Annie It's common sense that resisting arrest isn't the same as a criminal doing it.

Henry Arson is a criminal offence.

Annie Arson is burning down buildings. Setting fire to the wreath on the Cenotaph is a symbolic act. Surely you can see the difference?

Henry (*carefully*) Oh, yes . . . That's . . . easy to see.

  Not carefully enough. Annie looks at him narrowly.

Annie And, of course, he did get hammered by an emotional backlash.

  Pause.

Henry Do you mean real leopard skin or just printed nylon?

  She erupts and assails him, shouting.

Annie You don't love me the way I love you. I'm just a relief after Charlotte, and a novelty.

Henry You're a novelty all right. I never *met* anyone so silly. I love you. I don't know why you're behaving like this.

Annie I'm behaving normally. It's you who's abnormal. You don't care enough to *care*. Jealousy is normal.

Henry I thought you said you *weren't* jealous.

Annie Well, why aren't *you* ever jealous?

Henry Of whom?

Annie Of anybody. You don't care if Gerald Jones sticks his tongue in my ear – which, incidentally, he does whenever he gets the chance.

Henry Is that what this is all about?

Annie It's insulting the way you just laugh.

Henry But you've got no interest in him.

Annie I know that, but why should you assume it?

Henry Because you haven't. This is stupid.

Annie But why don't you *mind*?

Henry I do.

Annie No, you don't.

Henry That's true, I don't.
  Why *is* that?
  It's because I feel superior. There he is, poor bugger, picking up the odd crumb of ear wax from the rich man's table. You're right. I don't mind. I like it. I like the way his presumption admits his poverty. I like him, knowing that that's all there is, because you're coming home to me and we don't want anyone else.
  I love love. I love having a lover and being one. The insularity of passion. I love it. I love the way it blurs the

distinction between everyone who isn't one's lover.

Only two kinds of presence in the world. There's you and there's them.

I love you so.

Annie I love you so, Hen.

They kiss. The alarm on Henry's wristwatch goes off. They separate.

Henry Sorry.

Annie Don't get kicked by the horse.

Henry Don't get kicked by Brodie.

He goes to the door to leave. At the door he looks at her and nods. She nods at him. He leaves.

Annie goes slowly to Henry's desk and looks at the pages on it. She turns on the radio and turns it from pop to Bach. She goes back to the desk and, almost absently, opens one of the drawers. Leaving it open, she goes to the door and disappears briefly into the hall, then reappears, closing the door. She goes to one of the cardboard boxes on the floor. She removes the contents from the box. She places the pile of papers on the floor. Squatting down, she starts going through the pile, methodically and unhurriedly. The radio plays on.

Act Two

SCENE FIVE

Henry and Annie.
  Living-room/study. Three doors.
  Two years later. A different house. The two years
ought to show on Henry and on Annie. Perhaps he now
uses glasses when he is reading, as he is at the beginning
of the scene, or he may even have grown a moustache.
Annie may have cut her hair short. Opera (Verdi) is
playing on the record player. There is a TV and video
and a small radio on Henry's desk, on which there is also
a typewriter. Henry is alone, reading a script which
consists of a sheaf of typed pages.
  Henry reads for a few moments.
  Annie enters from bedroom or kitchen and glances
at Henry, not casually, then sits down and watches him
read for a moment. Then she looks away and listens to
the music for a moment. Henry glances up at her.
  Annie looks at him.

Annie Well?

Henry Oh – um – Strauss.

Annie What?

Henry Not Strauss.

Annie I meant the play.

Henry (*indicating the script*) Ah. The play.

Annie (*scornfully*) *Strauss*. How can it be Strauss? It's in Italian.

Henry Is it? (*He listens.*) So it is.
Italian opera.
One of the Italian operas.
Verdi.

Annie Which one?

Henry Giuseppe. (*He judges from her expression that this is not the right answer.*) Monty?

Annie I mean which *opera.*

Henry Ah. (*confidently*) *Madame Butterfly.*

Annie You're doing it on purpose. (*She goes to the record player and stops it playing.*)

Henry I promise you.

Annie You'd think that *something* would have sunk in after two years and a bit.

Henry I like it – I really do like it – quite, it's just that I can't tell them apart. Two years and a bit isn't very long when they're all going for the same sound. Actually, I've got a better ear than you – *you* can't tell the difference between the Everly Brothers and the Andrews Sisters.

Annie There isn't any difference.

Henry Or we could split up. Can we have something decent on now?

Annie No.

Henry All right. Put on one of your instrumental numbers. The big band sound. (*He does the opening of Beethoven's Fifth.*) Da – da – da – *da* . . .

Annie Get *on.*

Henry Right. (*He turns his attention to the script.*) Stop me if anybody has said this before, but it's interesting how many of the all time greats begin with B: Beethoven, the Big Bopper . . .

Annie That's all they have in common.

Henry I wouldn't say that. They're both dead. The Big Bopper died in the same plane crash that killed Buddy Holly and Richie Valens, you know.

Annie No, I didn't know. Have you given up on the play or what?

Henry Buddy Holly was twenty-two. Think of what he might have gone on to achieve. I mean, if Beethoven had been killed in a plane crash at twenty-two, the history of music would have been very different. As would the history of aviation, of course.

Annie *Henry.*

Henry The play. (*He turns his attention back to the script.*)

Annie How far have you got?

Henry Do you have a professional interest in this or is it merely personal?

Annie Merely?

Pause.

Henry Do you have a personal interest in this or is it merely professional?

Annie Which one are you dubious about?

Pause.

Henry Pause.

Annie I could do her, couldn't I?

Henry Mary? Oh, sure – without make-up.

Annie Well, then. *Three Sisters* is definitely up the spout.

Henry Nothing's definite with that lot.

Annie The other two are pregnant.

Henry Half a dozen new lines could take care of that.

Annie If this script could be in a fit state, say, a month from now –

Henry Anyway, I thought you were committing incest in Glasgow.

Annie I haven't said I'll do it.

Henry I think you should. It's classy stuff, Webster. I love all that Jacobean sex and violence.

Annie It's Ford, not Webster. It's Elizabethan, not Jacobean. *And* it's Glasgow.

Henry Don't you work north of Cambridge Circus, then?

Annie I was thinking you might miss me – pardon my mistake.

Henry I was thinking you might like me to come with you – pardon mine.

Annie You hadn't the faintest intention of coming to Glasgow for five weeks.

Henry That's true. I answered out of panic. Of course I'd miss you.

Annie Also, it *is* somewhat north.

Henry 'shoots' her between the eyes with his fore-finger.

198

Henry Got you. Is it rehearsing in Glasgow?

Annie (*nods*) After the first week. (*indicating the script*) Where've you got to?

Henry They're on the train.
'You're a strange boy, Billy. How old are you?'
'Twenty. But I've lived more than you'll ever live.'
Should I read out loud?

Annie If you like.

Henry Give you the feel of it.

Annie All right.

Henry I'll go back a bit where they first meet. All right?

Annie nods. Henry makes train noises. She is defensive, not quite certain whether he is being wicked or not.

(*Reading*) 'Excuse me, is this seat taken?'
'No.'
'Mind if I sit down?'
'It's a free country.'
'Thank you.'

He sits down opposite her. Mary carries on with reading her book

'Going far?'
'To London.'
'So . . . you were saying . . . So you think it's a free country.'
'Don't you?'
'This is it, we're all free to do as we're told. My name's Bill, by the way. What's yours?'
'Mary.'
'I'm glad to make your acquaintance, Mary.'
'I'm glad to make yours, Bill.'

'Do you know what time this train is due to arrive in London?'

'At about half-past one, I believe, if it is on time.'

'You put me in mind of Mussolini, Mary. Yes, you look just like him, you've got the same eyes.'

Annie If you're not going to read it properly, don't bother.

Henry Sorry.

'At about half-past one, I believe, if it is on time.'

'You put me in mind of Mussolini, Mary. People used to say about Mussolini, he may be a Fascist, but at least the trains run on time. Makes you wonder why British Rail isn't totally on time, eh?'

'What do you mean?'

'I mean it's a funny thing. The Fascists are in charge but the trains are late often as not.'

'But this isn't a Fascist country.'

'Are you quite sure of that, Mary? Take the army –'

You're not going to do this, are you?

Annie Why not?

Henry It's no good.

Annie You mean it's not literary.

Henry It's not literary, and it's no good. He can't write.

Annie You're a snob.

Henry I'm a snob, and he can't write.

Annie I know it's raw, but he's got something to say.

Henry He's got something to say. It happens to be something extremely silly and bigoted. But leaving that aside, there is still the problem that he can't write. He can burn things down, but he can't write.

Annie Give it back. I shouldn't have asked you.

Henry For God's sake, Annie, if it wasn't Brodie you'd never have got through it.

Annie But it is Brodie. That's the point. Two and a half years ago he could hardly put six words together.

Henry He still can't.

Annie You *pig*.

Henry I'm a pig, and he can't –

Annie I'll smash you one. It's you who's bigoted. You're bigoted about what writing is supposed to be like. You judge everything as though everyone starts off from the same place, aiming at the same prize. Eng. Lit. Shakespeare out in front by a mile, and the rest of the field strung out behind trying to close the gap. You all write for people who would like to write like you if only they could write. Well, sod you, and sod Eng. sodding Lit!

Henry Right.

Annie Brodie isn't writing to compete like you. He's writing to be heard.

Henry Right.

Annie And he's done it on his own.

Henry Yes. Yes . . . I can see he's done a lot of reading.

Annie You can't expect it to be Eng. Lit.

Henry No.

Annie He's a prisoner shouting over the wall.

Henry Quite. Yes, I see what you mean.

Annie Oh shut up! I can't bear you agreeing with me just to keep me quiet. I'd rather have your sarcasm.

Henry Why a play? Did you suggest it?

Annie Not exactly.

Henry Why did you?

Annie The committee, what's left of it, thought . . .
I mean, people have got bored with Brodie. People get
bored with anything after two or three years. The
campaign needs . . .

Henry A shot in the arm?

Annie No, it needs . . .

Henry A kick up the arse?

Annie (*flares*) For Christ's sake, will you stop finishing
my sentences for me!

Henry Sorry.

Annie I've lost it now.

Henry The campaign needs . . .

Annie A writer is harder to ignore. I thought, TV plays
get talked about, make some impact. Get his case
reopened. Do you think? I mean, Henry, what *do* you
think?

Henry I think it makes a lot of sense.

Annie No, what do you *really* think?

Henry Oh, *really* think. Well, I *really* think writing
rotten plays is not in itself proof of rehabilitation. Still
less of wrongful conviction. But even if it were, I think
that anyone who thinks that they're bored with Brodie
won't know what boredom is till they've sat through
his apologia. Not that anyone will get the chance, because
it's half as long as *Das Kapital* and only twice as funny.
I also think you should know better.

Annie You arrogant sod.

Henry You swear too much.

Annie Roger is willing to do it, in principle.

Henry What Roger? Oh *Roger*. Why the hell would Roger do it?

Annie He's on the committee.

Henry looks at the ceiling.

It just needs a bit of work.

Henry You're all bent.

Annie You're jealous.

Henry Of Brodie?

Annie You're jealous of the idea of the writer. You want to keep it sacred, special, not something anybody can do. Some of us have it, some of us don't. *We* write, *you* get written about. What gets you about Brodie is he doesn't know his place. You say he can't write like a head waiter saying you can't come in here without a tie. Because he can't put words together. What's so good about putting words together?

Henry It's traditionally considered advantageous for a writer.

Annie He's not a writer. He's a convict. *You're* a writer. You write *because* you're a writer. Even when you write *about* something, you have to think up something to write about just so you can keep writing. More well chosen words nicely put together. So what? Why should that be *it*? Who says?

Henry Nobody says. It just works best.

Annie Of *course* it works. You teach a lot of people what to expect from good writing, and you end up with a lot of people saying you write well. Then somebody who isn't in on the game comes along, like Brodie, who really has something to write about, something real, and you can't get through it. Well, *he* couldn't get through *yours*, so where are you? To you, he can't write. To him, write is all you *can* do.

Henry Jesus, Annie, you're beginning to appal me. There's something scary about stupidity made coherent. I can deal with idiots, and I can deal with sensible argument, but I don't know how to deal with you. Where's my cricket bat?

Annie Your cricket bat?

Henry Yes. It's a new approach. (*He heads out into the hall.*)

Annie Are you trying to be funny?

Henry No, I'm serious.

He goes out while she watches in wary disbelief. He returns with an old cricket bat.

Annie You better not be.

Henry Right, you silly cow –

Annie Don't you bloody dare –

Henry Shut up and listen. This thing here, which looks like a wooden club, is actually several pieces of particular wood cunningly put together in a certain way so that the whole thing is sprung, like a dance floor. It's for hitting cricket balls with. If you get it right, the cricket ball will travel two hundred yards in four seconds, and all you've done is give it a knock like knocking the top off a bottle of stout, and it makes a noise like a trout taking a fly . . .

(*He clucks his tongue to make the noise.*) What we're
trying to do is to write cricket bats, so that when we
throw up an idea and give it a little knock, it might . . .
travel . . . (*He clucks his tongue again and picks up the
script.*) Now, what we've got here is a lump of wood
of roughly the same shape trying to be a cricket bat,
and if you hit a ball with it, the ball will travel about
ten feet and you will drop the bat and dance about
shouting 'Ouch!' with your hands stuck into your
armpits. (*indicating the cricket bat*) This isn't better
because someone says it's better, or because there's a
conspiracy by the MCC to keep cudgels out of Lords.
It's better because it's better. You don't believe me, so
I suggest you go out to bat with this and see how you
get on. 'You're a strange boy, Billy, how old are you?'
'Twenty, but I've lived more than you'll ever live.' Ooh,
ouch!

> *He drops the script and hops about with his hands
> in his armpits, going 'Ouch!' Annie watches him
> expressionlessly until he desists.*

Annie I hate you.

Henry I love you. I'm your pal. I'm your best mate.
I look after you. You're the only chap.

Annie Oh, Hen . . . Can't you help?

Henry What did you expect me to do?

Annie Well . . . cut it and shape it . . .

Henry Cut it and shape it. Henry of Mayfair. Look – he
can't write. I would have to write it for him.

Annie Well, write it for him.

Henry I can't.

Annie Why?

Henry Because it's *balls*. Mary's part is the least of it –
it's merely ham-fisted. But when he gets into his stride,
or rather his lurch, announcing every stale revelation of
the newly enlightened, like stout Cortez coming upon the
Pacific – war is profits, politicians are puppets, Parliament is a farce, justice is a fraud, property is theft . . .
It's all here: the Stock Exchange, the arms dealers, the
press barons . . . You can't fool Brodie – patriotism is
propaganda, religion is a con trick, royalty is an anachronism . . . Pages and pages of it. It's like being run over
very slowly by a travelling freak show of favourite
simpletons, the india rubber pedagogue, the midget
intellectual, the human panacea . . .

Annie It's his view of the world. Perhaps from where
he's standing you'd see it the same way.

Henry Or perhaps I'd realize where I'm standing. Or at
least that I'm standing *somewhere*. There is, I suppose,
a world of objects which have a certain form, like this
coffee mug. I turn it, and it has no handle. I tilt it, and it
has no cavity. But there is something real here which is
always a mug with a handle. I suppose. But politics,
justice, patriotism – they aren't even like coffee mugs.
There's nothing real there separate from our perception
of them. So if you try to change them as though there
were something there to change, you'll get frustrated,
and frustration will finally make you violent. If you
know this and proceed with humility, you may perhaps
alter people's perceptions so that they behave a little
differently at that axis of behaviour where we locate
politics or justice; but if you don't know this, then you're
acting on a mistake. Prejudice is the expression of this
mistake.

Annie Or such is your perception.

Henry All right.

Annie And who wrote it, why he wrote it, *where* he wrote it – none of these things count with you?

Henry Leave me out of it. They don't count. Maybe Brodie got a raw deal, maybe he didn't. I don't know. It doesn't count. He's a lout with language. I can't help somebody who thinks, or thinks he thinks, that editing a newspaper is censorship, or that throwing bricks is a demonstration while building tower blocks is social violence, or that unpalatable statement is provocation while disrupting the speaker is the exercise of free speech . . . Words don't deserve that kind of malarkey. They're innocent, neutral, precise, standing for this, describing that, meaning the other, so if you look after them you can build bridges across incomprehension and chaos. But when they get their corners knocked off, they're no good any more, and Brodie knocks corners off without knowing he's doing it. So everything he builds is jerry-built. It's rubbish. An intelligent child could push it over. I don't think writers are sacred, but words are. They deserve respect. If you get the right ones in the right order, you can nudge the world a little or make a poem which children will speak for you when you're dead.

Annie goes to the typewriter, pulls out the page from the machine and reads it.

Annie 'Seventy-nine. Interior. Commander's capsule. From Zadok's p.o.v. we see the green glow of the laser strike-force turning towards us. BCU Zadok's grim smile. *Zadok:* "I think it's going to work. Here they come!" *Kronk,* voice over: "Hold your course!" *Zadok: –*'

Henry (*interrupts*) That's not words, that's pictures. The movies. Anyway, alimony doesn't count. If Charlotte made it legal with that architect she's shacked up with, I'd be writing the real stuff.

Annie lets the page drop on to the typewriter.

Annie You never wrote mine.

Henry That's true. I didn't. I tried.
I can't remember when I last felt so depressed.
Oh yes. Yesterday.
Don't be rotten to me. I'll come to Glasgow and I'll sit
in your dressing-room and I'll write Kronk and Zadok
every night while you're doing *'Tis Pity She's a Whore*.

Annie I'm not going to Glasgow.

Henry Yes, you bloody are.

Annie No I'm bloody not. We'll get Brodie's play off the
ground. I want to do it. *I* want to do it. Don't *I* count?
Hen? (*Pause.*) Well, I can see it's difficult for a man of
your fastidious tastes. Let's have some literacy. Something decent.

*Annie stabs her finger on to the small radio on
Henry's desk. Quietly it starts playing pop. She starts
to go out of the room.*

Henry (*exasperated*) Why Brodie? Do you fancy him or
what?

*She looks back at him and he sees that he has made a
mistake.*

I take it back.

Annie Too late. (*She leaves the room.*)

SCENE SIX

Annie and Billy.
*Annie is sitting by the window of a moving train. She
is immersed in a paperback book.*

Billy walks into view and pauses, looking at her for a moment. She is unaware of his presence. He carries a zipped grip bag. He speaks with a Scottish accent.

Billy Excuse me, is this seat taken?

Annie hardly raises her eyes.

Annie No.

Billy sits down next to or opposite her. He puts the grip on the seat next to him. He looks at her. She doesn't look up from her book. He looks at his watch and then out of the window and then back at her.

Billy You'd think with all these Fascists the trains would be on time.

Annie looks up at him and jumps a mile. She gives a little squeal.

Annie Jesus, you gave me a shock. (*She looks at him, pleased and amused.*) You fool.

Billy drops the accent.

Billy Hello.

Annie I didn't know you were on the train.

Billy Yes, well, there you are. How are you?

Annie All right. I gather you read it, then.

Billy Brodie's play? Yes, I read it.

Annie And?

Billy He can't write.

Small pause.

Annie I know. I just thought it was something you'd do well.

209

TOM STOPPARD

Billy Oh, yes. I could do a job on it. Are you going to do it?

Annie I hope so. Not as it is, I suppose. Thank you for reading it anyway.

Billy Do you mind me coming to sit with you?

Annie No, not at all.

Billy It doesn't mean we have to talk.

Annie It's all right.

Billy How do you feel?

Annie Scared. I'm always scared. I think, this is the one where I get found out.

Billy Well, better in Glasgow.

Annie Is anyone else on this train?

Billy No, we're completely alone.

Annie I mean any of *us*, the others.

Billy I don't know. Some of them are flying up, on the shuttle.

Annie I fancied the train.

Billy I fancied it with you.

  Annie meets his look.

Annie Billy . . .

Billy What did you think when you saw me?

Annie Just now?

Billy No. On the first day.

Annie I thought God, he's so young.

210

Billy (*Scottish*) I've lived more than you'll ever live.

Annie All right, all right.

Billy I'm the one who should be scared. You're smashing.

Annie I don't feel right.

Billy You seem right to me.

Annie I'm older than you.

Billy That doesn't matter.

Annie I'm a lot older. I'm going to look more like your mother than your sister.

Billy That's all right, so long as it's incest. Anyway, I like older women.

Annie Billy, you mustn't keep flirting with me.

Billy Why not?

Annie Well, because there's no point. Will you stop?

Billy No. Is that all right?

   Pause.

Annie Did you know I was going to be on this train?

Billy (*nods*) Watched you get on. I thought I'd come and find you when it got started.

Annie You certainly thought about it.

Billy I had to wait until the inspector came round. I haven't got a first-class ticket.

Annie What will you do if he comes back?

Billy I'll say you're my mum. How come you get a first-class ticket?

Annie I don't really. I'm afraid I upped it myself.

Billy You approve of the class system?

Annie You mean on trains or in general?

Billy In general. Travelling first-class.

Annie There's no system. People group together when they've got something in common. Sometimes it's religion and sometimes it's, I don't know, breeding budgies or being at Eton. Big and small groups over-lapping. You can't blame them. It's a cultural thing; it's not *classes* or *system*. (*She makes a connection.*) There's nothing really *there* – it's just the way you see it. Your perception.

Billy Bloody brilliant. There's people who've spent their lives trying to get rid of the class system, and you've done it without leaving your seat.

Annie Well . . .

Billy The only problem with your argument is that you've got to be travelling first-class to really appreciate it.

Annie I . . .

Billy Where do you get all that from? Did you just make it up? It's daft. I prefer Brodie. He sounds like rubbish, but you know he's right. You sound all right, but you know it's rubbish.

Annie Why won't you do his play, then?

Billy I didn't say I wouldn't. I'll do it if you're doing it.

Annie You shouldn't do it for the wrong reasons.

Billy Why not? Does he care?

Annie You said he can't write.

Billy He can't write like your husband. But your husband's a first-class writer.

Annie Are you being nasty about Henry?

Billy No. I saw *House of Cards*. I thought it was quite good.

Annie He'll be relieved to hear that.

Pause.

Billy Don't go off me.

Annie If you weren't a child, you'd know that you won't get anywhere with a married woman if you're snotty about her husband. Remember that with the next one.

Billy I'faith, I mean no harm, sister. I'm just scared sick of you. How is't with ye?

Annie I am very well, brother.

Billy Trust me, but I am sick; I fear so sick 'twill cost my life.

Annie Mercy forbid it! 'Tis not so, I hope.

Billy I think you love me, sister.

Annie Yes, you know I do.

Billy I know't, indeed. You're very fair.

Annie Nay, then, I see you have a merry sickness.

Billy That's as it proves. The poets feign, I read,
That Juno for her forehead did exceed
All other goddesses; but I durst swear
Your forehead exceeds hers, as hers did theirs.

Annie 'Troth, this is pretty!

Billy Such a pair of stars
    As are thine eyes would, like Promethean fire,
    If gently glanced, give life to senseless stones.

Annie Fie upon ye!

Billy The lily and the rose, most sweetly strange,
    Upon your dimpled cheeks do strive for change:
    Such lips would tempt a saint; such hands as those
    Would make an anchorite lascivious.

Annie O, you are a trim youth!

Billy Here! (*His 'reading' has been getting less and less discreet. Now he stands up and opens his shirt.*)

Annie (*giggling*) Oh, leave off. (*She looks around nervously.*)

Billy (*starting to shout*)
    And here's my breast; strike home!
    Rip up my bosom; there thou shalt behold
    A heart in which is writ the truth I speak.

Annie You daft idiot.

Billy Yes, most earnest. You cannot love?

Annie Stop it.

Billy My tortured soul
    Hath felt affliction in the heat of death.
    Oh, Annabella, I am quite undone!

Annie Billy!

SCENE SEVEN

Henry and Charlotte and Debbie.
    The living-room of Scene Two, without all the records.
Charlotte is searching through a file of newspaper

cuttings and programmes. A large, loaded ruck-sack is sitting by the door. Debbie is smoking.

Henry Since when did you smoke?

Debbie I don't know. Years. At school. Me and Terry used to light up in the boiler room.

Henry *I* and Terry.

Debbie I and Terry. Are you sure?

Henry It doesn't sound right but it's correct. I paid school fees so that you wouldn't be barred by your natural disabilities from being taught Latin and learning to speak English.

Charlotte I thought it was so that she'd be a virgin a bit longer.

Henry It was also so that she'd speak English. *Virgo syntacta.*

Debbie You were done, Henry. Nobody left the boiler room virgo with Terry.

Henry I wish you'd stop celebrating your emancipation by flicking it at me like a wet towel. Did the staff know about this lout, Terry?

Debbie He was on the staff. He taught Latin.

Henry Oh well, that's all right then.

Charlotte Apparently she'd already lost it riding anyway.

Henry That doesn't count.

Charlotte In the tackroom.

Henry God's truth. The groom.

Charlotte That's why he was bow-legged.

Henry I told you – I said you've got to warn her about being carried away.

Debbie You don't get carried away in jodhpurs. It needs absolute determination.

Henry Will you stop this.

Charlotte No. I can't find it. It was yonks ago. I mean, not being catty, I was nearer the right age.

Henry Does it really matter who played Giovanni to your Annabella in *'Tis Pity Shes a Whore*?

Charlotte I just think it's awful to have forgotten his name.

Debbie Perhaps he's forgotten yours.

Charlotte But it was *my* virginity, not his.

Debbie Was it actually on stage?

Charlotte Don't be silly – it was a British Council tour. No, it was in a boarding house in Zagreb.

Debbie A bawdy house?

Charlotte The British Council has a lot to answer for.

Henry Look, we're supposed to be discussing a family crisis.

Charlotte What's that?

Henry Our daughter going on the streets.

Debbie On the *road*, not the streets.

Charlotte Stop being so dramatic.

Henry I have a right to be dramatic.

Charlotte I see what you mean.

Henry I'm her father.

Charlotte Oh, I see what you mean.

Henry She's too young to go off with a man.

Charlotte She's certainly too young to go off without one. It's all right. He's nice. (*She has given up her search of the file and now leaves carrying the file. To Debbie*) If I'm in the bath when he comes I want to see you both before you disappear. (*She goes out.*)

Henry What does he play?

Debbie looks blank.

Ma said he's a musician.

Debbie Oh – um – steam organ . . .

Henry A travelling steam organist? (*Pause.*) He's not a musician.

Debbie Fairground.

Henry Well, swings and roundabouts.

Debbie Tunnel of love. How's Annie?

Henry In Glasgow.

Debbie Don't worry, Henry, I'll be happy.

Henry Happy? What do you mean happy?

Debbie Happy! Like a warm puppy.

Henry Dear Christ, is that what it's all come down to? – no philosophy that can't be printed on a T-shirt. You don't get visited by happiness like being lucky with the weather. The weather is the weather.

Debbie And happiness?

Henry Happiness is . . . equilibrium. Shift your weight.

Debbie Are you happy, Henry?

Henry I don't much like your calling me Henry. I liked being called Fa. Fa and Ma.

Debbie Happy days, eh? How're the Everlys getting on? And the Searchers. How's old Elvis?

Henry He's dead.

Debbie I did know that. I mean how's he holding up apart from that?

Henry I never went for him much. 'All Shook Up' was the last good one. However, I suppose that's the fate of all us artists.

Debbie Death?

Henry People saying they preferred the early stuff.

Debbie Well, maybe you were better then.

Henry Didn't you like the last one?

Debbie What, *House of Cards*? Well, it wasn't about anything, except did she have it off or didn't she? What a crisis. Infidelity among the architect class. Again.

Henry It was about self-knowledge through pain.

Debbie No, it was about did she have it off or didn't she. As if having it off is infidelity.

Henry Most people think it is.

Debbie Most people think *not* having it off is *fidelity*. They think all relationships hinge in the middle. Sex or no sex. What a fantastic range of possibilities. Like an on/off switch. Did she or didn't she. By Henry Ibsen. Why would you want to make it such a crisis?

Henry I don't know, why would I?

Debbie It's what comes of making such a mystery of it. When I was twelve I was obsessed. Everything was sex. Latin was sex. The dictionary fell open at *meretrix*, a harlot. You could feel the mystery coming off the word like musk. *Meretrix*! This was none of your *mensa*-a-table, this was a flash from the forbidden planet, and it was everywhere. History was sex, French was sex, art was sex, the Bible, poetry, penfriends, games, music, everything was sex except biology which was obviously sex but obviously not *really* sex, not the one which was secret and ecstatic and wicked and a sacrament and all the things it was supposed to be but couldn't be at one and the same time – I got that in the boiler room and it turned out to be biology after all. That's what free love is free of – propaganda.

Henry Don't get too good at that.

Debbie What?

Henry Persuasive nonsense. Sophistry in a phrase so neat you can't see the loose end that would unravel it. It's flawless but wrong. A perfect dud. You can do that with words, bless 'em. How about 'What free love is free of, is love'? Another little gem. You could put a 'what' on the end of it, like Bertie Wooster, 'What free love is free of is love, what?' – and the words would go on replicating themselves like a spiral of DNA . . . 'What love is free of love? – *free* love is what love, what? –'

Debbie (*interrupting*) *Fa*. You're going on.

Henry Yes. Well, I remember, the first time I succumbed to the sensation that the universe was dispensable minus one lady –

Debbie Don't write it, Fa. Just say it. The first time you fell in love. What?

Henry It's to do with knowing and being known. I
remember how it stopped seeming odd that in biblical
Greek knowing was used for making love. Whosit knew
so-and-so. Carnal knowledge. It's what lovers trust each
other with. Knowledge of each other, not of the flesh but
through the flesh, knowledge of self, the real him, the
real her, *in extremis,* the mask slipped from the face.
Every other version of oneself is on offer to the public.
We share our vivacity, grief, sulks, anger, joy . . . we
hand it out to anybody who happens to be standing
around, to friends and family with a momentary sense
of indecency perhaps, to strangers without hesitation.
Our lovers share us with the passing trade. But in pairs
we insist that we give ourselves to each other. What
selves? What's left? What else is there that hasn't been
dealt out like a deck of cards? A sort of knowledge.
Personal, final, uncompromised. Knowing, being known.
I revere that. Having that is being rich, you can be
generous about what's shared – she walks, she talks,
she laughs, she lends a sympathetic ear, she kicks off
her shoes and dances on the tables, she's everybody's and
it don't mean a thing, let them eat cake; knowledge is
something else, the undealt card, and while it's held it
makes you free-and-easy and nice to know, and when it's
gone everything is pain. Every single thing. Every object
that meets the eye, a pencil, a tangerine, a travel poster.
As if the physical world has been wired up to pass a
current back to the part of your brain where imagination
glows like a filament in a lobe no bigger than a torch
bulb. Pain.

Pause.

Debbie Has Annie got someone else then?

Henry Not as far as I know, thank you for asking.

Debbie Apologies.

Henry Don't worry.

Debbie Don't you. Exclusive rights isn't love, it's colonization.

Henry Christ almighty. Another *ersatz* masterpiece. Like Michelangelo working in polystyrene.

Debbie Do you know what your problem is, Henry?

Henry What?

Debbie Your Latin mistress never took you into the boiler room.

Henry Well, at least I passed.

Debbie Only in Latin.

  Doorbell.

Do me a favour.

Henry What?

Debbie Stay here.

Henry That bad, is he?

Debbie He's frightened of you.

Henry Jesus.

  Charlotte enters in a bath robe, a towel round her hair perhaps. She carries a bunch of postcards.

Charlotte Ten postcards – stamped and addressed. Every week I get a postcard you get ten quid. No postcards, no remittance. (*She gives Debbie the postcards.*)

Debbie Oh – Charley – (*Kisses Charlotte.*) See you, Henry.

Henry There; my blessing with thee. And these few precepts in thy memory . . .

Debbie Too late, Fa. Love you. (*Kisses him.*)

*Debbie leaves with the ruck-sack followed by
Charlotte. Henry waits until Charlotte returns.*

Charlotte What a good job we sold the pony.

Henry Musician is he? She's hardly seventeen.

Charlotte Almost over the hill for an Elizabethan
heroine. (*Pause.*) How's Annie? Are you going to
Glasgow for the first night?

Henry They don't open for a couple of weeks.

Charlotte Who's playing Giovanni?

Henry I don't know.

Charlotte Aren't you interested?

Henry Should I be?

Charlotte There's something touching about you, Henry.
Everybody should be like you. Not interested. It used to
bother me that you were never bothered. Even when
I got talked into that dreadful nudie film because it was
in Italian and Italian films were supposed to be art . . .
God, that dates me, doesn't it? Debbie's into Australian
films. *Australian.* Not Chips Rafferty – actual *films.*

Henry You've gone off again.

Charlotte Yes, well, it didn't bother you so I decided it
meant you were having it off right left and centre and it
wasn't supposed to matter. By the time I realized you
were the last romantic it was too late. I found it *didn't*
matter.

Henry Well, now that it doesn't . . . How many – um –
roughly how many –?

Charlotte Nine.

Pause.

Henry Gosh.

Charlotte And look what your one did compared to my nine.

Henry Nine?

Charlotte Feel betrayed?

Henry Surprised. I thought we'd made a commitment.

Charlotte There are no commitments, only bargains. And they have to be made again every day. You think making a commitment is *it*. Finish. You think it sets like a concrete platform and it'll take any strain you want to put on it. You're committed. You don't have to prove anything. In fact you can afford a little neglect, indulge in a little bit of sarcasm here and there, isolate yourself when you want to. Underneath it's concrete for life. I'm a cow in some ways, but you're an idiot. *Were* an idiot.

Henry Better luck next time.

Charlotte You too.
  Have a drink?

Henry I don't think so, thank you.
  How are things with your friend? An architect, isn't he?

Charlotte I had to give him the elbow. Well, he sort of left. I called him the architect of my misfortune.

Henry What was the matter with him?

Charlotte Very possessive type. I came home from a job, I'd been away only a couple of days, and he said, why did I take my diaphragm? He'd been through my bathroom cabinet, would you believe? And then, not finding it, he went through everything else. Can't have that.

Henry What did you say?

Charlotte I said, I didn't *take* my diaphragm, it just went with me. So he said, what about the tube of Duragel? I must admit he had me there.

Henry You should have said, 'Duragel! – no wonder the bristles fell out of my toothbrush.'

Charlotte (*laughs*) Cheers.

Henry (*toasting with an empty hand*) Cheers.

Henry stands up.

Charlotte Do you have to go?

Henry Yes, I ought to.

Charlotte You don't fancy one for the road?

Henry No, really.

Charlotte Or a drink?

Henry (*smiles*) No offence.

Charlotte Remember what I said.

Henry What was that? (*Pause.*) Oh . . . yes. No commitments. Only bargains. The trouble is I don't really believe it. I'd rather be an idiot. It's a kind of idiocy I like. 'I use you because you love me. I love you so use me. Be indulgent, negligent, preoccupied, premenstrual . . . your credit is infinite, I'm yours, I'm committed . . .

It's no trick loving somebody at their *best*. Love is loving them at their worst. Is that romantic? Well, good. Everything should be romantic. Love, work, music, literature, virginity, loss of virginity . . .

Charlotte You've still got one to lose, Henry.

SCENE EIGHT

In order to accommodate a scene change, Scene Eight was spoken twice, once as a 'word rehearsal' and then again as an 'acting rehearsal'.

Annie and Billy.
An empty space.
They are kissing, embracing: wearing rehearsal clothes.

Billy Come, Annabella, – no, more sister now,
But love, a name more gracious, – do not blush,
Beauty's sweet wonder, but be proud to know
That yielding thou hast conquered, and inflamed
A heart whose tribute is thy brother's life.

Annie And mine is his. O, how these stol'n contents
Would print a modest crimson on my cheeks,
Had any but my heart's delight prevailed!

Billy I marvel why the chaster of your sex
Should think this pretty toy called maidenhead
So strange a loss, when, being lost, 'tis nothing,
And you are still the same.

Annie 'Tis well for you;
Now you can talk.

Billy Music as well consists
In the ear as in the playing.

Annie O, you're wanton!
Tell on't you're best; do.

Billy Thou wilt chide me, then.
Kiss me: –

He kisses her lightly.

Annie (*quietly*) Billy . . . (*She returns the kiss in earnest.*)

TOM STOPPARD

SCENE NINE

Henry and Annie.
   The living-room. Henry is alone, sitting in a chair, doing nothing. It's like the beginning of Scene One and Scene Three.
   Annie is heard letting herself in through the front door. Then she comes in from the hall.
   Annie enters wearing a topcoat and carrying a suitcase and a small travelling bag.

Annie Hello, I'm back. (*She puts down the suitcase and the bag and goes to kiss Henry.*)

Henry Hello.

   She starts taking off her coat.

How was it?

Annie We had a good finish – a woman in the audience was sick. Billy came on with my heart skewered on his dagger and – ugh – whoops! (*She takes her coat out into the hall, reappears and goes to the travelling bag.*)

Henry I thought you were coming back overnight.

   From the travelling bag Annie takes a small, smart-looking carrier bag with handles, a purchase from a boutique.

Annie What have you been doing? How's the film? (*She gives the present to Henry, kissing him lightly.*)

Henry I thought you were on the sleeper.

Annie What's the matter?

Henry I was wondering what happened to you.

Annie Nothing happened to me. Have you had lunch?

226

Henry No. Did you catch the early train this morning, then?

Annie Yes. Scratch lunch, all right? (*She goes into the kitchen and returns after a moment.*) My God, it's all gone downhill since Sunday. Hasn't Mrs Chamberlain been?

Henry I phoned the hotel.

Annie When?

Henry Last night. They said you'd checked out.

Annie Did they?

> *She picks up her suitcase and goes out into the bedroom. Henry doesn't move. A few moments later Annie reappears, without the suitcase and almost walking backwards.*

Oh, God, Hen. Have we had burglars? What were you doing?

Henry Where were you?

Annie On the sleeper. I don't know why I said I came down this morning. It just seemed easier. I wasn't there last night because I caught the train straight from the theatre.

Henry Was the train late arriving?

Annie Do you want to see my ticket?

Henry Well, have you been to the zoo?

> *She meets his look expressionlessly.*

Who were you with?

Annie Don't be like this, Hen. You're not like this.

Henry Yes, I am.

Annie I don't want you to. It's humiliating.

Henry I really am not trying to humiliate you.

Annie For you, I mean. It's humiliating for you. (*Pause.*) I travelled down with one of the company. We had breakfast at Euston. He was waiting for a train. I stayed talking. Then I came home, not thinking that suddenly after two and a half years I'd be asked to account for my movements.

Henry You got off the sleeper and spent the morning sitting at Euston?

Annie Yes.

Henry You and this actor.

Annie Yes. Can I go now? (*She turns away.*)

Henry How did you sleep?

She turns to look at him blankly.

Well, did you?

Annie Did I what? What's the point? You'd only wonder if I was lying.

Henry Would you lie?

Annie I might.

Henry Did you?

Annie No. You see? I'm going to tidy up and put everything back.

Henry Do you want to know what I was looking for?

Annie No. (*She turns towards the bedroom.*)

Henry Was it Billy?

She turns back.

228

Annie Why Billy?

Henry I know it's him. Billy, Billy, Billy, the name keeps dropping, each time without significance, but it can't help itself. Hapless as a secret in a computer. Blip, blip. Billy, Billy. Talk to me. I'm sorry about the bedroom.

Annie You should have put everything back. Everything would be the way it was.

Henry You can't put things back. They won't go back. Talk to me.

I'm your chap. I know about this. We start off like one of those caterpillars designed for a particular leaf. The exclusive voracity of love. And then not. How strange that the way of things is not suspended to meet our special case. But it never is. I don't want anyone else but sometimes, surprisingly, there's someone, not the prettiest or the most available, but you know that in another life it would be her. Or him, don't you find? A small quickening. The room responds slightly to being entered. Like a raised blind. Nothing intended, and a long way from doing anything, but you catch the glint of being someone else's possibility, and it's a sort of politeness to show you haven't missed it, so you push it a little, well within safety, but there's that sense of a promise almost being made in the touching and kissing without which no one can seem to say good morning in this poncy business and one more push would do it. Billy. Right?

Annie Yes.

Henry I love you.

Annie And I you. I wouldn't be here if I didn't.

Henry Tell me, then.

Annie I love you.

Henry Not that.

Annie Yes, that. That's all I'd need to know.

Henry You'd need more.

Annie No.

Henry I need it. I can manage knowing if you did but I can't manage not knowing if you did or not. I won't be able to work.

Annie Don't blackmail.

Henry You'd ask me.

Annie I never have.

Henry There's never *been* anything.

Annie Dozens. For the first year at least, every halfway decent looking woman under fifty you were ever going to meet.

Henry But you learned better.

Annie No, I just learned not to care. There was nothing to keep you here so I assumed you wanted to stay. I stopped caring about the rest of it.

Henry I care. Tell me.

Annie (*hardening*) I did tell you. I spent the morning talking to Billy in a station cafeteria instead of coming straight home to you and I fibbed about the train because *that* seemed like infidelity – but all you want to know is did I sleep with him first?

Henry Yes. Did you?

Annie No.

Henry Did you want to?

Annie Oh, for God's sake!

Henry You can ask me.

Annie I prefer to respect your privacy.

Henry I have none. I disclaim it. Did you?

Annie What about your dignity, then?

Henry Yes, you'd behave better than me. I don't believe in behaving well. I don't believe in debonair relationships. 'How's your lover today, Amanda?' 'In the pink, Charles. How's yours?' I believe in mess, tears, pain, self-abasement, loss of self-respect, nakedness. Not caring doesn't seem much different from not loving. Did you? You did, didn't you?

Annie This isn't caring. If I had an affair, it would be out of need. Care about that. You won't play on my guilt or my remorse. I'd have none.

Henry Need? What did you talk about?

Annie Brodie mostly.

Henry Yes. I had it coming.

Annie Billy wants to do Brodie's play.

Henry When are you going to see Billy again?

Annie He's going straight into another show. I promised to see him. I want to see him.

Henry Fine, when should we go? It's all right to come with you, is it?

Annie Why not? Don't let me out of your sight, eh, Hen?

Henry When were you thinking of going?

Annie I thought the weekend.

Henry And where is it?

Annie Well, Glasgow.

Henry Billy travelled down with you from Glasgow and then took a train back?

Annie Yes.

Henry And I'm supposed to score points for dignity. I don't think I can. It'll become my only thought. It'll replace thinking.

Annie You mustn't do that. You have to find a part of yourself where I'm not important or you won't be worth loving. It's awful what you did to my clothes and everything. I mean what you did to yourself. It's not you. And it's you I love.

Henry Actually I don't think I can manage the weekend. I hope it goes well.

Annie Thank you. (*She moves towards the bedroom.*)

Henry What does Billy think of Brodie's play?

Annie He says he can't write.

She leaves. Henry takes his present out of its bag. It is a tartan scarf.

SCENE TEN

Billy and Annie.
  Annie sits reading on the train.
  Billy approaches the seat next to Annie. He speaks with a Scottish accent. He carries a grip.
  The dialogue is amplified through a mike.

Billy Excuse me, is this seat taken?

Annie No.

Billy Mind if I sit down?

Annie It's a free country.

   Billy sits down.

Billy D'you reckon?

Annie Sorry?

Billy You reckon it's a free country?

   Annie ignores him.

Going far?

Annie To London.

Billy All the way.

   Annie starts to move to an empty seat.

I'll let you read.

Annie Thank you. (*She sits in the empty seat.*)

Billy My name's Bill.

   She ignores him.

Can I just ask you one question?

Annie Mary.

Billy Can I just ask you one question, Mary?

Annie One.

Billy Do you know what time this train is due to arrive in London?

Annie At about half-past one, I believe, if it's on time.

Billy You put me in mind of Mussolini, Mary. People used to say about Mussolini, he may be a Fascist, but –

Annie No – that's wrong – that's the old script –

Billy (*swears under his breath*) Sorry, Roger . . .

Roger (*voice off*) OK, cut the tape.

Annie From the top, Roger?

Roger (*voice off*) Give us a minute.

A light change reveals that the setting is a fake, in a TV studio. Annie gets up and moves away. Billy joins her. They exchange a few words, and she moves back to her seat, leaving him estranged, an unhappy feeling between them.
  After a moment the scene fades out.

SCENE ELEVEN

Henry and Annie.
  Henry is alone listening to the radio, which is playing Bach's Air on a G String.
  Annie enters from the bedroom, dressed to go out, and she is in a hurry.

Henry (*urgently, on seeing her*) Listen –

Annie I can't. I'm going to be late now.

Henry It's important. *Listen.*

Annie What?

Henry *Listen.*

She realizes that he means the radio. She listens for a few moments.

What is it?

Annie (*pleased*) Do you like it?

Henry I *love* it.

Annie (*congratulating him*) It's Bach.

Henry The cheeky beggar.

234

Annie What?

Henry He's stolen it.

Annie *Bach?*

Henry Note for note. Practically a straight lift from Procul Harum. And he can't even get it right. Hang on. I'll play you the original.

He moves to get the record. She, pleased by him but going, moves to him.

Annie Work well.

She kisses him quickly and lightly but he forces the kiss into a less casual one. His voice, however, keeps its detachment.

Henry You too.

Annie Last day. Why don't you come?

Henry shrugs.

No, all right.

Henry I'm only the ghost writer anyway.

The phone rings.

Annie If that's them, say I've left.

Henry (*into the phone*) She's left . . . Oh . . . (*to Annie*) It's your friend.

She hesitates.

Just go.

Annie takes the phone.

Annie (*into phone*) Billy . . .? Yes – what? – yes, of course – I'm just late – yes – goodbye – all right . . . Yes, fine. (*She hangs up.*) I love you. Do you understand?

Henry No.

Annie Do you think it's unfair?

Henry No. It's as though I've been careless, left a door open somewhere while preoccupied.

Annie I'll stop.

Henry Not for me. I won't be the person who stopped you. I can't be that. When I got upset you said you'd stop so I try not to get upset. I don't get pathetic because when I got pathetic I could feel how tedious it was, how unattractive. Like Max, your ex. Remember Max? Love me because I'm in pain. No good. Not in very good taste.
  So.
  Dignified cuckoldry is a difficult trick, but it can be done. Think of it as modern marriage. We have got beyond hypocrisy, you and I. Exclusive rights isn't love, it's colonization.

Annie Stop it – please stop it.

  Pause

Henry The trouble is, I can't *find* a part of myself where you're not important. I write in order to be worth your while and to finance the way I want to live with you. Not the way you want to live. The way *I* want to live with *you*. Without you I wouldn't care. I'd eat tinned spaghetti and put on yesterday's clothes. But as it is I change my socks, and make money, and tart up Brodie's unspeakable drivel into speakable drivel so he can be an author too, like me. Not that it seems to have done him much good. Perhaps the authorities saw that it was a touch meretricious. *Meretrix, meretricis.* Harlot.

Annie You shouldn't have done it if you didn't think it was right.

236

Henry You think it's right. I can't cope with more than one moral system at a time. Mine is that what you think is right is right. What you do is right. What you want is right. There was a tribe, wasn't there, which worshipped Charlie Chaplin. It worked just as well as any other theology, apparently. They loved Charlie Chaplin. I love you.

Annie So you'll forgive me anything, is that it, Hen? I'm a selfish cow but you love me so you'll overlook it, is that right? Thank you, but that's not it. I wish I felt selfish, everything would be easy. Goodbye Billy. I don't need him. How can I need someone I spend half my time telling to grow up? I'm . . . – what's a petard?, I've often wondered.

Henry What?

Annie A petard. Something you hoist, is it, piece of rope?

Henry I don't think so.

Annie Well, anyway. All right?

Henry All right what? I keep marrying people who suddenly lose a wheel.

Annie I don't feel selfish, I feel hoist. I send out waves, you know. Not free. Not interested. He sort of got in under the radar. Acting daft on a train. Next thing I'm looking round for him, makes the day feel better, it's like love or something: no – love, absolutely, how can I say it wasn't? You weren't replaced, or even replaceable. But I liked it, being older for once, in charge, my pupil. And it was a long way north. And so on. I'm sorry I hurt you. But I meant it. It meant something. And now that it means less than I thought and I feel silly, I won't drop him as if it was nothing, a pick-up, it wasn't that, I'm not that. I just want him to stop needing me so I can stop behaving well. This is me behaving well. I have to choose who I hurt and I choose you because I'm yours.

Pause. The phone rings.

Maybe it's just me.

Henry (*into phone*) Roger –? She's left, about ten minutes ago – yes, I know, dear, but – don't talk to me about unprofessional, Roger – you lost half a day shooting the war memorial with a boom shadow all over it – OK, scream at me if it makes you feel better –

Annie takes the phone out of his hand.

Annie (*into phone*) Keep your knickers on, it's only a bloody play. (*She hangs up and starts to go. Going*) Bye.

Henry Annie. (*Pause.*) Yes, all right.

Annie I need you.

Henry Yes, I know.

Annie Please don't let it wear away what you feel for me. It won't, will it?

Henry No, not like that. It will go on or it will flip into its opposite.
What time will you be back?

Annie Not late.

He nods at her. She nods back and leaves. Henry sits down in his chair. Then he gets up and starts the record playing Procul Harum's 'A Whiter Shade of Pale', which is indeed a version of Air on a G String.
He stands listening to it, smiling at its Bach, until the vocals start. Then the smile gets overtaken.

Henry Oh, please, please, please, please, *don't*.

Then blackout, but the music continues.

238

SCENE TWELVE

Henry, Annie and Brodie.
In the blackout the music gives way to recorded
dialogue between Annie and Billy, who speaks with a
Scottish accent.

Billy (*voice*) Wait for me.

Annie (*voice*) Yes, I will.

Billy (*voice*) Everything's got to change. Except you.
Don't you change.

Annie (*voice*) No. I won't. I'll wait for you and for
everything to change.

Billy (*voice*) That could take longer. (*laughs*) I might
have to do it myself.

> *By this time, light has appeared starting with the faint*
> *glow from the television screen.*
> *Brodie, alone in the living-room, is twenty-five,*
> *wearing a cheap suit. He is holding a tumbler of neat*
> *scotch, his attention engaged by the television set and*
> *particularly by the accompanying video machine.*
> *From the television the dialogue has been followed*
> *by the echoing clang of a cell door, footsteps, credit*
> *music. Brodie turns the volume down.*
> *Henry enters from the kitchen carrying a small jug*
> *of water for Brodie's scotch. In the room there is wine*
> *for Henry and another glass for Annie.*
> *Brodie speaks with a Scottish accent.*

Brodie Very handy, these machines. When did they come
out?

Henry Well, I suppose they were coming out about the
time you were going in.

Brodie You can set them two weeks ahead.

Henry Yes.

Brodie How much?

Henry A few hundred. They vary.

Brodie I'll have to pinch one sometime.

Henry If you leave it a bit, they'll probably improve them so that you can have it recording concurrently with your sentence.

Brodie looks at Henry without expression.

Brodie Annie looked nice. She's come on a bit since *Rosie of the Royal Infirmary*. A good-looking woman.

Henry doesn't answer. Annie enters from the kitchen with a dip, peanuts, etc. on a tray. She puts the tray down. Henry pours wine into a third glass.

Just saying you looked nice.

Annie Oh, yes?

Brodie The pretty one was supposed to be me, was he?

Annie Well . . .

Brodie He's not a pansy, is he?

Annie I don't think so.

Henry hands her the glass of wine.

Thank you.

Henry (*to Brodie, indicating the TV*) What did you think?

Brodie I liked it better before. You don't mind me saying?

Henry No.

Annie It did work.

Brodie You mean getting me sprung?

Annie No, I didn't mean that.

Brodie That's right. I got sprung by the militarists.

Henry I don't think I follow that.

Brodie Half a billion pounds for defence, nothing left for prisons. So you get three, four to a cell. First off, they tell the magistrates, for God's sake go easy, *fine* the bastards. But still they keep coming – four, five to a cell. Now they're frightened it's going to blow up. Even the warders are going on strike. So: 'Give us the money to build more prisons!' 'Can't be done, laddie, we're spending the money to keep the world free, not in prison.' So they start freeing the prisoners. Get it? I'm out because the missiles I was marching against are using up the money they need for a prison to put me in. Beautiful. Can I have another?

He holds up his empty glass for Annie. Slight pause. Henry stays still.

Annie Please help yourself

Brodie does so.

Brodie Early release. There was eight of us just on my corridor. (*to Henry*) Not one of them a controversial TV author. I don't owe you.

Henry Is it against your principles to say thank you for *anything*, even a drink?

Brodie Fair enough. You had a go. You did your best. It probably needed something, to work in with their prejudices.

241

Henry Yes, they are a bit prejudiced, these drama producers. They don't like plays which go 'clunk' every time someone opens his mouth. They gang up against soap-box bigots with no idea that everything has a length. They think TV is a visual medium. (*to Annie, puzzled*) Is this *him*?

Brodie Don't be clever with me, Henry, like you were clever with my play. I lived it and put my guts into it, and you came along and wrote it clever. Not for me. For her. I'm not stupid.

Annie (*to Henry*) No, this isn't him.

Brodie Yes, it bloody is. That was me on the train, and this is me again, and I don't think you're that different either.

Annie And *that* wasn't him. (*She points at the TV.*) He was helpless, like a three-legged calf, nervous as anything. A boy on the train. Chatting me up. Nice. He'd been in some trouble at the camp, some row, I forget, he was going absent without leave. He didn't know anything about a march. He didn't know anything about anything, except *Rosie of the Royal Infirmary*. By the time we got to London he would have followed me into the Ku Klux Klan. He tagged on. And when we were passing the war memorial he got his lighter out. It was one of those big chrome Zippos – click, snap. Private Brodie goes over the top to the slaughter, not an idea in his head except to impress me. What else could I do? He was my recruit.

Henry You should have told me. That one I would have known how to write.

Annie Yes.

Brodie Listen – I'm still here.

Annie So you are, Bill. Finish your drink, will you?

Brodie Why not?

Brodie finishes his drink and stands up.

I can come back for some dip another time.

Annie No time like the present.

Annie picks up the bowl of dip and smashes it into his face. She goes to the hall door, leaving it open while she briefly disappears to get Brodie's coat.
Henry has stood up, but Brodie isn't going to do anything. He carefully wipes his face with his handkerchief.

Henry Well, it was so interesting to meet you. I'd heard so much about you.

Brodie I don't really blame you, Henry. The price was right. I remember the time she came to visit me. She was in a blue dress, and there was a thrill coming off her like she was back on the box, but there was no way in. It was the first time I felt I was in prison. You know what I mean.

Annie stands at the door holding Brodie's coat. He takes it from her, ignoring her as he walks out. She follows him, and the front door is heard closing. Annie returns.

Henry I don't know what it did to him, but it scared the hell out of me. Are you all right?

She nods.

Annie Are you all right?

The phone rings. Henry picks it up.

Henry Hello. (*into the phone, suddenly uncomfortable*) Oh, hello. Did you want to speak to Annie?

Annie No.

Henry (*suddenly relaxes*) Well, that's fantastic, Max! (*to Annie*) It's your ex. He's getting married. (*to phone*) Congratulations. Who is she?

Henry ferries this over to Annie with an expressive look, which she returns. Annie moves to Henry and embraces his shoulders from behind. She leans on him tiredly while he deals with the phone.

Oh, I think you're very wise. To marry one actress is unfortunate, to marry two is simply asking for it.

Annie kisses him. He covers the mouthpiece with his hand.

(*Into phone*) Really? Across a crowded room, eh?

Annie I've had it. Look after me.

He covers the mouthpiece.

Henry Don't worry. I'm your chap.
(*Into phone*) Well, it's very decent of you to say so, Max.
(*To Annie*) 'No hard feelings?' What does he mean? If it wasn't for me, he wouldn't be engaged *now*.

Annie disengages herself from him with a smile and goes around turning out the lights until the only light is coming from the bedroom door.

(*Into phone*) No. I'm afraid she isn't . . . She'll be so upset when I tell her . . . No, I mean when I tell her she missed you . . . No, she'll be delighted. I'm delighted, Max. Isn't love wonderful?

Annie finishes with the lights and goes out into the bedroom. Henry is being impatiently patient with Max on the phone, trying to end it.

Henry Yes, well, we look forward to meeting her. What? Oh, yes?

Absently he clicks on the little radio, which starts playing, softly, 'I'm a Believer' by the Monkees. He is immediately beguiled. He forgets Max until the phone crackle gets back through to him.

Sorry. Yes, I'm still here. (*He turns the song up slightly.*)

NIGHT AND DAY

To Paul Johnson

Characters

George Guthrie
Ruth Carson
Alastair Carson
Dick Wagner
Jacob Milne
Geoffrey Carson
President Mageeba
Francis

Notes on Characters

Guthrie is in his forties; perhaps quite short; fit, can look after himself; wears tough clothes, blue denim, comfortable boots.

Ruth is in her late thirties; probably tall; attractive in face, figure and, especially, voice; shoulder-length hair.

Alastair is eight, English prep school; fair.

Wagner is in his forties, a suit-and-tie man; big but not fat. An Australian; some accent.

Milne is twenty-two or twenty-three and definitely attractive in a way that is called boyish; casually dressed.

Carson, Ruth's husband, is somewhat older than her but also in good shape; casually but well dressed.

Mageeba, the President, is around fifty, a British-educated black African, a hard man if soft of voice; carefully dressed in freshly-laundered 'informal' army uniform.

Francis, Carson's black African servant and driver, is in his twenties; slacks and white clean short-sleeved shirt.

A Note on 'Ruth'

The audience is occasionally made privy to Ruth's thoughts, and to hers alone. This text makes no reference to the technique by which this is achieved. (It may be that – ideally – no technical indication is necessary.) When Ruth's thoughts are audible she is simply called 'Ruth' in quotes, and treated as a separate character. Thus, Ruth can be interrupted by 'Ruth'.

This rule is also loosely applied to the first scene of Act Two, where the situation is somewhat different.

The Set

An empty stage with a cyclorama, representing the open air, and a living room share the stage in various proportions, including total occupancy by the one or the other. Thus, the living room is mobile. Herewith, a few dogmatic statements tentatively offered. The play begins with the empty stage (possibly a low skyline in front of the cyclorama). The room makes its first appearance by occupying about half the stage, the rest of the stage becoming garden. For Alastair's entrance the room moves further round into view, leaving a corner of garden. The first act ends with a reverse transition to the empty stage. The second act presents the room in its position of total occupancy of the stage. There is, however, a limiting factor; we have to have a good view of the interior of an adjoining room, an office-study, which contains a telex machine. We see the machine through the door of the study, when the door is open; and the door can also shut it out of our view. When we first encounter the living room, the study door being open, we can see that the telex machine is operating, that is, the paper stuttering out of the machine. After Alastair's entrance, our view of the machine does not have to be so direct. But, again, when the room is in its Act Two position we need a clear view of a man sitting at the telex. The telex is like a large modern typewriter, on a desk. It has to be 'practical' and operate on cue.

We are in a fictitious African country, formerly a British Colony. The living room is part of a large and expensive house. The furniture is European with local colour. It looks comfortable and well used. Essentials include a telephone, marble-topped table or sideboard with bottles and glasses on it, and a large sofa. The verandah also has suitable furniture on it, including a small table and a couple of chairs at the downstage end. The garden will contain at least one long comfortable cane chair. The room should seat five people comfortably, possibly around a low table. This furniture might well be in a shallow well, so that people entering the room from further inside the house, or from the study, do so from a good vantage. The room could be connected with the rest of the house through a door, more likely double-doors, or it might continue out of sight into the wings.

The first act – after the prologue – starts just before sunset, the last rays illuminating the garden; twilight follows quickly on this, and darkness has overtaken the play by the time of Ruth's second entrance.

Night and Day was first performed at the Phoenix
Theatre, London, on 8 November 1978. The cast was
as follows:

George Guthrie William Marlowe
Francis George Harris
Ruth Carson Diana Rigg
Alastair Carson Jon Bentley
Dick Wagner John Thaw
Jacob Milne Peter Machin
Geoffrey Carson David Langton
President Mageeba Olu Jacobs

Directed by Peter Wood
Decor Carl Toms
Lighting Robert Bryan
Presented by Michael Codron

Act One

African sunset.

*An open, empty stage, the frame perhaps broken by
the branch of a tree. There may be a low skyline but not
necessarily. The 'cyc' looks very beautiful. The sun is
nearly down. The sky goes through rapid changes
towards darkness.*

*A distant helicopter is heard approaching. By the time
it reaches 'overhead', darkness has fallen and there is
moonlight.*

*Helicopter very loud. Shadow of blades whirling
on the floor of the stage. Violent shaking of foliage.
A spotlight from the helicopter traverses the stage.
It disappears. A jeep drives on to the stage with its
headlights on. Not much can be seen in the darkness.
Two or three people in the jeep. Guthrie is one of the
passengers. The jeep turns into the audience so one can
only see headlights.*

*By the time the jeep appears, a machine-gun has
started up. The noise is all very loud – helicopter and
machine-gun. The jeep probably isn't audible. Someone –
Guthrie – shouts something about the lights, and the
jeep's headlights are turned off. The jeep hasn't stopped
moving. It is turning in a circle. The spotlight comes
back and sweeps across the jeep. Guthrie jumps out of
the jeep and runs. He doesn't leave the stage. He just
runs out of the light. The light loses the jeep. The jeep
goes. Guthrie crouches in a down-stage corner. He is
shouting but it is hard to catch. He is shouting 'Press!
Press! You stupid fuckers!' Then the spotlight finds him.*

257

He stands up into the light with his arms spread out, shouting. The gun is firing bursts. He moves away from the corner. A burst catches him and knocks him over.

A late afternoon light reveals Guthrie stretched out on a long garden chair. Sundown. The steps to the verandah and the room are behind him. The telex is visible and chattering in bursts like the machine-gun; it is apparent that the noise of the telex had entered Guthrie's dream in the form of machine-gun fire. This noise has continued right through the transition of the scene. This sound is joined by the sound of an approaching car. The telex stops. Not far from Guthrie's chair is his camera-bag, with pockets for cameras, lenses, exposed and unexposed film, and other small objects. An empty glass is lying near the chair.

Guthrie is apparently asleep. Francis enters and removes the empty glass and goes again. The car arrives. The car door slams. Ruth enters carrying two or three packages which she puts down. She comes into the room expecting to find somebody there (Guthrie's car is outside) and then she sees him on the chair in the garden. She comes down and looks at him curiously. Guthrie doesn't move. Ruth notices the bag and bends down and touches it, perhaps to peer inside it.

Guthrie Please don't touch that.

Ruth I'm sorry.

Guthrie Christ. That wasn't nice at all.

Ruth I thought you were asleep.

Guthrie I thought I was dead.

He has barely moved and now doesn't move at all. Ruth looks at him.

Ruth Are you all right now? (*Pause.*) That's good.

(*Pause.*) I don't think we've met.

Guthrie half sits up, then relapses.

Guthrie Uh? Sorry, do you want to sit down?

Ruth (*drily*) Thank you.

She moves up the steps to the small table on the verandah and sits down. Guthrie seems to be coming to. He sits up slightly.

You shouldn't sleep in the sun.

Guthrie squints up at the sky.

Guthrie It moved.

Ruth It does that. It's called night and day.

Guthrie relapses again. Francis comes on with a tea-tray, a nice tea-set with one cup and saucer. He brings this to Ruth's table, while –

'Ruth' I think you're going to like it.
(*Sings*) 'Night and day . . . you are the one.'

With her right hand she plays imaginary piano keys on the table. We hear the piano.

'Only you beneath the moon and under the –'

A wrong note, caused by Francis placing the cup in the saucer. He has put the tray on the table in front of Ruth.

Ruth Thank you, Francis. Has the house been opened to the public?

Francis What's that, Mrs Carson?

This gets through to Guthrie.

Guthrie Oh – God – I'm terribly sorry –

Ruth I shouldn't get up; you look awful. (*to Francis who is leaving*) Another cup.

Ruth's manner is easy-going. Guthrie gets up.

Guthrie No – I'm fine. Sleeping on planes – you know. Ruins the complexion. From the inside. (*He has come up the steps towards Ruth.*) My name's Guthrie – George Guthrie.

Ruth How do you do? I'm Ruth Carson. Would you care for some tea?

Guthrie Wouldn't say no.

Ruth is pouring tea for Guthrie into the only cup.

Ruth Do you take sugar?

Guthrie No thank you.

Guthrie goes back down the steps to his bag and fishes about in it. Meanwhile Francis comes in with another cup.

Ruth (*to Francis*) Thank you. Would you take those parcels, Francis?

Guthrie is looking for something – saccharin tablets – in his bag. Francis leaves with the packages.

I'm sorry I wasn't here to greet you Mr . . . Guthrie. I had to go into Jeddu to pick up some things.

Guthrie The boy said it was OK to wait in the garden. Is that all right?

Ruth Of course. But I'm afraid I have no idea what time Geoffrey will be home. He's been in Malakuangazi – I was expecting him this afternoon.

Guthrie I've come to meet Dick Wagner.

*The name has the English form – Wag-ner. He has
found the saccharin and is coming back to the table.
Ruth remains perfectly still. Guthrie comes casually
back to the table and sits down. Ruth waits until he
looks at her.*

Ruth What are you talking about, Mr Guthrie?

Guthrie Dick Wagner. Do you know him?

Pause.

Ruth Is he a composer?

Guthrie No. He's a reporter. Writes for the *Sunday
Globe,* in London. I take the pictures. The pictures, as
you know, are worth a thousand words. In the case of
Wagner, two thousand. He was supposed to be at KC
to meet me.

Ruth Why in God's name do you expect to meet him at
my house?

Guthrie He told me. He left a message at the airport.

Ruth He told you to meet him *at my house?*

*Guthrie, sipping tea, catches her tone for the first
time, and hesitates.*

Guthrie Well, he didn't mention *you.*

Pause.

Ruth What kind of camera do you use?

Guthrie Do you know anything about cameras?

Ruth No. (*Pause.*) By the way, we don't call them boy
any more. The idea is, if we don't call them boy they
won't chop us with their machetes. (*brief smile*) Small
point.

Guthrie holds his arm out, palm to the ground.

Guthrie Boy about this high, fair hair, your mouth, knows about cameras, has a Kodak himself; said I could wait in the garden.

Ruth acknowledges her mistake, but Guthrie pushes it.

His name's Alastair.

He has pushed it too far and she snaps at him.

Ruth I know his bloody name.

Guthrie (*olive branch*) The one I use mainly is a motorized F2 Nikon. (*sips tea*) Lovely.

Ruth (*smiles*) Would you like a proper drink?

Guthrie (*relaxes; shakes his head*) The sambo gave me a lime squash. (*winces*) Sorry. (*His hand chops the air twice.*) Chop-chop.

Ruth gets up; moves.

Ruth Why is my husband filling my house with journalists?

Guthrie I thought he was one.

Ruth Geoffrey? Don't be silly.

Guthrie I saw the telex.

Ruth That's for his business. Did he ask this man to come here?

Guthrie I don't know.

Ruth What does he want?

Guthrie I don't know.

'Ruth' Help!

Piano chord.

Guthrie A story maybe.

'Ruth' I need somebody – help –

Piano chord: it's the Beatles' song, 'Help!'.

Guthrie What is his business?

'Ruth' (*picking up the rhythm*) Not just anybody –
He-e-e-lp!

Car approaching.

Guthrie Somebody coming.

*Guthrie stands up and moves back into the garden
looking out. Piano cuts out.*

'Ruth' You're a reasonable looking sort of chap,
Guthrie. How would you like to take me away from all
this? (*new voice*) My God, Ruth, not a *journalist*!

Ruth laughs briefly at herself.

Guthrie (*reporting from the garden*) Beat-up Mercedes.
Is that your husband?

Ruth It's a taxi.

Guthrie (*looking out*) Wagner.

*Ruth leaves. She goes into the house.
Helicopter approaching fast and low. Guthrie, in
the garden, looks up surprised. He sees the helicopter
apparently coming straight at him. He cowers and
goes into a crouch, his hands over his head. Shadow
whips across the garden. Then the helicopter has gone.
Alastair has entered. He sees Guthrie crouched.*

Alastair What's the matter? Mr Guthrie?

Guthrie Hello.

Alastair is carrying an old-fashioned leather-bound Kodak. The camera is folded and Alastair holds it by the strap. Guthrie straightens up.

Hello.

Alastair I've found it. Are you going to show me about it?

The receding helicopter noise has been succeeded by the taxi stopping outside the house. A dog barks, but not for long. Obscure voices of Wagner and Francis. Taxi departing.

Guthrie I think my friend has arrived.

Alastair I came before but you were asleep.

Guthrie I'm sorry.

Alastair Will you show me later?

Guthrie Sure.

Alastair I believe this is an excellent camera. It just needs some film.

Guthrie When does your daddy get home usually?

Alastair That was him. The helicopter.

Guthrie Oh.

Another car drives away from the house.

Alastair He buzzes us. Then Francis takes the car down to the compound to fetch him.

Guthrie The compound?

Alastair The mine. It's not daddy's own helicopter. He's just allowed to use it. A helicopter is extremely useful in a country like Africa. Have you ever flown in one?

Guthrie Yes, a few times.

Alastair In Africa?

Guthrie No, in Asia.

Alastair Well, you know how useful they can be.

Guthrie Yes. This is my friend, Dick Wagner.

Wagner has entered.

Wagner (*enthusiastically*) Hello Gigi, you lovely bastard! (*He moves down into the room and slaps Guthrie's shoulder.*) You look *terrific!*

Guthrie I look terrible.

Wagner (*fresh start; same tone*) You look *terrible!* How are you? House is wide open. Is Carson here?

Guthrie This is Alastair Carson.

Wagner (*talking down*) How do you do, Alastair? And how old are you?

Alastair Eight. How old are you?

Wagner Kid's a natural.

Female voice off, not Ruth, 'Allie!'

Alastair Got to have my bath now, anyway. (*to Guthrie*) Would you like to look at my camera 'til I get back?

Guthrie Sure.

Alastair You won't forget?

Guthrie No.

Alastair I'll come back. (*He goes.*)

Guthrie How are things here, Dick?

Wagner Not wonderful. Bloody thing won't catch fire. Where's this Carson?

Guthrie He's on his way. Who is he?

Wagner He runs the business end of the copper industry. Also manganese, potash . . . he's in mines generally.

Guthrie But not frequently.

Wagner How about Mrs Carson?

Guthrie She keeps herself nice, too.

Wagner Where is she?

Guthrie Inside somewhere. Are you a friend of the family?

Wagner Hardly. The one who came out here was an earl or something. Grandfather, I think. There's an elder brother defending the title in England. This one works for a living. As it were. She's his second wife.

Guthrie What are we doing here?

Wagner Looking up Carson.

Guthrie Why?

Wagner I don't know. I think Hammaker must know him. (*He takes a folded cablegram out of his pocket.*) I got this on Sunday. 'Guthrie arriving KC ex-Dacca Thursday. ETA ten hundred. Suggest uplook Geoffrey Carson at home Jeddu. Happy birthday. Hammaker.'

Guthrie takes the cable out of his hand.

How's Dacca?

Guthrie You know Dacca. It's not Paris.

Wagner (*nods; sings badly*) 'April in Dacca . . . I love Dacca in the springtime. I love Dacca in the . . .' Yeah.

It's not Paris. It's Dacca.

Guthrie (*handing back the cable*) Is it your birthday?

Wagner No. Sounds good, doesn't it?

Guthrie Did you clock the telex?

Wagner looks round and sees the telex.

Wagner Christ!

Guthrie (*nods*) Happy birthday.

Wagner I don't believe it.

Guthrie Do you think he's got a wire machine somewhere?

Wagner We're going to make them sick.

Guthrie Who's out here?

Wagner Everybody.

Wagner has gone to the machine. He taps a couple of keys and waits for the evidence that it is in working order. The machine chatters back at him briefly. Wagner looks at Guthrie wide-eyed.

We are going to make them *ill*.

Guthrie Doesn't the hotel have telex?

Wagner The hotel doesn't have cleft sticks. There's a post office in town which is a joke. Fritz Biedermeier said when he blew the dust off the counter there was an urgent message for Stanley from the *New York Herald*.

Guthrie That wasn't here, was it?

Wagner It was a joke.

Guthrie OK. Who's Biedermeier?

Wagner *Newsweek*. He was in Beirut that time.

Guthrie Oh yeah. Him. Has he got a photographer?

Wagner No, he's got a Pentax.

Guthrie That's bad for trade.

Wagner Yeah, I wouldn't like it if you learned to write. I think we'll do OK. Especially now we've got wheels. Which is yours?

Guthrie The Cortina.

Wagner Good. The taxi drivers have started to hire themselves out by auction.

Guthrie How did you get up from Kamba City, then?

Wagner In a Cessna.

Guthrie Bloody firemen.

Wagner Afraid of missing the war. It wasn't so expensive – I shared with a couple of photographers.

Guthrie (*interested*) Yeah? – who's that?

Wagner One was a Frog – Jean-Paul something. Belmondo, maybe. St Laurent army fatigues and a gold chain, very tough with the Gauloises, no filters – know what I mean? 'I was a Left Bank layabout 'til I discovered photo-journalism.'

Guthrie (*sharply, angrily*) Knock it off will you, Dick? (*Pause. Apologetically*) He's really very good.

Wagner Sorry.

Guthrie What about the other one?

Wagner A groupie. No sweat. He had one of those cameras with a little picture of a cloud and a little

268

picture of the sun and you slide it across according to the weather.

Guthrie (*smiles*) Well, I'm shooting Tri-X through two thousand quid's worth of lenses, but he'll get better pictures if he's in a better place. One time in Hué I was in a dug-out with Larry Barnes, and this American kid is there – he looked like a hippie, bummed his way into the country and got himself a letter from AP and a second-hand Leica, so he's accredited, right? – wouldn't know his arse from a hole in the ground except he's *in* a hole in the ground, and he's lost his light meter. He's reading his Kodak packet, and there's all kinds of shit coming over, mortars, and he says to Larry, 'Hey, do you think this is cloudy-bright or semi-dull?' Well, you can't see any sun because of the smoke, so Larry says, 'I think it's cloudy-bright.' This kid then starts walking forward behind a tank and the next time I see him he's got a set of prints of VC attacking the bridge, it looked like Robert Mitchum was just out of frame. Three pages in *Match*.

Wagner Maybe it's the same kid.

Guthrie Later he stepped on a land-mine.

Wagner (*pause*) It probably isn't, then.

Guthrie And Larry. And the other three in Larry's helicopter. Do you know how many people were killed in that war?

Wagner Not exactly.

Guthrie Fifty-four.

Wagner Oh. People.

Guthrie And eighteen missing.

Wagner Don't be morbid, Gigi.

Guthrie I'm not being morbid. (*Pause.*) Before you came I was sleeping, just over there, and I dreamed that I bought it – got killed by a helicopter. I was really quite spooked.

Wagner You were dreaming about Larry.

Guthrie No – not in a helicopter *crash* – we were in a jeep, and this gunship was shooting at us. And then it killed me. Is this going to be a helicopter war?

Wagner For Christ's sake!

Guthrie OK. How are they getting their stuff out?

Wagner Air freight from KC. There's nothing closer for pictures. Good chance of a pigeon, too – lots of people flying out at the moment. There's an overnight plane to London on Fridays – very handy; that gives you about twenty-four hours if you've got something for this week. And there's the AP wire on Saturday if you're pushed – they'll print up for you.

Guthrie Yeh. I checked them out on the way up. Either way, it's a four-hour drive for that lot.

Wagner You won't do any better.

Guthrie Carson's got a helicopter.

He sits down and picks up Alastair's camera and opens it. He's going to find a roll of film in his own bag and put it into Alastair's camera. But this is something which he takes his time over, checking the camera itself, etc. Also, he gets interrupted so the job isn't completed until later.

Wagner I can't take much more of this. Our own telex and a helicopter, and the competition on tom-toms. If this war starts on a Saturday morning you and I are going to be famous.

Guthrie You're famous in Dacca. I saw your name in the lavatory in the Inter-Continental.

Wagner How nice.

Guthrie It said, 'Dick Wagner before he dicks you'.

Wagner (*grins*) Sour grapes. That was a legitimate beat. I had my own source. By the time that Paki press officer handed it out with an embargo my story was in London – Jesus, it was on the *stone*.

Guthrie All right.

Wagner (*getting worked up*) I mean, I *cracked* that story, Gigi. The embargo was just shutting the stable door –

Guthrie Listen, it's nothing to me.

Wagner Yeh, but I know how those stuck-up bastards tell it around – the whole thing gets misreported.

Guthrie (*mildly*) And they're usually so accurate. Did you get me a room?

Wagner You're with me. There's two hotels, both dumps. Journalists hanging out the windows, and a Swedish TV crew sleeping in the lobby, and a lot of good friends from home too. We're going to make them ill. All we need is a story.

Guthrie Do you think we're in the right place?

Wagner What do you mean?

Guthrie I don't know what I mean.

Wagner Well, everybody else is here.

Guthrie Yeh. I suppose so.

Wagner There's nothing better. Except an interview with the President, and nobody has even *seen* that mad bastard for six months. Everybody's had a go.

Guthrie What's the story in Jeddu?

Wagner (*shrugs*) It's as near as we can get to Alf.

Guthrie Who's he?

Wagner Them. 'Who's he?' Don't you ever look at the bits between the photographs? Adoma Liberation Front. The Colonel. Colonel Shimbu.

Guthrie I was just testing you.

Wagner Didn't you know about my famous scoop?

Guthrie No.

Wagner Nor did I. Sunday, everyone gets cables. 'Globe finds Colonel Shimbu. Why Colonel unfound by you', etcetera. So everybody's screaming, where is he, Wagner, you bastard? Only, it isn't my story. *I* don't know where the bloody Colonel is. So they want to see my cable – they think it's a herogram from Hammaker. But of course I can't show it to them because I don't know what this happy birthday thing is all about. So then they're calling me a *lying* bastard, and following me to the lavatory when they aren't following armoured car patrols into the bush in broken-down taxis. You never saw anything like it.

Guthrie Yes I did.

Wagner Yes you did. There's a government press officer here who's the usual lying jerk, but there's no way of telling whether he's lying because he knows the truth or because he doesn't know anything, so you can't trust his mendacity either – he could be telling the truth half the time, by accident. His line was that the Adoma Liberation Front didn't exist, and the army had got it completely surrounded. Anyway, the BBC World Service picks up the *Globe* exclusive, and it turns out to be

272

date-lined up-country with the rebels, interview with the Colonel himself, a party political broadcast wouldn't have done it better, and furthermore it's not a rebellion, it's a secession – get the picture? *Media credibility!* Well, the press officer goes bananas. He wants to know which side the *Globe* thinks it's on. So I tell him, it's not on any side, stupid, it's an objective fact-gathering organization. And he says, yes, but is it objective-for or objective-against? (*Pause.*) He may be stupid but he's not stupid.

Guthrie I've got a present for you.

Guthrie gets up and walks towards the back of the room where he picks up a pile of newspapers. Wagner doesn't turn to see this.

Wagner So he spends the briefing attacking the *Globe* – God bless him, it's the only story I've filed this week – and he's in a flat spin trying to make everything fit. At the end, this very smooth guy from Reuters says, 'Let me see if I've got this right. It's not a *political* movement, it's just a lot – or rather *not* a lot – of completely illiterate ivory poachers who've been reading too much Marxist propaganda, and they're all armed with home-made weapons flown by Cuban pilots.'

Guthrie (*coming back*) Who's the *Globe* special correspondent?

Wagner I don't know. I'm famous in Jeddu. Scooped by my own paper. Bloody poaching, that's what it is. It's one of those ivory poachers moonlighting for Hammaker. I'd give anything for a copy of last Sunday's –

Guthrie dumps the newspapers into Wagner's lap.

Aw, Gigi!

Guthrie I couldn't get them all, just what they had when I changed planes at Karachi. Second lead.

The Sunday Globe *is a respectable English paper. The African story is the second most important story on the front page. The back page is a sports page. The other papers are: the* Sunday Express, *the* New York Times (*Monday not Sunday*), *the* Sunday Times, *the* Sunday Mirror, *the* Observer, *the* Sunday Telegraph *and the* News of the World. *Wagner of course looks at the* Globe *first.*

Wagner 'A special correspondent' –

Guthrie That's what I said.

Wagner What the hell does that mean? Fair old piece. (*He turns the paper to look over the fold.*) Took care of mine anyway – 'Richard Wagner adds from Jeddu' – two paragraphs. (*He puts the paper aside.*) Well, well. A world beat and no name on it.

Guthrie A freelance.

Wagner They have names. I don't get it.

Guthrie (*picking up the* Globe) Where is this place?

Wagner It's sort of North Wales.

Guthrie What do you mean North Wales?

Wagner I've given up on place names here – they all sound like games you play on board ship. If a place isn't called Tombola it's called Housey-housey. The way to look at it is, KC is London, Jeddu is up the A40 – Cheltenham – and the Colonel is somewhere in the Welsh hills. (*He has found the inside foreign page of the* Sunday Express *now.*) 'The smouldering heart of this coffee-laden, copper-loaded corner of Africa is being ripped apart by the ambitions of a cashiered Colonel whose iron fist, UN observers fear, may turn out to be holding a hammer and sickle . . .' (*scornfully*) And a

New York date-line, who needs it? (*He tosses that aside and reads from the front page of the* New York Times.) 'Jeddu, Saturday. This time last week Jeddu was a one-horse town on the road from Kamba City to nowhere. Today you can't see the town for cavalry, mainly armoured personnel carriers and a few T-47 tanks. In them thar hills to the north-west, the renegade Colonel Shimbu is given no more chance than Colonel Custer – if only he'd stand still. Unfortunately, no one can find the Colonel to tell him to stop playing the Indians and it may be that Jeddu is going to wake up one morning with its armoured cars drawn up in a circle.' (*He throws that aside.*) I hate them and their Pulitzer Prizes. All writing and no facts. (*The* Sunday Times) 'At five minutes past eight on Wednesday morning, an aide-de-camp on the staff of Supreme Commander and President Ginku Mageeba, his uniform distinguished by Christian Dior sunglasses and unbuttoned flies, drove a green and white jeep up to the Princess Alice Bar in downtown Jeddu and commandeered it as the nerve centre of Mageeba's victorious drive against the forces of darkness, otherwise known as the Adoma Liberation Front. The army itself appeared in time for elevenses, and by today the advance had nearly reached the Esso pump three hundred yards up the road towards the enemy.' Very funny. All facts and no news. (*He looks briefly through the* Mirror.) Nothing. Well, that's honest anyway. (*The* Observer) 'Sources close to President Mageeba are conceding that the peasant army of the ALF has the tacit support of the indigenous population of the interior and is able to move unhindered through the Adoma hills.' (*Considers this, nods sagely.*) True. (Sunday Telegraph) 'Evidence is emerging that the civilian population of the Adoma region has been intimidated into supporting the Russian-equipped rural guerillas of the ALF, but according to army sources, the self-styled Liberation

Front is penned up in the Adoma hills.' (*Considers this, nods sagely.*) True. (News of the World – *he only glances at the front page.*) 'Is this the laziest man in Britain?' I did that one once. Different bloke, mind you.

Wagner turns his attention back to the Globe, *which Guthrie has put down. He looks at it glumly. The dog barks. A car is arriving.*

Guthrie Carson.

Wagner (*still preoccupied with the paper*) I don't think it's anybody who's been around much. It's good stuff but it's too much I-was-there. It's somebody who wants to impress the world and doesn't know that the world isn't impressed by reporters and nobody is impressed by reporters except other reporters – who can work out that you were there without having it rammed down their throats.

We have heard car doors.

Yeah, I think I've got this one's number – he's not a star, he's a boy scout in an Austin Reed safari suit who somehow got lucky.

Milne appears at the edge of the room. Wagner's description is not far off. Wagner hasn't seen him.

(*Almost to himself*) Little prick.

Milne I say . . .

Guthrie and Wagner look at him.

I say, that wouldn't be a *Sunday Globe*, would it?

Guthrie and Wagner look at each other.

Wagner Care to have a look?

Milne Not last Sunday's?! I say – *thanks.*

Wagner Have you just come with Mr Carson?

Milne Yes, that's right. He's just gone up to see his wife.

Wagner gives him the Globe. *Milne ignores the front page and thumbs through to the foreign page inside. His disappointment is silent but immense. He tries another page.*

(*Miserably; scanning the paper*) He's just gone up to see his wife.

Wagner and Guthrie, especially Wagner, watch him like people watching a play, tensely waiting for Milne to find his Story. Milne gives up and closes the paper, giving the front page a casual glance. Then he sees his story and the jolt he gets is audible. Wagner and Guthrie relax. Milne reads for a few seconds, lost in himself.

(*To Wagner*) Do you need this paper?

Wagner No. I'd like you to have it.

Milne Thanks awfully. (*reading again*) Carson's just gone up to see his wife and boy.

Wagner Yes, you said.

Milne Are you in mining as well?

Wagner As well as what?

Milne giggles and goes on reading.

Anything interesting in the paper?

Milne finally puts the paper down.

Milne Actually, I'm a journalist.

Wagner Oh.

Milne Actually, I'm on the *Sunday Globe*.

Wagner Ah.

Milne Well, I'm not actually *on* the *Sunday Globe*.

Wagner What are you doing here, actually?

Milne I'm covering the rebellion. This is my interview with Colonel Shimbu on the front page.

Wagner That's very good. How did you find him?

Milne A bit excitable but quite –

Wagner (*hard edge*) How did you find him?

Milne Oh. It was a bit of luck really. Some of his men stopped a bus I was on.

Wagner What for? Food? Money?

Milne No. They give out leaflets and lecture the passengers for a while and let them carry on. But they took me off the bus. I was the only white. That was a month ago before the story broke properly – I mean, the story was there all the time but no one was taking any notice of it, you just heard talk about it. I was in KC so I thought I'd have a recce, and I got kidnapped by this ALF group.

Guthrie Lucky.

Milne Yes. I moved around with them for two weeks and finally I persuaded Shimbu he should let his case be properly reported. So he did the interview.

Wagner How did you get the story out?

Milne He got it out for me.

Wagner A pigeon?

Milne (*laughing patronizingly*) A *pigeon*? No, we've got a little beyond that in Fleet Street. He gave it to one of

278

his chaps to take over the border and he posted it for
me.

Wagner glances at Guthrie.

Wagner (*expressionless*) Posted it.

Milne To tell you the truth the interview was ten days
old but luckily I had Shimbu to myself. By the time the
foreign press started to arrive in Kambawe the
government got wise and attached the reporters to the
army, which sounds promising but it takes away their
freedom of movement. On a story like this it's no good
at all until the real shooting starts. The story has got to
be with the rebels. They should have known that.

Guthrie smiles at Wagner.

Wagner Where was your last job?

Milne The *Grimsby Evening Messenger.*

Wagner The *Grimsby Evening Messenger.*

Milne That's an evening paper in Grimsby, in England.
By the way, my name is Jacob Milne.

Wagner What are you doing here, Jacob?

Milne In this house?

Wagner In Africa.

Milne Oh. I lost my job in Grimsby.

Wagner Yes?

Milne My idea was to get myself in on a good foreign
story without too much competition. I thought, Eritrea.

Wagner This isn't Eritrea. Is it?

Milne No – no. Eritrea is up north.

Wagner I thought it was.

Milne I couldn't get in. Then I heard that there was this interesting situation developing in Kambawe.

Wagner Where did you hear that?

Milne In Grimsby.

   Wagner waits for more.

In *Time Magazine.*

Wagner Ah.

Milne Incredible how it's worked out. Carson says there's fifty reporters in Jeddu. They've got themselves thoroughly lumbered. There's no story in Jeddu. (*Reading from the* Globe) '. . . sources close to President Mageeba . . .' Sheer desperation . . . Richard Vahgner. I bet I've made him sick. Well, he's not going to be very pleased about my exclusive, and the awful thing is (*looking Wagner in the eye*) *I've got another one.* (*He sees the awful truth in Wagner's eyes.*) Oh, Christ.

Wagner Sit down, Jacob.

Milne Look, I'm sorry – (*He turns to Guthrie.*) Are you with –?

Guthrie George Guthrie. Hello.

Milne *Guthrie?* – Christ. I thought your Lebanon pictures were just –

Wagner Sit down. I'm Dick Wagner. Where have you just come from?

Milne The Kaminco Complex – you know – where the Kaminco mines are – I can never get these places right – what's it called?

Guthrie Deck tennis.

Milne No.

Guthrie Ping pong.

Wagner Shut up.

Milne Malakuangazi. About a hundred and fifty miles north.

Guthrie What's Kaminco?

Wagner Kambawe Mining Corporation. Carson's outfit. (*to Milne*) How did you get *there?*

Milne With the ALF of course. Shimbu captured it this morning. That's my story. They shelled it and then went in and killed the garrison.

Wagner stares at him.

Wagner Jesus wept.

Carson enters, heading for the study. Wagner's interception is slightly ingratiating.

Mr Carson – I'm Richard Wagner, *Sunday Globe.*

Carson Yes. Are you helping Jake on his story?

Wagner decides to swallow that.

Wagner That's right. Fred Hammaker suggested I look you up. Sends his regards. And to Mrs Carson.

Carson I'm afraid I've never heard of him. Excuse me.

Leaving Wagner looking at the closed study door.

Guthrie He's never heard of him.

Wagner I'm thinking about it. (*to Milne*) How did Hammaker know about Carson?

Milne I told him.

Guthrie When you sent your Colonel Shimbu piece.

Milne That's right. I thought Jeddu would be the next place I'd have a chance to file. I was right about that, though for the wrong reasons – like everybody else I thought the Colonel was heading this way.

Wagner You haven't filed yet?

Milne I couldn't. The land cable was cut in the shelling. That's why I came out with Carson. Do you know what Carson has got here?

Wagner Seen it. Happy birthday.

Milne I knew Geoff Carson slightly. I met him in KC. He spends time in KC and Malakuangazi, it's a dog-leg with Jeddu at the bend, and he's also got a small potash operation just down the road from here – where the helicopter came down. Kaminco is mainly copper but there's some potash and also manganese –

Wagner Just get on with it.

Milne Well, I interviewed Carson for a background piece I sent Hammaker when I first arrived in the country. He didn't use it. Sent me a cable, saying 'Think stuff unwanted.'

Wagner Too right.

Milne It paid off anyway. Carson wanted to check his quotes so he gave me his home telex number. I had it in my book. I told Hammaker it was one place he might be able to reach me.

Wagner And here you are.

Milne With bells on.

He takes his 'copy' from his pocket and flourishes it. Wagner takes it from him.

Wagner Well, you're a bloody idiot. You should have stayed inside and got Carson to carry your story out.

He was the pigeon of a lifetime, with his own little helicopter. *Now* how are you going to get back in?

Milne Carson said he'd lend me a Kaminco car.

Wagner Don't be a clown – no one's going to get into Malakuangazi now without a tank.

Guthrie Why did Shimbu let Carson leave?

Milne I don't know. (*Pause. Apologetically*) I thought you meant a real pigeon . . . before. Sorry.

Wagner (*to Guthrie*) What do you think?

Guthrie (*to Milne*) Carson's using you for something.

Milne Does it matter?

Guthrie Maybe not. I'll come with you.

Milne Fine. I never thought I'd be on a story with you.

Guthrie Me neither. (*He relaxes, having settled his immediate future. He picks up Alastair's camera and completes the business of inserting a film.*)

Milne How interesting – I always imagined you'd have one of those flashy Japanese jobs with lenses and things . . .

Guthrie (*smiles*) There you go.

Wagner (*with Milne's story*) Is all this going to stand up? Twelve Mig-17s, three Ilyushin-28s – who told you?

Milne I watched them land this morning.

Wagner Where did they come from?

Milne Yemen. But Shimbu already had the American T-28s stashed away on strip which the Russians put down for him in the desert. He's got three of those. Flown in by Kambawe Airforce deserters.

Wagner (*to Guthrie*) True to form. No matter how far left you plant your flag, there's always a few who'll go with you.

Milne Actually, no – this was tribal, not political. This was very early on and no more have come over since, which probably means the Airforce have grounded anyone they're not sure of. That's probably worth checking into.

Wagner (*drily*) Thank you.

Milne You can see why Shimbu went for Malakuangazi – I should have worked it out. It's not the mine, it's the airstrip. There's no strip at Jeddu for anything bigger than a light plane. In the hills he had to make do with Mi-8 choppers to supply him from across the border.

Wagner Who flies them?

Milne Cubans. It's in there.

Wagner Did you actually see a Cuban flying a helicopter?

Milne Not exactly –

Wagner (*flaring up*) Listen, Jacob – I know what it's like in Grimsby. You can say that Cubans have taken over the fishing fleet and next day you say that they haven't, *actually,* and nobody gives a bugger, because it's Grimsby. But this is the *Sunday Globe* and if you say Shimbu's got Cuban pilots you've got to have something better than his word and a Havana cigar – so who says they're Cuban?

Milne They do.

Wagner (*pause*) You interviewed them?

Milne Not exactly interviewed – they wouldn't let me. We played cards a few times. I was just improving my

Spanish. (*His irritation gets the better of him.*) And if
you don't mind my saying so, Mr Wagner, you know
fuck all about the *Grimsby Evening Messenger,* which is
a great deal more important around Grimsby than the
Sunday Globe is around the globe on any bloody day
of the week!

Wagner Please call me Dick. This guy with the field
battery – did you talk to *him*? (*He is referring to Milne's
pages.*)

Milne Yes.

Wagner He spoke English?

Milne No, but I know a little Russian – it was my
optional language at school.

Wagner (*exasperated*) Tell me something, Jacob – what
did you get fired *for*?

Milne I didn't exactly get fired. It was after the trouble
in the provinces – you know, the strike.

Wagner Strike?

Milne The provincial reporters' strike. There were
several reports in the *Globe,* including one from Grimsby
which was not as accurate as one might have wished.

Wagner I don't understand. You got fired for going on
strike?

Milne (*laughs*) Are you serious?

Wagner (*pause*) Oh no.

Milne Yes. It all seems a bit silly out here, doesn't it?

Wagner Milne. You're one of those blokes all the fuss
was about in . . .

Milne Grimsby.

Wagner (*to Guthrie*) Do you see who we've got here? It is the Grimsby scab.

Milne I say, that's not very nice.

Wagner Is it not?

Milne No. I don't keep an abusive vocabulary ready for anyone who acts on different principles.

Wagner Oh, acting on principle were you?

Milne Yes, I was, as a matter of fact.

Wagner Is it your principle to betray your fellow workers when they're in confrontation with management?

Milne can't believe this. He almost laughs.

Milne Come again?

Wagner (*furious*) Don't patronize *me*, you little berk.

Milne I'm sorry – I was just taken aback. I never got used to the way the house Trots fell into the jargon back in Grimsby – I mean, on any other subject, like the death of the novel, or the sex life of the editor's secretary, they spoke ordinary English, but as soon as they started trying to get me to join the strike it was as if their brains had been taken out and replaced by one of those little golf-ball things you get in electric typewriters . . . 'Betrayal' . . . 'Confrontation' . . . 'Management' . . . My God, you'd need a more supple language than that to describe an argument between two amoebas.

But Wagner has already turned away to Guthrie – well worked up.

Wagner 'Special Correspondent'! That's why Hammaker didn't give him a by-line! He knew Derek would never have worn it for a minute –

Guthrie What Derek?

Wagner Battersby – Derek Battersby – Branch Secretary.

Guthrie Battersby? I went on something with him once . . . bloody useless reporter.

Wagner He's bloody good at squeezing the management. They don't always go together.

Guthrie Do they *ever* go together?

Milne I thought foreign correspondents would find the whole thing a bit parochial.

Wagner (*acidly*) I am not a foreign correspondent. A foreign correspondent is someone who lives in foreign parts and corresponds, usually in the form of essays containing no new facts. Otherwise he's someone who flies around from hotel to hotel and thinks the most interesting thing about any story is the fact that he has arrived to cover it. I am a fireman. I go to fires. Brighton or Kambawe – they're both out-of-town stories and I cover them the same way. I don't file prose. I file facts. So don't imagine for a moment you've stumbled across a fellow member of the Travellers' Club. To me you're the Grimsby scab. Jacob Milne. Yeah. What happened to the others?

Milne What do you mean?

Wagner It wasn't just you, was it? Getting out the paper like bob-a-job week?

Milne No.

Wagner Well I hope they're all making out as stringers up the Limpopo.

Milne They're all still on the *Messenger*. After the strike was settled the union expelled us, but the others appealed and got fined. Of course, the union didn't really want to expel me, they expected me to appeal too.

Wagner Why didn't you?

Milne I was feeling a bit wicked. The *Messenger* isn't officially a closed shop, you see – they'd just got used to having a hundred per cent membership. I gave them a problem.

Wagner Smarty-boots.

Milne I'm afraid so. But it backfired. By a majority decision they refused to work with me, and it looked as if the paper was going to shut down again, this time because of me.

Wagner So the management dumped you. You had to learn the hard way, didn't you? Bosses are bosses, and that's what it's all about, kid.

Milne I resigned.

Wagner Oh yeah.

Milne They refused to sack me.

Wagner They just heaved a huge sigh of relief when you went.

Milne Possibly.

Wagner Well, I hope the experience radicalized you a little. We're working to keep richer men than us richer than us, and nothing's going to change that without worker solidarity.

Milne I bet they don't come much more solid than you.

Wagner (*wide-eyed to Guthrie*) Did you hear what he just said to me?

Milne The *Globe* is losing a million a year, and nobody's getting rich on the *Messenger* either. It's not a private coal-mine sending somebody's son to Eton, it's a limited liability company publishing a reasonably honest and not particularly wonderful local paper in the last two-paper town of its size in the country that began the whole idea of the right to publish, and you'd close it down out of pique –

Wagner What are you burbling about?

Milne We were called out for the same reason as the *Mirror* last year – because the *printers* had got a new deal.

Wagner (*high*) Well, there were printers getting more than journalists!

Milne Yes, I know, but you make it sound as if the natural order has been overthrown. Fish sing in the streets, rivers run uphill, and the printers are getting more than the journalists. OK – you're worth more than a printer. But look at some of this – (*With his hand, or perhaps his foot, he spreads the newspapers and the News of the World lies in front of him.*) 'Exposed! The Ouija Board Widow Who's Writing Hitler's Memoirs' . . . 'It Was Frying Tonight And Every Night In The Back Of The Chip Shop!' . . . (*and the* Mirror) 'Some Like It Hot And Sweet – Sally Smith is a tea lady in a Blackpool engineering works, but it was the way she filled those C-cups which got our cameraman all stirred up!' It's *crap*. And it's written by grown men earning maybe ten thousand a year. If I was a printer, I'd look at some of the stuff I'm given to print, and I'd ask myself what is supposed to be so special about the people who write it – is that radical enough for you – Dick?

The feeling is that Wagner might actually hit him. Before we can find out whether he would have done or not, the study door opens and Carson comes out, head bent over a sheet of telex paper in his hands. He comes out reading.

Carson 'Onpass Milne. Congratulations Shimbu interview worldwide interest. Hammaker.' (*He hands this to Milne.*)

Milne Oh . . . thanks.

Carson Sorry I had to leave you so long. (*He nods at Guthrie.*)

Guthrie George Guthrie.

Carson George.

They shake hands.

. . . and . . .

Wagner Dick Wagner.

Carson Good. Geoff is my name. Should we have a beer? Or would you prefer something stronger?

Guthrie Beer is fine.

Carson Dick?

Wagner Thank you.

Carson Sure you wouldn't rather have a scotch?

Wagner Much rather. Thanks.

Carson looks again at Guthrie.

Guthrie No – beer is fine.

Carson Jake?

Milne seems to be still reading the telex.

Milne Yes?

Carson Beer or scotch?

Milne Yes – fine.

Carson (*giving up*) I'll go and tell Francis. (*to Milne*) You can try London now if you like.

Wagner We're very grateful to you . . . Geoff . . . most grateful.

Carson (*to Milne*) By the way you've got the spare room.

Milne Thank you.

   Carson leaves.

Wagner I want to use that thing.

Milne How do you get London anyway?

Wagner You may be wasting your time.

Milne Why?

Guthrie You're kidding.

Wagner No, I'm an officer of the *Globe* chapel.

Guthrie That doesn't make it your responsibility.

Wagner That's right. Let Hammaker fight it out with Battersby at branch level.

Milne What is this?

Wagner (*by way of answer*) 'Onpass Battersby. Must protest employment of special correspondent Milne, non-member ex-Grimsby.' All right?

Milne (*pause*) We went in under heavy sniper fire. If there'd been a paid-up member around he could have had the job with pleasure.

Wagner Nothing personal. Send the piece. I'm not stopping you.

Milne Thanks a lot.

Guthrie You *are* kidding.

Wagner Watch me.(*He goes to the study door and then invites Milne.*) Watch me?

> *Milne goes into the study with Wagner, who shuts the door. Guthrie takes a camera out of the camera bag and hangs it round his neck. Carson returns.*

Carson Ruth's just coming down.

Guthrie OK if I take a picture?

Carson What for?

Guthrie I don't know. Can I?

Carson I suppose there's no harm.

> *Guthrie gets ready to take pictures, and is taking them over the next few moments until Ruth's entrance.*

Guthrie How can you get back into that place?

Carson Malakuangazi? There's no way you can get me back. I was lucky to get out.

Guthrie I mean . . .

Carson Oh . . . How can *you* . . .

Guthrie Me and Jake.

Carson Jake asked me to help him.

Guthrie Can you?

Carson Mageeba will have got his armour up there. You can't just stroll through.

Guthrie What then?

Carson We'll see.

Guthrie Do you know Shimbu?

Carson Yes.

Guthrie Why did he let you out? (*Pause.*) I wondered if you were some kind of . . . I don't mean messenger –

Carson Emissary.

Guthrie Yes.

> *Carson doesn't reply. Guthrie takes pictures. The telephone rings. Guthrie had just finished but this gives him a different sort of picture to take and he takes some while Carson is on the phone. Carson does hardly any talking, much more listening. What he says isn't audible anyway.*
>
> *Behind Carson, on phone, and Guthrie, Wagner comes out of the study, closing the door behind him just as Ruth enters from within the house. When they see each other they pause, looking at each other. Wagner smiles.*
>
> *Carson hangs up and turns and sees them. Francis enters with a tray of drinks, beers and scotches.*

Carson Ah, darling – have you met?

Ruth No, we haven't. Mr Guthrie told me you were expected . . . (*offering her hand*) Mr . . . Strauss . . .? (*She takes a scotch off the tray.*) Thank you, Francis. (*Her manner is amused, relaxed.*)

Wagner Wagner.

Ruth Wagner. Exactly. I knew it was Richard.

Wagner How nice to meet you, Mrs Carson.

Francis is moving around and the drinks are being taken off his tray. Ruth and Wagner move down through the room and end up downstage.

Carson We're Geoff and Ruth to everyone around here. (*He takes a beer off the tray.*) Isn't that right, Francis?

Francis Yes sir, Mr Carson.

Wagner (*taking a scotch off the tray*) Ruth, then.

Ruth And I'll call you Richard.

Wagner Most people call me Dick.

Ruth I'm not terribly fond of Dick.

Wagner You could have fooled me.

Their position in the room has enabled him to say this evenly.

Ruth Well, that's that settled. Why don't we sit down?

Guthrie (*to Francis but for Ruth's benefit; taking his beer off the tray*) Thank you, sir . . .

Ruth Where's the other chap? The one who came with you?

Carson Jacob Milne.

Wagner He's in there trying to raise London. Do you know London, Ruth?

Ruth Oh, rather. Good old London eh? . . . the red buses scattering the pigeons in Trafalgar Square . . .

Carson Yes, indeed.

Ruth Covent Garden porters with baskets of fruit and veg piled on their heads, threading their way among the flower girls and professors of linguistics.

Carson All gone now.

Ruth Flexing their native wit against the inimitable banter of the pearly kings . . . The good old London bobby keeping a fatherly eye on the children feeding the beefeaters outside Buckingham Palace . . .

Carson Oh, all right.

Ruth . . . giving himself a glancing blow with his riot shield every time a tourist asks him the time. (*She turns her wrist to look at her watch and staggers back from an imaginary blow to the forehead.*)

Carson Don't be a rotter. (*to Wagner*) How is London really?

Guthrie Don't ask him – he's a bloody colonial, knows nothing.

> *Deep pause. Ruth is amused. Carson is forgiving. Guthrie apologetic. Wagner helps out.*

Wagner It's quite true about me. When I first arrived in London I thought Fleet Street was between the Strand and Trafalgar Square. I was working from a Monopoly board.

Ruth We play Monopoly with Alastair.

Carson Do we?

Ruth On Boxing Day. As far as I remember Fleet Street was yellow and rather cheap. Is that right, Dick?

Wagner Not necessarily. Leicester Square and Coventry Street were yellow. To be fair you'd never confuse Fleet Street with Soho on the ground, you never saw anything so sleazy – the whole place has given itself over to crude titillation and eye-catching junk.

Ruth And how about Soho?

Wagner (*catching up*) Soho. You're a caution.

Ruth Where are you from, George?

Guthrie London Wall. In the City. Of course, it's all been knocked down now. Bloody shame.

Carson Yes, indeed.

Guthrie You should see it now. Do you know St Paul's?

Ruth I've heard of it.

Guthrie Sitting there surrounded by giant boxes. It looks like it's just been unpacked and nobody's cleared up.

Carson Actually, Ruth was born in London.

Guthrie Really? Well, you wouldn't know it now. When were you last there?

Ruth Friday.

Guthrie (*pause*) I think I'll just sit and drink my beer.

Carson (*to Ruth*) You're a rotter.

The telephone rings and he gets up to answer it. Again he does more listening than talking.

Ruth I'm a rotter, George. I'm a frightful rotter. I was picking up Allie from prep school, his first term at Ascot Heath.

Alastair comes in wearing pyjamas and dressing gown and slippers.

Hello, darling, your mummy's a rotter. Have you come to say goodnight?

Alastair (*outraged*) Goodnight? I haven't even had supper.

Ruth Well, go and see Winnie, she'll have it ready.

Alastair I want to talk to Mr Guthrie.

Ruth Mr Guthrie will come and see you, won't you, George?

Guthrie Never fear. (*He stands and moves to the verandah and looks out, and yawns.*)

Alastair Will you come and see me in my room?

Guthrie Promise.

Ruth So will I. Say goodnight to Mr Wagner.

Alastair Goodnight.

Wagner Goodnight, Alastair.

Alastair You won't forget, George?

Ruth Mr Guthrie to you – hop it.

Alastair goes. Guthrie sits in a comfortable chair on the verandah.

Oh dear, he's taken rather a fancy to George. Next thing, he'll want to be a journalist when he grows up. What is a mother to do?

Carson hangs up the phone.

Should I tell him it'll send him blind, and risk psychological damage, or should I sew a war correspondent's badge on his pyjamas and hope he grows out of it?

Carson (*leaving the room*) Darling, these gentlemen may not be used to your sense of humour. (*calling*) Allie!

Ruth Well I'm going to *need* a sense of humour if Alastair's going to go around the house putting his foot in the doors and asking impertinent questions. Perhaps I'll get him a reporter doll for Christmas. Wind it up and it gets it wrong. (*She seems in high good humour.*) What does it say when you press its stomach? Come on, Dick!

297

Wagner I name the guilty man.

Ruth (*laughs*) Very good.

> *Carson comes back and takes his place. Ruth gets up to replenish her glass.*

Yes, that's a question which has loomed large in my life – who's the guilty man? Until Geoffrey of course. Geoffrey is entirely blameless.

Carson Steady on, Ruth.

Wagner Who is the guilty man this time, Geoff?

'Ruth' Don't get cheeky, Wagner.

Wagner Shimbu or Mageeba?

Carson Oh . . .

'Ruth' Jesus!

Carson Depends which paper you read, doesn't it?

'Ruth' Don't do that to me.

> *Ruth takes her drink and sits apart from the men.*

Wagner What did the President have to say?

Carson Are you interviewing me, Dick?

Wagner Is that all right?

Carson No, it isn't.

Wagner Off the record, then.

'Ruth' Tell him to bugger off.

Wagner No attribution.

'Ruth' I'll tell him. Elizabeth Taylor in *Elephant Walk*. (*shouts*) 'Get out of this house! This is no longer Geoffrey Carson's bachelor quarters, I'm his beautiful bride from England, and I'm sick of all you hooligans playing bicycle polo in my sitting-room!'

Carson realizes that Guthrie has fallen asleep holding his beer glass. Carson goes over and gently takes the glass out of Guthrie's hands.

Carson George tells me he'd like to get into Malakuangazi.

Wagner We both would.

Carson What about Jake?

Wagner Jake is a freelance. I'm the *Globe*'s man on this story.

'Ruth' He's got hair in his nostrils. I must have been drunk.

Carson He did well.

'Ruth' I *was* drunk.

Wagner Yes, he did well. He had some luck.

Carson Was that it?

'Ruth' I name the guilty men – J and B.

Wagner OK, but now it's up to me to go where I can get ahead of the competition. There'll be a lot of journalists with the same idea.

Carson They haven't got a hope. The army won't let them through.

Wagner Can you help?

Carson Yes. I can give you a car, a driver who speaks the lingo, and a pass signed by the President.

Wagner My God, what am I doing for you?

'Ruth' Don't ask.

Carson Colonel Shimbu didn't let me go for old times' sake. I was taking a message. You'll be taking the reply.

Wagner A reply from the President?

Carson Use your imagination.

Wagner Unprofessional. What *I* use has to check out.

Carson Well, I'm flying down to KC. I'll be back in the morning, early, with a letter and the pass.

Wagner Signed by Mageeba.

Carson That's it.

Wagner And the letter too? (*Pause.*) Just say yes – what's the matter?

Carson It's called giving you as much information as you need to know.

'Ruth' Terrible title. (*sings, improvising*) 'Giving you as much information . . .'

'Ruth' worries away at this song, at intervals, until Ruth speaks out loud.

Wagner Has Shimbu offered a deal?

Carson Come on, Dick. Well, you can assume I wouldn't ask you if I thought there'd be a war going on.

Wagner Why a journalist?

Carson Who else wants to go? I was thinking of Jake.

Wagner No. How long is the drive?

Carson About five hours. Lunch in Malakuangazi.

Wagner Friday lunch. Twenty-four hours to get back here and file. That's nice going if the Colonel cooperates.

Carson It might be better if Jake went. Shimbu likes him.

Wagner Shimbu will like me. I'm very popular.

Ruth I've always wanted to meet a popular journalist. I mean socially, I don't mean under one's bed or outside the law courts. One is not normally introduced to journalists. I mention that as a matter of circumstance, not as a piece of social etiquette. Though, of course, it is that, too.

Carson *I thought* you were being unnaturally silent.

Wagner You don't much care for the media, do you, Ruth?

Ruth The media. It sounds like a convention of spiritualists.

Carson Ruth has mixed feelings about reporters.

Ruth No, I haven't. I despise them. Not foreign correspondents, of course – or the gardening notes. The ones in between. I'm sure you know what I mean.

Wagner You've met one or two, have you?

Ruth Under the bed, outside the law courts . . . But don't imagine that I despise them because of any injury done to me – on the contrary I looked jolly nice in my divorce hat, and being on the front page of four morning newspapers did my reputation nothing but good in my part of Highgate – 'Hasn't she done well?' And even the indignities with which the whole saga began . . . well, there are worse things than being pursued across Shropshire by the slavering minions of a philistine press lord; in fact, it brought Geoffrey and me closer together. I loved him for the way he out-drove them in his Jaguar, and it wasn't his fault at all that the early morning tea in our hideaway hotel was brought in by a Fleet Street harpie in a tweeny . . . no, no, it isn't that. It isn't even – or anyway not entirely – the way it was written up, or rather snapped together in that Lego-set language they have, so that poor Geoffrey's wife, a notably hard-boiled zoologist who happens to breed rare parakeets, and who incautiously admitted to a reporter that, yes she would like Geoff to give me up, and yes, she would have him back, was instantly dubbed Heartbreak Parrot Woman In Plea For Earl's Brother. Earl's Brother. That's the bit. Of all the husbands who ran off with somebody's wife that week, Geoffrey qualified because he had a measly title and if the right three-hundred people went down on the Royal Yacht he'd be Duke of Bognor. *Has anyone ever bothered to find out whether anybody really cares?* The populace and the popular press. What a grubby symbiosis it is. Which came first? The rhinoceros or the rhinoceros bird?

The study door opens.

Milne Dick! I got a line!

The study door closes. Wagner gets up to go.

Wagner Titled people haven't had the greatest luck with journalists. Infatuation gave way to resentment without any intervening period of indifference. I remember you now. Just. The beginning of the Red Guard phase. Nick Webster was allowed thirty thousand pounds a year for tip-off money. Thought he was the scourge of privilege. Thought the paper was behind him. Don't you love it? If someone had convinced the paper that the AB readership has gone over to astronomy, Nick would have found himself on the roof with a telescope. (*He goes out into the study closing the door behind him.*)

Carson You're riding him a little hard, aren't you? Is anything the matter? (*He goes to the telephone and is using it during this scene.*)

Ruth Geoffrey, there's something I have to tell you.

Carson Mm? (*into phone*) Carson. Yes.

'Ruth' Darling, there's something I have to tell you.

Carson What's up?

'Ruth' My darling, there's something I have to tell you that happened when I was in London.

Carson (*turning to her from the telephone*) Ruth?

'Ruth' Geoffrey, darling, when I was in London I did something rather silly . . .

Carson Eh, Ruth?

'Ruth' (*American*) We're two grown up people, Geoffrey, let's try to be mature about this.

Carson temporarily free from the phone but still holding on.

Carson Aren't you talking to me?

Ruth turns towards him for the first time.

Ruth I'm sorry I'm a rotten wife.

Carson You're not a rotten wife. I've had one of those.

Ruth Geoff –

Carson is caught by the phone.

Carson I'm sorry. (*into phone*) Yes? . . . yes.

Carson is occupied on the phone now. Ruth lights a cigarette. She smokes long cigarettes and usually stubs them out after a few puffs.

'Ruth' (*loudly*) I have brought shame on the house of Carson! Yes! It's Dick! He took advantage of me, Geoffrey! I fought it, my God how I fought it! But I couldn't help myself!

Carson listening at the phone, half turns with his free hand stretched out towards her, his fingers ready to receive a lit cigarette.

Don't shoot. Geoffrey!

Distant echo of gun-shot. She puts her cigarette between his fingers.

(*Casually*) By the way, Geoffrey, I let Wagner take me to bed in London, in the Royal Garden Hotel, view over Kensington High Street, chosen for its proximity to the Embassy, in the visa section of which I met him while he was fixing his papers. I was fixing Alastair's. 'Going out to Kambawe?' 'Actually, I live there.' 'How interesting. I'm going out for the *Sunday Globe*. I say, you couldn't spare the time for a chat, could you? – spot of lunch – dinner – drinks – nightcap – and so on.' And so on. I believe it's called de-briefing. Not half bad either, though not as good as he thinks. Next day I picked up Allie and flew home.

Carson hangs up the phone.

Carson It's on.

His back is to Ruth. He is looking at a document, taken from his pocket; not absorbed in it, perhaps talking to Ruth though we can't see his face.

'**Ruth**' I didn't blame Wagner at all, 'til he showed up here looking for a second helping. I thought I let him off lightly. That man is not a gentleman. Thinks I hop into bed with strange men because I hopped into bed with a strange man. (*Pause.*) I'm sorry.

Carson Are you listening, Ruth?

Ruth I'm sorry –

Carson I've told Allie to get dressed.

Ruth What?

Carson He can stay with the Krebs for a couple of days. I don't want him here.

Ruth Is it on, then?

Carson Looks like it. You really ought to go, too. I trust Mageeba less than I trust Shimbu, and I don't trust Shimbu.

Ruth Do you want me to go with Allie?

Carson No. I don't.

Ruth kisses him. Nothing too special.

Ruth Then I'll stay.

Wagner, re-entering from the study, almost catches this.

Wagner Sorry.

Carson All right.

Wagner would have retired, but now closes the study door and comes forward.

I'll go and see how Allie's getting on.

Carson goes.

Wagner Is it safe to come in?

Ruth Why not? (*She goes to the drinks shelf, and pours the remainder of a bottle of J and B into a glass for herself. It makes a large double scotch.*)

Wagner I thought I detected feelings of bitterness and bad news.

Ruth Whatever gave you that idea? I name this ship *Titanic* – (*She smashes the neck of the empty bottle on*

305

the marble shelf.) – long may she sail. (*She drops the rest of the bottle into the bin at her feet. She picks up her glass and turns to Wagner.*)

Wagner You seemed to find me agreeable enough in London.

Ruth And you thought I might find you just as agreeable in Jeddu, eh? That's something I forgive. It's crass but I forgive it. And just in case finding-you-agreeable-enough is supposed to be Australian understatement for wetting myself down to my socks, let me tell you something, Wagner – if I had fancied you *at all* when you chatted me up in the visa office, I would have run a mile. That's what we honourable ladies with decent husbands do – didn't you know that? Every now and again we meet a man who attracts us, and we run a mile. I let you take me to dinner because there was no danger of going to bed with you. And then because there was no danger of going to bed with you a second time, I went to bed with you. A lady, if surprised by melancholy, might go to bed with a chap, once; or a thousand times if consumed by passion. But twice, Wagner, *twice* . . . a lady might think she'd been taken for a tart.

Wagner takes his cable out of his pocket and gives it to Ruth.

Wagner This is a cable I got on Sunday, from my editor. I didn't come here to sniff at your skirts.

While Ruth is reading the cable.

Believe it or not, I like to read. I like modern fiction and historical biography best. One of the things that makes novels less plausible than history, I find, is the way they shrink from coincidence. (*He waits until Ruth looks up.*) And also the way that so few women in fiction are in love with their husbands.

Ruth I'm not in love with anybody. I just like some people a great deal more than I like others, and I like Geoffrey a great deal more than I like you. Is that all right?

Wagner Yes, that's fine.

Ruth Good. (*She gives him back the cable.*) Happy Birthday.

Alastair comes in dressed to travel.

Come to give me a kiss, Allie?

Alastair No – I want my camera.

Ruth Be quick then.

Ruth goes out. Alastair goes to where Guthrie is sleeping. He kneels down and whispers to him.

Alastair Mr Guthrie . . .

Wagner Don't wake him. I'll find your camera.

Alastair He said he'd show me how it works.

Wagner He put a film in for you. (*He finds the camera where Guthrie had been sitting.*) Here you are.

Alastair Oh . . . gosh, thanks. It's my dad's old camera really.

Wagner I say, I thought you were going to bed.

Alastair Daddy's taking me to Kamba City.

Wagner Why's that?

Alastair I'm going to stay with Krebs. Do you know him?

Wagner No.

Alastair He lives in KC. He's my friend.

307

Wagner Oh.

Alastair I bet you don't know who my dad is going to see. I'll give you a hundred guesses.

Wagner The President.

Alastair He told you.

Wagner Do you know the President?

Alastair No, I'm too young. That's why daddy's sending me to KC. He doesn't want me here when the President comes.

Wagner (*pause*) Well, you'll meet the President another time, I expect. When is he coming here?

Alastair Tomorrow night, probably. Don't tell daddy I know it's him – he just said it was somebody coming.

Wagner And who told you, then?

Alastair My mum.

Offstage Carson calls 'Allie!'

Wagner Don't worry, I won't tell him.

Carson enters.

(*With camera*) You have to guess how far it is – you turn this, you see – three feet – six feet – and that's infinity, which means as far as you can see.

Carson Come on, Allie, into the car. (*to Wagner, as Allie goes*) Allie was going to visit a pal in KC – so I'm taking him now –

Wagner I see.

Carson Might as well. Two birds with one stone.

Wagner What a childhood, eh?

Carson Yes. He's quite used to helicopters.

Wagner Yes, he was saying. Well, I hope everything goes well for you.

Carson See you in the morning.

Wagner Thanks, Geoff.

Carson goes out. Wagner stands still, thinking, and listens to the sounds of farewell, the car doors slamming, the car leaving. Wagner is tense, and then he gives an inarticulate cry of triumph and punches his fist through the air like a goal-scorer. He moves quickly to Guthrie and slaps his hands together by Guthrie's ear, calls his name, and wakes him unceremoniously. Guthrie comes awake, and stands up in the same moment, talking.

Guthrie I'm fine – I'm fine – where are we going?

Wagner is as high as a kite.

Wagner I'm going back to the hotel. Need the car.

Guthrie relapses into the chair.

Keys!

Wagner goes to the study door and opens it.

How are you doing?

He comes back and leaves the door ajar. The telex audible.

(*To Guthrie*) Listen, you're going to Malakuangazi, you and Jake, in the morning.

Guthrie I should bloody think so.

Wagner I've got you a car, a driver and a pass, and I've arranged a cease-fire. The *Globe* never sleeps.

Guthrie (*bitterly*) I know.

Wagner I'll cover this end.

Ruth returns to the room.

Ruth George – poor George – when did you last sleep in a bed?

Guthrie I was just pretending to be asleep. It's an old photographer's trick.

Ruth Oh yes, I'm sure.

Guthrie I promised to go and see Alastair –

Ruth Oh dear – you've missed him –

Guthrie Missed him?

Wagner I gave him the camera. You'll see him next time. (*to Ruth*) I'm taking George to the hotel.

Ruth There's room in the dorm. Geoffrey arranged it.

Wagner Well, that *would* be better. It's going to be quite an early start.

Guthrie Yes, thanks. I'll get my stuff out of the car. (*He goes out.*)

Ruth I hope you don't mind sharing a room?

Wagner You're a sport, Mrs Carson, but let's just be friends.

Ruth Bastard.

Wagner I made an excuse and left.

Wagner is leaving but Milne comes out of the study holding a piece of telex. Milne doesn't see Ruth.

Milne Dick, I've got your reply

Wagner What?

Milne (*slightly embarrassed*) The reply to your, um, protest . . .

Wagner Oh yes? From Battersby?

Milne No.

Wagner Well, what does it say?

Milne 'Onpass Wagner. Upstick protest arsewards. Hammaker.'

Wagner This is Jacob Milne. He'll be making the trip with George.

Milne Oh – how do you do?

Ruth How do you do?

Wagner You're staying the night here, Jake, leaving early tomorrow. Geoffrey will fill you in.

Milne Fine.

Wagner If the land-line is still out, one of you'd better get back here to file early Saturday to be safe. Either give Gigi your copy or bring his film out.

Milne OK. Don't worry. What will you do?

Wagner Best I can. (*to Ruth*) Thanks for everything. (*to Milne*) See you.

Milne No hard feelings?

Wagner It was your story anyway. (*He's going but a thought strikes him.*) Why did you choose the *Globe*?

Milne Well, Hammaker started on the *Messenger*. Didn't you know that?

Wagner No, I didn't.

Milne Yes. He's famous in Grimsby.

Wagner (*smiles*) I bet.

Wagner goes. Ruth sits down.

Ruth What was that about no hard feelings?

Milne Dick isn't very happy about the *Globe* using me. He's a strong union man.

Ruth And you're not.

Milne It's not that. It's just that I think journalism is . . . special. Dick thinks I'm naïve about newspapers.

Ruth And you're not?

Milne Do you think I am?

Ruth I haven't really had time to form an opinion.

Milne He thinks the *Globe* is a million packets of journalism manufactured every week by businessmen using journalists for their labour, along with typesetters, dispatchers and all the rest.

Ruth That *is* what the *Globe* is.

Milne No, it's not. A free press, free expression – it's the last line of defence for all the other freedoms.

Ruth I've formed an opinion.

Milne (*laughs*) No, really –

Ruth Why don't you sit down?

Milne No, thanks. I'm still – you know . . .

Ruth Would you like a drink?

Milne No, thanks.

Ruth (*holding out her empty glass*) Would you be good enough . . .? Straight scotch.

Milne (*taking the glass*) Of course.

Ruth gets up.

'Ruth' Watch yourself, Tallulah. (*She walks to the verandah steps.*)

Milne (*doing the drink*) Dick wants union membership to be a licence to practise. 'This man has been judged fit.'

He joins Ruth and gives her the scotch. She goes further into the garden and Milne follows her. At some point the room pivots out leaving us with the two of them in the garden. The room is no doubt visible at the side of the stage.

Like doctors and lawyers, I suppose.

Ruth Nothing wrong with that. Otherwise you'd have lawyers amputating the wrong leg. And doctors, um, trying their patients, ho, ho –

'Ruth' You're giggling. Shut up.

Ruth Mining engineers have the same sort of thing, I believe. (*earnestly*) Terribly interesting.

Milne What is?

'Ruth' He's got you there.

Ruth No – do go on. Professional standards. Don't you think they're important?

Milne Oh, yes. But nothing could be further from Dick's mind. He's honest about that. Others are less so. The fact is nobody's going to be drummed out of the NUJ for professional incompetence – persistent inaccuracy or illiteracy or getting drunk at the Lord Mayor's dinner. On the contrary it's the union which is going to keep them in their jobs. No, what Dick wants is a *right-thinking press* – one that thinks like him.

Ruth So what? You'd like a right-thinking press, too. One that thinks like you.

Milne Sure I would, but I don't intend to get it by denying employment to *him*.

Ruth Perhaps you should.

Milne Think about it.

Ruth (*pause*) Yes, quite.

'Ruth' Clarissa, who's this rather interesting young man?

Milne Once you establish the machinery it'll be there for someone else to use. Drum you out if you're too left-wing, or not left-wing enough, or the wrong colour, or something.

Ruth Well, it would be up to you, wouldn't it? Everybody's got a vote.

Milne Everybody who's allowed in would have a vote, yes.

Ruth You're an alarmist, Jacob. On the whole people behave responsibly.

Milne On the whole because their behaviour is observed. Reported.

Ruth You're a cynic.

Milne Me?

Ruth No, that can't be right.

Milne It wouldn't be like the Law Society or the BMA.

Ruth It would in principle. If some group got control of the Law Society, they'd be just as free to have only right-thinking solicitors. What then?

Milne Then you'd *really* need a free press, otherwise you may never find out about it. That's the whole point. No matter how imperfect things are, if you've got a free press everything is correctable, and without it everything is concealable.

Ruth I'm with you on the free press. It's the newspapers I can't stand.

Milne (*laughs*) I know what you mean. They let *me* down too. Arguing with the Trots in the reporters room 'The press is the last hope for democracy!!' . . . and I'd find I'm thumping my fist on some starlet's left nipple. You don't have to tell me, I know it better than you – the celebration of inanity, and the way real tragedy is para-phrased into an inflationary spiral of hackneyed melo-dramas – Beauty Queen In Tug-Of-Love Baby Storm . . . Tug-Of-Love Baby Mum In Pools Win . . . Pools Man In Beauty Queen Drug Quiz. I *know*. It's the price you pay for the part that matters.

'Ruth' I like that one who's doing all the talking.

Milne It's not easy to defend, but it's mainly attacked for the wrong reasons. People think that rubbish-journalism is produced by men of discrimination who are vaguely ashamed of truckling to the lowest taste. But it's not. It's produced by people doing their best work. Proud of their expertise with a limited number of cheap devices to put a shine on the shit. Sorry. I know what I'm talking about because I started off like that, admiring it, trying to be *that good*, looking up to Fleet Street stringers, London men sometimes, on big local stories. I thought it was great. Some of the best times in my life have been spent sitting in a clapped-out Ford Consul outside a suburban house with a packet of Polos and twenty Players, waiting to grab a bereaved husband or a footballer's runaway wife who might be good for one front page between oblivion and oblivion. I felt part of a privileged group, inside society and yet outside it, with a licence to scourge it and a duty to defend it, night and day, the street of adventure, the fourth estate. And the thing is – I was dead right. That's what it was, and I *was* part of it because it's indivisible. Junk journalism is the evidence of a society that has got at least one thing right, that there should be nobody with the power to dictate where responsible journalism begins. (*Pause.*) I'm sorry. I go on a bit. I'm not usually so wound up. It's been an amazing day. I was the only reporter in Malakuangazi, you know. I mean, that story I sent over, it's probably the best story I'll ever get in my life.

Ruth You must be tired.

Milne Not a bit.

Ruth Hungry?

Milne Starving.

Ruth Then let's eat.

Milne I'm sorry I talked so much.

Ruth No. I like you to talk.

She looks at him steadily, too long for his comfort.

Milne Thanks very much for having me here. I'll go and sort myself out.

Milne goes into the lighted house. Ruth stays in the dark.

'Ruth' Run. Run, you stupid bitch.

Night into day.
  Ruth has gone.
  Dawn.
  The jeep drives in. Francis at the wheel. Carson comes out of the house, shortly followed by Guthrie.

Guthrie has changed some of his clothes, still blue denim or something non-military. He has his camera bag and another shoulder bag. Carson shouts up as though to an upstairs window.

Carson Jake! (*He turns and sees Guthrie.*) All set? Where's Jake?

Guthrie What's that?

Carson Your jeep.

Carson goes to the jeep to say something to Francis. Guthrie stays right downstage.

Guthrie I can see it's a jeep. Wagner said a car.

Carson What's the difference? Car, jeep. This isn't a trip for a family saloon.

Guthrie is very angry and upset but still controlled.

Guthrie A family saloon is neutral. A jeep is a target. Listen – I know the game. I know the edge on every hand I'm dealt. It was the same in the Congo, Angola, Somalia. And it's the same here.

Then he sees that Milne has come out of the house wearing army type clothing, including a camouflage-coloured cotton bush hat.

(*Explodes*) Oh, *bloody hell*, he's dressed up like action man! (*He takes the hat off Milne's head and throws it on the ground.*)

Milne What's the matter? (*He picks up the hat.*)

Guthrie You don't drive into an African war in a khaki shirt with epaulettes!

Carson What war? There isn't going to be any war today.

Milne I've got a tennis shirt in my bag – I'll change if you like.

Guthrie Did you bring your racket? *This is crazy.* Wagner should have done the trip.

Milne Thought you were on my side. Come on, Gigi – (*He goes towards the jeep, and towards Carson.*)

Carson Got it?

Milne pats the small bag he's carrying.

Milne Got it.

Milne gets into the jeep. Francis guns the engine a little. Guthrie stands looking at the ground.

Well, are you coming or not?

Guthrie (*quietly*) Oh, shit.

Then he moves quickly to the jeep, puts his camera bag on board and swings on behind as the jeep starts to move.

Blackout.

Act Two

The room at night.
   The room occupies the whole stage now.
   *Ruth sits in one of the comfortable chairs. She is
wearing a long dress, not formal but loose and comfortable, perhaps a kaftan; more dressed up than we have
seen her, rich material but not gaudy. She sits facing the
audience.*
   *The room is not brightly lit, and the edges are in
gloom.*
   *Milne stands at the edge of the room, having just
entered. He is dressed the way we first saw him.*
   Ruth doesn't turn round.

Ruth Hello, Jacob, I'm glad it's you. I've been holding
my breath since I heard the jeep. I'm glad you're back.
I missed you, Jake. Actually, Jake, I . . . Christ, I've been
missing you, Jake . . . (*She turns round.*)

Milne Hello.

Ruth Oh – hello!

Milne Thought you were having a snooze.

Ruth No, no. Good trip?

Milne Yes, thanks. Piece of cake.

Ruth Lots of scoops?

Milne Masses.

Ruth Come and sit down. Have a drink.

Milne No thanks. Where's Geoffrey?

Ruth He's away.

Milne I thought everybody would be asleep.

Ruth I felt like waiting up. Are you all right?

Milne Never better.

   Ruth laughs.

What's up?

Ruth Nothing. I like the way you have such a good time. Dashing around for the glory of the *Globe*. Grimsby man in *Globe* glory dash.

Milne You do think I'm naïve.

Ruth No I don't.

Milne Too young and romantic.

Ruth That's different.

Milne I expect I'll end up like Dick.

Ruth I hope not.

Milne Dick's all right. He's a bit . . .

Ruth Wagnerian. (*English pronunciation*)

Milne I suppose he's gone off with the press corps.

Ruth I suppose so. It's nice that you've got us to come back to.

Milne Yes – a line to London on tap – one couldn't ask for more. Oh – and present company included, of course.

'Ruth' Help.

Milne Well, I expect you'd like to go to bed.

'Ruth' I'm over here.

Milne I've got a piece to write.

'Ruth' To hell with that.

Milne You won't mind if I try to get London later?

'Ruth' And to hell with London.

Milne I'm sure Geoffrey wouldn't mind. Is he in KC?

'Ruth' Why don't you shut up and kiss me.

Milne He said I could help myself.

'Ruth' So kiss me.

Milne Perhaps I should try for a line first – let them know I'm here.

Ruth I would prefer you to kiss me.

Milne Kiss you?

Pause. Ruth blinks and turns to him.

Ruth Yes.

Milne Well . . . um, I was just saying, I ought to establish contact with the office.

Ruth Yes. I think that would be a very sensible idea.

Milne Thank you.

Ruth But isn't it rather late, or early, or something?

Milne It is here.

Ruth Oh yes. We seem to have got off the subject.

Milne Have you been out this evening?

Ruth No. Why?

Milne You look – a bit dressed up.

Ruth This old thing? I just threw it on as I stepped out of the shower.

Milne Ah. Jolly nice.

Ruth Wouldn't do for the club at all.

Milne Is there a club?

Ruth The Jeddu Country Club. Very quiet since independence. They used to have Coronation dances, I believe. Now it's billiards, bar and smoking room. I don't play billiards but I drink and smoke. And they get all the important magazines – *Country Life, Mining Review, Kambawe Today* . . . and, you'll be pleased to know, some of the London papers.

Milne Doesn't sound bad at all. Are they flown in?

Ruth I don't think so. We're still getting the *Morning Post*. It's all right, you don't have to kiss me at all.

Milne It isn't that I don't think you're attractive.

Ruth No. It's just that Geoffrey has been damned decent to you . . .

Milne Well, yes. And even if he hadn't . . .

Ruth It wouldn't be right to make free with his possessions – his ox, his ass, his wife –

Milne Wait a minute. (*He pauses, concentrating for four or five seconds – he looks at her.*) No.

Ruth Well, I'm glad it wasn't instantaneous.

Milne I mean your argument. It sounds good but it's not. I *might* make free with his ox and his ass – or his jeep – because they *are* merely his possessions. But if I indulged my desire for you I would be numbering you among them. As it is, it seems I regard a wife as different

322

from a jeep, which puts me in the forefront of enlightened thinking. (*smiles*) Wouldn't you say?

Ruth What desire for me?

Milne Oh, crikey.

Ruth Had any lewd thoughts?

Milne I told you I found you attractive.

Ruth Tell me about the lewd thoughts.

Milne No.

Ruth Oh, come on. Don't be such a spoil-sport. There you are, in the jeep. The sun beats down. Bwana Guthrie is taking pictures of nature and poverty for the colour magazine. Tracker Francis is keeping his eye on the road. Your thoughts drift . . . 'I say, that Ruth Carson, she's all woman.' Carry on from there.

Milne won't.

Did you undress me?

Milne No.

Ruth I kept my clothes on?

Milne You undressed yourself.

Ruth Ah. Was it dark or daylight? On a bed? On the floor? Long grass? In the jeep? (*Pause.*) It was in the jeep.

Milne (*sharply*) No, it wasn't. (*Pause.*) It was in a parallel world. No day or night, no responsibilities, no friction, almost no gravity.

Ruth I know it. How was I?

Milne (*exasperated*) Ruth.

Ruth You were *good*. It's about *time* you called me Ruth.

Milne Show some, then. Ruth: that which is lacking in ruthlessness. It comes into Milton. 'Look homeward angel, now, and melt with ruth.' Compassion – contrition. Something like that.

Ruth I'm not really a tart.

Milne No – of course.

Ruth I was almost a tart with my first husband, but he was a rotter in his own way. He was frankly proud of his left-hook.

Milne Was he?

Ruth Unjustifiably so. You could slip it quite easily and get him with a right-cross. What a way to live. To get *me,* all Geoffrey had to do was clear his throat and hold the door.

Milne Did you love him too?

Ruth Of course I loved him – loved Africa. Just like Deborah Kerr in *King Solomon's Mines* before the spider got into her underwear. And I haven't been a tart with Geoffrey. Slipped once, but that was in a hotel room and hotel rooms shouldn't count as infidelity. They constitute a separate moral universe. Anyway, I had terrible PCR, and a tart wouldn't, would she?

Milne What's PCR?

Ruth Post-coital remorse. Post-coital ruth. Quite needlessly – I mean, it's a bit metaphysical to feel guilt about the idea of Geoffrey being hurt if Geoffrey is in a blissful state of ignorance – don't you think?

Milne No.

Ruth No. Fresh start. Hello! – had a good trip? (*Pause.*) I don't know. I got into a state today.

Ruth's fingers play on the arm of her chair: distant piano is heard – 'I've Got You Under My Skin' – just a fragment of it – it is interrupted by Milne.

Milne What sort of state?

Ruth Itchy. I'm telling you this because it is interesting, you understand. Went to bed feeling nothing more dangerous than a heightened sense of you being in the house. Woke up fluttering with imminent risk. Quite a pleasant feeling, really. Like walking along the top board knowing you don't have to jump. But a desperate feeling, too, because if you're not going to jump what the hell are you doing up there? So I got dressed to say goodbye to you. Really. Dressed for it. 'What shall I wear to say goodbye to Jake?' Don't feel flattered. You look like you look, and you've got a way of being gauche which suggests that you've got the edge on people who know the ground and prepare their effects – I was attracted, as it happens, but it's like throwing a pair when you've got three-of-a-kind on the table. This time, bingo, but no use at all to anyone looking for a straight. Anyway, while I was dressing for this intensely laconic farewell, you'd been gone an hour. Geoffrey hadn't wanted to wake me. He's thoughtful about things like that. Saying goodbye would have taken care of it, I expect. It was finding you gone that did it. Quietus interruptus. I went peculiar. I lost my view of myself. I was unembarrassable. Your sheets were cold. Pillow had no smell. You say something.

Milne You were good, too. (*Pause.*) You shouldn't try to make it sound like a free ride. 'Geoffrey will never know and I'm not his chattel so there's nothing to pay.' There are no free rides. You always pay.

Ruth Take it, then, and pay. Be a bastard. Behave badly.

Milne That's better.

Ruth Betray your benefactor.

Milne That's right.

Ruth Corrupt me.

Milne Put it like that, I might.

Ruth Steal me.

Milne I want to.

Ruth Good. Mess up my life. I'll pay.

Milne Stupid.

Ruth Don't be frightened.

Milne And tomorrow –

Ruth I'll pack if you like. If you don't like, I'll stay and deadhead the bougainvillaea. Either way I'll pay.

> *They kiss on the mouth, but not passionately and not holding each other.*

Milne Leave me alone. You should know better.

Ruth I do know better. To hell with that. (*She lets herself fall over backwards on to the sofa. [At least that would be one way of doing this moment.] Only her calves and feet are visible.*)

Milne You're really something, Ruth. I don't know what.

> *Milne turns and walks upstage into the dark and disappears. Ruth's feet disappear out of sight behind the sofa and then 'she' (double) stands up with her*

back to the audience looking towards where Milne disappeared, undoes her dress and steps out of it (she has nothing on underneath) holding on to the dress with one hand and trailing it after her as she follows Milne into the dark. Before she has disappeared Carson has walked unhurriedly, relaxed, into the room from the side of the stage. He lights a cigarette and stands thoughtfully watching as Ruth moves into the dark. After a moment or two, behind him, Ruth's voice:

Ruth Got a cigarette?

She is lying on the sofa behind Carson. He turns and offers her a cigarette. Ruth's hand comes into view to take it.

Thanks.

Carson offers his lighter and Ruth's head comes up to meet it. She stands and lights her cigarette from his lighter.

Carson There's no need for you to stay up.

Ruth I want to.

Carson He may not come for hours.

Ruth I'm all right. What time is it?

Carson (*looks at his watch*) Saturday. Nearly one. You got dressed up for him.

Ruth Well, he is the President.

The dog starts barking. Carson moves to a light switch and the exterior lights come on. Sound of an approaching vehicle. Carson leaves the room. Ruth moves to a chair. She puts out her cigarette. The vehicle has arrived. Carson's voice audible offstage.

Carson (*offstage*) Oh – God!

Wagner (*a few yards off*) Hello!

Carson (*offstage*) Any other time, old man –

Wagner (*offstage*) I saw your lights from the road.

Carson (*entering*) Ruth and I were just going to bed.

Wagner comes in behind Carson.

Wagner Good evening. I brought a nightcap. (*He's carrying a bottle of Cutty Sark whisky, not a full one.*) Compliments of the firm. I'm afraid I've started without you. (*He's making himself at home. He puts the bottle down.*) I saw the lights as I was passing.

Ruth The lights weren't on as you were passing.

Carson Look, Dick, not this time, there's a good fellow.

Wagner Have a heart – all this way for a nightcap –

Carson You said you were passing –

Wagner To see if you were up.

Carson Well, we were just turning in, weren't we, darling? Why don't you drop in tomorrow – *today*, for heaven's sake – for a sundowner.

Ruth Leave off, Geoffrey – he knows. (*to Wagner*) You do know, don't you?

Wagner Oh, absolutely.

Carson Knows what?

Ruth He knows we're waiting for Mageeba.

Carson (*angrily*) Ruth . . .

Wagner Mageeba – that's the fellow.

Carson It's a social call. He likes to eat late.

Wagner Doesn't he, though?

Carson Well, there you are.

Wagner Yes, indeed. When is Colonel Shimbu supposed to be coming?

Carson He's not coming.

Ruth (*simultaneously*) In the morning. He's not coming in the morning.

Carson This is dreadful.

Wagner I'll be as quiet as a mouse.

Carson Mageeba is going to be furious. You'll be lucky if you don't end up under arrest.

Wagner I'm your house guest.

Carson No, you're not.

Ruth Oh, do let him. He could crawl under the sofa. (*to Wagner*) You'll feel quite at home, it's almost like a bed. I'll bet you're better under a bed than in it.

Carson Stop this.

Wagner Vouch for me, then. Lobby basis, I promise.

Carson What do you mean, lobby basis? – this is the President of Kambawe, not some Downing Street PR man. Journalists here get hung up by their thumbs for getting his medals wrong.

Wagner Charming fellow, your boss.

Carson He's not my boss. He's the President, that's all, I can't help who's President. I'm a mining engineer.

Wagner They're his mines.

Carson They were here first and so was I. They're my bloody mines more than his.

Ruth And more Shimbu's than yours now.

Wagner True. Do you think Shimbu will show up?

Carson As it happens I don't. Not unless he's got a fool-proof triple-cross to put over on the double-cross he'd be expecting from Mageeba.

Wagner It *is* like Downing Street.

Carson How did you know about all this?

Wagner I was guessing about Shimbu. On Mageeba I had my own source.

Carson Yes, I bet – Canadian loud-mouth.

Wagner What Canadian loud-mouth is that?

Carson You know about the UN team, do you?

Wagner Up to a point, Lord Copper.

Carson UN observers, they've been in KC since Sunday.

Wagner Shimbu's letter was to the UN not to Mageeba . . .?

Carson I'll brief you if you promise to leave.

Wagner Sounds fair.

Carson Mageeba wants his mines back. Last year they produced nearly sixty per cent of his copper – you read that in the *Kambawe Citizen*. The mines are no good to Shimbu because the railway goes the wrong way. You saw that on a map. So Shimbu will swop the mines for recognition of Adoma. Pretty good going – I steal your clothes and offer to give back your trousers if I can keep your shirt. He wants to talk through the UN people. To show good faith he says he won't fire a shot until he's fired upon.

Wagner Sounds sincere.

Carson Sounds as if he hasn't got all his armour up. Anyway, Mageeba bought it, he said he'd show up here with the Canadians at dawn, ready to talk. Half-way house, you see.

Wagner I'll believe the Canadians when I see them.

Carson Me too. Everybody's lying.

Wagner Tell me what you think.

Carson I think Shimbu wants the whole apple, and is using the time to get his supply line working. I think Mageeba isn't going to let Shimbu secede anywhere except into a ditch, and at breakfast time when he sees Shimbu hasn't fallen for it, he's going to go in with air-strikes and tanks and lose half of them in a week, and appeal to the free world about Russian interference. I also think that the British and the Americans will protest, and all the time they're protesting the Russians will be interfering the shit out of Mageeba's army, until Kambawe is about as independent as Lithuania, and that the British and Americans will protest.

Wagner I see. I'll make sure the *Globe* puts that over.

Carson You'll what –?

Wagner I said I'll make sure the *Globe* –

But Carson is already laughing heartily.

Carson Oh good! Oh wonderful! The *Globe* will pro-nounce! We're saved – the Prime Minister will be straight on to the Foreign Office – (*He mimes winding up an old-fashioned telephone while holding the ear-piece.*)

331

'Now look here, have you seen what those Russkies are up to in Africa? – the Queen is absolutely *furious* and so is Albert!'

Wagner All right.

Ruth Poor Dick.

Carson Well . . . there you are.

Wagner Thanks, Geoff.

Carson You said you'd leave.

Wagner I was lying.

Carson I'm beginning to wonder if you can be altogether trusted.

Wagner I'm sorry, but nobody on this story has got a sight of Mageeba since it broke. Let alone a quote. Let alone an interview. Let alone this Shimbu deal. It's too big to pass up and I'm greedy for it – I admit that. I'm going to put the *Globe* so far out in front this Sunday, those roving correspondents and African specialists and line-shooters and bullshitters won't keep down their dinner for a week.

Carson Serve you right if he doesn't show up. He seldom does what he says.

But a car is becoming audible.

Wagner If he hadn't shown up I'd still be watching the compound. I saw him land fifteen minutes ago. Also two Sea King helicopters. Do you think they're full of Canadian lawyers?

The car is getting louder.

Carson Are you going?

Wagner No.

Carson Be careful if he laughs. (*He goes out to meet the car.*)

Ruth You're shaking.

Wagner That's because I'm scared.

Ruth I'm beginning to like you a little. Now that I can see through you. You're just like Jake, really. My paper 'tis of thee. If you two were just a little brighter you'd remind me of Batman and Robin.

Wagner What do I call him?

Ruth He likes to be called boy.

Wagner For Christ's sake. Don't leave the room.

Then Mageeba is in, followed by Carson. Mageeba is in uniform, open-necked shirt, informal but well laundered and wearing medal-ribbon. He carries a short cane with a metal knob.

Ruth Good evening, Your Excellency . . . how kind of you to honour us.

Mageeba Mrs Carson . . . a pleasure . . . a beautiful home and a beautiful hostess. Please forgive this late hour.

Ruth It's never too late – welcome . . . we're night birds here.

Mageeba How gracious . . . I, too, sleep very little.

Ruth (*gaily*) Well – uneasy lies the head that –

'Ruth' (*loudly*) Idiot!

Ruth I mean the sheer volume of work must be enormous, the cares of State, and –

'Ruth' Shut up, you silly woman –

Ruth May I introduce Mr Richard Wagner?

Mageeba Mr Wagner.

Wagner Sir – your most – er – Excellency –

'Ruth' Compose yourself, Wagner.

Mageeba You are a visitor to Kambawe?

Wagner Yes, sir.

Carson Would you care for anything, sir?

Mageeba What brings you to Kambawe?

Wagner You do, sir – your determined stand against Russian imperialism in Africa has won the admiration of the British people, sir –

'Ruth' Jesus Christ.

Wagner And I feel very privileged myself to have the opportunity to –

Mageeba stops him with an upraised hand.

Mageeba (*triumphantly*) Ah! (*to Carson*) Your guest is a journalist.

Carson I'm very sorry about this, sir – Mr Wagner arrived a few minutes ago quite by chance – he was just leaving –

Ruth For London.

Mageeba How I envy him. I have very happy memories of London. Student days, you know. I learned everything about economic theory. It has proved a great handicap. (*to Ruth*) How are things in London, Mrs Carson?

Ruth Oh – did you know I'd been?

334

Mageeba My cousin tells me of all interesting and distinguished travellers.

Ruth You have a cousin at the airport?

Mageeba No, at the Court of St James.

'Ruth' Say goodnight, Gracie.

Mageeba But I also have a cousin at the airport, of course.

Ruth Oh good.

Mageeba You see, I know everything. How is young Alexander finding London?

Ruth Oh . . . he's a wild success, I believe, much respected . . .

Carson (*hurriedly*) He's staying with friends in Kamba City, sir – school-friend, you know

Ruth Oh yes . . . young Allie . . .

Mageeba You see, Mrs Carson, I am like a father to all Kambaweans. In your case, of course, I have to say an adopted father.

Ruth Of course.

'Ruth' Wrong!

Mageeba Such is our legacy of racial and cultural prejudice.

Ruth Yes, indeed.

'Ruth' (*loudly*) Geoffrey!!

Wagner decides to make his pitch and to do so quite formally. The effect is more wooden than formal.

Wagner Your Excellency – Sir . . . I hope you will forgive my presence but as I say, the British people are watching with intense and sympathetic interest your courageous stand against the communist menace in Africa, and if you, sir, have any words of reassurance – however few – any message for the British people – and indeed the world – the *Sunday Globe* would be privileged to publish them.

Pause. Mageeba has been deciding on a chair and sinking himself into it. Now he looks up and looks at Wagner apologetically.

Mageeba I'm so sorry – Mr Wagner – were you speaking to me?

Wagner (*bravely*) Yes, sir. I was saying, Your Excellency, that the British people are following with intense admiration and interest your . . . er . . . courageous stand against the communist threat in Africa . . . sir . . .

Mageeba Yes?

Wagner Yes, sir, and if you have any message for the British people – and indeed the world – well, my paper would be privileged to publish it.

Mageeba (*pause*) The *Sunday Globe*.

Wagner nods.

'Ruth' You're bitched, Wagner.

Carson Well, Dick, it's time you were off.

Mageeba Is Mr Wagner a friend of yours, Geoffrey?

Carson No –

Ruth (*simultaneously*) Oh, rather. We met in London. I'm terribly fond of him. (*to Wagner*) I'll see you to the door.

Mageeba Please! Do you have to leave, Mr Wagner?

Wagner Not at all.

Mageeba Then you must stay. I am interested to meet you. We must have a good talk. Sit down there.

Wagner Thank you, sir.

Carson Your Excellency . . .

Mageeba Yes, you were saying, Geoffrey – a little whisky and water, then.

Carson Of course. Would you like the malt?

Mageeba Not with water.

Carson No – of course.

Mageeba The blended, about half and half, no ice.

Carson Whisky and water, no ice.

Wagner That will do me nicely, without the water. (*He is transformed, secure, pleased with himself.*) So I don't mind a bit of malt if you can spare it.

> *Carson uses Wagner's bottle of Cutty Sark for the drinks.*

Carson (*to Ruth*) Darling?

Ruth Nothing.

Carson Ruth has arranged for a little late supper to be laid out in the dining room if you should care for something, sir.

'Ruth' He's not going to have room for a thing after Wagner.

Mageeba Mr . . . Wagner.

Wagner Mr . . . President. Sir.

Mageeba Mr Wagner, it is not you, is it, who has to be congratulated on the *Sunday Globe*'s interview with Colonel Shimbu?

Wagner That wasn't me, sir, no. As a matter of fact, it wasn't a *Globe* reporter at all, it was a young freelance chap who found himself caught up with Shimbu quite by accident. Of course when he sent it to the *Globe,* they were bound to use it, because – well, all the news that's fit to print, as they say.

Mageeba 'The press lives by disclosure.'

Wagner Ah, you know that one.

Mageeba Delaney of *The Times* – we had all that at the LSE. The political history of communications, or some such course. (*He accepts his drink from Carson.*) Thank you. And C. P. Scott of the *Manchester Guardian,* of course – 'Comment is free but facts are sacred.'

Wagner Yes, and 'Comment is free but facts are on expenses.'

Mageeba Scott?

Wagner Wagner. (*He takes his drink.*) Cheers.

Mageeba What did you think of the interview by the way?

Wagner Ah, well, (*He looks for safe ground.*) – these chaps, they even talk like puppets, don't they? I think it's useful in a way to let them have their say. For that reason. Of course, sir, if you felt that some reply – or refutation – was indicated, I need hardly say that I, or rather the *Globe* –

Mageeba You would give me equal space?

Wagner Oh – absolutely –

Mageeba That's very fair. Isn't it Geoffrey? Mr Wagner says I can have equal space.

Wagner And some space is more equal than others. I think, sir, I could more or less guarantee that an interview with you at this juncture of the war would be treated as the main news story of the day, and of course would be picked up by newspapers, and all the media, round the world.

Mageeba What war, Mr Wagner?

Wagner Sorry?

Mageeba Kambawe is not at war. We have a devolution problem. I believe you have one, too.

Wagner A devolution problem? Yes . . . I see. Do you mind, sir, if I make a note or two?

Mageeba waves permission and Wagner takes a note book from his pocket.

Mageeba If it is a war it is not of my waging. I am a man of peace . . . (*He waits for Wagner and repeats as he writes.*) . . . man of peace. When a man strikes me without cause or warning, I invite him to breakfast. Don't I, Geoffrey?

Carson I have told Mr Wagner that this is a social call, sir.

Mageeba Quite right. I am going to have breakfast with Shimbu. At least – I have invited him to breakfast, I can do no more than that, and I don't mind at all, Mr Wagner, that you are here to witness my good faith.

Wagner Do you think Shimbu will come?

Mageeba I think he might come if he is still his own master. He would come *early*, perhaps, and bring his own food, but I think he would come. It would be to his advantage now to come to the breakfast table with a reasonable and peace-loving man. His methods have been piratical but his cause is not without interest. Our frontiers, you know, are still the frontiers of colonialism. Adoma has its own language, an ancient culture, and the people are of distinct appearance. This does not mean that Adoma could prosper as an independent nation – frankly it could not, except as the hand-maiden of its so-called liberators, and I think Shimbu will see that there is more true independence in being, let us say, an autonomous state federated to Kambawe.

Wagner Are you offering that, sir?

Mageeba I would consider a referendum. But of course that would depend on an immediate withdrawal from his present aggressive positions.

Wagner The Malakuangazi mines.

Mageeba I don't think Geoffrey would accept anything less.

Carson He did rather come in without knocking.

Mageeba And of course there is the question of uninvited foreigners. At this moment on Kambawe soil we have Russians, Cubans, Yemeni and Libyans. We even have a few Czech and German mechanics, I'm told. The American Ambassador asked me if I would let the United Nations come in. I said, half of them are already here – working for Shimbu.

Wagner Is there any UN presence in Kamba City yet?

Mageeba No.

Wagner I see. And what if Shimbu doesn't come to the table and doesn't withdraw?

Mageeba Then, Mr Wagner, you may call it a war.

Wagner When may I do that, sir?

Mageeba Would ten o'clock suit you?

Wagner grins, drains his glass and holds it out to Carson.

Wagner (*to Carson*) May I . . .? (*to Mageeba*) Do you have what you need to win the war?

Mageeba If it's a short war.

Wagner And if it's not? Are you looking to us and the Americans?

Mageeba I'd be a fool to do that. Your record of cowardice in Africa stretches from Angola to Eritrea.

Carson Lobby basis, Dick.

Mageeba No – no – I don't believe in that. They asked me if they could appoint a lobby correspondent in KC. I said, fine, tell him to go and sit in the Sheraton, it's the most comfortable lobby in town. I know the British press is very attached to the lobby system. It lets the journalists and the politicians feel proud of their traditional freedoms while giving the reader as much of the truth as they think is good for him. I have some experience of the British press. When you granted us our independence – as the rules of hospitality oblige me to refer to the military victory of the Nationalist Front – the Kambawe paper was the property of an English gentleman. Isn't that so, Geoffrey?

Carson Well, not exactly, sir –

Mageeba Not *exactly* a gentleman, no, but a rich English-man with a title. So there we were, an independent country, and the only English newspaper was still part of a British Empire – a family empire – a chain of news-papers – a fleet of newspapers, shall I say? Yes, that's very good, not a chain but a fleet of newspapers. That's good, isn't it, Mr Wagner?

Wagner Yes . . . you mean like a convoy?

'Ruth' He means like Fleet Street, you fool.

Mageeba Fleet Street –

Wagner Oh yes – very good –

Mageeba Of course, we had many businesses controlled by overseas interests, we still have many, and we have many more partnerships – even the Kambawe Mining Corporation is such a partnership and you can see from that, can you not, Mr Wagner, that we have no prejudice against English gentlemen as such – but a newspaper, a newspaper is not like a mine, or a bank, or an airline; it is the voice of the people and the Kambawe paper was the voice of an English millionaire.

Wagner Which one?

Carson Yours, Dick.

Wagner Oh . . . somewhat before my time, sir.

Mageeba Nothing personal, Mr Wagner.

Wagner Good God, I hold no brief for *him*.

Mageeba I realize of course that you are only an able-seaman on the flag-ship.

Wagner Well, sir, we've come a long way since we were galley slaves. Northcliffe could sack a man for wearing the wrong hat. Literally. There was a thing called the

Daily Mail hat and he expected his reporters to wear it. Until he got interested in something else. Aeroplanes or wholemeal bread . . . Those days are gone.

Mageeba Indeed, Mr Wagner, now the hat is metaphorical only.

Wagner With respect, sir, you underestimate the strength of the organized workers – the journalists. I admit that even when *I* started in newspapers a proprietor could sack any reporter, who, as it were, insisted on wearing the wrong hat, but things are very different now.

Ruth Now the union can sack him instead.

Wagner I see that young Milne has been bending your car.

Ruth Young Milne? (*She doesn't quite hide her anger.*) Yes, I suppose you can afford to patronize him now.

Carson Perhaps we're getting a little off the President's point.

Mageeba And perhaps not. I'm most interested in what you have to say, Mr Wagner.

Wagner We have a mutual friend who believes that the freedom of the journalist is safer in the hands of the proprietors than in the hands of his fellow journalists.

Ruth Well, of course it is, you fool. Even Northcliffe could only sack you from his *own* newspapers, and nowadays he'd be answerable to one of those industrial tribunals which make banks compensate their sacked embezzlers . . . *and* he'd have to think twice if you were anything special because he'd know that in short order you would be working for the competition. But you'd better be damned careful if you cross your fellow journalists because they would stop you working for any

343

newspaper in the land, no matter how good a reporter you are; and they are answerable to nobody.

Wagner They are answerable to a democratically elected body representing the membership.

Ruth Wagner, are you completely daft?

Carson Ruth . . .

Ruth In your utopia will the burglars be answerable to a democratically elected body of safe crackers?

Mageeba (*enjoying this*) Ha! Mr Wagner?

Wagner Well, without the democracy, that was very much the situation when rich and powerful men in commerce were only answerable to rich and powerful men in the establishment. I'm with the President on this one, if I may say so. I believe that a newspaper, although it is a business, is too important to be merely somebody's property. And I'm not talking about protecting my job but my freedom to report facts that may not be congenial to, let us say, an English millionaire.

Mageeba Mrs Carson?

Ruth I think I'll have that drink after all.

Carson goes to get it for her.

I have difficulty in controlling myself when I'm completely sober.

Carson This comes of having journalists in the house, I suppose . . . I didn't know you felt so passionately about newspapers, Ruth. *Against* them, perhaps.

Ruth I'm against cant. 'Congenial to English million-aires!' The whole country is littered with papers pushing every political line from Mao to Mosley and back again, and I bet even Allie could work out for himself that it

344

is the very free-for-all which guarantees the freedom of each. You don't have to be a millionaire to contradict one. It isn't the millionaires who are going to stop you, it's the Wagners who don't trust the public to choose the marked card.

Wagner I'm talking about *national* papers. It's absurd to equate the freedom of the big battalions with the freedom of a basement pamphleteer to challenge them.

Ruth You are confusing freedom with ability. The *Flat Earth News* is *free* to sell a million copies. What it lacks is the ability to find a million people with four pence and a conviction that the earth is flat. Freedom is neutral. Free expression includes a state of affairs where *any* millionaire can have a national newspaper, if that's what it costs. A state of affairs where only a particular, approved, licensed and supervised non-millionaire can have a newspaper is called, for example, Russia.

Mageeba Or, of course, Kambawe.

'Ruth' (*shouts*) Geoffrey!

Carson I'm sorry, sir – I know Ruth didn't mean –

Mageeba (*placatingly*) Please!

Ruth No – of course not – I mean, the *Daily Citizen* isn't state-controlled.

Mageeba Please don't concern yourself. I enjoy a free and open debate. It is a luxury which a man in my position can seldom afford. And I admit that by the highest ideals the *Daily Citizen is* open to criticism. But you must remember it is the only English language paper we have. The population cannot yet support a number of competing papers offering a natural balance of opinion.

Carson Exactly.

Mageeba At the time of independence the *Daily Citizen* was undoubtedly free. It was free to select the news it thought fit to print, to make much of it, or little, and free to make room for more and more girls wearing less and less underwear. You may smile, but does freedom of the press mean freedom to choose its own standards?

Carson Absolutely.

Mageeba Mrs Carson?

Ruth What's the alternative?

Mageeba That was the question. Easy enough to shut the paper down, as I would have been obliged to do had it not been *burned* down during the state of emergency which followed independence. But what to put in its place? The English millionaire folded his singed tents and stole away the insurance money, which didn't belong to him since I had nationalized the paper well before the fire was out. Never mind – the field was open. I did not believe a newspaper should be part of the apparatus of the state; we are not a totalitarian society. But neither could I afford a return to the whims of private enterprise. I had the immense and delicate task of restoring confidence in Kambawe. I could afford the naked women but not the naked scepticism, the carping and sniping and the public washing of dirty linen which represents freedom to an English editor. What then? A democratic committee of journalists? – a thicket for the editor to hide in. No, no – freedom with responsibility, that was the elusive formula we pondered all those years ago at the LSE. And that is what I found. From the ashes there arose, by public subscription, a new *Daily Citizen,* responsible and relatively free. (*He leans towards Wagner.*) Do you know what I mean by a relatively free press, Mr Wagner?

Wagner Not exactly, sir, no.

Mageeba I mean a free press which is edited by one of my relatives.

He throws back his head and laughs. Wagner joins in uncertainly. Ruth smiles nervously. Carson looks scared. Mageeba brings the weighted end of his stick down on Wagner's head.

(*Shouting*) So it doesn't go crawling to uppity niggers! – so it doesn't let traitors shit on the front page! – so it doesn't go sucking up to liars and criminals! 'Yes sir, Colonel Shimbu, tell us about the exploitation of your people! – free speech for all here, Colonel Shimbu, tell us about the wonderful world you're going to build in that vulture's garbage dump you want to call a country' – yes, you tell us before you get a machine-gun up your backside and your brains coming down your nostrils! – who's going to interview you *then*, Colonel, sir!

Mageeba has stood up and moved away from Wagner. Wagner's head is bleeding slightly above the hairline.

(*Evenly*) I'll give him equal space. Six foot long and six foot deep, just like any other traitor and communist jackal.

Guthrie has entered. He is somewhat the worse for wear. He glances round the room and then ignores everybody and walks diagonally right downstage to where Wagner is. His words are only for Wagner.

Guthrie Dick. Jacob's dead.

Carson (*in response to Mageeba's glance of enquiry*) This is Mr Guthrie, Your Excellency, he is also from – er – London –

Guthrie crosses to Mageeba and stands close to him.

347

Guthrie Are you the President of this shit-house country?

Wagner George . . .

Guthrie Is it you runs that drunken duck-shoot calls itself an army?

Wagner and Carson are moving in on him. Wagner grabs Guthrie and starts pulling him away.

(*Shouts*) I don't call that a fucking cease-fire! I hope they blow their fucking heads off!

Wagner has got Guthrie back down into a chair, and holds him down. Ruth comes forward and kneels on the floor by Guthrie and talks straight into his face.

Ruth Where's Jacob?

Guthrie In the jeep.

Ruth In the jeep? What's he doing there?

Guthrie Not a lot.

Ruth starts to leave.

(*Sharply*) Don't turn him over – he'll come away in your hand.

Ruth moans and sinks down where she is.

Wagner Jesus.

Carson I'm sorry. What happened?

Guthrie We never got to Shimbu.

Mageeba Your messenger, Geoffrey?

Carson Yes. (*to Guthrie*) Have you got the letter?

Guthrie Jake had it. I suppose it's still in his bag.

Carson leaves the room.

(*To Wagner*) You've got blood on your head.

Mageeba Well, Mrs Carson. I must say goodnight. Thank you for your gracious hospitality. (*to Wagner*) I will remember what you said, Mr Wagner.

Wagner What was that . . . sir?

Mageeba Why, that my determined stand against communist imperialism is being watched with admiration by the British people.

Wagner Oh, yes.

Mageeba I enjoyed our discussion. I'm sorry if I was rude about your hat. (*He leaves.*)

Guthrie He hit you? Because he didn't like your hat?

Wagner That's right. What happened to Jacob?

Guthrie It was right outside Malakuangazi. Just getting dark. It took us twice as long to get there as Geoffrey said. Mageeba's pass worked but it worked slowly. Everybody scared stiff of getting their ears chopped off for letting us through, and also for *not* letting us through. Same thing round here, I mean the road to the house. There's soldiers behind every tree. A real back-up to the peace initiative.

Wagner Yeah. he was going to have Shimbu for breakfast all right.

Guthrie These are the good guys. We get accredited by the good guys.

Ruth I want to know what happened.

Mageeba's car has been heard to leave. Carson enters.

Guthrie We eventually got to the front, which is where the cover runs out. You could see Malakuangazi across a strip of open land, no dead ground. We had the headlights on, acting friendly, and a white handkerchief tied to the aerial, but it was just about dark, they couldn't see what was coming. We got a couple of hundred yards, and they put up a flare. That was OK. But somebody behind us got nervous and let off a few rounds. You know – shooting at a town with a rifle – that sort of discipline. So that gets somebody else excited, and pretty soon there's a cross-fire, and another flare, and we're the only moving object in sight. There's only one smart thing to do and the driver knows it. He stops the jeep and runs and I shouted to Jake to run and I got fifty yards and when I looked back he's in the driving seat trying to turn the jeep round. He got it round, and then he was hit. Knocked him into the back seat. I should have looked after him better. Stupid sod. Up 'til then he was having a good time.

Wagner You went back to the jeep.

Guthrie I didn't know if he was dead. Engine was OK. Only the windscreen smashed. So I killed the lights and drove it back. But he was dead all right. A whole burst, head and shoulders. Heavy machine-gun, I should think, just spraying around. He didn't know anything about it anyway.

Carson Where's Francis?

Guthrie He ran the other way, towards Shimbu.

Carson Why?

Guthrie I don't know. Maybe he knew something.

Carson My God. You were taking a hell of a chance, going in after dark.

Guthrie We were already six hours behind.

Carson Shimbu was a long shot anyway.

Guthrie Not Shimbu. The *Globe* is a Sunday paper. If you miss it by an hour you've missed it by a week. Story could be dead as a – I mean – (*to Wagner*) he wanted to go in, Dick. It wasn't just me.

Wagner nods. Carson touches Ruth's shoulder.

Carson I've got to follow Mageeba to KC. There's nothing to worry about. He needs to talk to me about the mines, doesn't want to bomb the bits that matter. (*to Wagner*) I'm taking the helicopter. I'll dump you two at the airport, but after that you're on your own. Get on any plane you can, and with luck you'll be out of the country before Mageeba has time to think about you. He's got bigger problems at the moment.

Wagner I want to file from here.

Carson I'm already sticking my neck out for you. You've got time to get out and file.

Wagner No, I don't like that – planes can be late. Let me think.

Guthrie You can file first from KC. Get an AP wire. You have to risk that. And then a plane. Gives you two chances.

Wagner Yes, that's good. OK. What about Jake?

Carson There's no proper morgue in Jeddu. I'll take the body to KC. Do you know anything about his family? Who to tell?

Wagner Only the *Globe*. I'd better let them know that at least. All right?

Carson You can try.

Wagner goes to the telex and switches it on, and taps some keys.

We'll take the jeep down to the compound.

Wagner (*over his shoulder to Guthrie*) Jeep picture?

Guthrie pats his camera bag.

Guthrie I shot a couple of rolls before starting back. It was an artillery war when I left.

Carson (*to Wagner*) If you can't get straight through you'll have to leave it.

Wagner All my stuff's at the hotel.

Carson Forget it.

Wagner And the car?

Carson I'll get it picked up some time.

Guthrie It's my car. I want it.

Wagner leaves the telex and comes back to Guthrie.

Wagner What do you mean?

Guthrie is putting rolls of exposed film into linen envelopes which are pre-prepared, labelled.

Guthrie Here. The guy in the AP office is called Chamberlain. Ask him to print up this one – I marked it – and wire anything which looks worthwhile. Tell him to push it to eight hundred and bugger the grain, I was using moonlight and flares. This one is for the London plane if you can get a pigeon.

Carson I don't think you understand. Mageeba is unpredictable. He may decide he was amused by your effrontery and give you a decoration, or he may feed you to the crocodiles. If I were you I wouldn't take the chance. He can always post you the decoration.

Guthrie No, I don't think so.

Carson *Look* – first that Shimbu interview, and now you calling him names – he's not going to think the *Globe* is on his side.

Guthrie We're not here to be on somebody's side, Geoffrey. That was World War II. We try to show what happened, and what it was like. That's all we do. It's bloody difficult, and sometimes people bitch about which side we're supposed to be on. (*to Wagner*) Remember what that Yank admiral said to Malcolm Browne that time in Saigon? (*to Carson*) This brass-hat showed up and he *knew* that all the bad news was just the fault of the reporters. He knew them by name. He said to the AP man, 'Oh, so you're Browne. When are you going to get on the team?' (*to Wagner*) Remember that? The team. Give me the keys. I'll go by the hotel and get your stuff out.

Wagner hands over the car keys.

Wagner Use my room. You should crash for a few hours.

Guthrie No, I want to get back. It'll all be happening this morning.

Wagner I'll see you then. Take care, George.

Carson Good luck, George.

Ruth I hope they blow your head off, George.

Carson Come on, Ruth.

Ruth No, I won't. (*to Guthrie*) Tell me something, George. Which page is it on?

Guthrie What?

The newspapers are still in the room and Ruth picks up one of them.

353

Ruth This thing that's worth dying for.

Guthrie I don't intend to die for anything.

Ruth Jake did.

Guthrie Yes.

Ruth (*with the paper*) Show me where it is. It can't be on the back page – 'Rain Halts Australian Collapse.' That's not it, is it? Or the woman's page – 'Sexy Or Sexist? – The Case For Intimate Deodorants.' Is that it, George? What about readers' letters? – 'Dear Sir, If the Prime Minister had to travel on the seven fifty-three from Bexhill every morning we'd soon have the railwaymen back on the lines.' Am I getting warm, George?

Wagner You're belittling his death.

Ruth (*angrily*) You bet I am. I'm not going to let you think he died for free speech and the guttering candle of democracy – crap! You're all doing it to impress each other and be top dog the next time you're propping up a bar in Beirut or Bangkok, or Chancery Lane. Look at Dick and tell me I'm a liar. He's going to be a hero. The wires from London are going to burn up with congratulations. They'll be talking about Wagner's scoop for years, or anyway Wagner will. It's all bloody ego. And the winner isn't democracy, it's just business. As far as I'm concerned, Jake died for the product. He died for the women's page, and the crossword, and the racing results, and the heartbreak beauty queens and some-where at the end of a long list I suppose he died for the leading article too, but it's never worth *that* – (*She has started to swipe at Guthrie with a newspaper and she ends up flinging it at him.*)

Guthrie Yes, all that. But also the other thing. I've been around a lot of places. People do awful things to each other. But it's worse in places where everybody is kept in the dark. It really is. Information is light. Information, in itself, about anything, is light. That's all you can say, really. (*to Wagner*) What's the name of the hotel?

Wagner I forget. Green awnings.

Carson The Sandringham.

Wagner Oh yeah. I should have used that.

Guthrie There'll always be an England, though maybe not there. I'll see you. (*He goes.*)

Carson Go to bed, darling. I'm sorry about having to go. I'll bring Allie back anyway.

Ruth Will it be all right for him here?

Carson Oh yes. If it's not, I don't want you here either. I'll have some news before I leave KC. (*to Wagner*) Fit?

The telex has started chattering.

If that's London make it quick. (*to Ruth*) Do we have an old blanket or something like that?

Ruth Just take anything.

Carson goes out. Wagner has gone to the chattering telex. It doesn't chatter for long. Wagner stands reading the message as it comes off the machine. The machine stops. Wagner continues to stare at it for a few moments. Then he turns away and goes to his Cutty Sark bottle and pours himself a drink and then takes the drink back to his chair and sits down.

London?

Wagner Yes.

Ruth Well?

Wagner There's no hurry.

Carson comes back with a ground-sheet.

Carson Allie's ground-sheet. I'll get him another one. (*to Wagner*) OK –? What are you doing? (*He's crossing to the telex.*) Did you get it? (*He tears the message out of the machine and looks at it. He comes back into the room with it.*) It's yours. From someone called Battersby. 'Milne copy blacked by subs, full chapel and machine room support. Total confrontation and dismissal notices tonight, weekend shut down definite. Wotwu –' – is that a garble? – 'Wotwu – Battersby.' What's that?

Wagner There's no paper this week.

Pause.

Carson That's rotten luck, Dick. (*He gives Wagner the telex message.*)

Wagner Yeah. Wotwu.

Carson What is that?

Wagner Workers of the world unite.

Carson I see. What will you do now?

Wagner I'm just thinking. Would you air-freight George's film for me? There's no rush.

Carson receives the envelopes from Wagner, or just picks them up.

Carson Yes, all right.

Wagner Telex the way-bill number to the office and they'll pick them up COD. I'll call the hotel and get George to come back and fetch me. There may be a paper next week, and as he says, it'll all be happening this morning. I ought to be there.

Ruth Aren't you supposed to be withdrawing your labour?

Wagner (*snaps at her*) Don't get clever with me, damn you. (*Pause. To Carson*) I'm sorry.

Ruth That's all right.

Carson What about your story? Can't they do anything with it?

Wagner Yes, they could make paper aeroplanes with it. We'll see. Thanks for everything, Geoff.

Carson Drop by again.

Wagner I will.

Carson (*to Ruth*) I'll phone from KC.

Carson leaves. Wagner empties his glass and stands up.

Wagner Could I have another drink?

Ruth You brought it. (*She takes his glass.*) I think I'll have one too. Nightcap.

Wagner goes to the telex and is tapping at it while she is pouring the rest of the Cutty Sark equally into two glasses.

What are you doing?

Wagner Short piece about Jake. Onpass *Grimsby Messenger*.

Ruth Good idea.

The jeep is heard leaving.

No point in staying sober now he's gone, eh?

357

Wagner Jake?

Ruth The President.

Wagner Oh.

She takes his drink and puts it on top of the telex.

Ruth Are you going to call George?

Wagner In a while. He won't be there yet. Did you have a thing for Jake?

Ruth No.

Wagner Just wondered.

Wagner is working the keyboard, pausing for thought. He stops to loosen his tie and light a cigarette. Ruth takes her drink back into the room.

Ruth Well, it was a very elevated, intellectual sort of thing. I wanted to undress him with my teeth. Oh God, I'm tired as hell and I'm not going to get to sleep.

Wagner Don't you have a pill for that?

Ruth There *are* no pills for that. I want to be hammered out, disjointed, folded up and put away like linen in a drawer. (*She goes back to the whisky bottle and holds it upside down over her glass, and examines the label.*) You can use the phone upstairs if you like.

Wagner I thought you didn't want to be a tart . . .

Ruth How do I know until I've tried it? I name this bottle 'Cutty Sark'.

She breaks the bottle against the marble shelf and drops the remainder into the bin. She looks at Wagner: he's at the keyboard, tie loose, cigarette in mouth, whisky on the 'piano lid'. It looks like a

358

familiar piano-player-plus-singer scene. We hear the piano. Something fast. Ruth sings. Just a few bars. Wagner disrupts this by tearing the paper out of the machine.

Is that it?

Wagner That's it.

Blackout.

INDIAN INK

Dedicated to the memory of
Laura Kendal

Characters

Flora Crewe
Coomaraswami
Nazrul
Eleanor Swan
Eldon Pike
Anish Das
Nirad Das
David Durance
Dilip
Resident
Englishwoman
Englishman
Rajah/Politician
Nell
Eric

In addition

Indian Questioner(s)
Club Servant(s)
Rajah's Servant(s)

Indian Ink was first performed at the Yvonne Arnaud Theatre, Guildford, and opened at the Aldwych Theatre, London, on 27 February 1995. The cast was as follows:

Flora Crewe Felicity Kendal
Coomaraswami Rashid Karapiet
Nazrul Ravi Aujla
Eleanor Swan Margaret Tyzack
Eldon Pike Colin Stinton
Questioner Akbar Kurtha
Nirad Das Art Malik
Anish Das Paul Bhattacharjee
David Durance Dominic Jephcott
Dilip Akbar Kurtha
Englishman Kenneth Jay
Englishwoman Diana Oxford
Resident Peter Wickham,
Club Servant Ravi Aujla
Rajah/Politician Derrick Branche
Rajah's Servant Naim Khan-Turk
Nell Nickie Rainsford
Eric Daniel Wellon

Produced by Michael Codron
Directed by Peter Wood
Designed by Carl Toms
Lighting by Mark Henderson

The play is set in two periods, 1930 (in India) and mid-1980s (in England and India).

It is not intended that the stage be demarcated between India and England, or past and present. Floor space, and even furniture, may be common. In this respect and in others, the play profited greatly from Peter Wood's direction. The stage directions generally follow the original production but are not offered as a blueprint for the staging.

Act One

Dusk. Flora sits alone on a moving train. Her suitcase is on the rack above her head. The train is approaching a station. Flora, already speaking, stands to lift down her suitcase. By the end of her first speech, she is on the station platform at Jummapur.

Flora 'Jummapur, Wednesday, April the second. Darling Nell, I arrived here on Saturday from Bombay after a day and a night and a day in a Ladies Only, stopping now and again to be revictualled through the window with pots of tea and proper meals on matinee trays, which, remarkably, you hand back through the window at the next station down the line where they do the washing up; and from the last stop I had the compartment to myself, with the lights coming on for me to make my entrance on the platform at Jummapur. The President of the Theosophical Society was waiting with several members of the committee drawn up at a respectful distance, not quite a red carpet and brass band but garlands of marigolds at the ready, and I thought there must be somebody important on the train –'

Coomaraswami (*interrupting*) Miss Crewe!

Flora '– and it turned out to be me.'

Coomaraswami Welcome to Jummapur!

Flora '– which was very agreeable.' Thank you! (*And as she is garlanded by Coomaraswami*) How nice! Are you Mr Coomar . . .

Coomaraswami Coomaraswami! That is me! Is this your only luggage?! Leave it there! (*He claps his hands imperiously for assistance, and then shakes hands enthusiastically with Flora.*) How do you *do*, Miss Crewe!

> *The handshake which begins on the station platform ends on the verandah of the 'Dak Bungalow', or guesthouse. The guesthouse requires a verandah and an interior which includes, or comprises, a bedroom. On the verandah is a small table with at least two chairs. There is an electric light, unlit, and an oil lamp, lit. The bedroom contains a bed under a mosquito net, a washstand, a bedside table, an electric fan and a 'punkah'. There is a door to a bathroom offstage.*
>
> *A servant, Nazrul, carries Flora's suitcase into the bedroom, and then retreats to his quarters, out of sight.*

Flora (*completing the handshake*) Thank you!

Coomaraswami Welcome, my dear Miss Crewe! And farewell! A day of rest!

Flora Thank you – you were so kind to . . .

Coomaraswami I will leave you! Tomorrow, a picnic! Do you like temples?

Flora Well, I don't know . . . I'm sure I . . .

Coomaraswami Leave everything to me!

> *Coomaraswami leaves her, shouting in Hindi for his buggy-driver.*
> *The Shepperton garden is now visible. Here, Mrs Swan and Pike are having tea while occupied with a shoebox of Flora's letters.*

Flora 'And in no time at all I was installed in a little house, two good-sized rooms under a tin roof with electric light . . . (*She tries the electric light switch without result.*) . . . and an oil lamp just in case . . .' (*She looks out from the verandah.*) '. . . a verandah looking out at a rather hopeless garden . . . but with a good table and chair which does very well for working . . .' (*She tries out the chair and the table.*) '. . . and a wicker sofa of sorts for not working . . . and round the back . . .'

She has a brief look around the corner of the verandah where it goes out of sight, while Mrs Swan turns a page of the letter.

(*Reappearing*) '. . . a kitchen bit with a refrigerator! But Nazrul, my cook and bottle-washer, disdains the electric stove and makes his own arrangements on a little verandah of his own.' (*She goes into the interior, into the bedroom, where she tries the switch for the ceiling fan, again without result.*) 'My bedroom, apart from the ceiling fan, also has a punkah which is like a pelmet worked by a punkah-wallah who sits outside and flaps the thing by a system of ropes and pulleys, or would if he were here, which he isn't. And then off the bedroom . . .'

She disappears briefly through a door. Mrs Swan passes the page to Pike and they continue to read in silence.

(*Reappearing*) '. . . is a dressing room and bathroom combined, with a tin tub, and a shower with a head as big as a sunflower – a rainflower, of course . .

Pike grunts approvingly.

'. . . and all this is under a big green tree with monkeys and parrots in the branches, and it's called a duck bungalow . . .'

Mrs Swan *Dak* bungalow.

Flora '. . . although there is not a duck to be seen.' (*She disappears into the bathroom with her suitcase.*)

Mrs Swan Dak was the post; they were post-houses, when letters went by runner.

Pike Ah . . .

Mrs Swan I wish I'd kept the envelopes, they'd be worth something now, surely, the Indian ones at least.

Pike Oh, but it's the wine, not the bottles! These letters are a treasure. They may be the only *family* letters anywhere.

Mrs Swan I dare say, since I'm the only family. I like to have two kinds of cake on the go. The Madeira is my own.

Pike I'm really not hungry.

Mrs Swan I wouldn't let that stop you, Mr Pike, if you hope to get on my good side.

Pike I would love some. The Madeira.

She cuts him a slice.

And won't you please call me Eldon? (*He takes the slice of cake.*) Thank you. (*He takes the bite and gives a considered verdict.*) Wonderful.

Mrs Swan I should think so.

Pike It's the excitement. There's nothing like these in the British Library, you know!

Mrs Swan (*amused*) The British Library!

Pike The University of Texas has Flora Crewe indexed across twenty-two separate collections! And I still have the Bibliothèque Nationale next week. The *Collected Letters* are going to be a year of my life!

Mrs Swan A whole year just to collect them?

Pike (*gaily*) The notes, the notes! The notes is where the fun is! You can't just *collect* Flora Crewe's letters into a book and call it 'The Collected Letters of Flora Crewe', I'm not even sure if it's legal where I come from.

Mrs Swan America?

Pike The Department of English Studies, University of Maryland. Luckily, the correspondence of well-known writers is mostly written without a thought for the general reader. I mean, they don't do their own foot-notes. So there's an opportunity here. Which you might call a moral enterprise. No, OK, an opportunity. Edited by E. Cooper Pike. There isn't a page which doesn't need – look – you see here? – 'I had a funny dream last night about the Queen's Elm.' Which Queen? What elm? Why was she dreaming about a *tree*? So this is where I come in, wearing my editor's hat. To lighten the darkness.

Mrs Swan It's a pub in the Fulham Road.

Pike Thank you. This is why God made writers, so the rest of us can publish. Would that be a *chocolate* cake?

Mrs Swan Why, would you . . .?

Pike No, I just thought: did your sister like chocolate cake particularly?

Mrs Swan What an odd thing to think. Flora didn't like chocolate in any form.

Pike Ah. That's interesting. May I?

*Pike takes the next page of the letter from the
tea-table. Flora approaches, accompanied by
Coomaraswami, who has a yellow parasol, furled.*

Flora 'The sightseeing with picnic was something of a
Progress with the president of the Theosophical Society
holding a yellow parasol over me while the committee
bicycled alongside, sometimes two to a bike, and children
ran before and behind – I felt like a carnival float representing Empire – or, depending how you look at it, the
Subjugation of the Indian People, and of course you're
right, darling, but I never saw anyone less subjugated
than Mr Coomaraswami.'

Coomaraswami We have better temples in the south.
I am from the south. You are right to be discriminating!

Flora (*apologetically*) Did I seem discriminating? I'm
sure it wasn't their fault. The insides of churches . . .

Coomaraswami I understand you completely, Miss
Crewe!

Flora But I don't know what I'm trying to say!

Coomaraswami That is not a requirement.

Flora I'm afraid I'm without religion, you see.

Coomaraswami I *do* see! Which religion are you afraid
you are most without?

Flora Now, Mr Coomaraswami, turning a phrase may
do for Bloomsbury but I expect better from *you*.
    'And I told him about Herbert's lady decorator being
asked on her deathbed what was her religion and telling
the priest, "I'm afraid I worship mauve".'

Coomaraswami (*thoughtfully*) For me, it is grey.

Flora 'I'm going to like India.'

Pike (*with letter*) Who was Herbert?

Mrs Swan Wells.

Pike Ah. (*catching on*) H. G. Wells? Really? (*cautiously*) You don't mean he and Flora . . .?

Mrs Swan You should see your face. Flora met him not long before she went out.

Pike Out?

Mrs Swan To India. It must have been round Christmas or New Year. I think I got a postcard from Paris . . . (*She delves into the shoebox.*) Flora loved Paris. Here, look . . . is that it?

Pike Paris, yes . . . no, 1924 . . . it's a souvenir of the Olympic Games.

Mrs Swan Oh yes, the hurdler. Flora apologized publicly in the Chelsea Arts Club. No medals for us in the *hurdles*.

Pike Is that *true*, Eleanor?

Mrs Swan Now, Eldon, you are *not* allowed to write a book, not if you were to eat the entire cake. The *Collected Poems* was a lovely surprise and I'm sure the *Collected Letters* will be splendid, but *biography* is the worst possible excuse for getting people wrong.

Flora 'So far, India likes me. My lecture drew a packed house, Mr C's house, in fact, and a much more sensible house than mine, built round a courtyard with a flat roof all round so I had an audience in the gods like gods in the audience . . .'

There is the sound of the applause. Coomaraswami faces the audience with Flora. It is night.

'. . . and it all went terribly well, until . . .'

373

Coomaraswami Miss Crewe in her wisdom and beauty has agreed to answer questions!

Flora '– and the very first one went –'

Questioner Miss Crewe, it is said you are an intimate friend of Mr H. G. Wells –

Flora '– and I thought, "God, how unfair! – to have come all this way to be gossiped about as if one were still in the Queen's Elm" –'

Pike A public house in the Fulham area of Chelsea.

Flora '– but it turned out nothing was meant by it except –'

Questioner Does Mr Wells write his famous books with a typewriter or with pen and ink?

Flora (*firmly*) With pen and ink, a Waterman fountain pen, a present from his wife.

There is an appreciative hubbub.

'Not that I had the least idea – Herbert showed small inclination to write his famous books while I was around.'

Pike FC had met Wells no earlier than December and the affair was therefore brief, possibly the weekend of January 7th and 8th; which she spent in Paris.

Flora 'After which there was a reception with lemonade and Indian Scotch. . . '

Flora and Coomaraswami are offered drinks from a tray of drinks. They are joined in due course by the questioner.

'. . . and delicious snacks and conversation – darling, it's so moving, they read the *New Statesman* and the *TLS* as if they were the Bible in parts, well, I don't mean the

Bible but you know what I mean, and they know who wrote what about whom; it's like children with their faces jammed to the railings of an unattainable park. They ask me –'

Questioner What is your opinion of Gertrude Stein, Miss Crewe?

Flora Oh . . .
   '– and I can't bring myself to say she's a poisonous old baggage who's travelling on a platform ticket . . .'

Pike FC's aversion to Gertrude Stein was reciprocated at their first and only meeting when Stein and her companion Alice B. Toklas invited Flora to tea at 27 Rue de Fleurus in 1922. Even so, the legend that FC enthused over Miss Toklas's chocolate cake and that Stein threatened to gouge out FC's eyes, or possibly Miss Toklas's eyes, cannot be trusted. FC did not like chocolate in any form.

Flora 'Then I met my painter . . .'

Das Miss Crewe, may I congratulate you on your lecture. I found it most interesting!

Flora Thank you . . .!

Das I was surprised you did not mention Virginia Woolf.

Flora I seldom do.

Das Have you met George Bernard Shaw?

Flora Yes. I was nearly in one of his plays once.

Das But you are not an actress . . .?

Flora No, that was the trouble.

Das What do you think of Jummapur?

Flora Well, I only arrived the day before yesterday but –

Das Of course. How absurd of me!

Flora Not at all. I was going to say that my first impression –

Das Jummapur is not in any case to be compared with London. Do you live in Bloomsbury?

Flora No, I live in Chelsea.

Das Chelsea – of course! My favourite part of London!

Flora Oh! You . . .?

Das I hope to visit London one of these days. The Chelsea of Turner and the Pre-Raphaelite Brotherhood! – Rossetti lived in Cheen Walk! Holman Hunt lived in Old Church Street! 'The Hireling Shepherd' was *painted* in Old Church Street! What an inspiration it would be to me to visit Chelsea!

Flora You are a painter!

Das Yes! Nirad Das.

Flora How do you do?

Das I am top hole. Thank you. May I give you a present?

Flora Oh . . .

Das Please do not judge it too harshly, Miss Crewe . . .

Flora Thank you!

Das Of course, I work in oils, Winsor and Newton. If it would please you to sit for your portrait I would like to repay you for your superfine portrait-in-words of the rough-and-tumble of literary life in London.

Flora Would you really?

Das I would very much! (*He produces a small sketch pad and tears off a sheet. He gives it to her shyly.*)

Flora '. . . and he gave me a pencil sketch of myself holding forth on the literary life.'

Flora retraces her steps with Coomaraswami.

Pike She mentions a pencil sketch. Do you know what happened to it?

Mrs Swan I'm sure I never saw it. I would have remembered if it had been among what was called her effects. It was only one suitcase.

Pike Do you still have it?

Mrs Swan What? Her suitcase? Heavens, it was a battered old thing even then, and being always on the move, Eric and I, one shed things . . .

Pike You threw away Flora Crewe's suitcase?

Mrs Swan What is it you're up to, Eldon? A *luggage* museum? Really, you're like an old woman about her; except, of course, that I'm not.

Pike But she was Flora Crewe!

Mrs Swan (*crisply*) Well, if so, where was everybody sixty years ago?

Mrs Swan replenishes the teacups. Pike takes one or two more letters from the shoebox and scans them.
At the guesthouse, Nirad Das arrives by bicycle. He has his wooden workbox strapped to the pillion-rack. His folded easel is strapped to his back. He rides one-handed, holding a canvas in his free hand. Flora, in her cornflower-blue dress, comes out from the interior.

Flora Good morning!

Das Miss Crewe! Here I am! A little late! Forgive me!

377

Flora I didn't realize – I've been writing a letter. Does this look all right?

Das (*nervously*) Very, very good.

Flora Now . . . this will be nice, we'll both be working. Poet and painter. Work in progress.

> *Das unstraps his work-box and establishes himself on the verandah. Flora establishes herself at her work table. Pike is puzzling over a letter.*

Pike She says paint on paper.

Mrs Swan Yes.

Pike '. . . a smudge of paint on paper' . . . 'Perhaps my soul will stay behind as a smudge of paint on paper' . . . She's referring to an actual painting, isn't she?

Mrs Swan I don't know.

Pike And 'undressed'. She says 'undressed'. Like a nude. On *paper*. That would be a watercolour, wouldn't it?

Mrs Swan What would? There isn't any 'it'.

Pike Well, if it doesn't mean a portrait of Flora undressed, what do you think it means?

Mrs Swan As much or as little as you like. Isn't that the point of being a poet?

Pike I don't know, I'm not a poet, but it reads quite specific, the deserted house . . . where is the bit?

Mrs Swan Between your teeth, Eldon.

Pike Here. 'In an empty house . . . Perhaps my soul will stay behind as a smudge of paint on paper, as if I'd always been here, like . . . Radha?'

Mrs Swan Radha.

Pike '– the most beautiful of the herdswomen, undressed –'

Mrs Swan (*interrupting, briskly*) Well, the portrait, as it happens, is on canvas and Flora is wearing her cornflower dress.

Pike Portrait?

Mrs Swan She mentions the portrait somewhere. It was rolled up in the suitcase.

Pike Eleanor . . . do you mean there's a portrait of Flora?

Mrs Swan Would you like to see it?

Pike Oh my God.

Mrs Swan It's fairly ghastly, like an Indian cinema poster. I think I know where it is but I'll need you to get it down for me. Should we go in? We're about to lose the sun.

Pike Oh my God. But this is . . . Oh my God. There's never been one, not a real portrait.

Mrs Swan That's true. Apart from the Paris portrait; but that was on canvas, too.

Pike The *Paris* portrait . . .?

Mrs Swan Yes, Flora's first time in Paris, she was driving an ambulance, officially, in the last year of the war . . . so she was twenty-three, I suppose, when she met Modigliani.

Pike Modigliani?

Mrs Swan Oh, Flora met everybody. Not that Modigliani was anybody at the time.

Pike *A portrait by Modigliani?*

Mrs Swan I was nine at the Armistice, so that was, my goodness, sixty-six years ago! I'm coming up to seventy-five, you know.

Pike Eleanor . . . I can hardly believe my ears.

Mrs Swan I'm afraid so. I was born in 1909. But thank you, Eldon. Have another slice of cake.

Pike No – thank you – I – excuse me: a painting of Flora by Modigli –

Mrs Swan Yes. A nude. I never saw it myself. I was at school, of course, and then, it was too late.

Pike Too late?

Mrs Swan Yes, isn't that bad luck? The Technicolor Flora like a cork in a storm, washed up on top of a wardrobe in a bungalow in Shepperton, and the Modigliani, which would have paid for the bungalow several times over, burned to ashes in a bathtub in the Ritz.

By now she has assembled the tea-tray and she leaves with it.

Pike Could you run that by me again?

Pike totters after her.
Flora, in her blue dress, is at the table on the verandah, writing in her notebook with a fountain pen. She pauses, thinking, sitting quite still. Her feet are bare and her shoes are placed neatly to one side. Das is painting her portrait.

Flora (*recorded*)
'Yes I am in heat like a bride in a bath
without secrets, soaked in heated air
that liquifies to the touch and floods,
shortening the breath, yes
I am discovered, heat has found me out,

380

a stain that stops at nothing,
not the squeezed gates or soft gutters,
it slicks into the press
that prints me to the sheet
yes, think of a woman in a house of net
that strains the oxygen out of the air
thickening the night to Indian ink
or think if you prefer –'

*Flora has unconsciously crossed her legs, which brings
Das's work to a halt. He waits, patiently. She notices
that Das has stopped.*

Oh . . .

Das No, please be comfortable.

Flora I'm sorry! (*She puts her feet side-by-side.*) There.
Is that how I was?

Das You are patient with me. I think your nature is very
kind.

Flora Do you think so, Mr Das?

Das I am sure of it. May I ask you a personal question?

Flora That *is* a personal question.

Das Oh my goodness, is it?

Flora I always think so. It always feels like one. Carte
blanche is what you're asking, Mr Das. Am I to lay
myself bare before you?

Das (*panicking slightly*) My question was only about
your poem!

Flora At least you knew it was personal.

Das I will not ask it now, of course.

Flora On that understanding I will answer it. My poem is about heat.

Das Oh. Thank you.

Flora I resume my pose. Pen to paper. Legs uncrossed. You know, you are the first man to paint my toe-nails.

Das Actually, I am occupied in the folds of your skirt.

Flora Ah. In that you are not the first.

Das You have been painted before? – but of course you have! Many times, I expect!

Flora You know, Mr Das, your nature is much kinder than mine.

> *Flora resumes. Das resumes.*
> *Anish Das comes into the Shepperton garden.*
> *He has a soft briefcase; he sits in one of the garden chairs.*

Mr Das, I have been considering whether to ask you a delicate question, as between friend and artists.

Das Oh, Miss Crewe, I am transported beyond my most fantastical hopes of our fellowship! This is a red-letter day without dispute!

Flora If you are going to be so Indian I shan't ask it.

Das But I cannot be less Indian that I am.

Flora You could if you tried. I'm not sure I'm going to ask you now.

Das Then you need not, dear Miss Crewe! You considered. The unasked, the almost asked question, united us for a moment in its intimacy, we came together in your mind like a spark in a vacuum glass, and the redness of the day's letter will not be denied.

Flora You are still doing it, Mr Das.

Das You wish me to be less Indian?

Flora I did say that but I think what I meant was for you to be *more* Indian, or at any rate *Indian*, not Englished-up and all over me like a labrador and knocking things off tables with your tail – so *waggish* of you, Mr Das, to compare my mind to a vacuum. You only do it with us, I don't believe that left to yourself you can't have an ordinary conversation without jumping backwards through hoops of delight, *with* whoops of delight, I think I mean; actually, I do know what I mean, I want you to be with me as you would be if *I* were Indian.

Das An Indian Miss Crewe! Oh dear, that is a mental construction which has no counterpart in the material world.

Flora So is a *unicorn*, but you can imagine it.

Das You can imagine it but you cannot mount it.

Flora Imagining it was all I was asking in my case.

Das (*terribly discomfited*) Oh! Oh, my gracious! – I had no intention – I assure you –

Flora (*amused*) No, no, you cannot unwag your very best wag. You cleared the table, the bric-a-brac is on the Wilton – the specimen vase, the snuff box, the souvenir of Broadstairs –

But she has misjudged.

Das (*anguished*) You are cruel to me, Miss Crewe!

Flora (*instantly repentant*) Oh! I'm so sorry. I didn't want to be. It's my nature. Please come out from behind your easel – look at me.

Das May we fall silent, please. I prefer to work in silence.

Flora I've spoiled everything. I'm very sorry.

Das The shadow has moved. I must correct it.

Flora Yes, it has moved. It cannot be corrected. We must wait for tomorrow. I'm so sorry.

> *Das resumes working at the easel. Flora maintains her pose, but screws the cap on to her fountain pen.*
> *Anish stands up at the approach of Mrs Swan who comes from the bungalow with tea for two on a tray, and two kinds of cake.*

Anish Let me help you.

Mrs Swan I've forgotten your sugar.

Anish Actually, I don't take it.

Mrs Swan Oh. I thought you'd be more Indian.

> *They settle the tray and themselves at the garden table.*

Anish This is so kind of you.

Mrs Swan Oh no. Your letter was irresistible. Having an artist to tea was beyond my fondest hopes for my dotage. We'll let it sit a minute. Do you think you take after your father?

Anish I don't know. I would like to think so. But my father was a man who suffered for his beliefs and I have never had to do that, so perhaps I will never know.

Mrs Swan I really meant being a painter. You are a painter like your father.

Anish Oh . . . yes. Yes, I am a painter like my father. Though not at all like my father, of course.

Mrs Swan Your father was an Indian painter, you mean?

Anish An Indian painter? Well, I'm as Indian as he was. But yes. I suppose I am not a particularly *Indian* painter . . . not an Indian painter *particularly*, or rather . . .

Mrs Swan Not particularly an Indian painter.

Anish Yes. But then, nor was he. Apart from being Indian.

Mrs Swan As you are.

Anish Yes.

Mrs Swan Though you are not at all like him.

Anish No. Yes. My father was a quite different kind of artist, a portrait painter, as you know . . .

Mrs Swan I can't say I do, Mr Das. Until I received your letter your father was unknown to me. In fact, the attribution 'Unknown Indian Artist' described the situation exactly . . .

Anish He was not unknown in Jummapur!

Mrs Swan . . . if indeed it was your father who did the portrait of Flora.

Anish Oh, the portrait is certainly my father's work, Mrs Swan! You cannot imagine my feelings when I saw the book in the shop window – my excitement! You see, I carry my copy everywhere.

He takes The Collected Letters *from his briefcase. The dustjacket has the portrait of Flora by Nirad Das.*

Mrs Swan Well, I hope there'll be lots like *you*, Mr Das.

Anish There will be no one like me, Mrs Swan! It was not the book, of course, but the painting on the jacket and reproduced inside. If only he could have known that one day his portrait of Flora Crewe . . .

Mrs Swan He might have been more pleased to be in the window of an art gallery than a bookshop.

Anish Perhaps not. I'm sure my father never had a single one of his paintings reproduced, and that is an extraordinary pleasure for an artist. I know! The painting under one's hand is everything, of course . . . unique. But replication! *That* is popularity! Put us on book jackets – calendars – biscuit tins! Oh, he would have been quite proud!

Mrs Swan By the way, what *were* your father's beliefs?

Anish (*surprised*) Why . . . we are Hindu . . .

Mrs Swan You said he had suffered for his beliefs.

Anish Oh. I meant his opinions.

Mrs Swan How did he suffer?

Anish He was put in prison.

Mrs Swan Really? By whom?

Anish Well, by you.

Mrs Swan By me? Oh . . . by us. But how did we know what his opinions were?

Anish It seems he took part in some actions against the Raj during the Empire Day celebrations in Jummapur.

Mrs Swan Then he was put in prison for his actions, not his opinions, Mr Das, and obviously deserved what he got. Will you have a slice of cake?

Anish Thank you.

Mrs Swan Victoria sponge or Battenberg?

Anish Oh . . .

Mrs Swan The sponge is my own, raspberry jam included.

Anish I would love some . . . thank you.

Mrs Swan Tea? But all that must have been before you were born.

Anish Oh, yes, I was the child of my father's second marriage. I was born long after Independence, and my father went to prison in Jummapur in 1930.

Mrs Swan 1930! But that was when Flora was in Jummapur!

Anish Yes, I know. That is why I am here.

Mrs Swan administers tea. Flora takes the cap off her fountain pen.

Flora Are we friends this morning?

Das I hope so! Why do you ask that? Has something happened?

Flora Oh. No.

She laughs. He frowns, painting.

Well, I thought if we're friends I'll ask you to write something on the drawing you did of me. (*She produces the pencil sketch.*)

Das Oh, but that was only a poor scribble! Not even a good likeness!

Flora Even so.

Das Oh. (*He is taken aback but then realizes he is being teased. He laughs.*)

Flora Yes, you won't get anywhere with that.

Nazrul, the servant, brings a jug of fresh lemonade and two glasses, which he puts on the table.

Namby pani time!

Nazrul Nimbupani!

Flora (*getting up*) Thank you, Nazrul . . . Shukriya!

Nazrul responds and leaves.

Das Actually, I have something for you, a little present.

Flora Have you? You mustn't keep giving me things, Mr Das!

Das Well, it is a kind of birthday present, you see.

Flora Especially not birthday presents when it isn't my birthday.

Das gives her an old but well-preserved book. It is green with a brown spine. In fact it is a copy of Up the Country *by Emily Eden (1866).*

Das I did not buy it, it is a book of my father's which I would like you to have. Letters by an English lady travelling in India a hundred years ago.

Flora (*truly pleased*) Oh, but this will be just my book! Thank you! *Up the Country* . . . Emily Eden. Oh, it's a lovely present!

Das Well . . . I will write, 'To remind you of Jummapur and your friend and fellow artist Nirad Das'. And I will draw myself listening to you.

Flora pours the nimbupani. Das writes on the pencil drawing with his own fountain pen, and settles down to draw her.

Anish When my father met Flora Crewe he had been a widower for several years, although he was still quite a young man, younger than her, yes, the beginning of the Hot Weather in 1930 . . . he had his 34th birthday on April 2nd, just after he met your sister. He had lost his wife to cholera and he was childless. I knew nothing of my father's life before me. In my earliest memory, my father was an old gentleman who spoke very little except when he sometimes read aloud to me. He liked to read in English. Robert Browning, Tennyson, Macaulay's *Lays of Ancient Rome*, and Dickens, of course . . .

Mrs Swan How surprising.

Anish Oh yes – he went from a vernacular school to Elphinstone College in Bombay, and you only have to look at Elphinstone College to see that it was built to give us a proper English education.

Mrs Swan I meant, in view of his 'opinions'. But I spoke without thinking. Your father took part in actions against the British Raj and loved English literature, which was perfectly consistent of him.

Anish (*laughs*) Usually, the education succeeded admirably! In Jummapur we were 'loyal' as you would say, we had been loyal to the British right through the first War of Independence.

Mrs Swan The . . .? What war was that?

Anish The Rising of 1857.

Mrs Swan Oh, you mean the Mutiny. *What* did you call it?

Anish Dear Mrs Swan, Imperial history is merely . . . no, no – I promise you I didn't come to give you a history lesson.

Mrs Swan You seem ill-equipped to do so. We were your Romans, you know. We might have been your Normans.

Anish And did you expect us to be grateful?

Mrs Swan That's neither here nor there. I don't suppose I'd have been grateful if a lot of Romans turned up and started laying down the law and teaching Latin and so forth. 'What a cheek,' is probably what I would have thought. 'Go away, and take your roads and your baths with you.' It doesn't matter what I would have thought. It's what I think now that matters. You speak English better than most young people I meet. Did you go to school here?

Anish No, I went to a convent school in . . . You are spreading a net for me, Mrs Swan!

Mrs Swan What net would that be? Have some more cake.

Anish Mrs Swan, you are a very wicked woman. You advance a preposterous argument and try to fill my mouth with cake so I cannot answer you. I will resist you and your cake. *We* were the Romans! We were up to date when you were a backward nation. The foreigners who invaded *you* found a third-world country! Even when you discovered India in the age of Shakespeare, we already had our Shakespeares. And our science – architecture – our literature and art, we had a culture older and more splendid, we were rich! After all, that's why you came.

But he has misjudged.

Mrs Swan (*angrily*) We made you a proper country! And when we left you fell straight to pieces like Humpty Dumpty! Look at the map! You should feel nothing but shame!

Anish Oh, yes . . . I am a guest here and I have been . . .

Mrs Swan (*calming down*) No, only provocative. Will you be going home?

Anish (*bewildered*) I . . . would you like me to go?

Mrs Swan (*equally bewildered*) No. What do you mean?

Anish (*understanding*) Oh – home! I didn't mean I was a guest in *England*. England is my home now. I have spent half my life here. I married here.

Mrs Swan An English girl?

Anish Yes. We met at art school.

Mrs Swan (*approvingly*) Artists together.

Anish Actually she was not a student, she was earning money as a model. Life class, you see.

Mrs Swan Of course. Is she still your model?

Anish No. My work is not figurative now.

Mrs Swan What is it now?

Anish Well, deconstructive.

Mrs Swan What a shame.

Anish I can still draw if I wish. May I draw you?

Mrs Swan Oh no, the last thing I need –

Anish No, for myself.

Mrs Swan Oh. Why?

Anish Only a little sketch with a pencil. We must not resist when life strives to close one of its many circles!

Mrs Swan Is that Hinduism?

Anish Oh . . . I don't know. Perhaps.

Mrs Swan Well, it sounds very east of Suez. All right then. You may draw me.

Anish It will make us friends.

> *Anish takes an artist's block from his briefcase and begins to draw her.*
> *Flora and Das sit at the table with lemonade.*

Flora While having tiffin on the verandah of my bunga-low I spilled kedgeree on my dungarees and had to go to the gymkhana in my pyjamas looking like a coolie.

Das I was buying chutney in the bazaar when a thug escaped from the choky and killed a box-wallah for his loot, creating a hullabaloo and landing himself in the mulligatawny.

Flora I went doolally at the durbar and was sent back to Blighty in a dooley feeling rather dikki with a cup of char and a chit for a chotapeg.

Das Yes, and the burra sahib who looked so pukka in his topee sent a coolie to the memsahib –

Flora No, no. You can't have memsahib *and* sahib, that's cheating – and anyway I've already said coolie.

Das I concede, Miss Crewe. You are the Hobson-Jobson champion!

Flora You are chivalrous, Mr Das. So I'll confess I had help. I found a whole list of Anglo-Indian words in my bedside drawer, for the benefit of travellers.

Das But I know both languages, so you still win on handicap.

Flora Where did you learn everything, Mr Das?

Das From books. I like Dickens and Browning, and Shakespeare, of course – but my favourite is Agatha

Christie! *The Mysterious Affair at Styles*! – oh, the woman is a genius! But I would like to write like Macaulay.

Flora Oh dear.

Das I have to thank Lord Macaulay for English, you know. It was his idea when he was in the government of India that English should be taught to us all. He wanted to supply the East India Company with clerks, but he was sowing dragon's teeth. Instead of babus he produced lawyers, journalists, civil servants, he produced Gandhi! We have so many, many languages, you know, that English is the only language the nationalists can communicate in! That is a very good joke on Macaulay, don't you think?

Flora Are *you* a nationalist, Mr Das?

Das (*lightly*) Ah, that is a very interesting question! But we shouldn't have stopped all this time. It's getting late for you, I must work more quickly tomorrow.

Flora It's only half-past ten.

Das No, it's already April, and that is becoming late.

Flora Yes, it seems hotter than ever. Would you like some more lemonade?

Das No, thank you, no lemonade. Miss Crewe, you haven't looked at my painting yet.

Flora No. Not yet. I never look. Do you mind?

Das No.

Flora You do really. But I once asked a painter 'Can I look?' and he said, 'Why? When I paint a table I don't have to show it to the table.'

Das I said you had been painted before.

Flora Only once.

Das A portrait?

Flora Not in the way you mean. It was a nude.

Das Oh.

Flora Unusually. He painted his friends clothed. For nudes he used models. I believe I was his friend. But perhaps not. Perhaps a used model only. It hardly matters. He was dead so soon afterwards. (*Pause.*) He was not so kind to me as you are.

Das Do you have the painting?

Flora No.

Das Where is it?

Flora Nowhere. A man I thought I might marry burned it. My goodness, what a red-letter day you are having. There's a man on a horse.

We have already heard the horse. We do not see the horse.

Durance (*offstage*) Good morning! Miss Crewe, I think!

Flora (*standing up*) Yes – good morning! (*to Das*) Do you know him?

Das He is the Assistant.

Durance (*offstage*) May I get down a moment?

Flora Of course. What a beautiful animal! (*(to Das)* Assistant what?

Das (*to Flora*) Captain Durance!

Durance Thank you!

Flora Come on up, do join us.

Durance arrives on foot.

Durance Oh – it's Mr Das, isn't it?

Das Good morning, sir. But we have never met.

Durance Oh, but I know you. And Miss Crewe, your fame precedes you.

Flora Thank you . . . and you . . .

Durance I'm from the Residency. David Durance.

Flora (*shaking hands*) How do you do?

Durance Oh, but look here – I'm interrupting the artist.

Flora We had stopped.

Durance May one look? Oh, I say! Coming along jolly well! Don't you think so, Miss Crewe?

Das I must be going. I have overstayed my time today.

Flora But we'll continue tomorrow?

Das Yes. Perhaps a little earlier if it suits you. I can leave everything . . .

Das prepares to remove the canvas from the easel.

Flora Why don't you leave the canvas too? It will be quite safe.

Das (*hesitates*) Yes, all right . . . I have a drape for it. Thank you.

He drapes a cloth over the canvas on the easel.

Flora Like shutting up the parrot for the night.

Das There we are. Thank you for the lemonade, Miss Crewe. An absolute treat. I promise you! Goodbye, sir – and – yes – and until tomorrow . . . (*He goes down the verandah steps and wheels his bicycle away.*)

Flora Yes . . . goodbye! (*to Durance*) I'll put my shoes on. Sorry about my toes, but I like to wriggle them when I'm working.

Durance I'll only stay a moment. My chief asked me to look in. Just to make sure there's nothing we can do for you.

Flora Would you like some lemonade?

Durance No, nothing for me. Really. We might have found you more comfortable quarters, you know, not quite so in-the-town.

Flora How did you know I was here?

Durance Now, there's a point. Usually we know of arrivals because the first thing they do is drop in a card but in your case . . . rumours in the bazaar, so to speak. Are you an old hand here, Miss Crewe?

Flora No, I've never been to India before. I came up from Bombay just a few days ago.

Durance But you have friends here, perhaps?

Flora No. I got on a ship and I came, knowing no-one. I have friends in England who have friends here. Actually, one friend.

Durance In Jummapur, this friend?

Flora No – the *friend* – my friend – is in London, of course; Mr Joshua Chamberlain. *His* friends are in different places in Rajputana, and I will also be going to Delhi and then up to the Punjab, I hope.

Durance Now I see. And your friend in London has friends in Jummapur.

Flora Yes.

Durance Like Mr Das?

Flora No. Are you a policeman of some kind, Mr Durance?

Durance Me? No. I'm sorry if I sound like one.

Flora Well, you do a bit. I'm travelling with letters of introduction to a number of social clubs and literary societies. I speak on the subject of 'Literary Life in London', in return for board and lodging . . . So you see I couldn't have taken advantage of your kindness without giving offence to my hosts.

Durance The game is different here. By putting up at the Residency you would have gained respect, not lost it.

Flora Thank you, but what about self-respect?

Durance Well . . . as long as all is well. So you are following in Chamberlain's footsteps. All is explained.

Flora I don't think *I* explained it. But yes, I am. He spoke in Jummapur three years ago, on the subject of Empire.

Durance Yes. Is he a good friend?

Flora Well . . .

Durance Did you know he was some sort of Communist?

Flora I thought he might be. He stood twice for Parliament as the Communist candidate.

Durance (*unoffended, pleasant as before*) I amuse you. That's all right, amusing our distinguished visitors is among my duties.

Flora Well, don't be so stuffy.

Durance How long will you be with us?

Flora I'm expected in Jaipur but they don't mind when I come.

Durance I'm sure you'll have a marvellous time. There are wonderful things to see. Meanwhile, please consider yourself an honorary member of the Club – mention my name, but I'll put you in the book.

Flora Thank you.

Durance Well . . .

He offers his hand and she shakes it.

Flora Call again, if you like. I wish I had a lump of sugar for your horse. Next time.

Durance He's my main indulgence. I wish I'd been here when a good horse went with the job.

Flora Yes . . . what is your job? You mentioned your chief.

Durance The Resident. He represents the government here.

Flora The British government?

Durance Delhi. The Viceroy, in fact. Jummapur is not British India . . . you understand that?

Flora Yes . . . but it's all the Empire, isn't it?

Durance Oh yes. Absolutely. But there's about five hundred Rajahs and Maharajahs and Nabobs and so on who run bits of it, well, nearly half of it, actually, by treaty. And we're here to make sure they don't get up to mischief.

Flora I knew you were a kind of policeman.

Durance laughs and goes down the steps of the verandah. He hesitates shyly.

Durance Miss Crewe, would you have dinner with us while you are here?

Flora With you and your wife, do you mean?

Durance No . . . at the Club. Us. With me. I don't run to a wife, I'm afraid. But do come. We're a reasonably civilized lot, and there's usually dancing on Saturdays, only a gramophone but lots of fun.

Flora I'd love to. On Saturday, then.

Durance Oh . . . splendid! I'll come by.

Flora I haven't got a horse, you know.

Durance We have a Daimler at the Residency. I'll see if I can wangle it. Pick you up about eight?

Flora Yes.

Durance We don't dress, normally, except on dress nights. (*Laughs at himself.*) Obviously.

Flora I'll be ready.

Durance Jolly good.

    He exits and mounts the horse, which snorts.

Flora Goodbye!

Durance (*offstage*) Goodbye!

Flora (*calling out*) Wangle the Daimler!

    Flora waves and turns aside. She sits at her table and starts to write. Anish is drawing Mrs Swan.

Mrs Swan But Jummapur was a Native State.

Anish Yes.

Mrs Swan So *we* didn't put your father in gaol.

Anish (*politely dissenting*) Ah well . . .

Mrs Swan (*firmly*) Whatever your father may have done, the Resident would have had no authority to imprison an Indian. The Rajah of Jummapur had his own justice.

Anish Ah, but His Highness the Rajah . . .

Mrs Swan Oh, I'm not saying we wouldn't have boxed his ears and sent him packing if he forgot which side his bread was buttered, but facts are facts. The Rajah put your father in the choky. How long for, by the way?

Anish Six months.

Mrs Swan There you are. In British India he would have got a year at least. After the War it may have been different. With Independence round the corner, people were queuing up to go to prison, it was their ticket to the top. They'd do their bit of civil disobedience and hop into the paddy-waggon thoroughly pleased with themselves. Eric – that's my husband – would let them off with a small fine if he thought they were Johnny-come-latelies, and they'd be furious. That was when Eric had his District. We were right up near Nepal . . .

Anish Yes, the tea-tray . . .

Mrs Swan You spotted it. In India we had pictures of coaching inns and foxhunting, and now I've landed up in Shepperton I've got elephants and prayer wheels cluttering up the window ledges, and the tea-tray is Nepalese brass. One could make a comment about human nature but have a slice of Battenberg instead.

Anish Thank you.

Mrs Swan I got it specially, an artistic sort of cake, I always think. What kind of paintings are they, these paintings that are not like your father's? Describe your latest. Like the cake?

Anish (*eating*) Delicious. Thank you.

Mrs Swan No, are they like the cake?

Anish Oh. No. They are all. . . like each other really. I can't *describe* them.

Mrs Swan Indescribable, then.

Anish completes the drawing, and passes it to her.

Anish There.

Mrs Swan (*pleasantly surprised*) Ah. That's a proper drawing. You could do portraits if you wanted. (*She gives the drawing back to Anish.*)

Anish Thank you.

Mrs Swan Now, what are we going to tell Eldon about your father?

Anish Eldon?

Mrs Swan E. Cooper Pike. He calls me Eleanor so I have to call him Eldon, so as not to seem toffee-nosed. If he starts calling me Nell I suppose I'll have to call him El. He's waiting for me to die so he can get on with Flora's biography which he thinks I don't know he's writing.

Anish (*referring to his copy of the book*) Oh yes. 'Edited by E. Cooper Pike.'

Mrs Swan That means he does the footnotes.

Anish Oh yes, I see.

Mrs Swan Far too much of a good thing, in my opinion, the footnotes; to be constantly interrupted by someone telling you things you already know or don't need to know at that moment. There are pages where Flora can hardly get a word in sideways. Mr Pike teaches Flora Crewe. It makes her sound like a subject, doesn't it, like biology. Or in her case, botany. Flora is widely taught in America. I have been written to, even visited, and on one occasion telephoned, by young women doing Flora Crewe. Almost always young women. And from all over, lots from America. Flora has become quite a heroine. Which she always was to me. I was only three when Mother died, so it was Flora who . . . Oh dear, I'm going to need a hanky.

Anish Oh – I say! I'm sorry –

Mrs Swan Found it. (*She blows her nose.*) It makes me so cross that she missed it all, the *Collected Poems,* and now the *Letters,* with her name all over the place and students and professors so *interested* and so sweet about her poetry. Nobody gave tuppence about her while she was alive except to get her knickers off. How is your tea?

Das arrives at the guesthouse and props his bicycle against the verandah. Flora, working, barely acknowledges him.

Anish It's very nice. Mrs Swan . . . it says, 'The portrait of Flora Crewe is reproduced by permission of Mrs Eleanor Swan.' Does that mean you have it?

Mrs Swan Yes.

Anish Here? In your house?

Mrs Swan Would you like to see it?

Anish Very much! I half expected to see it hanging the moment I arrived.

Mrs Swan That's because you're a painter. Come on, I'll show you. Yes, I can't get the tea here to taste as it should. I expect it's the water. A reservoir near Staines won't have the makings of a good cup of tea compared to the water we got in the Hills. It came straight off the Himalayas.

They leave. Flora and Das are at work.

Flora (*recorded*)
'– or think if you prefer, of a corpse in a ditch
I have been left for dead before –
heat crawls in my hair like insects –'

Oh, fiddlesticks! May we stop for a moment. (*She gets up.*) I'm sticking to myself.

Das Of course! Forgive me!

Flora You mustn't take responsibility for the climate too, Mr Das.

Das No, I . . .

Flora No, I'm sorry. I'm bad tempered. Should we have some tea? I wouldn't mind something to eat too. (*calls out*) Nazrul! (*to Das*) There's a jar of duck pâté in the refrigerator . . .

Nazrul appears from round the corner of the verandah.

Oh, Nazrul . . . char and . . .

Nazrul (*in Hindi*) Yes, madam, I will bring tea immediately . . .

Flora . . . bread . . . and in the icebox, no, don't go, listen to me –

Das Would you allow me, please?

Das and Nazrul speak in Hindi. Das orders bread and butter and the duck pâté from the fridge.

Flora (*over the conversation*) A jar with a picture of a *duck* . . .

But Nazrul has dramatic and tragic disclosures to make. Thieves have stolen the pâté. Das berates him. Nazrul leaves the way he came.

What was all that?

Das He will bring tea, and bread and butter and cake. The pâté has been taken by robbers.

Flora What?!

Das (*gravely*) Just so, I'm afraid.

Flora But the refrigerator is padlocked – Mr Coomaraswami pointed it out to me particularly.

Das Where do you keep the key?

Flora Nazrul keeps it, of course.

Das Ah well . . . the whole thing is a great mystery.

Flora splutters into laughter and Das joins in.

Flora But surely, isn't it against his religion?

Das Oh, certainly. I should say so. Not that I'm saying Nazrul stole the pâté, but stealing would be against his religion, undoubtedly.

Flora I don't mean stealing, I mean the pork.

Das But I thought you said it was duck.

Flora One must read the small print, Mr Das. 'Duck pâté' in large letters, 'with pork' in small letters. It's normal commercial practice.

Das Yes, I see.

Flora We must hope he only got the duck part . . .

Das That is your true nature speaking, Miss Crewe!

Flora . . . though of course, if they use one pig for every duck, he'll be lucky to have got any duck at all.

Das The truth will never be known, only to God who is merciful.

Flora Yes. Which God do you mean?

Das Yours if you wish, by all means.

Flora Now, Mr Das, there is such a thing as being too polite. Yours was here first.

Das Oh, but we Hindus can afford to be generous; we have gods to spare, one for every occasion. And Krishna said, 'Whichever god a man worships, it is I who answer the prayer.'

Flora I wasn't sure whether Krishna was a god or a person.

Das Oh, he was most certainly a god, one of the ten incarnations of Vishnu, and a favourite subject of the old Rajasthani painters. He had a great love affair, you see, with a married lady, Radha, who was the most beautiful of the herdswomen. Radha fell passionately in love with Krishna and she would often escape from her husband to meet him in secret.

Flora I think that's what confused me. Come and sit down, Mr Das.

Das I will . . . but I will start on my tree while we wait.

Flora Put a monkey in it.

Das Yes. Like Hanuman, he is my favourite in the Ramayana. The monkey god.

Flora Mr Coomaraswami showed me the temples.

Das Did you find them interesting?

Flora I liked some of the sculptures, the way the women are often smiling to themselves. Yes, that was quite revealing, I thought.

Das About Indian women?

Flora No, about Indian sculptors. And breasts like melons, and baby-bearing hips. You must think me ill-favoured.

Das No. My wife was slightly built.

Flora Oh . . .

Nazrul enters with the tea-tray.

Thank you, Nazrul . . . And two kinds of cake!

Nazrul replies smilingly and leaves.

Das But your face today . . . I think your work was troublesome.

Flora Yes.

Das Is it the rhyming that is difficult?

Flora No.

Das The metre?

Flora No. The . . . emotion won't harmonize. I'm afraid I'm not much good at talking about it.

Das I'm sorry.

Flora That's why I don't keep nipping round to your side of the easel. If I don't look there's nothing to say. I think that that's better.

Das Yes. It is better to wait. My painting has no *rasa* today.

Flora What is *rasa?*

Das *Rasa* is juice. Its taste. Its essence. A painting must have its *rasa* which is not *in* the painting exactly. *Rasa* is what you must feel when you see a painting, or hear music; it is the emotion which the artist must arouse in you.

Flora And poetry? Does a poem have *rasa*?

Das Oh yes! Poetry is a sentence whose soul is *rasa*. That is a famous dictum of Vishvanata, a great teacher of poetry, six hundred years ago.

Flora *Rasa* . . . yes. My poem has no *rasa*.

Das Or perhaps it has two *rasa* which are in conflict.

Flora Oh . . .

Das There are nine *rasa*, each one a different colour. I should say mood. But each mood has its colour – white for laughter and fun, red for anger, pale yellow for tranquillity . . .

Flora (*interrupting*) Oh . . . is there one for grey?

Das Grey is for sorrow.

Flora Sorrow? I see.

Das Each one has its own name and its own god, too.

Flora And some don't get on, is that it?

Das Yes. That is it. Some do and some don't. If you arouse emotions which are in opposition to each other the *rasa* will not . . . harmonize, you said.

Flora Yes.

Das Your poem is about heat.

Flora Yes.

Das But its *rasa is* perhaps anger?

Flora Sex.

Das (*unhesitatingly*) The *rasa* of erotic love is called
Shringara. Its god is Vishnu, and its colour is *shyama*,
which is blue-black. Vishvanata in his book on poetics
tells us: Shringara requires, naturally, a lover and his
loved one, who may be a courtesan if she is sincerely
enamoured, and it is aroused by, for example, the moon,
the scent of sandalwood, or being in an empty house.
Shringara goes harmoniously with all other *rasa* and
their complementary emotions, with the exception of
fear, cruelty, disgust and sloth.

Flora I see. Thank you. Empty house is very good.
Mr Das, you sounded just like somebody else. Yourself,
I expect. I knew you could. The other one reminded me
of Dr Aziz in Forster's novel. Have you read it? I kept
wanting to kick him.

Das (*offended*) Oh . . .

Flora For not knowing his worth.

Das Then perhaps you didn't finish it.

Flora Yes, perhaps. Does he improve?

Das He alters.

Flora What is your opinion of *A Passage to India*?

Das Was that the delicate question you considered to
ask me?

Flora (*laughs happily*) Oh, Mr Das!

> *Pike enters, dressed for India. He is staying at the best*
> *hotel in Jummapur, and looks it. He carries a smart*
> *shoulder-bag. He stares around him in a vaguely*
> *disappointed way.*
>   *Modern street sounds, distinctly Indian, accompany*
> *Pike's entrance.*

Flora is at her table, writing. Das is at the easel, painting.

Flora (*writing*) 'Jummapur, Saturday April 5th. Darling Nell. I'm having my portrait painted, I mean the painter is at it as I write, so if you see a picture of me in my cornflower dress, you'll know I was writing *this* – some of the time anyway. He thinks I'm writing a poem. Posing as a poet, you see, just as the Enemy once said of me in his rotten rag.'

Pike 'The Enemy' was J. C. Squire (1884–1958), poet, critic, literary editor of the *New Statesman* and editor of the *London Mercury*. An anonymous editorial in the *London Mercury* (April 1920) complained about, 'an outbreak of versifying flappers who should stop posing as poets and confine themselves to posing as railway stations'. The magazine was sued by the poets Elizabeth Paddington (1901–1980) and Meredith Euston (1899–1929), both cases being settled out of court. FC poured a pint of beer over Squire's head in the Fitzroy Tavern in January 1921.

Dilip enters with a bottle of cola.

Dilip Dr Pike . . .

Pike Eldon, please.

Dilip . . . will you have a cola, Eldon?

Pike Oh, thanks. What kind of . . . (*His suspicion has been aroused.*) *Thumbs Up* Cola? You know, I think maybe I won't.

Dilip (*misunderstanding*) I got two – really – I drank mine while I was talking to the shopkeeper. It is as I thought. The dak bungalow was exactly here, in the courtyard. Of course, the flats did not exist. I'm afraid nothing you can see goes back to before the war.

Pike No . . . That's a shame.

Dilip Except the tree, perhaps.

Pike (*brightening*) Oh, yes. The tree. That's right. She mentions a tree.

Dilip The old man remembers the bungalow very well. It was destroyed. A casualty of Partition.

Pike Taken apart?

Dilip Burned, in the riots. There were many people killed here in '47.

Pike *Partition*. Oh, yes . . . terrible . . . Would this be the same tree?

Dilip It looks old.

Pike Would you take my picture? . . . on the spot.

Dilip Yes, certainly.

Pike takes a camera from his bag and gives it to Dilip.

Pike It's self-focusing . . . just press the . . . (*He positions himself.*) I could take out an ad . . . in the newspaper. Someone may remember an artist . . . Go back a bit . . . show more of the . . .

Dilip No, the 35 is fine. Do you mind if I take it off auto? . . . stop it down for the background . . . F8 . . .

Pike Oh . . . sure.

Dilip Yes, why not? – put an advert in the paper. Ready? (*He takes the photo.*)

Pike Thank you. I'll take one of you.

Dilip All right. (*adjusting the camera*) On 50. More of Dilip.

They change places, Pike taking the camera.

After all . . . fifty-six years . . . he could be still alive . . . he'd only have to be . . .

Pike Ninety.

Dilip Yes, probably not. Is this all right?

Pike The other thing is . . . What do I do?

Dilip Just point it.

Pike The other thing is, Dilip . . . Here we go. (*He takes the picture.*)

Dilip Thank you.

Pike The other thing is, there was the watercolour. A lost picture. That's the way it reads to *me*. Don't you think so?

Dilip (*laughs*) Oh yes, I think that's the way it reads to you, Eldon, but she was a poet . . . and you're a biographer! A lost picture would be just the ticket.

Pike How about offering a reward?

Dilip A reward?

Pike For information leading to. If the local paper did a story about it . . . I bet that would get results.

Dilip Undoubtedly. The Jummapur Palace Hotel will be stormed by a mob waving authentic watercolour portraits of English ladies in every stage of undress. But the newspaper is a good idea, if the files go back to 1930 . . . A portrait painter must advertise.

Pike This is so good of you, Dilip! – I should get a shot from above, with the tree . . . Could one get on the roof, do you think?

Dilip I'm sure. Let me go and see. (*He leaves.*)

Flora 'Yours arrived overland, and thank you for it, darling, but you mustn't expect me to be Intelligence from Abroad. You obviously know much more about the Salt March than I do.'

Pike Gandhi's 'March to the Sea' to protest the Salt Tax began at Ahmedabad on March 12th. He reached the sea on the day this letter was written.

Flora 'Nobody has mentioned it to me. If I remember I'll ask at the Club tonight – I've had a visit from a clean young Englishman who asked me to dinner. It was a bit of an afterthought really. I think I made a gaffe by not announcing myself to the Resident, and the young man, he was on a horse, was sent to look me over. I think he ticked me off but he was so nice it was hard to tell. I've a feeling I'm going to have to stop in a minute. My artist is frowning at me and then at the canvas as if one of us is misbehaving. He is charming and eager and reminds me of Charlie Chaplin, not the idiotic one in the films, the real one who was at Sir Herbert's lunch party.'

Pike It was Sir Herbert Beerbohm Tree who, soon after the Crewe family arrived in London from Derbyshire, gave FC her first employment, fleetingly as a cockney bystander in the original production of *Pygmalion*, and, after objections from Mrs Patrick Campbell, more permanently 'in the office'. It was this connection which brought FC into the orbit of Tree's daughter Iris and her friend Nancy Cunard, and thence to the Sitwells, and arguably to the writing of poetry.

Flora 'My poem, the one I'm not writing, is about sitting still and being hot. It got defeated by its subject matter, and I should be gone to the hills, I'm only waiting for my artist to finish. The Hot Weather, they tell me, is about to start, but I can't imagine anything hotter than this, and it will be followed by the Wet Season, though

I already feel as though I'm sitting in a puddle. I don't think this is what Dr Guppy meant by a warm climate.'

Pike Dr Alfred Guppy had been the Crewe family doctor since the move from Derbyshire to London in 1913. His notes on FC's illness, with reference to pulmonary congestion, are first dated 1926.

Flora Oh, shut up!

> *It is as though she has turned on Pike. Simultaneously, Das, losing his temper, is shouting in Hindi, 'Get off! Get off!' But they are both shouting at a couple of unseen pi-dogs who have been heard yapping and barking and are now fighting under the verandah. In the middle of this, Dilip calls out for Eldon. The fuss resolves itself. Pike follows Dilip off. The dogs go whining into oblivion.*

Das Oh – fiddlesticks!

Flora I'm sorry – is it my fault?

Das No – how can it be?

Flora Is that so silly?

Das No . . . forgive me! Oh dear, Miss Crewe! Yesterday I felt . . . a communion and today –

Flora Oh! . . . It *is* my fault! Yesterday I was writing a poem, and today I have been writing a letter to my sister. That's what it is.

Das A letter?

Flora I am not the same sitter. How thoughtless of me.

Das Yes. Yes.

Flora Are you angry?

Das I don't know. Can we stop now? I would like a cigarette. Would you care for a cigarette? They are Goldflake.

Flora No. But I'd like you to smoke.

Das Thank you.

Mrs Swan, attended by Anish, opens a cupboard.

Mrs Swan Pride of place!

Anish In here?

Mrs Swan Yes, that must seem rather unkind but Flora didn't care to be on show.

Anish That's all right.

The canvas is inside a cardboard tube.

Mrs Swan This is how it came back from the publishers. I tuck things away. You hold her and I'll pull the tube.

Anish Thank you.

Mrs Swan Well, there she is.

Anish Oh . . .!

Mrs Swan Yes, a bit much, isn't it?

Anish Oh . . . it's so vibrant.

Mrs Swan Vibrant. Yes . . . oh, *you're* not going to blub too, are you?

Anish (*weeping*) I'm sorry.

Mrs Swan Don't worry. Borrow my hanky . . .

He takes her handkerchief.

Anish Please excuse me . . .

Mrs Swan It just goes to show, you need an eye. And your father, after all, was, like you, an Indian painter.

Anish I'm sorry I . . . you know.

Mrs Swan No, I should not have been disparaging. I'm sorry. Let me see. (*She takes the painting from Anish and looks at it.*) Yes, book jackets and biscuit tins are all very well, but obviously there's something that stays being in the painting after all.

Anish Yes. Even unfinished.

Mrs Swan Unfinished?

Anish It wasn't clear from the book, the way they cropped the painting. You see where my father has only indicated the tree, and the monkey . . . He would have gone back to complete the background only when he considered the figure finished. Believe me. I wondered why he hadn't signed it. Now I know. My father abandoned this portrait.

Mrs Swan Why?

Anish He began another one.

Mrs Swan How do you know, Mr Das?

Anish Because I have it. (*He opens his briefcase and withdraws the painting which is hardly larger than the page of a book, protected by stiff boards. He shows her the painting which is described in the text.*)

Mrs Swan Oh heavens! Oh . . . yes . . . *of course.* How like Flora.

Anish More than a good likeness, Mrs Swan.

Mrs Swan No . . . I mean, *how like Flora*! (*She continues to look at the painting.*)

Das You were writing to your sister? She is in England, of course.

Flora Yes, in London. Her name is Eleanor. She is much younger than me.

Das And also beautiful like you?

Flora Routine gallantry is disappointing from you.

Das (*surprised*) Oh, it was not.

Flora Then, thank you.

Das Where does your sister live?

Flora That's almost the first thing you asked *me*. Would it mean anything to you?

> *Das is loosening up again, regaining his normal good nature.*

Das Oh, I have the whole of London spread out in my imagination. Challenge me, you will see!

Flora All right, she lives in Holborn.

Das (*pause*) Oh. Which part of London is that?

Flora Well, it's – oh dear – between the Gray's Inn Road and –

Das Holl-born!

Flora Yes. Holborn.

Das But of course I know Holl-born! Charles Dickens lived in Doughty Street.

Flora Yes. Eleanor lives in Doughty Street.

Das But, Miss Crewe, *Oliver Twist* was written in that very street!

Flora Well, that's where Eleanor lives, over her work. She is the assistant to the editor of a weekly, *The Flag*.

Das *The Flag*!?

Flora You surely have never read that too?

Das No, but I have met the editor of *The Flag* –

Flora (*realizing*) Yes – of course you have! That is how I came to be here. Mr Chamberlain gave me letters of introduction.

Das His lecture in Jummapur caused the Theosophical Society to be suspended for one year.

Flora I'm sorry. But it's not for me to apologize for the Raj.

Das Oh, it was not the Raj but the Rajah! His Highness is not a socialist! Do you agree with Mr Chamberlain's theory of Empire? I was not persuaded. Of course I am not an economist.

Flora That has never deterred Mr Chamberlain.

Das It is not my impression that England's imperial adventure is simply to buy time against revolution at home.

Flora I try to keep an open mind. Political theories are often, and perhaps entirely, a function of temperament. Eleanor and Mr Chamberlain are well suited.

Das Your sister shares Mr Chamberlain's opinions?

Flora Naturally.

Das Being his assistant, you mean.

Flora His mistress.

Das Oh.

Flora You should have been a barrister, Mr Das.

Das I am justly rebuked!

Flora It was not a rebuke. An unintended slight, perhaps.

Das I am very sorry about your sister. It must be a great sadness for you.

Flora I am very happy for her.

Das But she will never be married now! Unless Mr Chamberlain marries her.

Flora He is already married, otherwise he might.

Das Oh my goodness. How different things are. Here, you see, your sister would have been cast out – for bringing shame on her father's house.

Flora snorts.

Yes – perhaps we are not so enlightened as you.

Flora Yes, perhaps. Well, you have had your cigarette. Are we going to continue?

Das No, not today.

Flora I'll go back to my poem.

Das There is no need.

Flora Well, I'll copy out my poem for my sister. I do that for safe keeping, you see. I'm sending her the drawing you did of me at the lecture.

Das (*pause*) I have an appointment I had forgotten.

Flora Oh.

Das Actually you mustn't feel obliged . . . (*He begins gathering together his paraphernalia, apparently in a hurry now.*)

Flora What have I done?

Das Done? What should you have done?

Flora Stop it. Please. Stop being Indian.

Das And you stop being English! (*Pause.*) You have looked at the portrait, Miss Crewe?

Flora Oh, I see. Yes, yes . . . I did look.

Das Yes.

Flora I had a peep. Why not? You wanted me to.

Das Yes, why not? You looked at the painting and you decided to spend the time writing letters. Why not?

Flora I'm sorry.

Das You still have said nothing about the painting.

Flora I know.

Das I cannot continue today.

Flora I understand. Will we try again tomorrow?

Das Tomorrow is Sunday.

Flora The next day.

Das Perhaps I cannot continue at all.

Flora Oh. And all because I said nothing. Are you at the mercy of every breeze that blows? Are you an artist at all?

Das Perhaps not! A mere sketcher – a hack painter who should be working in the bazaar! (*He snatches up the 'pencil sketch' from under Flora's hand.*)

Flora (*realizing his intention*) Stop it!

Das tears the paper in half.

Das Or in chalks on the ghat!

Flora Stop!

But Das tears the paper again, and again and again, until it is in small pieces.

I'm ashamed of you!

Das Excuse me, please! I wish to leave. I will take the canvas –

Flora You will not!

It becomes a physical tussle. A struggle. She begins to gasp.

Das You need not see it again!

Flora You will not take anything! We will continue!

Das I do not want to continue, Miss Crewe. Please let go!

Flora *I won't* let you give up!

Das Let go, damn you, someone will see us!

Flora – and stop crying! You're not a baby!

Das (*fighting her*) I will cry if I wish!

Flora Cry, then, but you will finish what you started! How else will you ever . . . Oh! (*And suddenly she is helpless, gasping for breath.*)

Das Oh . . . oh, Miss Crewe – oh my God – let me help you. I'm sorry. Please. Here, sit down –

She has had an attack of breathlessness. He helps her to a chair. Flora speaks with difficulty.

Flora Really, I'm all right. (*Pause. She takes careful breaths.*) There.

Das What happened?

Flora I'm not allowed to wrestle with people. It's a considerable nuisance. My lungs are bad, you see.

Das Let me move the cushion.

Flora It's all right. I'm back now. Panic over. I'm here for my health, you see. Well, not *here* . . . I'll stay longer in the Hills.

Das Yes, that will be better. You must go high.

Flora Yes. In a day or two.

Das What is the matter with you?

Flora Oh, sloshing about inside. Can't breathe under water. I'm sorry if I frightened you.

Das You did frighten me. Would you allow me to remain a little while?

Flora Yes. I would like you to. I'm soaking.

Das You must change your clothes.

Flora Yes. I'll go in now. I've got a shiver. Pull me up. Thank you. Ugh. I need to be rubbed down like a horse.

Das Perhaps some tea . . . I'll go to the kitchen and tell –

Flora Yes. Would you? I'll have a shower and get into my Wendy house.

Das Your . . . ?

Flora My big towel is on the kitchen verandah – would you ask Nazrul to put it in the bedroom?

> *Das runs towards the kitchen verandah, shouting for Nazrul.*
>   *Flora goes into the interior, into the bedroom, undressing as she goes, dropping the blue dress on the floor, and enters the bathroom in her underwear.*

Das returns, hurrying, with a white towel. He enters the interior cautiously, calling 'Miss Crewe . . .' He enters the bedroom and finds it empty. From the bathroom there is the sound of the water pipes thumping, but no sound of water.

Flora (*offstage*) Oh, damn, come on!

Das Miss Crewe . . .

The thumping in the pipes continues. Das approaches the bathroom door.

(*Louder*) Miss Crewe! I'm sorry, there's no –

Flora (*offstage, shouts*) There's no water!

The thumping noise continues.

Das Miss Crewe! I'm sorry, the electricity –

The thumping noise suddenly stops.

(*In mid-shout*) The electric pump –

Flora (*entering naked*) I have to lie down.

Das Oh! (*Thrusting the towel at her.*) Oh, I'm so sorry! (*Relieved of the towel, Das is frozen with horror.*)

Flora I'm sorry, Mr Das, but really I feel too peculiar to mind at the moment.

Das (*turning to leave hurriedly*) Please forgive me!

Flora No, please, there's water in the jug on the wash-stand. (*She stands shivering, hugging the towel.*) Do be quick.

Das (*getting the water*) It's the electricity for the pump.

Flora Is there any water?

Das Yes, it's full . . . Here – (*He gives her the jug, and turns away.*

Flora Thank you. No, you do it. Over my head, and my back, please.

Das pours the water over her, carefully.

Oh, heaven . . . Oh, thank you . . . I'm terribly sorry about this. Oh, that's good. Tip the last bit on the towel.

Das There . . .

She wipes her face with the wet corner of the towel . . .

Flora I feel as weak as a kitten.

Das I'm afraid that's all.

Flora Thank you. (*She wraps the towel around herself.*) Could you do the net for me?

Das lifts one side of the mosquito net and Flora climbs onto the bed.

I'll be all right now.

Das (*misunderstanding; leaving*) Yes, of course.

Flora Mr Das, I think there's soda water in the refrigerator. Would you . . .?

Das Oh yes. But is it locked? I cannot find Nazrul.

Flora Oh . . . I'm already hot again. And no electricity for the fan. It's too late for modesty (*She discards the towel and gets under the sheet.*) Anyway, I'm your model.

Das I will fetch soda water from the shop.

Flora That was the thing I was going to ask you.

Das When?

Flora The delicate question . . . whether you would prefer to paint me nude.

Das Oh.

Flora I preferred it. I had more what-do-you-call it.

Das *Rasa.*

Flora (*laughs quietly*) Yes, *rasa.*

Das leaves the bedroom and goes along the verandah towards the servants' quarters and disappears round the corner. Nazrul returns to the dak bungalow, with shopping, the worse for wear, disappearing towards the kitchen area where Das starts shouting at him and Nazrul is heard protesting. Das returns to view with a bottle of soda water. He speaks first from outside the bedroom.

Das Nazrul has returned, most fortunately. I was able to unlock the refrigerator. I have soda water.

Flora Thank you, Mr Das!

Das enters the bedroom.

Das (*approaching the bed*) Should I pour the water for you?

On the little table by the bed, outside the mosquito net, there is a glass with a beaded lace cover. Das pours the water.

Nazrul was delayed at the shops by a riot, he says. The police charged the mob with lathis, he could have easily been killed, but by heroism and inspired by his loyalty to the memsahib he managed to return only an hour late with all the food you gave him money for except two chickens which were torn from his grasp.

Flora Oh dear . . . you thanked him, I hope.

Das I struck him, of course. You should fine him for the chickens.

Flora lifts the net sufficiently to take the glass from Das, who then steps back rather further than necessary.

Flora (*drinking*) Oh, that's nice. It's still cold. Perhaps there really was a riot.

Das Oh yes. Very probably. I have sent Nazrul to fetch the dhobi – you must have fresh linen for the bed. Nazrul will bring water but you must not drink it.

Flora Thank you.

The punkah begins to flap quite slowly, a regular beat.

Das I'm sure the electricity will return soon and the fan will be working.

Flora What's that? Oh, the punkah!

Das I have found a boy to be punkah-wallah.

Flora Yes, it makes a draught. Thank you. A *little* boy?

Das Don't worry about him. I've told him the memsahib is sick.

Flora The memsahib. Oh dear.

Das Yes, you are memsahib. Are you all right now, Miss Crewe?

Flora Oh yes. I'm only shamming now.

Das May I return later to make certain?

Flora Are you leaving now? Yes, I've made you late.

Das No, not at all. There is no one waiting for me. But the servant will return and . . . we Indians are frightful gossips, you see.

Flora Oh.

Das It is for yourself, not me.

Flora I don't believe you, Mr Das, not entirely.

Das To tell you the truth, this is the first time I have been alone in a room with an Englishwoman.

Flora Oh. Well, you certainly started at the deep end.

Das We need not refer to it again. It was a calamity.

Flora (*amused*) A calamity! That's not spoken like an artist.

Das Then perhaps I am not an artist, as you said.

Flora I did not. All I did was hold my tongue and you had a tantrum. What would you have done in the rough and tumble of literary life in London? I expect you would have hanged yourself by now. When *Nymph in Her Orisons* came out one of the reviewers called it *Nymph In Her Mania,* as if my poems which I had found so hard to write were a kind of dalliance, no more than that. I met my critic somewhere a few months later and poured his drink over his head and went home and wrote a poem. So that was all right. But he'd taken weeks away from me and I mind that now.

Das Oh! – you're not dying are you?!

Flora I expect so, but I intend to take years and years about it. You'll be dead too, one day, so let me be a lesson to you. Learn to take no notice. I said nothing about your painting, if you want to know, because I thought you'd be an *Indian* artist.

Das An Indian artist?

Flora Yes. You *are* an Indian artist, aren't you? Stick up for yourself. Why do you like everything English?

Das I do not like everything English.

Flora Yes, you do. You're enthralled. Chelsea, Blooms-bury, Oliver Twist, Goldflake cigarettes, Winsor and Newton . . . even painting in oils, that's not Indian. You're trying to paint me from my point of view instead of yours – what you *think* is my point of view. You *deserve* the bloody Empire!

Das (*sharply*) May I sit down please?

Flora Yes, do. Flora is herself again.

Das I will move the chair near the door.

Flora You can move the chair onto the verandah if you like, so the servants won't –

Das I would like to smoke, that is what I meant.

Flora Oh. I'm sorry. Thank you. In that case, can you see me through the net from over there?

Das Barely.

Flora Is that no or yes? (*She raises the sheet off her body and flaps it like a sail and lets it settle again.*) Oof! – that's better! That's what I love about my little house – you can see out better than you can see in.

Das (*passionately*) But you are looking at such a house! The bloody Empire finished off Indian painting! (*Pause.*) Excuse me.

Flora No, that's better.

Das Perhaps your sister is right. And Mr Chamberlain. Perhaps we have been robbed. Yes; when the books are balanced. The women here wear saris made in Lancashire. The cotton is Indian but we cannot compete in the weaving. Mr Chamberlain explained it all to us in simple

Marxist language. Actually, he caused some offence. He didn't realise we had Marxists of our own, many of them in the Jummapur Theosophical Society.

Flora Mr Coomaraswami . . .?

Das No, not Mr Coomaraswami. *His* criticism is that you haven't exploited India *enough*. 'Where are the cotton mills? The steel mills? No investment, no planning. The Empire has failed us!' That is Mr Coomaraswami. Well, the Empire will one day be gone like the Mughal Empire before it, and only their monuments remains – the visions of Shah Jahan! – of Sir Edwin Lutyens!

Flora 'Look on my works, ye mighty, and despair!'

Das (*delighted*) Oh yes! Finally like the empire of Ozymandias! Entirely forgotten except in a poem by an English poet. You see how privileged we are, Miss Crewe. Only in art can empires cheat oblivion, because only the artist can say, 'Look on my works, ye mighty, and despair!' There are Mughal paintings in London, in the Victoria and Albert Museum.

Flora I just didn't like you thinking English was better because it was English. Can't you paint me without thinking of Rossetti or Millais? Especially without thinking of Holman Hunt. Did you consider my question?

Das When you stood . . . with the pitcher of water, you were an Alma-Tadema.

Flora Well, I don't want to be painted like that either – that's C. B. Cochran, if only he dared.

Das I don't understand why you are angry with me.

Flora You were painting me as a gift, to please me.

Das Yes. Yes, it was a gift for you.

Flora If you don't start learning to *take* you'll never be shot of us. *Who whom.* Nothing else counts. Mr Chamberlain is bosh. Mr Coomaraswami is bosh. It's your country, and we've got it. Everything else is bosh. When I was Modi's model I might as well have *been* a table. When he was done, he got rid of me. There was no question who whom. You'd never change his colour on a map. But please light your Goldflake.

Pause. Das lights his cigarette with a match.

Das I like the Pre-Raphaelites because they tell stories. That is my tradition, too. I am Rajasthani. Our art is narrative art, stories from the legends and romances. The English painters had the Bible and Shakespeare, King Arthur . . . We had the Bhagavata Purana, and the Rasikpriya which was written exactly when Shakespeare had his first play. And long before Chaucer we had the Chaurapanchasika, from Kashmir, which is poems of love written by the poet of the court on his way to his execution for falling in love with the king's daughter, and the king liked the poems so very much he pardoned the poet and allowed the lovers to marry.

Flora Oh . . .

Das But the favourite book of the Rajput painters was the Gita Govinda which tells the story of Krishna and Radha the most beautiful of the herdswomen.

The ceiling fan starts working.

Flora The electricity is on.

Das You will be a little cooler now.

Flora Yes. I might have a sleep.

Das That would be good.

Flora Mr Durance has invited me to dinner at the Club.

Das Will you be well enough?

Flora I am well now.

Das That is good. Goodbye, then.

Flora Were Krishna and Radha punished in the story?

Das What for?

Flora I should have come here years ago. The punkah boy can stop now. Will you give him a rupee? I'll return it tomorrow.

Das I will give him an anna. A rupee would upset the market.

Das leaves.
Flora remains in the bed.

Act Two

The Jummapur Club after sundown. Gramophone music. Three couples are dancing: Flora and Durance, the Resident and the Englishwoman, and a third couple, an Englishman and English Lady.

Somewhat removed from the dance floor is a verandah, which is spacious enough not only for the necessary furniture but also for two gymnasium horses, fitted out with stirrups and reins. These 'horses' are used for practising polo swings and there are indeed a couple of polo sticks, a couple of topees and odd bits of gear lying in the corner.

Pike is sitting alone on the verandah. He is tieless, wearing a Lacoste-type short-sleeved sports shirt.

Englishwoman Are you writing a poem about India, Flora?

Flora Trying to!

Englishman Kipling – there's a poet! 'Though I've belted you and flayed you, by the living Gawd that made you, you're a better man than I am Gunga Din!'

Resident The only poet I *know* is Alfred Housman. I expect you've come across him.

Flora (*pleased*) Oh yes, indeed I have!

Resident A dry old stick, isn't he?

Flora Oh – come *across him* –

Resident He hauled me though 'Ars Amatoria' when I was up at Trinity.

431

Flora 'The Art of Love'?

Resident When it comes to love, he said, you're either an Ovid man or a Virgil man – *omnia vincit amor* – that's Virgil – 'Love sweeps all before it, and we give way to love' – *et nos cedamus amori*. Housman was an Ovid man – *et mihi cedet amor* – 'Love gives way to me'.

Flora I'm a Virgil man.

Resident Are you? Well, it widens one's circle of acquaintance.

Englishwoman Will you be here for the Queen's Ball, Flora?

Flora The . . .?

Englishwoman It comes off next month, Queen Victoria's birthday, and there's the gymkhana!

Flora Oh . . . I can't, I'm afraid. I'll be going up the country soon; is that the expression?

Resident Of course, you're here on doctor's orders, I believe.

Flora Why . . . yes . . .

Resident If there's anything you need or want you tell David – right, David?

Durance Yes, sir.

Flora Thank you. He's already promised me a go in the Daimler.

Durance (*embarrassed*) Oh . . . Flora's keen on autos.

Englishwoman If you like cars, the Rajah has got about eighty-six of them. Collects them like stamps.

Another record begins to play.

Resident Well, don't let us stop you enjoying yourselves.

Durance Would you like to dance, Flora?

Flora I'm out of puff. Do you think there might be more air outside?

Durance On the verandah? Any air that's going. Should we take a peg with us?

. . . The Kipling fan, unseen, is singing:

Englishman
  'On the road to Mandalay
  Where the flyin' fishes play,
  An' the dawn come up like thunder outer China
    crost the Bay!'

The dancers disperse.
  Dilip, now smartly dressed in a jacket and tie, enters the verandah from within, in something of a hurry, carrying a jacket and a tie. The jacket is a faded beige gabardine with metal buttons, the skimpy jacket of a servant. On the breast, however, not instantly apparent, is a short strip of grimy campaign ribbons.

Dilip Here I am at last! – I am so sorry, my fault entirely for not thinking to mention – but, look – all will be well in a jiffy! – and I have terrifically good news.

Pike (*getting up*) Thank you, Dilip – what . . .?

Dilip (*helping him on with the jacket, which is too small for Pike*) Put it on and I will tell you. The jacket is a miserable garment, and our benefactor, I'm afraid, isn't quite your size.

Pike (*implausibly*) This is fine.

Dilip The tie, on the other hand, is tip-top, Jummapur Cricket Club. My friend Mr Balvinder Lal keeps a small stock on the premises. I spared you the blazer.

Pike obligingly starts putting on the striped tie.

Pike Do you mean you can't come in here without a jacket and tie, not ever?

Dilip Not in the dining-room after sunset. Oh these rules are absurd! But – Eldon – something wonderful has come of it. I have discovered the name of your painter!

Pike You *have*?

Dilip I have! His name was Nirad Das. Now we can *research*!

Pike But Dilip – but that's – how did you –?

Dilip It was God. If you had been wearing a jacket we would still be in the dark. But in borrowing the jacket, you see – oh, don't think that I discuss your affairs – it only seemed, shall I say, tactical to point out your distinction –

Pike Dilip, never mind about that –

Dilip Nor, for that matter, was the owner of the jacket indulging in impertinent curiosity about your private business, I assure you – actually, I know him well, he is an Old Soldier, formerly in the 6th Rajputana Rifles –

Pike Dilip – *please*!

Dilip He remembers the English lady who stayed in the dak house.

Pike He . . . he *remembers* . . .? But are you sure it was the same –?

Dilip Oh yes – he saw Miss Crewe having her portrait painted.

Pike (*when he recovers*) I have to talk to him.

Dilip Of course. After dinner we will –

434

Pike *After dinner?* He could *die* while I'm eating! Where is he? Ask him to have dinner with us.

Dilip Oh, that is not possible, you see.

Pike Why not?

Dilip He would not like that. Anyway, he does not have a jacket.

Pike We're getting off the point there –

Dilip Also, he is working now.

Pike What, he works here?

Dilip Exactly. He works here. He is in charge of supervising the cloakroom.

Pike Well, that's wonderful. Show me the way.

Dilip Eldon, please be guided by me. We will not rush at the fences in the lavatory. (*He points at the ribbons on Pike's breast.*) One of these is the ribbon for '39 to '45. This one, I think, is the Burma Star. He is without one leg. He has no sons. He has three daughters, two of them unmarried and to marry the third he sold his army pension and secured for himself a job which is cleaning toilets. Tomorrow there is time, there is reflection, there is . . . esteem . . . We can take a cup of tea together on the *maidan* and talk of old times. Believe me.

Pike Esteem. If he dies I'll kill you.

Dilip (*laughs*) He will not die. Let me go and see if our table's ready. Oh, how terrible –! with all this excitement I have not offered you an aperitif.

Pike What's his name, Dilip?

Dilip Mr Ram Sunil Singh, formerly Subadar, B Company, 6th Rajputana Rifles.

Pike He must be pretty ancient.

The gramophone music creeps back in. Flora, alone, comes out onto the verandah.

Dilip No, not at all. He was only a small boy, you see. One day the Memsahib was sick and Ram Sunil Singh worked the punkah to cool the air. Mr Nirad Das gave him two annas. One does not forget such things. (*Leaving now.*) I won't be a jiff. I must say, I could eat a horse! (*He leaves.*)

Flora 'My suitor – I suppose I must call him that, though I swear I've done nothing to encourage him – came to fetch me in an open Daimler which drew such a crowd, and off we went with people practically falling off the mud-guards, rather like leaving Bow Street – my God, how strange, that was ten years ago almost to the day.'

Pike In fact, nine. See 'The Woman Who Wrote What She Knew', E. C. Pike, *Modern Language Review,* Spring 1979.

Flora 'And everyone at the Club was very friendly, going out of their way to explain that although they didn't go in much for poetry, they had nothing against it, so that was all right, and dinner was soup, boiled fish, lamb cutlets, sherry trifle and sardines on toast, and it beats me how we're getting away with it, darling, I wouldn't trust some of them to run the *Hackney* Empire. Well, it's all going to end. That's official. I heard it from the horse's mouth –'

The Resident and the Englishwoman dance into view, in a cheerful mood.

Resident (*dancing*) (a) It is our moral duty to remain and (b) we will shirk it.

The Resident and the Englishwoman, dancing, spin out of view.

Flora 'I thought the Club would be like a commercial hotel in the hotter part of Reigate, but not at all – it was huge and white and pillared, just like the house of your first memory, perhaps – poor mama's nearly-house, which was ours for six months and then no more. I've never been back to Maybrook. Perhaps we should make a pilgrimage one day.'

Pike The Crewe family met Sir George Dewe-Lovett of Maybrook Hall, Lancashire, in August 1911 on the promenade at Llandudno.

Durance appears now, followed by a servant with two tumblers of whisky and a soda syphon on a salver.

Durance Here we are. Two burra-pegs.

Pike Catherine Crewe never returned to the house at Ashbourne.

Flora Lots of soda with mine, please.

Pike She eloped with Dewe-Lovett, a director of the White Star Shipping Line, and took her daughters to live at Maybrook.

Durance I'll do it.

The servant bows and leaves.

Pike Percival Crewe proved to be co-operative and divorce proceedings were under way when the girls returned to Ashbourne to stay with their father for the Easter holidays of 1912, while their mother joined Dewe-Lovett at Southampton.

Durance Say when. (*He deals with the drinks.*)

Flora When.

Pike The Titanic sailed on April 10th and FC never saw her mother or Maybrook again.

Flora Cheers.

Durance Cheers.

Dilip reappears with the menus.

Dilip Eldon! We can eat! I hope you will like my Club. The Jummapur Palace is a beautiful hotel, naturally, but *this* was the place in the old days when the palace was still the private residence of the rajah.

Pike (*following him out*) Where does he live now?

Dilip (*leaving*) In the penthouse! The fish curry is usually good, and on no account miss the bread-and-butter pudding!

Flora I'm sorry I packed up on you.

Durance This is nicer. So you've come to India for your health . . .

Flora Is that amusing?

Durance Well, it is rather. Have you seen the English cemetery?

Flora No.

Durance I must take you there.

Flora Oh.

Durance People here drop like flies – cholera, typhoid, malaria – men, women and children, here one day, gone the next. Are you sure the doctor said India?

Flora He didn't say India. He said a sea voyage and somewhere warm. I wanted to come to India.

438

Durance Good for you. Live dangerously. In a month, you can't imagine it, the heat. But you'll be gone to the hills, so you'll be all right. (*referring to the chair*) There we are. Long-sleever. Good for putting the feet up.

Flora Yes – long-sleever. Thank you. It's a nice Club.

Durance Yes, it's decent enough. There are not so many British here so we tend to mix more.

Flora With the Indians?

Durance No. In India proper, I mean *our* India, there'd be two or three Clubs. The box-wallahs would have their own and the government people would stick together, you know how it is – and the Army . . .

Flora Mr Das called you Captain.

Durance Yes, I'm Army. Seconded, of course. There are two of us juniors – political agents we call ourselves when we're on tour round the States. Jummapur is not one of your twenty-one-gun salute states, you see – my Chief is in charge of half a dozen native states.

Flora In charge?

Durance Oh yes.

Flora Is he Army? No – how silly –

Durance He's Indian Civil Service. The heaven-born. A Brahmin.

Flora Not seriously?

Durance Yes, seriously. Oh no, not a Brahmin seriously. But it might come to that with I-zation.

Flora . . .?

Durance Indianization. It's all over, you know. We have Indian officers in the Regiment now. My fellow Junior here is Indian, too, terribly nice chap – he's ICS, passed the exam, did his year at Cambridge, learned polo and knives-and-forks, and here he is, a pukkah sahib in the Indian Civil Service.

Flora Is he here?

Durance At the Club? No, he can't come into the Club.

Flora Oh.

Durance Cheers. Your health, Flora. I drink to your health, for which you came. I wish you were staying longer. I mean, only for my sake, Flora.

Flora Yes, but I'm not. So that's that. Don't look hangdog. You might like me less and less as you got to know me.

Durance Will you come riding in the morning?

Flora Seriously.

Durance Yes, seriously. Will you?

Flora In the Daimler?

Durance No. Say you will. We'll have to go inside in a minute if no one comes out.

Flora Why?

Durance There's nothing to do here except gossip, you see. They're all agog about you. One of the wives claims . . . Were you in the papers at home? Some scandal about one of your books, something like that?

Flora I can see why you're nervous, being trapped out here with me – let's go in –

Durance No – I'm sorry. Flora . . .? Pax? Please.

Flora All right, Pax.

He kisses her, uninvited, tentatively.

Durance Sealed with a kiss.

Flora No more. I mean it, David. Think of your career.

Durance Are you really a scandalous woman?

Flora I was for a while. I was up in court, you know. Bow Street.

Durance (*alarmed*) Oh, not really?

Flora Almost really. I was a witness. The publisher was in the dock, but it was my poems – my first book.

Durance Oh, I say.

Flora The case was dismissed on a technicality, and the policemen were awfully sweet, they got me away through the crowd in a van. My sister was asked to leave school. But that was mostly my own fault – the magistrate asked me why all the poems seemed to be about sex, and I said, 'Write what you know' – just showing off. I was practically a virgin, but it got me so thoroughly into the newspapers my name rings a bell even with the wife of a bloody jute planter or something in the middle of Rajputana, damn, damn, damn, no, let's go inside.

Durance Sit down, that's an order.

Durance, who has been standing, swings himself aboard one of the gymnasium horses.

Flora Oh dear, you're not going to be masterful, are you?

Durance (*laughs*) Do you like polo?

Flora Well, I don't play a lot.

Durance Measure your swing, you see . . . (*He swings the polo mallet.*) How's your whisky?

Flora Excellent. All the better for being forbidden. My God, where did that moon come from?

441

Durance Better. I love this country, don't you?

Flora What's going to happen to it? The riot in town this morning . . . does that happen often?

Durance Not here, no. The jails are filling up in British India.

Flora Well, then.

Durance It wasn't against us, it was Hindu and Moslem. Gandhi's salt march reached the sea today, did you hear?

Flora No. I want to know.

Durance Our Congress Hindus closed their shops in sympathy, and the Moslems wouldn't join in, that's all it was about.

Flora My cook came home minus two chickens.

Durance The Indian National Congress is all very well, but to the Moslems, Congress means Gandhi . . . a Hindu party in all but name.

Flora Will Gandhi be arrested?

Durance No, no. The salt tax is a lot of nonsense actually.

Flora Yes, it does seem hard in a country like this.

Durance Not that sort of nonsense. It works out at about four annas a year. Most Indians didn't even know there *was* a salt tax.

Flora Well, they do now.

Durance Yes. They do now.

Flora Let me have a go.

There is a solar topee on the second horse. She puts the topee on her head, and puts her foot in the stirrup.

Durance, laughing, helps Flora to heave herself on board the second horse.

Oh yes, nothing to it. Yes, I can see the point of it, what fun, polo and knives-and-forks. Is that all you need to govern India?

Durance (*laughs*) Oh yes. There's about twelve hundred ICS, that's four of our chaps for every million Indians.

Flora Why do the Indians let them?

Durance Why not? They're better at it.

Flora Are they?

Durance Ask them.

Flora Who?

Durance The natives. Ask them. We've pulled this country together. It's taken a couple of hundred years with a hiccup or two but the place now works.

Flora That's what you love, then? What you created?

Durance Oh no – it's India I love. I'll show you.

The horses whinny. Flora's horse lurches just enough to almost throw her. She squeals, quite happily.

Durance Knees together!

The scene becomes exterior. The actors remain astride the gym horses.
Sunrise.
Ground mist.
The horses whinny, the riders shift and rebalance themselves, Flora whooping with alarm, and birds are crying out, distancing rapidly.

Durance Sand grouse! Are you all right?

Flora They startled me.

Durance Time to trot – sun's up.

Flora Oops – David – I'll have to tell you – stop! It's my first time on a horse, you see.

Durance Yes, I could tell.

Flora (*miffed*) Could you? Even walking? I felt so proud when we were walking.

Durance No, no good, I'm afraid.

Flora Oh, damn you. I'm going to get off.

Durance No, no, just sit. He's a chair. Breathe in. India smells wonderful, doesn't it?

Flora Out here it does.

Durance You should smell chapattis cooking on a camel-dung fire out in the Thar Desert. Perfume!

Flora What were you doing out there?

Durance Cooking chapattis on a camel-dung fire. (*laughs*) I'll tell you where it all went wrong with us and India. It was the Suez Canal. It let the women in.

Flora Oh!

Durance Absolutely. When you had to sail round the Cape this was a man's country and we mucked in with the natives. The memsahibs put a stop to that. The memsahib won't muck in, won't even be alone in a room with an Indian.

Flora Oh . . .

Durance Don't point your toes out. May I ask you a personal question?

444

Flora No.

Durance All right.

Flora I wanted to ask *you* something. How did the Resident know I came to India for my health?

Durance It's his business to know. Shoulders back. Reins too slack.

Flora But I didn't tell anybody.

Durance Obviously you did.

Flora Only Mr Das.

Durance Oh well, there you are. Jolly friendly of you, of course, sharing a confidence, lemonade, all that, but they can't help themselves bragging about it.

Flora (*furious*) Rubbish!

Durance Well . . . I stand corrected.

Flora I'm sorry. I don't believe you, though.

Durance Righto.

Flora I'm sorry. Pax.

Durance Flora.

Flora No.

Durance Would you marry me?

Flora No.

Durance Would you think about it?

Flora No. Thank you.

Durance Love at first sight, you see. Forgive me.

Flora Oh, David.

Durance Knees together.

Flora 'Fraid so.

She laughs without malice but unrestrainedly.
The horses trot.

Mrs Swan and Anish are sitting in the garden with
gin-and-tonic, and with the watercolour painting.
The small painting has remained on the garden table.

Mrs Swan I was a shandy drinker until I went out.
G-and-T takes me right back to Rawalpindi. The bottles
used to say *Indian* tonic water. I was quite surprised to
discover when Eric got home leave that it was Indian
everywhere, and always had been. Quinine, you see.
Very good for staving off malaria, though interestingly
quite useless, it seemed, without the gin. Eric swore by it,
the gin part, he pointed out how it got dozens of our
friends through malaria until their livers gave out. Then
he had a stroke on the cricket field, silly goose, umpiring
without a hat. What happened to your father?

Anish I was in England when my father died. It was
Christmas Day. My first Christmas in London, in a
house of student bedsits in Ladbroke Grove. An unhappy
day. All the other students had gone home to their
families, naturally. I was the only one left. No one had
invited me.

Mrs Swan Well, having a Hindu for Christmas can be
tricky. Eric would invite his Assistant for Christmas Day
lunch. It quite spoiled the business of the paper hats.

Anish The telephone rang all day.

Mrs Swan The mistletoe was another problem.

Anish It would stop and then start again. I ignored it.

The phone was never for me. But finally I went up and answered it, and it was my uncle calling from Jummapur to say my father was dead.

Mrs Swan Oh, and at Christmas!

Anish I went home. It was still 'home'. But to my shame I found the rituals of mourning distasteful. I wanted to return to England, to my new friends. And I did. I was in England when I learned that my father had léft me his tin trunk which had always stood at the foot of his bed. It arrived finally and it was locked. So I broke the hasp. There was nothing of value in the trunk that I could see. It was full of paper, letters, certificates, school report cards . . . There was a newspaper cutting, however – a report of a trial of three men accused of conspiring to cause a disturbance at the Empire Day celebrations in Jummapur in 1930. My father's name was there. Nirad Das, aged thirty-four. That is how I know the year. His birthday was in April and Empire Day was in May.

Mrs Swan May the 24th, Queen Victoria's birthday.

Anish This is how I found out. My father never told me.

Mrs Swan And this painting?

Anish Yes. Underneath everything was this painting. A portrait of a woman, nude, but in a composition in the old Rajasthani style. Even more amazing, a European woman. I couldn't imagine who she was or what it meant. I kept it, of course, all these years. Then, a week ago, in the shop window . . . It was like seeing a ghost. Not her ghost; his. It was my father's hand, his work, I had grown up watching him work. I had seen a hundred original Nirad Dases, and here was his work, not once but repeated twenty times over, a special display. *The Collected Letters of Flora Crewe*, and I saw that it was the same woman.

Mrs Swan Yes. Oh yes, it's Flora. It's as particular as an English miniature. A watercolour, isn't it?

Anish Watercolour and gouache.

Mrs Swan He hasn't made *her* Indian.

Anish Well, she was *not* Indian.

Mrs Swan Yes, I know, I'm not gaga, I'm only old. I mean he hasn't painted her flat. Everything else looks Indian, like enamel . . . the moon and stars done with a pastry cutter. The birds singing in the border . . . and the tree in bloom, so bright. Is it day or night? And everything on different scales. You can't tell if the painter is in the house or outside looking in.

Anish She is in a house within a house. The Mughals brought miniature painting from Persia, but Muslim and Hindu art are different. The Muslim artists were realists. But to us Hindus, everything is to be interpreted in the language of symbols.

Mrs Swan And an open book on the bed, that's Flora.

Anish Yes. That is her. Look where this flowering vine sheds its leaves and petals, they are falling to the ground. I think my father knew your sister was dying.

Mrs Swan Oh . . .

Anish She is not posing, you see, but resting. The vine embraces the dark trunk of the tree.

Mrs Swan Now really, Mr Das, sometimes a vine is only a vine. Whether she posed for him or whether it's a work of the imagination . . .

Anish Oh, but the symbolism –

Mrs Swan Codswallop! Your 'house within a house', as anyone can see, is a mosquito net. And the book is Emily

Eden, it was in her suitcase. Green with a brown spine.
You should read the footnotes!

Pike enters.

Pike The book was *Up the Country* (1866). Miss Eden
was accompanying her brother, the Governor-General
Lord Auckland, on an official progress up country. The
tour, supported by a caravan of ten thousand people,
including Auckland's French chef, lasted thirty months,
and Emily wrote hundreds of letters to sisters and friends
at home, happily unaware that the expedition's diplomatic
and strategic accomplishment was to set the stage for the
greatest military disaster ever to befall the British under
arms, the destruction of the army in Afghanistan.

> *Dilip enters and joins Pike. They are in the garden/
> courtyard of the Jummapur Palace Hotel, which was
> formerly the Palace of the Rajah of Jummapur. They
> are brought drinks – reassuringly American cola –
> served by a waiter decked out in the authentic livery
> of the old regime. Thus, the servants operate freely
> between the two periods.*

Pike I started off shoving rupees . . . you know . . .
through the window . . . But it gets impossible. You
can't . . . there's more of them than you can ever . . .
I mean there's nothing to be in between, you have to be
St Francis or some rich bastard who ignores them, there's
nothing between that can touch it, the problem. Not St
Francis, I didn't mean any disrespect, they're not *birds* –
but Mother Teresa, some kind of saint. I lock the doors
now. That's the truth. First thing I do now when the taxi
hits a red light, I check the doors, wind up the window.
But this one, she had this baby at the breast, I mean she
looked *sixty,* and – well, this is the thing, she had a
stump, you see, she had no hand, just this stump, up

449

against the glass, and it was . . . raw . . . so when the
light changed, the stump left this . . . smear . . .

Dilip You have to understand that begging is a profes-
sion. Like dentistry. Like shining shoes. It's a service.
Every so often, you need to get a tooth filled, or your
shoes shined, or to give alms. So when a beggar presents
himself to you, you have to ask yourself – do I need a
beggar today? If you do, give him alms. If you don't,
don't. You have beggars in America.

Pike We have bums, winos, people down on their luck . . .
it's not a *service,* for God's sake.

Dilip Ah well, we are in a higher stage of development.

Pike Is that Hinduism, Dilip?

Dilip (*kindly*) It was a witticism, Eldon.

Pike Oh . . . right. What are you, actually?

Dilip I am a book critic, Eldon, but I have many fish to
fry before I depart this vale of tears.

    Pike laughs experimentally.

Oh, but I do.

Pike Sorry. When you're in India a lot of things sound . . .
you know, Indian.

Dilip Now you see why the Theosophical Society trans-
planted itself from America. (*with his drink*) Let's drink
to Madame Blavatsky.

Pike Who's she?

Dilip What? Don't you know 'Bagpipe Music'?

Pike Oh . . . (yeah).

Dilip 'It's no go the yogi man, it's no go Blavatsky . . .'

Pike MacNeice, right.

Dilip Madame Blavatsky was a famous name in India, she *was* the Theosophical Society. Of course, she was long dead by 1930, and now long forgotten, except in my favourite poem in the Oxford Book of English Verse.

Pike Why are you so crazy about English, Dilip?

Dilip I'm not!

Pike You love it!

Dilip Yes, I do. I love it.

Pike Yes. You do.

Dilip (*cheerfully*) Yes, it's a disaster for us! Fifty years of Independence and we are still hypnotized! Jackets and ties must be worn! English-model public schools for the children of the elite, and the voice of Bush House is heard in the land. Gandhi would fast again, I think. Only, this time he'd die. It was not for this India, I think, that your Nirad Das and his friends held up their home-made banner at the Empire Day gymkhana. It was not for this that he threw his mango at the Resident's car. What a pity, though, that all his revolutionary spirit went into his life and none into his art.

Pike Do you think he had a relationship with Flora Crewe?

Dilip But of course – a portrait is a relationship.

Pike No, a *relationship*.

Dilip I don't understand you.

Pike He painted her nude.

Dilip I don't think so.

Pike Somebody did.

Dilip In 1930, an Englishwoman, an Indian painter. . . it is out of the question.

Pike Not if they had a relationship.

Dilip Oh . . . a *relationship*? Is that what you say? (*amused*) A relationship!

Pike This is serious.

Dilip (*laughing*) Oh, it's very serious. What do you say for – well, for 'relationship'?

Pike Buddies.

Dilip almost falls off his chair with merriment.

Please, Dilip . . .

Dilip (*recovering*) Well, we will never know. You are constructing an edifice of speculation on a smudge of paint on paper, which no longer exists.

Pike It must exist – look how far I've come to find it.

Dilip Oh, very Indian! Well, if so, there are two ways to proceed. First, you can go around Jummapur looking at every piece of paper you come to. Second, you can stand in one place and look at every piece of paper that comes to you.

A waiter brings a note to Pike, and leaves.

Pike (*reading the note*) He's coming down. I thought maybe he'd ask us upstairs.

Dilip Don't be offended.

Pike I'm not offended.

Dilip He is not the Rajah now, he is an ordinary politician. He has your letter. I hope he can help you. In any case, it is better if I leave you so he does not need to wear two hats.

Pike What do I call him?

Dilip Your Highness. He will correct you.

Dilip leaves.
Flora enters, dressed for tiffin with his Highness the
Rajah of Jummapur.

Flora 'Interrupted – by a Rolls Royce, darling, so now
it's tomorrow so to speak, and yesterday I got several
days' worth of India all in one, dawn to dawn, starting
off on horseback with my suitor, lunch, to say the least
of it, with a Rajah, and – oh dear, guess what. You won't
approve. Quite right. I think it's time to go. Love 'em
and leave 'em.'

Pike The man was probably the Junior Political Agent at
the Residency, Captain David Arthur Durance, who took
FC dancing and horse riding. He was killed at Kohima in
March 1944 when British and Indian troops halted the
advance of the Japanese forces.

Flora 'I feel tons better, though. The juices are starting
to flow again, see enclosed.'

Pike 'Pearl', included in *Indian Ink* (1932).

Flora 'I'll send you fair copies of anything I finish in case
I get carried away by monsoons or tigers, and if you get
a pound for them put it in the Sasha Fund.'

Pike The reference is obscure.

Flora 'I was let off church parade, being a suspected
Bolshie, and I was writing the last bit on my verandah
after my early-morning ride when what should turn up
but a Rolls circa 1912 but brand new, as it were, with a
note from his Highness the Rajah of Jummapur going
on about my spiritual beauty and inviting me to tiffin.'

Rajah (*entering*) The spiritual beauty of Jummapur has been increased a thousandfold by your presence, Miss Crewe! I understand you are a connoisseur of the automobile.

Flora 'Well, what is a poor girl to do? Hop into the back of the Rolls, that's what.'

The Rajah is not very formally dressed – mostly in white, a long tight-fitting coat and leggings. He shakes hands with Flora who has stood up.

Rajah How delightful that you were able to come!

Flora Oh, how sweet of you to ask me . . . your Highness.

Rajah Unfortunately I cannot show them all at once because I have many more motor cars than mechanics, of course. But we can sit and chat between the scenes.

Flora I would be happy to walk around them, your Highness.

Rajah Oh, but that would deny them their essential being! They would not be automobiles, if we did the moving and they did the sitting.

A stately concours d'elegance *of motor cars, as distinguished as they are invisible, begins to pass in front of them.*

Flora Oh –! What a beauty! A Duesenberg! And what's that? – Oh, my goodness, it's a Type 41 Bugatti! I've never seen one! And a . . . is it an Isotta-Fraschini?

Rajah Possibly. I acquired it by way of settlement of a gambling debt at Bendor Westminster's. Do you know him?

Flora I don't know any dukes.

Rajah He's my neighbour in the South of France. I go to the South of France every year, you see, for my health. (*He laughs.*) But you have come to India for your health!

Flora (*not pleased*) Well . . . yes, Your Highness. Everybody seems to know everything about me.

Rajah Mr Churchill was in the house party. He paints. Do you know Mr Churchill?

Flora Not very well.

Rajah I was at school with him, apparently. I can't remember him at all, but I read Mr Churchill's speeches with great interest, and . . .

Flora Oh – look at that!

Rajah (*looking*) Ah yes, I couldn't resist the headlamps. So enormous, like the eggs of a chromium bird.

Flora Yes – a Brancusi!

Rajah You know them all, Miss Crewe! . . . Yes, Mr Churchill is perfectly right, don't you agree, Miss Crewe?

Flora About what exactly, Your Highness?

Rajah In his own words, the loss of India would reduce Britain to a minor power.

Flora That may be, but one must consider India's interests, too.

Rajah I must consider Jummapur's interests.

Flora Yes, of course, but aren't they the same thing?

Rajah No, no. Independence would be the beginning of the end for the Princely States. Though in a sense you are right, too – Independence will be the end of the unity of the Subcontinent. Look at the hullabaloo in the town yesterday. You tell Mr Churchill from me, Miss Crewe.

My grandfather stood firm with the British during the First Uprising.

Flora The . . .?

Rajah In 1857 the danger was from fundamentalists –

Flora The Mutiny . . .

Rajah – today it is the progressives. Marxism. Civil disobedience. But I told the Viceroy, you have to fight them the same way, you won't win by playing cricket.

There is a pause in the cavalcade of motor cars. A servant appears with a tray of drinks, fruit, a cigarette box, finger bowls and napkins.

Ah, the first interval. Do you smoke? No? I enjoy a cigarette. You must tell me when you have had enough of automobiles. There are one or two things in my apartments which have drawn favourable comment from historians of Indian art, even exclamations of delight if I may be honest with you. Do you enjoy art, Miss Crewe? But of course you do, you are a poet. I would be happy to show you.

Flora I would like that very much.

Rajah You would really? Yes, I can see you are a true seeker. My ancestors' atelier produced some work which in my opinion compares with the best workshops of Rajasthan.

Flora I would like to see *everything*!

Rajah So you shall. Well, not quite everything, perhaps. Some of the most exquisite work, alas, is considered indelicate.

Flora Considered by whom? By you?

456

Rajah Oh no. In my culture, you see, erotic art has a long history and a most serious purpose.

Flora (*unangrily*) But only for men, your Highness?

Rajah I have made you angry. I am terribly sorry. I should not have mentioned it.

Flora I'm very glad you did. Otherwise I should not have seen it.

Rajah (*comfortably*) Oh, my dear Miss Crewe, you are making me uncomfortable! What can I say?

Flora What do you usually say, Your Highness? Well . . . here are some more cars . . . I'm going to leave it to you.

Another car purrs by in front of them

(*Pleased*) Oh – a Silver Ghost. Goodness, that's beautiful.

Rajah Will you not have some fruit, Miss Crewe?

Flora Yes, I think I might. Thank you. (*From the tray, which is piled up with tangerines, bananas, lychees, etc., she takes an apricot. She bites into it.*) Apricot is my favourite word.

Rajah Miss Crewe, you shall see all the paintings you wish to see; on the condition that you allow me to choose one to present to you.

Flora Oh. . . . thank you, Your Highness, but if there are going to be conditions, I'm not sure I want to see *any*.

Rajah The English ladies came, Mrs Tuke, Mrs Stokely-Smith, Mrs Blane . . . a dozen of them, to see the lily pools, the flower garden . . . They drank tea with me and I offered them fruit, but they would only eat the fruit which had a skin they could remove, you see.

Flora Yes. I see. Then I accept.

*One of the next cars makes Flora gasp and almost
jump out of her chair.*

Oh! – I *know* that one!

Rajah Of course you do, Miss Crewe!

Flora No, I really know it. Where did you get it?

Rajah Well . . . from a car shop.

Flora Could you make him stop a moment.

*Flora stands up. The Rajah signals for the car to
stop and it does so, idling. Flora takes a step or two
towards the unseen car.*

Rajah Would you like a ride in it?

Flora shakes her head.

Flora 'And oh my darling, it was Gus's Bentley! I mean
it was absolutely the one I broke my engagement in
when I took Gus to the French pictures at Heals – it still
had the AB number-plate! I almost started to cry, not for
the car, for Modi.' (*Going to the car, she leaves the
stage.*)

Pike Augustus de Boucheron enjoyed brief celebrity as
a millionaire philanthropist and patron of the arts. FC
met him – and received his proposal of marriage – on
December 3rd 1917. The occasion was Modigliani's first
show, in Paris. FC sat for the artist soon afterwards.
At the exhibition of Modern French Art at Heal and
Sons in the Tottenham Court Road, London, in August
1919, Modigliani was one of several newer artists shown
with the better known Matisse, Picasso and Derain.
FC arrived at Heals with de Boucheron, expecting to see
her portrait, but before they got out of the Bentley she
discovered that her fiancé had bought the painting from
the artist and, as he triumphantly confessed, taken it

back to the Ritz Hotel and burned it in a bathtub. In the ensuing row, FC returned de Boucheron's engagement ring, and made plans to sit for Modigliani again in the autumn of that year. But she delayed, arriving in Paris only on the morning of January 23rd, unaware that Modigliani had been taken to hospital. He died on the following evening, without regaining consciousness, of tuberculosis, aged thirty-five. De Boucheron, under his real name Perkins Butcher, went to prison in 1925 for issuing a false prospectus. His end is unknown.

The Rajah looks around the courtyard seeking someone . . . and spots Pike. Pike has not noticed him. The Rajah, soi disant, approaches Pike.

Rajah Professor Pike . . .?

Pike (*jumping up*) Oh! – indeed, yes – thank you.

Rajah (*shaking hands*) How do you do?

Pike An honour, sir.

Rajah (*waving Pike back into his chair*) Please . . . I'm so sorry to have kept you waiting. But what I say is, a punctual politician is a politician who does not have enough to do. In other words, an impossibility.

Pike I'm so grateful to you for this.

Rajah No, no – delighted. I hope you find the hotel comfortable? We are not one of the international chains, you know. You mustn't be deluded on that point, no matter how much we exert ourselves to delude you.

Pike The hotel is excellent, your Highness.

Rajah Actually, I am, in fact, just one of 542 members of the Lok Sabha, the House of the People, popularly elected, I am happy to say, by this District. Thank you so much for your book. I have already read the Indian letters. Perhaps you are wondering what happened to my grandfather's motor cars.

Pike No, I hadn't really . . . what did happen to them?

Rajah My father presented them to the war effort. I can't think what he had in mind. Despatches carried by Rolls Royce, Staff Officers reporting for duty in snazzy Italian racing models . . . But by that time the collection had suffered the attrition of my grandfather's generosity. He gave several away, sometimes as farewell presents to his lady friends. Which brings me to your letter. To begin with, there was a disappointment. There is no Flora Crewe in the visitors book in April 1930. However, my archivist has excelled himself. (*He takes a letter from his pocket.*) The *Collected Letters* are not complete!

Pike A letter from Flora?

Rajah A thank-you note.

Pike May I?

The Rajah gives him the letter and waits while Pike reads it.

He gave her a painting.

Rajah I believe we have identified it. Or rather, the volume from which it came. A miniature. From our Gita Govinda of about 1790, artist unknown. The series is by no means complete, but even so, I wish my grandfather had given her a motor car.

Pike Thank you. Yes, indeed. (*He gives the letter back.*)

Rajah I had a copy made for you. (*He gives Pike the copy of the letter.*)

Pike Thank you. That was thoughtful of you. The Gita Govinda . . . would that be anything to do with a herdswoman, Radha?

Rajah But absolutely. It is the story of Radha and Krishna.

Pike Yes. And . . . erotic? She could have been nude?

Rajah Well, let us say, knowing His Highness, the painting would have been appropriate to the occasion.

Pike A watercolour, of course. On paper.

Rajah Are you not feeling well, Professor Pike?

Pike No, I'm fine. Thank you. Actually, I'm just head of the Department, we don't have a Chair . . . Please call me Eldon.

Rajah (*getting up*) Well, Eldon . . .

> *They shake hands.*

I hope I have been of some service to your biography of Miss Crewe.

Pike Yes. You could say that. But thanks anyway. (*correcting*) A lot. Thanks a lot. (*remembering himself*) Thank you, Your Highness. (*correcting*) Sir.

Rajah (*in Hindi*) Farewell!

Pike Is that your Christian name?

Rajah Actually, I am not Christian. No, I was saying goodbye. (*in Hindi*) Farewell!

Pike (*alone; under his breath*) Oh, shit.

Nirad Das and Coomaraswami are sitting on Flora's verandah. It is evening, nearly dark. They have not lit the lamp. A car is heard delivering Flora back to the guesthouse. Possibly the sweep of the headlights shows Das and Coomaraswami rising to greet Flora. She approaches the verandah, dark again, not seeing them, and is startled.

Flora Oh, Mr Das!

Das Good evening, Miss Crewe! I'm sorry if we frightened you.

Flora And Mr Coomaraswami!

Coomaraswami Yes, it is me, Miss Crewe.

Flora Good evening. What a surprise.

Coomaraswami I assure you – I beg you – we have not come to presume on your hospitality –

Flora I wish I had some whisky to offer you, but will you come inside.

Coomaraswami It will be cooler for you to remain on the verandah.

Flora Let me find Nazrul.

Coomaraswami He is not here, evidently. But perhaps now that the mistress has returned it is permitted to light the lamp?

Flora Yes, of course.

Coomaraswami So much more pleasant than sitting in the electric light. (*He lights the oil lamp.*) There we are. And the moon will clear the house-tops in a few minutes . . .

Flora Please sit down.

Coomaraswami May I take this chair?

Flora No, that's Mr Das's chair. And this is mine. So that leaves you with the sofa.

Coomaraswami (*sitting down*) Oh yes, very comfortable. Thank you, Miss Crewe. Mr Das told me that I was exceeding our rights of acquaintance with you in coming to see you without proper arrangement, and even more so to lie in wait for you like *mulaquatis*. If it is so, he is blameless. Please direct your displeasure to me.

Das Miss Crewe does not understand *mulaquatis*.

Coomaraswami Petitioners!

Flora In this house you are always friends.

Coomaraswami Mr Das, what did I tell you!

Flora But what can I do for you?

Das Nothing at all! We require nothing!

Flora Oh . . .

Coomaraswami Have you had a pleasant day, Miss Crewe?

Flora Extremely interesting. I have been visiting his Highness the Rajah.

Coomaraswami My goodness!

Flora I believe you knew that, Mr Coomaraswami.

Coomaraswami Oh, you have found me out!

Flora He showed me his cars . . . and we had an interesting conversation, about art . . .

Coomaraswami And poetry, of course.

Flora And politics.

Coomaraswami Politics, yes. I hope, we both hope – that your association with, that our association with, in fact – if we caused you embarrassment, if you thought for a moment that I personally would have knowingly brought upon you, compromised you, by association with –

Flora Stop, stop. Mr Das, I am going to ask *you*. What is the matter?

Das The matter?

Flora I shall be absolutely furious in a moment.

Das Yes, yes, quite so. My friend Coomaraswami, speaking as President of the Theosophical Society, wishes to say that if His Highness reproached you or engaged you in any unwelcome conversation regarding your connection with the Society, he feels responsible, and yet at the same time wishes you to know that –

Flora His Highness never mentioned the Theosophical Society.

Das Ah.

Coomaraswami Not at all, Miss Crewe?

Flora Not at all.

Coomaraswami Oh . . . well, jolly good!

Flora What has happened?

Coomaraswami Ah well, it is really of no interest. I am very sorry to have mentioned it. And we must leave you, it was not right to trouble you after all. Will you come, Mr Das?

Flora I hope it is nothing to do with my lecture?

Coomaraswami (*getting up*) Oh no! Certainly not!

Das Nothing!

Coomaraswami Mr Das said we should not mention the thing, and how truly he spoke. I am sorry. Goodnight, Miss Crewe –

> *Coomaraswami shouts towards somebody distant, in Hindi, and the explanation is an approaching jingle*

*of harness, horse and buggy; Coomaraswami goes
offstage to meet it.*

Das I am coming, Mr Coomaraswami. Please wait for
me a moment.

Flora If you expect to be my friends, you must behave
like friends and not like whatever-you-called-it. Tell me
what has happened.

Coomaraswami (*offstage*) Mr Das!

Das (*shouts*) Please wait!

Flora Well?

Das The Theosophical Society has been suspended, you
see. The order came to Mr Coomaraswami's house last
night.

Flora But why?

Das Because of the disturbances in the town.

Flora The riot?

Das Yes, the riot.

Flora I know about it. The Hindus wanted the Moslems
to close their shops. What has that to do with the Theosophical Society?

Coomaraswami (*offstage*) I am going, Mr Das!

Das (*shouts*) I come now! (*to Flora*) Mr Coomaraswami
is a man with many hats! And His Highness the Rajah is
not a nationalist. I must leave you, Miss Crewe. (*He
hesitates.*) I think I will not be coming tomorrow. Do
you mind if I fetch my painting away now?

Flora I think that's up to you, Mr Das. I put everything
inside.

Das asks permission to put on the electric light.

Das May I?

He starts gathering his possessions. Flora turns down the oil lamp.

Flora I think I should leave tomorrow.

Das Tomorrow?

Flora I think I must. Every day seems hotter than the day before.

Das Yes, you are right of course. The humidity . . .

Flora Mr Das, did you tell people I was ill?

Das What do you mean?

Flora That I came to India for my health?

Coomaraswami (*more distant*) I cannot wait, Mr Das!

Das (*shouts*) A moment! (*to Flora*) Why do you ask me that?

Flora He is leaving you behind.

The horse and buggy are heard departing.

Das I will walk, then.

Flora It seems that everyone from the Rajah to the Resident knows all about me. I told no one except you. If I want people to know things, I tell them myself, you see. I'm sorry to mention it but if there's something wrong between two friends I always think it is better to say what it is.

Das Oh . . . my dear Miss Crewe . . . it was known to all long before you arrived in Jummapur. Mr Chamberlain's letter said exactly why you were coming. This is how it is with us, I'm afraid. The information was not considered to be private, only something to be treated with tact.

Flora Oh . . .

Das As for the Rajah and the Resident, I am sure they knew before anybody. A letter from England to Mr Coomaraswami would certainly be opened.

Flora Oh . . .

Das is embarrassed by her tears.

Das You must not blame yourself. Please.

Flora Oh, Mr Das . . . I'm so glad . . . and so sorry. How idiotic I am. Have you got a hanky?

Das Yes . . . certainly . . .

Flora Thank you. And now I have made you walk. Leave everything here.

Das It is not far and the moon is rising, I can manage everything without difficulty. (*He brings the easel and his box on to the verandah and returns for the canvas.*)

Flora Mr Das. Don't take it. (*Pause.*) If it is still a gift, I would like to keep it, just as it is.

Das Unfinished?

Flora Yes. All portraits should be unfinished. Otherwise it's like looking at a stopped clock. Your handkerchief smells faintly of . . . something nice.

Das The portrait is yours, if you would like it. Of course, I must take it off the stretcher for you, or it will not travel easily in your luggage. Perhaps I can find a knife in the kitchen, to take out the little nails.

Flora There are scissors on the table.

Das Ah, yes. Thank you. No – I think I would damage them. May I call Nazrul?

Flora I thought –

Das Yes – Mr Coomaraswami sent him away. He is suspicious of everyone. I'm sorry.

Flora It doesn't matter.

A power cut. All the lights go out. The scene continues in moonlight.

Oh!

Das Yes. It is Jummapur, I'm afraid.

Flora Never mind.

Das Will we meet again?

Flora Perhaps, if I come back this way. I must be in Bombay by July the 10th at the latest. My ship sails on the 11th.

Das You may take a later ship.

Flora No, I cannot. My sister . . . oh, you'll be horrified, but never mind – my sister is having a baby in October.

Das That is joyful news.

Flora Oh good.

Das Miss Crewe . . . actually, I have something . . . I decided I must not show it to you, but if we are friends again . . . I would like you to see it.

Flora Then I would like to see it.

Das takes a small watercolour out of his pocket.

Das I have wrapped it, although it is itself only a sheet of paper. (*He gives it to her.*) I can light the lamp.

Flora There is enough light. Mr Coomaraswami was quite right about the moon. (*She unwraps the paper.*) It's going to be a drawing, isn't it? . . . Oh!

468

Das (*nervous, bright*) Yes! A good joke, is it not?
A Rajput miniature, by Nirad Das!

Flora (*not heeding him*) Oh . . . it's the most beautiful
thing . . .

Das (*brightly*) I'm so pleased you like it! A quite witty
pastiche –

Flora (*heeding him now*) Are you going to be Indian?
Please don't.

Das (*heeding her*) I . . . I am Indian.

Flora An Indian artist.

Das Yes.

Flora Yes. This one is for yourself.

Das Yes. You are not offended?

Flora No, I'm pleased. It has *rasa*.

Das I think so. Yes. I hope so.

Flora I forget its name.

Das (*pause*) Shringara.

Flora Yes. Shringara. The *rasa* of erotic love. Whose god
is Vishnu.

Das Yes.

Flora Whose colour is blue-black.

Das Shyama. Yes.

Flora It seemed a strange colour for love.

Das Krishna was often painted shyama.

Flora Yes. I can see that now. It's the colour he looked
in the moonlight.

They stand still, and in the moment the moonlight clouds to darkness.

Flora (*recorded*)
'Heat collects and holds as a pearl at my throat,
let's go and slides like a tongue-tip down a Modigliani,
spills into the delta, now in the salt-lick,
lost in the mangroves and the airless moisture,
a seed-pearl returning to the oyster –
et nos cedamus amori . . .'

Dawn.
Flora lies inside the mosquito net. She looks at her watch on the bedside table, and drinks from the water glass.
Approaching unseen, Pike and Dilip are heard reciting/chanting.

Pike and Dilip
'It's no go the merrygoround, it's no go the rickshaw,
All we want is a limousine and a ticket for the
    peepshow.
Their knickers are made of crêpe de Chine, their
    shoes are made of python,
Their halls are lined with tiger rugs, and their walls
    with heads of bison.'

During this, Flora, naked and pulling on a robe, gets out of bed. She goes into the bathroom.
Pike and Dilip enter. It is dawn for them, too. They have been up all night. They each have a bottle of beer. They are happy, not drunk.

Pike and Dilip
'It's no go the yogi-man, it's no go *Blavatsky,*
All we want is a bank balance and a bit of skirt in
    a taxi!'

Pike (*toasting*) Madame Blavatsky and Louis MacNeice!

Dilip (*toasting*) Madame Blavatsky and the Theosophical Society, coupled with Indian nationalism!

Pike Really?

Dilip Oh yes. That's why the Jummapur branch was suppressed. The study of Indian religions is a very fine thing, no doubt, but politics is always the baby in the bathwater. Excuse me, I'll have a little rest. (*He lies on the ground on his back.*)

Pike It's no go the records of the Theosophical Society, it's no go the newspaper files partitioned to ashes . . . All we want is the facts and to tell the truth in our fashion . . . Her knickers were made of crêpe-de-Chine, her poems were up in Bow Street, her list of friends laid end to end . . . could make a hell of a story. But it's no go the watercolour, it's no go the Modigliani . . . The glass is falling hour by hour, and we're back in the mulligatawny . . . But we will leave no Das unturned. He had a son. God, this country is so *big*! – Dilip –?

Dilip is asleep. Pike shakes him.

Dilip! It's morning!

Dilip wakes refreshed.

Dilip Ah yes. Would you like to come home for breakfast?

Pike Oh . . . Thanks!

Dilip It's going to be hot today.

Pike It's hot *every* day.

Dilip No, Eldon, you haven't been hot yet. But you're off to the hills, so you will be all right.

A car is heard approaching. Flora comes from the bathroom, now wearing her slip and putting on her robe. She comes to meet Durance at the steps of the verandah.

Flora David . . .?

Durance You're up!

Flora Up with the dawn. What on earth are *you* doing?

Durance (*approaching*) I'm afraid I came to wake you. Don't you sleep?

Flora Yes, I slept early and woke early.

Durance I promised you a turn with the Daimler – remember?

Flora Yes.

Durance I wanted to show you the sunrise. There's a pretty place for it only ten minutes down the road. Will you come?

Flora Can I go in my dressing-gown?

Durance Well . . . better not.

Flora Right-o. I'll get dressed.

Durance Good.

Flora Come up.

Durance comes up the verandah steps.

I'll be quick. (*She goes into the bedroom. She hurriedly puts on a dress.*)

Durance (*calling from the verandah*) The damnedest thing happened to me just now.

Flora Can't hear you!

Durance steps into the interior, outside the bedroom door.

Durance That fellow Das was on the road. I'm sure it was him.

Flora (*dressing*) Well . . . why not?

Durance He cut me.

Flora What?

Durance I gave him a wave and he turned his back. I thought – 'well, that's a first!'

Flora Oh! There's hope for him yet.

Durance They'll be throwing stones next. (*then registering her remark*) What?

Flora Come in, it's quite safe.

Durance enters the bedroom. Flora, dressed, puts on her shoes, drags a hairbrush through her hair . . .
Durance picks up Flora's book from beside the unmade bed.

Durance Oh . . .! You're reading Emily Eden. I read it years ago.

Flora We'll miss the sunrise.

Durance (*with the book*) There's a bit somewhere . . . she reminds me of you. 'Off with their heads!'

Flora Whose heads?

Durance Hang on, I'll find it – it was Queen Victoria's birthday . . . (*He discovers the Rajah's gift.*) Oh!

Flora What?

Durance Nothing. I found your bookmark.

Flora I'm ready. It's not my bookmark, I put it there for safe keeping.

Durance Where did you get such a thing?

Flora His Highness gave it to me.

Durance Why?

Flora Because I ate an apricot. Because he is a Rajah. Because he hoped I'd go to bed with him. I don't know.

Durance But how could he . . . feel himself in such intimacy with you? Had you met him before?

Flora No, David –

Durance But my dear girl, in accepting a gift like this don't you see – (*Pause*.) Well, it's your life, of course . . .

Flora Shall we go?

Durance . . . but I'm in a frightfully difficult position now.

Flora Why?

Durance Did he visit you?

Flora I visited him.

Durance I know. Did he visit you?

Flora Mind your own business.

Durance But it is my business.

Flora Because you think you love me?

Durance No, I . . . Keeping tabs on what His Highness is up to is one of my . . . I mean I write reports to Delhi.

Flora (*amused*) Oh heavens!

Durance You're a politically sensitive person, actually, coming here with an introduction from that man Chamberlain . . . I mean this sort of thing –

Flora Oh, darling policeman.

Durance How can I ignore it?

Flora Don't ignore it. Report what you like. I don't mind, you see. You mind. But I don't. I have never minded. (*She steps on to the verandah. In despair*) Oh – look at the sky! We're going to be too late!

Durance (*to hell with it*) Come on! Our road is due west – if you know how to drive a car we'll make it.

They dash towards the car . . . the car doors are heard slamming, the engine roars into life and the Daimler takes off at what sounds like a dangerous speed.

Mrs Swan and Anish are walking away. He carries his briefcase. She has Flora's copy of Emily Eden.

Anish Mrs Swan . . . Flora's letter said, 'Guess what – you won't approve . . .' and Mr Pike's footnote implies that it was the Political Agent, Captain Durance, who . . .

Mrs Swan Mr Pike presumes too much.

Anish Yes! Why wouldn't you approve of Captain Durance? Surely it's more likely she meant . . .

Mrs Swan Meant what, Mr Das?

Anish I don't mean any offence.

Mrs Swan Then you must take care not to give it.

Anish But would you have disapproved of a British Army Officer, Mrs Swan? More than of an Indian painter?

Mrs Swan Certainly. Mr Pike is spot-on there. In 1930 I was working for a communist newspaper. Which goes to show that people are surprising. But you know that from your father, don't you?

Anish Why?

Mrs Swan He must have surprised you too. The terror of the Empire Day gymkhana, the thrower of mangoes at the Resident's Daimler.

Anish Yes. Yes. He must have – altered.

Mrs Swan Yes. One alters. (*She gives Anish the book by Emily Eden.*) This is yours. It belonged to your father. It has his name in it.

Anish takes the book wordlessly and opens it.

I hope you're not going to blub. And you mustn't make assumptions. When Flora said I wouldn't *approve*, she did not mean this man or that man. Cigarettes, whisky and men were not on the menu. She didn't need Dr Guppy to tell her that. No, I would not have approved. But Flora's weakness was always romance. To call it that.

Anish She had a romance with my father.

Mrs Swan Quite possibly. Or with Captain Durance. Or His Highness the Rajah of Jummapur. Or someone else entirely. It hardly matters, looking back. Men were not really important to Flora. If they had been, they would have been fewer. She used them like batteries. When things went flat, she'd put in a new one . . . I'll come to the gate with you. If you decide to tell Mr Pike about the watercolour, I'm sure Flora wouldn't mind.

Anish No. Thank you, but it's my father I'm thinking of. He really wouldn't want it, not even in a footnote. So we'll say nothing to Mr Pike.

Mrs Swan Good for you. I don't tell Mr Pike everything either. It's been an unusually interesting day, thanks to you, Mr Das.

Anish Thank you for tea. The Victoria sponge was best! The raspberry jam too.

Mrs Swan I still have raspberries left to pick, and the plums to come. I always loved the fruit trees at home.

Anish At home?

Mrs Swan Orchards of apricot – almond – plum –
I never cared for the southern fruits, mango, paw-paw and such like. But up in the North West . . . I was quite unprepared for it when I first arrived. It was early summer. There was a wind blowing. And I have never seen such blossom, it blew everywhere. There were drifts of snow-white flowers piled up against the walls of the graveyard. I had to kneel on the ground and sweep the petals off her stone to read her name.

They stroll out of view.

Nell is bending over a gravestone . . . watched by Eric.

Nell 'Florence Edith Crewe . . . Born March 21st 1895 . . .
Died June 10th 1930. *Requiescat In Pace.*'

Eric I'm afraid it's very simple. I hope that's all right.

Nell Yes. It was good of you.

Eric Oh no, we look after our own. Of course.

Nell I think she would have liked 'Poet' under her name. If I left some money here to pay for it . . .?

Eric There are funds within my discretion. You may count on it, Miss Crewe. Poet. I should have thought of that. It is how *we* remember your sister.

Nell Really?

Eric She read one evening. The Club has a habit of asking guests to sing for their supper and Miss Crewe read to us . . . from her work.

Nell Oh dear.

Eric (*laughs gently*) Yes. Well, we're a bit behind the times, I expect. But we all liked her very much. We didn't know what to expect because we understood she was a protegee of Mr Chamberlain who had lectured in the town some years before. Perhaps you know him.

Nell Yes. I'm not really in touch with him nowadays.

Eric Ah. It was just about this time of year when she was here, wasn't it? It was clear she wasn't well – these steps we just climbed, for instance, she could hardly manage them. Even so, death in India is often more unexpected, despite being more common, if you under-stand me. I'm talking far too much. I'm so sorry. I'll wait at the gate. Please stay as long as you wish, I have no one waiting for me.

Nell I won't be a moment. Flora didn't like mopers.

Eric leaves her.

(*Quietly*) Bye bye, darling . . . oh – damn!

. . . *because she has burst into sobs. She weeps unrestrainedly.*

Eric (*returning*) Oh . . . oh, I say . . .

Nell Oh, I'm sorry.

Eric No – please . . . can I . . .?

Nell stops crying after a few moments.

Nell I've messed up your coat. I've got a hanky some-where.

Eric Would you like to . . .? Here . . .

Nell Yes. Thank you. (*She uses his handkerchief.*) I came too soon after all. I hated waiting a whole year but . . .

well, anyway. Thank you, it's a bit wet. Should I keep it? Oh look, I've found mine, we can swap.

Eric Don't you worry about anything. What a shame you had to come on your own. You have another sister, I believe. Or a brother?

Nell No. Why?

Eric Oh. Flora was anxious to return to England to be an *aunt,* she said.

Nell Yes. I had a baby in October. He only lived a little while, unfortunately. There was something wrong.

Eric Oh. I'm so sorry.

Nell It's why I couldn't come before.

Eric Yes, I see. What rotten luck. What was his name?

Nell Sasha. Alexander, really. Alexander Percival Crewe. How nice of you to ask. Nobody ever does. I say, how about that blossom!

Eric Yes, it's quite a spot, isn't it? I hope you stay a while. First time in India?

Nell Yes.

Eric Mind the loose stone here. May I . . .?

Nell Thank you. I'm sorry I blubbed, Mr Swan.

Eric I won't tell anyone. Do call me Eric, by the way. Nobody calls me Mr Swan.

Nell Eric, then.

Eric Do you like cricket?

Nell (*laughs*) Well, I don't play a *lot*.

Eric There's a match tomorrow.

Nell *Here?*

Eric Oh yes. We're going to field a Test team next year, you know.

Nell We?

Eric India.

Nell Oh.

As they go, Pike enters, looking for the right grave. He finds it, he takes his hat off and stands looking at it.

Flora is on the verandah, placing the rolled-up canvas, Nirad Das's portrait of her, into her suitcase.

Flora 'Darling, that's all from Jummapur, because now I'm packed, portrait and all, and Mr Coomaraswami is coming to take me to the station.' (*She closes the suitcase. She holds on to her copy of the Emily Eden book.*) 'I'll post this in Jaipur as soon as I get there. I'm not going to post it here because I'm not. I feel fit as two lops this morning, and happy, too, because something good happened here which made me feel halfway better about Modi and getting back to Paris too late. That was a sin I'll carry to my grave, but perhaps my soul will stay behind as a smudge of paint on paper, as if I'd always been here, like Radha who was the most beautiful of the herdswomen, undressed for love in an empty house.'

Elsewhere, Nell kneels on the floor, going through the contents of Flora's suitcase. She looks at the blue dress briefly. She finds the rolled-up canvas. She looks at it and puts it back.

Nazrul enters to take Flora's suitcase to the train.

The train makes its reappearance. Coomaraswami, holding his yellow parasol, is on the station platform

*to take leave of Flora. He garlands her. Nazrul puts
Flora's suitcase on the rack above her seat. Flora
enters the train-compartment, gives Nazrul a tip, and
bids him farewell.*

   *Nell finds Flora's copy of the Emily Eden book in
the suitcase. She opens it and finds the Rajah's gift in
the book. She replaces the 'bookmark' and glances
through the book.*

   *During all these actions, following Pike's speech,
the voice of Flora reading Emily Eden is being heard.
During Emily's letter the train, in sound only, sets off
on its journey, and Flora opens her copy of Emily
Eden and begins to read to herself.*

Flora (*recorded*) 'Simla, Saturday, May 25th, 1839. The
Queen's Ball "came off" yesterday with great success . . .
Between the two tents there was a boarded platform for
dancing, roped and arched in with flowers and then in
different parts of the valley, wherever the trees would
allow of it, there was "Victoria", "God Save The Queen"
and "Candahar" in immense letters twelve feet high.
There was a very old Hindu temple also prettily lit up.
Vishnu, to whom I believe it really belonged, must have
been affronted. We dined at six, then had fireworks, and
coffee, and then they all danced till twelve. It was the
most beautiful evening; such a moon, and the mountains
looked so soft and *grave*, after all the fireworks and
glare. Twenty years ago no European had ever been here,
and there we were with a band playing, and observing
that St Cloup's Potage à la Julienne was perhaps better
than his other soups, and that some of the ladies' sleeves
were too tight according to the overland fashions for
March, and so on, and all this in the face of those high
hills, and we one hundred and five Europeans being
surrounded by at least three thousand mountaineers,
who, wrapped up in their hill blankets, looked on at

what we call our polite amusements, and bowed to the ground if a European came near them. I sometimes wonder they do not cut all our heads off and say nothing more about it.'

The train clatters loudly and fades with the light.

HAPGOOD

For Oliver with love and thanks

We choose to examine a phenomenon which
is impossible, *absolutely* impossible, to explain in any
classical way, and which has in it the heart of quantum
mechanics. In reality it contains the *only* mystery . . .
Any other situation in quantum mechanics, it turns out,
can always be explained by saying, 'You remember the
case of the experiment with the two holes?
It's the same thing.'

Richard P. Feynman
'Lectures on Physics'/'The Character of Physical Law'

Characters

Hapgood aged thirty-eight
Blair probably twenty years older, but in good shape
Kerner forty-ish
Ridley mid-thirties
Wates either side of forty-five
Maggs twenties
Merryweather twenty-two
Joe eleven
Russian any age, thirty to fifty

Hapgood was first performed at the Aldwych Theatre, London, on 8 March 1988. The cast was as follows:

Hapgood Felicity Kendal
Blair Nigel Hawthorne
Kerner Roger Rees
Ridley Iain Glen
Wates Al Matthews
Merryweather Adam Norton
Maggs Roger Gartland
Joe Christopher Price *or* Andrew Read
Russian Patrick Gordon

Directed by Peter Wood
Designed by Carl Toms
Lighting by David Hersey
Presented by Michael Codron

Act One

Scene One The Pool, Wednesday morning
Scene Two The Zoo, Wednesday noon
Scene Three The Rugby Pitch, Wednesday afternoon
Scene Four The Office, Thursday morning
Scene Five The Shooting Range, Thursday afternoon

Act Two

Scene One The Office, Thursday evening
Scene Two The Studio, Friday morning
Scene Three The Zoo, Friday noon
Scene Four The Office, Friday afternoon
Scene Five The Hotel, Friday evening
Scene Six The Pool, Friday night
Scene Seven The Rugby Pitch, Saturday afternoon

Act One

SCENE ONE

*We are looking at part of the men's changing room of
an old-fashioned municipal swimming-baths. It is ten
o'clock in the morning. The cubicles are numbered, and
they have doors which conceal occupancy although they
don't meet the ground. There is a wash-basin or two,
a place to shave facing front. Four of the cubicles have
to 'work'. There are four ways of coming and going:
'Lobby', 'Pool', 'Showers', and, for the sake of
argument, 'Upstage'.*

The lobby doors have MEN *in reverse on the glass.
Signs saying* POOLS, SHOWERS, GENTS *and* EXIT *may be
used. One of the showers is evidently in use – we can
hear it. When we encounter this scene, Wates is shaving.
He is a black man, an American, who is normally
impressively tailored and suave but at present is dressed
in cast-offs and looks as if he spent last night on a park
bench. His tackle is basic – shaving brush, shaving stick,
old-fashioned safety razor.*

*Before anything else happens we have a short radio
play. What we can hear is two people (a man and a
woman, Hapgood) talking to each other on shortwave
radio. The voices have a slight distort.*

Radio OK, we have a blue Peugeot . . . stopping.

Single male.

It's not Georgi.

Anybody know him? No briefcase, repeat negative on
briefcase.

Are you getting this, Mother? – we have the Peugeot
but it's not Georgi.

He's crossing the road. Fancy tracksuit, running shoes. No sign of the follower. Are you getting this? – target is approaching, negative on Georgi, negative on briefcase, negative on follower, give me a colour.

Hapgood (*on radio*) Green. You should be seeing Kerner.

Radio Negative. They changed the plot. Confirm Green.

Hapgood (*on radio*) Green. Tell me when Kerner shows.

Wates (*live*) If he shows.

Hapgood (*on radio*) Tell me when Kerner shows, he'll be walking.

Wates (*live, no emotion*) Kerner is thirty thousand feet up on Aeroflot, I feel sick.

Radio Who is that?

Hapgood (*on radio*) Wates – just shave.

Wates (*live*) Yes, Ma'am.

Radio Target inside. Negative on Kerner. Target in lobby. Ridley has seen him. Still negative on Kerner. Do I hear yellow? Mother, give me a colour, we're still – OK, we have a walker.

OK, we have Kerner . . . three hundred yards . . . affirmative on briefcase.

Target's got his key.

Hapgood (*on radio*) Say when.

Radio Four – three – two –

The lobby door opens.

You're looking at him.

A man enters from the lobby. He wears a colourful tracksuit and running shoes. He carries a towel rolled

490

up into a sausage, we assume the swimming trunks
and cap are inside. He carries a key on a loop of
string which might make it convenient to wear as a
pendant. He is otherwise empty-handed. We call this
man Russian One, because he is Russian and because
there are going to be two of them.

Russian One enters Cubicle One. (This numbering
has nothing to do with the actual numbers on the
cubicles, it is only for our convenience.) Russian One
enters his cubicle and closes the door behind him.

Ridley enters from the lobby. He is carrying a
briefcase (but the briefcase may be inside a sports
holdall.) Ridley now goes on a perambulation. The
essence of the situation is that Ridley moves around
and through, in view and out of view, demonstrating
that the place as a whole is variously circumnavigable
in a way which will later recall, if not replicate, the
problem of the bridges of Konigsberg (and which will
give Russian One time to undress).

Back to the Plot. Russian One, dressed to swim,
leaves his cubicle, locks it, swings his towel up and
over the lintel and leaves it hanging there, and goes
off to the pool. When he has gone Ridley posts his
briefcase under the door of Cubicle One, and pulls the
towel off the door. (As a matter of interest, the Ridley
who posts the briefcase is not the same Ridley who
entered with it.) Ridley enters Cubicle Two and closes
the door behind him. The towel appears, flung over
the lintel, hanging down. Wates continues to shave.
The shower continues to run. Kerner enters from the
lobby. He carries a briefcase. He has a towel and a
key. He looks around and posts his briefcase under
the door with the towel showing (Cubicle Two).
Kerner pulls the towel off the door and tosses it over
the door into the cubicle. Kerner enters another
cubicle (Cubicle Three) and closes the door behind

him. A moment later his towel appears over the lintel.

Ridley leaves Cubicle Two, bringing Kerner's brief-case with him, and also the towel. He chucks the towel over the door of Cubicle One. With the brief-case he disappears in the direction of the showers. The shower cubicle may be in full view, in which case we see Ridley delivering his briefcase to the occupant. Russian One leaves the pool, wet of course, and re-enters his cubicle.

Ridley comes back into view, from the showers, without the briefcase. He goes to the pool.

Russian Two enters from the lobby. He is the twin of Russian One, and dressed like Russian One. He carries a similar rolled-up towel. However, he also carries a briefcase. He glances round briefly, and notes the towel on Kerner's door (Cubicle Three). He posts his briefcase under Kerner's door. He enters a cubicle, Cubicle Four.

Merryweather, a boyish twenty-two-year-old in sports jacket and flannels, enters from the lobby. His manner is not as well calculated as Ridley's had been. He is at first relieved and then immediately disconcerted by the absence of Russians.

Russian One now dressed, leaves his cubicle, carrying his rolled-up towel but leaving the briefcase (which Ridley posted) behind. Russian One leaves to the lobby.

Merryweather, whose idea of making himself inconspicuous has been, perhaps, to examine himself in Wates's mirror, follows Russian One out to the lobby.

Kerner, dressed, leaves Cubicle Three, with the briefcase which had been posted there, and leaves to the lobby.

Russian Two reappears, from Cubicle Four, and enters Cubicle One to collect the briefcase which had

been posted there by Ridley. As he leaves the cubicle,
Ridley re-enters from the pool.

Russian Two leaves to the lobby. Ridley follows him
out.

Wates has finished shaving. He is packing up his
shaving tackle. The shower stops running. There is a
pause, and then the occupant of the shower, Hapgood,
approaches, somewhat encumbered by a briefcase
(Kerner's original) a leather rectangular clutch hand-
bag with a shoulder strap, and an umbrella which she
is at the moment taking down and shaking out. From
her appearance, the umbrella has been an entire success.
She comes down into the light and leans the umbrella
carefully against the cubicles, and stands pensively
for a moment. She is apparently too preoccupied to
acknowledge Wates, who is himself preoccupied with
something which makes him shake with silent laughter.
He is putting a heavy steel wrist-watch on his right
wrist. (Note: All the foregoing action may be done to
music and lightly choreographed.)

Wates Young guy in a sports coat, college haircut, nasty
wart on the back of his right hand, no, left, it was in the
mirror.

Hapgood Merryweather.

Wates Merryweather, right. Followed the man in,
followed the wrong man out, meanwhile Merryweather's
man turns around and leaves with the goods. Sort of
dummy.

Hapgood Yes, he is rather.

The lobby doors open. Ridley enters in a somewhat
excited, even delighted, state.

Ridley (*greeting her*) Mother.

493

Hapgood This is Ridley.

Ridley You didn't tell me it was twins.

Hapgood This is Wates.

Hapgood puts the briefcase on the ground, then lays it flat. She undoes the catches and raises the lid. During this Wates and Ridley shake hands.

Wates Ben Wates.

Ridley (*friendly*) Ridley.

Hapgood has stood up, taking from the case a flat white cardboard box, a few inches square, the sort of thing that might contain a computer disc, which is what in fact it does contain. However, she is not the slightest interested in the box. She stands staring down at the open briefcase.

Hapgood (*bad news*) Wates.

Now Wates looks at her and at the briefcase.

Wates Oh, Lord.

Hapgood Where's yours, Ridley?

Ridley In the Peugeot.

Merryweather returns, looking sheepish. Hapgood tosses the disc-box back into the briefcase.

Merryweather Sorry, Mother – I –

Hapgood Where did he go, Merryweather?

Merryweather Actually, I lost him – a taxi came round the corner –

Hapgood He's in the taxi?

Merryweather nods.

Ridley (*to Hapgood*) Chamberlain's cab, I love it. Listen, how the hell –

Hapgood (*politely*) Be quiet, Ridley.

She is opening her handbag and taking out a small radio transmitter/receiver.
These gadgets are going to get quite a lot of use and evidently the state of the art has arrived at a radio which is no larger and somewhat slimmer than twenty cigarettes. The radio speaks quietly.

(*To Merryweather*) Have a look round the pool.

Merryweather Right. What for exactly?

Hapgood Anything there is, I'll want to see it. (*to radio*) Cotton.

Radio Mother.

Wates and Merryweather dovetail with Hapgood and her radio.

Wates (*shaking hands*) Ben Wates.

Merryweather How do you do, sir? Merryweather.

Merryweather goes out to the pool. Ridley is probably contemplating the briefcase.
Wates moves quietly up towards the cubicles and calmly investigates them, one after another without fuss. During this:

Hapgood (*to radio*) Where is he?

Radio In the Peugeot.

Hapgood (*patiently*) Thank you, Cotton, and where is the Peugeot?

Radio Camden High Street.

Hapgood Pick him up and I want everything, I want him in a plastic bag.

Radio Yes, ma'am.

Hapgood Contents of briefcase. I'm here to be told.

Radio You know it's twins?

Hapgood Yes, I know it's twins.
  (*To Ridley*) You take Kerner – go through him, do it properly.
  (*To radio*) Chamberlain.

Ridley Kerner's clean.

Radio P.O.B.

Hapgood (*to radio*) I know.

Ridley I did the switch.

Hapgood (*to Ridley, more sharply*) Move.

  Ridley exits to the lobby.

(*To radio*) Where are you?

Radio Chalk Farm, turning west on Adelaide.

Hapgood Bring him in.

Radio Say again?

Hapgood Just do it.

Radio OK, guv.

Hapgood Taxi needs back-up.

Radio (*new voice*) Roger.

Hapgood I'm here to be told. (*She turns the gadget off, hesitates, and turns it on again. To radio*) Paul . . .

Her tone for Paul is different – she is not giving orders. No answer.

Paul . . .

Still no answer. She turns the radio off.
    Wates is coming back to her.

What are you thinking?

Wates I guess we took our eye off the ball.

Hapgood closes the briefcase.

Hapgood What happened to the bleep?

Wates (*shrugs*) It's dead.

Hapgood I'll need when.

Wates You'll get it. Why did he take the film?

Hapgood Who?

Wates Yeah, that's the other thing.

Hapgood goes to collect her umbrella.

Hapgood (*to radio*) I'm leaving.

Radio Car out front.

Hapgood (*to radio*) Thank you. (*She puts the radio back into her bag.*) Wates . . .

Wates Yes, ma'am.

Hapgood Thank you for your co-operation.

Wates You bet.

He holds the briefcase out for her and she takes it.

Hapgood Well, we'll talk. You're invited.

Wates Appreciate it.

Hapgood starts off to the lobby door. Merryweather comes back in from the pool.

Merryweather Nothing, Mother – the whole place is clean.

Hapgood (*continuing out*) Drain the pool.

The doors swing shut behind her.

Merryweather (*thoughtfully, not entirely happy*) Drain the pool.

He goes back to the pool. Wates is alone. He is evidently a man with a burden. He is getting ready to leave, perhaps he has a coat to put on. From the pocket he takes a similar radio and walks towards the doors, raising the radio to his mouth; at which point everything changes for him. He stops to listen, his head turned back towards the upstage, by which time, gracefully and without making a big thing of it, he has tossed his radio from right hand to left, and produced from somewhere about his person a short barrelled revolver. He stands listening, holding the gun down by his side. He has to be patient but after a while a figure comes out of the dark upstage between the cubicles. This turns out to be a man wearing a hat and a good tweed overcoat, his hands in the pockets, a slightly surprising colourful silk scarf tucked inside the coat. He walks down in his own time, a careful stroll. Wates does not move until the downstage light falls across Blair's face. Blair comes to a halt. Wates puts his gun away, gets the radio back into his right hand and resumes.

Wates (*to radio*) Wates – I need the sweeps. (*He nods at Blair.*) Paul.

Blair (*greets him back*) Ben.

Radio Sweeps coming up.

Wates (*to radio*) Thank you. (*He puts the radio in his pocket and, in leaving, speaks to Blair without reproof, just information.*) She blew it.

He goes out through the lobby doors. Blair takes a radio from his pocket. The scene begins to change.

Blair (*to radio*) Ridley.

Ridley (*on radio*) Ridley.

Blair (*to radio*) I want Kerner in Regent's Park, twelve o'clock sharp.

He puts the radio away and looks at his wrist-watch. The next time he moves, it is twelve o'clock and he is at the Zoo.

SCENE TWO

Kerner has been brought by Ridley to the Zoo. Blair, having checked the time on his watch, nods at Ridley to dismiss him. Ridley moves out.

Perhaps we are looking at Blair and Kerner through the bars of a cage. There could be a bench, there could be paper cups of coffee . . . The bars make hard-edged shadows. We need one particular and distinct demarcation of light and shadow on the floor, perhaps thrown by the edge of a wall.

Kerner speaks with a Russian accent, which is not too heavy; in fact, attractive.

Blair You're blown, Joseph.

Kerner I love it. You blew it and I'm blown: well, I'll be blowed. Nobody teaches that, you know. They teach you so you can almost read *David Copperfield* and then you

499

find out David talks like a language student, he must have been put in as a sleeper.

Blair Well . . . you're blowed, Joseph. Your career is over.

Kerner Except as a scientist, you mean.

Blair Yes, that's what I mean.

Kerner My career as your man at the Pool.

Blair Or theirs. Just an observation. The meet at the pool came unstuck this morning. We have to consider you blown as our joe. The Russians must consider you blown as their sleeper. Either way your career is over. *Which* way, is perhaps an academic question.

Kerner And yet, here you are.

Blair One likes to know what's what.

Kerner Oh, you think there's a what's-what? Your joe. Their sleeper. Paul, what's-what is for zoologists: 'Oh yes – definitely a giraffe.' But a double agent is not what's-what like a giraffe, a double agent is more like a trick of the light.

Blair Joseph –

Kerner Look. (*He points.*) Look at the edge of the shadow. It is straight like the edge of the wall that makes it. This means light is particles: little bullets. Bullets go straight. They cannot bend round the wall and hit you. If light was *waves* it would bend round the wall a little, like water bends round a stone in the river.

Blair (*irritated*) Yes. Absolutely.

Kerner So that's what. When you shine light through a gap in the wall, it's particles. Unfortunately, when you shine the light through *two* little gaps, side by side, you don't get particle pattern like for bullets, you get wave pattern like for water. The two beams of light mix together and –

Blair Joseph. I want to know if you're ours or theirs, that's all.

Kerner I'm telling you but you're not listening. Now we come to the exciting part. We will watch the bullets to see how they make waves. This is not difficult, the apparatus is simple. So we look carefully and we see the bullets, one at a time. Some go through one gap and some go through the other gap. No problem. Now we come to my favourite bit. The wave pattern has disappeared. It has become particle pattern again.

Blair (*obliging*) All right – why?

Kerner Because we looked. Every time we don't look, we get wave pattern. Every time we look to see how we get wave pattern we get particle pattern. The act of observing determines what's what.

Blair How?

Kerner Nobody knows. Somehow light is continuous and also discontinuous. The experimenter makes the choice. You get what you interrogate for. And you want to know if I'm a wave or a particle. Every month at the pool, I and my friend Georgi exchange material. When the experiment is over, you have a result. I am your joe. But they also have a result: because you have put in my briefcase enough information to keep me credible as a Russian sleeper activated by my KGB control; which is what Georgi thinks he is. So naturally he gives me enough information to keep me credible as a British joe. Frankly, I can't remember which side I'm supposed to be working for, and it is not in fact necessary for me to know.

Pause.

Blair It wasn't Georgi today.

Kerner No?

Blair No, it was different today.

Kerner Today you decided to look. Why was that?

Blair Some of your research has turned up in Moscow. Real secrets, not briefcase stuff.

Kerner Tsk, tsk, tsk.

Blair That's what the Americans said, roughly.

Kerner The one shaving.

Blair Mm. Ben Wates, CIA. You'd appreciate him, he makes waves with a Smith and Wesson.

Kerner I'm sorry, Paul.

Blair (*shrugs*) Cousin-trouble is nothing new. This thing with you is trouble, though. Oh yes. If the Evil Empire has a tap into *you*, that's quite another ballroom as Wates put it –

Kerner Ballgame. I think.

Blair I assure you it wasn't. Ballpark. Anyway, Wates flies in and says, 'I have come from Washington to help you. How about Kerner for a start? Do we know anything about Joseph Kerner?' Well, we do as a matter of fact. He's Russian from Kaliningrad. The Russians put him in as a sleeper years ago but we turned him round and now he's really working for us, they only *think* he's working for them.

Kerner What did he say?

Blair He said: you guys.

Kerner Poor Paul. What happened at the Pool?

Blair Wates wanted us to abort the meet and put you through the mangle. But Mrs Hapgood insisted you were straight. And she wanted to keep the channel open. She made Wates an offer. She duplicated the contents of your briefcase. So now we had everything twice, in two brief-cases. Ridley showed up before you at the Pool –

Kerner What is a mangle?

Blair I'm trying to tell you what happened at the Pool.

Kerner You already did. Your Mr Ridley delivered to my Russian control and I delivered where Ridley put his towel. Quite nice. If I'm putting something extra in my briefcase, you get it all back.

Blair That sort of thing.

Kerner And was there something extra in my briefcase?

Blair No. There was something missing. The computer disc was there but the films were gone.

Kerner A puzzle.

Blair Now we come to the exciting part. Wates had booby-trapped your briefcase. He sprayed the inside with an aerosol can, like radioactive deodorant – did you ever hear of such a thing?

Kerner An isotope solution. If I open the briefcase I give a Geiger reading.

Blair Yes, Wates shakes your hand and he has a counter which goes on the wrist and looks like a Rolex. We're working with people who tried to kill Castro with an exploding cigar. It's a joke shop.

Kerner So, did I give a Geiger reading?

Blair No.

Kerner (*pleased*) Oh, good.

Blair We also had a bleep in your briefcase.

Kerner A bleep?

Blair A radio transmitter.

Kerner Oh – a *bug*.

Blair gives him a look.

Sorry. A bleep in my briefcase. Go on.

Blair Wates tracked the signal all the way to the meet. There the signal died. And the transmitter went missing from the briefcase, which nobody opened. The job was done by Mr Nobody.

Kerner Well I'm blown. Blow me for a monkey's uncle. Can I say that?

Blair I would avoid it. Any thoughts, Joseph?

Kerner Mr Nobody put something extra in my briefcase. Then he found out my delivery was going to be intercepted. So he had to take it out again.

Blair But why remove our rolls of film? He'd only have to take out what he put in, and we'd be none the wiser.

Kerner Obviously because he put *in* a roll of film and they all look the same; he had to take them all.

Blair (*pause*) Obviously. By the way do you know anything about twins?

Kerner Twins?

Blair That was the other thing. It wasn't Georgi today, it was twins.

Kerner laughs.

Yes, that's my favourite bit too. Give it some thought. Will you?

Kerner Oh, yes. But excuse me, now it is time for the feeding of the seals.

Kerner strolls away, jerking his head at the unseen Ridley to follow him. Ridley re-enters and follows Kerner out at a comfortable distance.
Blair stands looking out front. The next time he moves he is on the touch-line of a rugger pitch.

SCENE THREE

Blair is standing in an open exterior against a grey sky on a cold October afternoon. He is watching thirty eleven-year-old boys playing rugby. This, alas, is not as rich in sound effects as one might think: there is the referee's whistle, there are occasional piping exhortations to 'Heel', 'Drive', 'Shove', and so on, and the occasional sound of the ball being kicked, but much of all this is happening at a distance, and so the general effect is sporadic anyway. Nevertheless it would be nice to work out where Blair is before the next thing happens – which is that Hapgood comes hurtling crabwise and in full cry along the touch-line. She is shod and dressed for the conditions and is carrying a boy's two-piece tracksuit, the top half of which is perhaps tied round her neck. Her momentum takes her a good way along the front of the stage, passing in front of Blair.

Hapgood Come on, big shove now, St Christopher's! Heel! – *break! well tackled*, darling! – I mean, Hapgood – oh, sugar . . . (*The match recedes but she always gives it as much attention as she can spare or as she is allowed.*) Look at their little knees. Don't you love little boys?

Blair It's never been encouraged in the Service. Which one is he?

Hapgood The handsome one.

Blair Oh, yes.

Hapgood Don't wave.

Blair I wasn't going to.

Hapgood I used to wave. He told everyone he was adopted. You are nice wearing the scarf, you don't have to.

Blair I like the scarf. I wanted to see you –

Hapgood – wanted to see *you* –

Blair – before you see Wates. Washington wants –

Hapgood Kick! – kick for touch! – oh, sugar! – Tackle! – tackle low . . .

Referee's whistle. Bad news for Hapgood.

Oh . . . Bad luck, St Christopher's! Little darlings, they look so cold. Sixteen love.

Blair Nil. Washington wants us to take Kerner off everything.

Hapgood What have the Americans got against Kerner?

Blair Well, this is just an educated guess but I suppose if they're going to spend a hundred million dollars over here on Kerner's SDI research they'd rather he didn't continue swapping briefcases with the high dive champion of the Russian Embassy.

Hapgood Paul, Kerner is my star.

Blair Means nothing.

Hapgood Do you want me to tell you or not? I had six months' work in Kerner's delivery, long-term reflectors on countdown.

Blair Do talk English.

Hapgood Disinformation that had to be launched, I couldn't *afford* to abort the meet just because Washington got into a flap about Kerner.

Blair You can't blame Washington. Kerner's pure gold, the man with the anti-particle trap, and if he's leaking his own stuff to Moscow we're making it awfully easy for him.

Hapgood Kerner's all right – I run him and he's just doing what I tell him.

Blair Wates made the same point. Don't take it personally.

Hapgood Why would I? It isn't personal.

The referee's whistle – the conversion of the try.

Eighteen. Come on, St Christopher's! Lets get one back! This is personal. Everything else is technical. You're personal sometimes; but not this minute which is all right, so what can I tell you? – it isn't Kerner.

Blair So what happened at the pool? It's a technical question, it almost looks as if you could solve it with pencil and paper: cubicles A, B, C, D, briefcases P, Q, R, find X when the angles are Kerner and the Russian twins, which is a question in itself – are these the famous KGB twins? Now that's what I call a double agent. Who's in charge and is he sane?

Hapgood I hate it, Paul.

Blair Yes, why aren't we pleased?

Hapgood It reeks. The KGB twins are like an old joke that keeps coming back, we've been hearing it for years and I never believed it. And suddenly here they are, identical and large as life. I hate it. (*Pause.*) But it's about the twins. The answer. I nearly got it, then I lost it.

Blair Do you want to keep them for a while?

Hapgood No – chuck 'em out. They're stooges, Paul. The meet this morning went exactly as the Russians planned it, including the arrests. The twins were expendable, they were meant to be seen, they were a success – 'Now he's here, now he's there, oh my God, there's two of them!' Wates nearly cut himself shaving he was so fascinated. He's doing a diagram, on pink paper, showing who was where when, all the coming and going.

Blair He showed me. Guess who was holding the briefcase when the transmitter went off the air.

Hapgood Who was?

Blair You were.

Referee's whistle – a try is scored.

Our side isn't doing too well. Well, if it's you I don't care which side traps its particles. Anti-particles. Do you know what they are? They were never mentioned by Democritus who was the pro-particle chap when I was at school.

Hapgood When a particle meets an anti-particle they annihilate each other, they turn into energy – bang, you understand. You can produce anti-particles in a collider and bottle them in a magnetic field but then you're stuck – the bottle is as big as a barn, and when you open the door you've got a billionth of a second so you have to be quick. If you could slow them down enough to get hold of you'd be in business, and Kerner thinks he can. Do you want me to tell you how?

Blair You know, I don't really . . .

Hapgood (*shouts*) Break! Blind!

Blair . . . I gave a chap a job with us once because he said he'd read physics and I thought he meant the book by Aristotle.

Hapgood Was that last try converted?

Blair No.

Hapgood You weren't looking.

Blair They re-started with a drop-kick.

Hapgood Joe's worried about something too, we've both got the same look.

Blair I've lost him again – you can't tell one from the other when they're all in the same get-up.

Hapgood Once when he was really little, he got unhappy about something, he was crying, he couldn't tell me what it was, he didn't *know* what it was, and he said, 'The thing is, Mummy, I've been unhappy for *years*.' He was only as big as a gumboot. (*Pause. She freezes, thinking.*) Oh . . . ssh – sugar! – Paul, you just said it.

Blair What did I?

Hapgood You can't tell one from the other when they're all in the same get-up. That was what it was. Listen. Ridley's by the pool, Ridley's Russian is getting dressed. Merryweather's Russian arrives. Merryweather follows his Russian in and he follows the other Russian out, and why not? – they're identical and he only saw them one at a time, it could happen to anybody, especially to Merryweather, he probably still doesn't know there were two of them. Now Ridley comes from the pool and the same thing happens to him. He followed one Russian in and he follows the other one out, and why not? – they're identical and he only saw them one at a time. Then he comes back inside and he says, 'You didn't tell me it was twins.'

Referee's whistle, a longer one indicating the end of the game.

It's true. I didn't.

Distantly the two rugby teams call for three cheers for each other, first for St Christopher's, secondly for St Codron's.

Blair So how did he know?

Hapgood He was expecting twins. I think it's Ridley, Paul. I've left my own back door open.
(*Clapping*) Well played, St Christopher's . . . bad luck –

Blair Oh, f-f-fiddle!

Joe enters.

Hapgood Hello, darling.

Joe Hello, Mum. (*He is very muddy and glad to see her. His boots are a size too large.*)

Hapgood Bad luck – well played anyway. Put this on.

Joe Thanks.

He takes the tracksuit and puts it on. Hapgood helps him a little.

Blair Hello, Joe. I'm afraid they were rather good, weren't they?

Joe Yess'a.

Blair How are you otherwise?

Joe All rights'a, thank-yous'a. We always get beaten.
I wish you wouldn't watch, Mum.

Hapgood Well, I like watching, I don't mind if you get
beaten.

Joe But nobody watches except you.

Hapgood There's lots of people watching – look over
there.

Joe That's the *firsts* – that's what I *mean*, nobody watches
Junior Colts B –!

Hapgood I do.

Joe I *know*, Mum –

Hapgood Well, I won't, then.

Joe I like you *coming* –

Hapgood I didn't shout this time –

Joe You did a bit, Mum.

Hapgood Hardly at all, whose boots are those?

Joe Mine.

Hapgood No, they're not.

Joe Yes they are, I bought them.

Hapgood Where?

Joe From Sandilands.

Hapgood Who's Sandilands?

Joe He's had his kidney out so he does art.

Hapgood Oh. How much?

Joe A pound.

Hapgood A pound? What was wrong with yours?

Joe I lost one.

Hapgood You lost a rugby boot?

Joe Yes. Well, not exactly, I mean I haven't *got* any rugger boots.

Hapgood (*irked*) Of course you have, what were you playing in before?

Joe My running shoes – it doesn't matter, nobody minds –

Hapgood You mean you *never* had any rugby boots?

Joe Only this term, Mother –

Hapgood Why didn't you say? – those look too big anyway, how old is Sandilands?

Joe It's *all right*, it's silly to buy new boots for Colts B.

Hapgood And now you've lost a running shoe? How did that happen?

Joe It's not lost, it's on the roof.

Hapgood I don't wish to know about this.

Joe I borrowed the key for Mr Clark's garage where there's the ladder, I was going to get it down in break with the ladder but then I lost it.

Hapgood The ladder?

Joe No, *the key*, Mum – I put it somewhere and Mr Clark will have an epi if I don't find it.

Hapgood Is that what you're worried about, Mr Clark's garage key?

Blair I'll send one of the burglars.

Joe It's all right, don't do anything, Mum –

Hapgood I won't. When was all this?

Joe Today after breakfast – oh: thank you for the parcel. Your card came too. When were you in Austria? Did you go to the Spanish horses?

Hapgood No. I was too busy. What was in the parcel?

Joe The chocolate animals.

Hapgood Oh, yes.

Joe I gave one to Roger.

Hapgood How is Roger?

Joe I think he's pregnant.

Hapgood Oh dear.

Joe Well, he's awfully fat and he only eats chocolate.

Hapgood Oh, well . . .

Joe I've got to go –

Hapgood Yes, don't miss tea – have you told Mr Clark you've lost his garage key?

Joe No, I mean he doesn't know I borrowed it.

Hapgood Don't tell him yet – do the grid for me. From getting up, to when you couldn't find it. You remember how we do that?

Joe It's all right, Mother –

Hapgood I know it's all right. Just do the grid – five minutes for every square, don't leave any out because the key is in one of them, and phone me in first break if you haven't found it.

Joe Yes, all right, thanks, Mum – thanks for coming –

Blair Goodbye, Joe.

Joe Goodbyes'a.

Hapgood Bye, darling – I'll let you know when I can come again –

They exchange a kiss and he runs off.

Blair (*suddenly hearty*) I say – what a jolly nice young chap! Excellent knees. You know, you should go to the Spanish Riding School some time when you're next in Vienna – really worth it.

Hapgood (*tightly*) Right, fine, thanks, point taken – I sent him a postcard; sorry. Oh, sugar, Paul!

Blair I merely said –

Hapgood No, you're right, I break the rules, but I keep *missing* things, last time I missed him in *Robin Hood* even if he was only a tree, and if I can't send him a rotten postcard you can take Vienna and stick it up your –

Blair Right, fair enough –

Hapgood – jumper! Oh, fiddle! – I already run the only intelligence network in the Western world which exhibits seasonal fluctuations, and it's only a matter of time before somebody works out it's the school holidays. And now there's Ridley. Really I should pack it in.

Blair Oh, yes, Ridley. You could be right about him. It makes one wonder about that Bulgarian we lost in Paris . . .

Hapgood Ganchev, I thought so too. And Athens.

Blair Yes, Athens. Wates will like that one.

Hapgood It's a mess.

Blair Yes. Frankly I'd rather it were Kerner. That's just a better mousetrap. The real secrets are about intentions and deployment, and Ridley could make it shit city around here. I like the way they talk, the Americans, don't you? – no, of course you don't. What do you say when you burn your hand on a saucepan? 'Oh, sugar'?

Hapgood I don't cook.

Blair I didn't know you knew. Well, what are we going to do about Ridley? We could reel him in for a hostile interview but I'd rather catch him at it.

Hapgood Yes, that's right. We missed our chance today, we'll have to make him do it all again.

Blair (*surprised*) He won't come back to the well, it's been poisoned.

Hapgood I know. It's difficult. I'll think about it. Do you want some tea? They lay it on for parents and he's entitled to two.

Blair (*shakes his head*) I think I'd better get the search going in back numbers. Perhaps you could organize a relief team from eight o'clock.

Hapgood I've done that.

Blair And someone should tell Downing Street we're standing by Kerner.

Hapgood I've done that too.

Blair Well . . . (*He nods goodbye at her.*) Don't pack it in yet, I need you.

Hapgood I was calling you at the pool this morning.

Blair I was there.

Hapgood I needed *you*.

Blair No, no, that was only personal. But you're going to need me now.

Hapgood I'll see you tomorrow. I'll be twenty minutes late in, there's something I have to do.

> *Blair watches her go. The next time he moves he's in Hapgood's office giving his hat to Maggs and taking off his overcoat.*

SCENE FOUR

Hapgood's office, ten a.m.
There is a door from Maggs's office. A window would be nice but is not necessary. There is a desk with the usual stuff including at least two telephones one of which is red. Push-button dialling. You can dial without picking up the receiver, and you can talk to Maggs without picking up anything. There is a photograph frame on the desk, not too large. There is a safe. There is a decent old polished table big enough for six people to meet though we never need it for more than four. It might be nice to make the conference table and the desk all one thing so long as Hapgood doesn't look like Mussolini at work. An armchair would be useful but not if it has to be carried on. Anyway, there should be room to walk around. Maggs is Hapgood's secretary. He is young, calm, professional.

Maggs Mrs Hapgood will be late. I've told Mr Wates.

Blair Is he here? I didn't see him.

Maggs He's washing his hands and can he have a word.

Blair Well, I'm here.

Maggs He said to say he's washing his hands and can he have a word.

Blair Don't be silly.

Maggs That's what he said. Can I get you some tea?

Blair No, I don't think so, thank you, I had some. Was that Merryweather out there?

Maggs Yes, sir.

Blair Well, somebody should go and tell Mr Wates to stop washing his hands.

Maggs I'll ask Mr Merryweather.

Maggs takes Blair's hat and coat and scarf out. Under the coat Blair looks a bit rumpled, yesterday's shirt, that sort of feeling. He has a Daily Telegraph. *He makes himself comfortable and opens it up.*
The red telephone rings. It has its own sound. Blair takes no notice.
Maggs hurries in.

Blair It's the red line, I thought I wouldn't get in the way.

Maggs (*into phone*) Mrs Hapgood's office . . . oh, hello, I'm sorry she isn't in . . . Yes, I'm fine, thanks, how are things your end?

Wates enters, looking terrific: suit, white shirt, tie, polished shoes. The clothes are loose enough for a gun and the radio to be in there somewhere but not baggy.
Blair gets up to greet him.

Blair Ben! Good morning!

Wates Paul.

Blair Come in – sit down –

Maggs (*into phone*) Uh, hold on a moment –

Blair Mrs Hapgood won't be long.

Maggs (*to Blair*) Excuse me – should I . . .?

Blair No, no – it's perfectly all right.
(*To Wates*) Downing Street.

Wates Uh-huh.

Maggs (*into phone, baffled*) You lost Mr Clark's garage key?

Blair (*hastily*) The *Telegraph* has got a lot better, I notice
. . . doesn't come off on your hands the way it used to.
Maggs said you were washing your hands, but he didn't
say of what.

Wates You guys.

Blair (*cheerfully*) Yes, it's wit city around here.

Wates No, you're funny like funny money, it doesn't
mean everything it says.

Maggs (*into phone*) He threw your boot on the roof.

Wates I'm not listening.

Maggs (*into phone*) Five minutes for every square.
Uh-huh. One square finding Whitaker for Matron. In
the toilet, all right – two squares just dossing about,
all right –

Wates What number Downing Street?

Maggs (*into phone*) Oh! Have you got another coin? I'll
call you straight back from my office. (*He puts down the
red phone and leaves, closing the door.*)

Blair You wanted a word, I think . . .

Wates Well . . .

Blair . . . in the washroom.

Wates gets up, or perhaps he hasn't sat down, his manner is restless. He picks up the photo on Hapgood's desk.

Wates (*quietly*) Mother.

Blair Mm?

Wates Ridley and the other one, Merryweather, they call her Mother.

Blair Yes.

Wates There's a son.

Blair There is a son but she was called Mother when she joined the Defence Liaison Committee – the tea would arrive and the Minister would say, 'Who's going to be mother?'

Wates She was the only woman.

Blair Yes. She's still the only woman.

Wates Is there a Mr Hapgood?

Blair No.

Wates Dead?

Blair Is this idle curiosity?

Wates You tell me.

Blair Hapgood is her own name. Mrs is a courtesy title. It saves a lot of explanation. Usually.

Wates Do you mind if I ask you something, Paul?

Blair I'm beginning to.

Wates puts the frame carefully back on the desk. Suddenly impatient.

Wates Look, it's simple: do you know who the kid's father is or not?

Blair stares back at him, quite blank, and Wates lets it go. Wates has a complaint now.

She calls me Wates.

Blair It's a sort of compliment.

Wates It doesn't sound friendly.

Blair Mister wouldn't be friendly.

Wates You call me Ben.

Blair That's another sort of compliment.

Wates She doesn't call me Ben.

Blair That would be friendly but not necessarily a compliment.

Wates She calls you Paul.

Blair Yes, but we're friends.

Wates Can you explain this in some way I'd understand it?

Blair considers the question.

Blair No, I don't think so.

Wates You guys.

Blair What did you want to talk about?

Wates Ridley.

Blair All right.

Wates You don't look surprised.

Blair It's deceptive.

Wates I was thinking about Ridley. Kerner delivers but Ridley intercepts. Ridley intercepts and delivers to Hapgood.

Ridley and Hapgood. Hapgood and Ridley. I know the tune. You didn't tell me it was him in Athens.

Blair Oh, yes, Athens.

Wates Talk to me about Athens, Paul, since we're friends.

Blair Well, we targeted a radio operator in the Russian Embassy in Athens who was cheating on his wife with a local girl we put in his way, a straightforward honeytrap. Mrs Hapgood came out from London to put the squeeze on him. Ridley was at that time number three in the Athens station, he took the photographs. But it went wrong and as you know we had to pull Ridley out of Athens in a hurry.

Wates He killed an American agent.

Blair That isn't how I'd put it.

Wates How would you put it?

Blair He killed a Greek national who turned out to be on the Company payroll. Anyway, it was a sideshow. The target's wife found out he was cheating. Next thing, the KGB goons busted our Russian in the girl's flat. Simply bad luck. The girl got roughed up in the process and her pimp took it into his head that Ridley set her up. He tried to shoot Ridley on the stairs of his apartment and Ridley shot him first. Most embarrassing.

Wates Embarrassing?

Blair For Her Majesty's Government. It nearly cost us the Elgin Marbles.

Wates Look at the score. One American source dead, one Russian target blown, one honeytrap busted – that's three nothing to them, and Ridley moves on to Paris. (*Pause.*) Now I'm thinking about Ganchev, you remember Ganchev?

Blair Ganchev. I can't quite place him –

Wates Bulgarian. He was one of your joes, shot dead in Paris. He was your Bulgarian – he got blown – the Bulgarians took him out – boom! – and you can't quite place him.

Blair Oh, yes, Ganchev.

Wates Right, Miron Ganchev. He was Ridley's joe, wasn't he?

Blair Yes, that's right.

Wates He was making a meet with Ridley and he was killed in a safe house in the rue Velásquez except it wasn't a safe house any more.

Blair Yes.

Wates It was Ridley's meet. Two doorkeys, whoever gets there first waits for whoever gets there second. Ridley was second.

Blair I think I can see what you're getting at but unfortunately Ganchev was shot at a range of about nine inches and Ridley was in a taxi in a traffic jam on the wrong side of the river. We went into it.

Wates No, you don't see. Who says he was in a taxi?

Pause.

Blair (*quietly*) Ben, I really wouldn't want you to make an ass of yourself.

Wates Who says he was in a taxi?

Blair Fuck off.

Wates It was Hapgood. She was in the taxi too. And you went into it. Did you get the taxi driver? No. You had Ridley's boss.

Blair (*flares up*) What is this – couldn't you sleep? This is stood on *nothing*: if Ridley did it, Hapgood must have alibi'd him: if Hapgood alibi'd him Ridley must have done it. You've got nothing, Ben, except insomnia.

Wates That's what it was. Nine p.m. Washington time I'm in Grosvenor Square, going through the whole thing again, I'm thinking about the radio signal in Kerner's briefcase. It gets to the meet, no question. Kerner delivers, Ridley collects, Ridley delivers to Hapgood. The signal goes dead.

Blair It's still insomnia.

Wates (*imperturbably*) It's still insomnia and I'm still thinking about Kerner's bleep. It went off the air but what does that mean? Maybe it went off the air, maybe we lost the frequency, maybe it hopped frequencies, maybe there was an override, you know what I mean? I didn't believe any of it, I just wanted to get rid of these things so I could forget the bleep and think about some-thing else. So my guy's radio-finder is sitting on the desk and I put on the phones and I tune it in . . . and, Paul, it was alive. It was transmitting like a bullfrog.

Blair Two o'clock in the morning?

Wates (*nods*) I start waking people up. I have a vector on it, I need co-ordinates. By four o'clock I know which street, I know the building, I know which corner of the building, I know how high up the building within eight feet, I mean, shit, I know which *room*. It was coming from this office. The bleep has come back home. It's here.

Blair Why didn't you wake me?

Wates Where were you sleeping?

Pause.

Blair Where is she now?

Wates You're asking me?

Blair (*snaps*) Yes, I'm asking you.

Wates Excuse me. (*He takes the radio out of his coat. To radio*) Wates – who's in the Toyota?

Radio Collins, sir.

Wates Where're you at?

Radio Outside. Target is home.

Wates puts the radio back in his pocket.

Wates She just walked in.

Blair Good.

Wates We should hold back a little, feel this thing out.

Blair Don't worry. Incidentally, where did she go this morning?

Wates Shopping.

Blair Shopping.

Wates As I say, it makes sense to hold back, Paul, give her a little room, you understand me?

Blair Of course.

*The door opens and Hapgood enters briskly. She has
her shopping with her. There is a Lillywhites' carrier
bag and a little Fortnum's bag.*

Hapgood Good morning! – Paul – Wates –

Blair Good morning! – Guess what – Kerner's bleep
came alive in the night, it seems to be coming from your
office.

Wates Aw, shit.

Hapgood Golly, Wates.

Wates I meant golly.

Hapgood Sit down.

Wates I've been sitting, I like standing, ma'am.

*Maggs enters. He comes from the outer office with
stuff for Hapgood's attention; a wooden tray (shallow
box) overflowing with open letters, memos, etc., and a
separate lot of sensitive material which might even be
in a little attaché case or a closable file. The tray is put
on the desk; it's the other lot of stuff which Hapgood
looks through first.*

Maggs Good morning. Do you want to see the decrypts?

*Hapgood is behind her desk. Blair has sat down again
where he was sitting, and Wates probably stays standing. Maggs stands.*

Hapgood (*to Maggs*) Thank you. Anything else?

Maggs Joe telephoned. I wrote down the grid.

Hapgood Thank you – don't go. (*to Wates*) What time,
Wates?

Wates One fifty – two o'clock . . .

Hapgood Uh-huh.

She has scooped the decrypts, etc., out of their case. Maggs gets the case. Hapgood starts going through the pile of stuff. There's not very much of it. But unless otherwise stated she is reading the material continuously, making notes on pages which one by one go back to Maggs and back into the case. She reads while she listens and she also reads while she talks to Wates. But for Blair she looks up.

(*To Blair*) Did you see this from the Listeners?

Blair Mm. I'll believe it when it happens.

Hapgood (*to Wates*) It was alive when you checked, so you don't know when it came on air.

Wates That's right.

Hapgood (*to Maggs*) This one to Special Branch in the pouch. This one to the Russian Desk by hand.

(*To Wates*) And you got a triangulation and the beams crossed in this office.

Wates Yes, ma'am.

Hapgood Is it still giving out?

Wates As far as I know.

Hapgood And you would know, wouldn't you?

It is clear now that he is not popular with her this morning.

(*Icy*) Why didn't you call me?

He doesn't reply so she gives him a glance.

Yes, I see. (*She bangs a few buttons on her telephone console and then lifts the handset. Into phone*) Get me the form on a white Toyota –

Wates (*pleading guilty*) Yeah, all right.

Hapgood (*into phone*) Cancel. (*She puts the phone down. To Wates*) I'll get back to that. So did you bring a radio-finder with you? (*to Maggs*) This one upstairs, this one reconfirm.

Wates No, ma'am.

Hapgood You thought you'd give me first crack. That's all right.

Wates Ma'am, this is a 500 millisecond-repeat transponder-transmitter locked on seventeen megahertz with a lithium battery and a gate interrupter . . . it . . .

He falters because she appears to be absorbed in her next paper.

Hapgood Interrupter.

Wates It gives it a signature, it has to be the same bleep.

She scribbles on the last decrypt, hands it to Maggs and takes the top sheet off the other pile.

Hapgood So it went dead at ten-oh-seven yesterday morning and it was alive again at two a.m. Can they come and go like that?

Wates Not that I ever heard. My guy couldn't figure it either. They're either fixed or broke, they don't fix themselves.

Hapgood Uh-huh. Did he mention a hamster?

Wates A what?

Hapgood (*to Maggs*) Roger.

Maggs No.

Hapgood You sure? – empty square before assembly –

Maggs No Roger-the-hamster.

Hapgood Oh, the chump. (*relieved*) That's all, Maggs. Tea.

Maggs goes back to his office. Wates has had enough of this.

Wates Excuse me – we don't need to know about this stuff. When I put on the phones I felt foolish like putting on a stethoscope for a corpse that's been ten hours dead in the water – but, ma'am, we've got a situation now and I'm glad Paul is here because I'm asking him to ask you if you would open up that safe you have there and then I won't have to worry about it any more.

Hapgood has stopped listening. She sits thinking.

Paul? (*He gets no help.*)

Hapgood Wates, I could kiss you. (*She goes to the door.*) Merryweather. (*She heads back to her desk.*)

Merryweather (*entering*) Thanks, Mother, I don't need long, it was just that I had a thought about our Russian friend –

Hapgood (*sitting down*) In a minute. You drained the pool.

Merryweather Yes, that's right.

Hapgood How long did that take?

Merryweather Ages – most of the day – right down to the filter –

Hapgood And?

Merryweather I put it in Maggs's box last night.

He means an envelope on Maggs's pile. Hapgood tears the envelope across.

Looked interesting to me. Any good?

The envelope contains a 'poker chip' transmitter. She tosses it to Wates who catches it.

Hapgood Ten hours dead in the water. It only drowns the signal, when Merryweather fished it out it was back on the air.

Maggs comes in with Hapgood's tea. It's like having tea at the Ritz without the sandwiches – nice china, tea pot, hot water jug, etc.
Blair, who has been sitting too still for too long, now stretches all the tension out of his body, sprawling in his chair, languid again.

Blair I think I might change my mind about that tea, Maggs . . . how about you, Ben?

Wates Yes. Thank you.

Hapgood Just the cups, Maggs. Mr Wates takes it with lemon.

Maggs We haven't got a lemon.

Hapgood Tsk, tsk, you must always keep a lemon.

Maggs (*leaving*) The reply from Ottawa came in.

Hapgood Oh yes?

Maggs Exchange bishops, and queen to king one.

Hapgood Exchange bishops, my eye – he'll be lucky.

Maggs leaves. Hapgood broods for a moment. From his pocket, Wates produces his pink-paper 'diagram'. He looks at it and passes it to Blair. Meanwhile –

Merryweather Mother . . .

Hapgood Oh, I'm sorry, Merryweather –

Merryweather It's just that I had a thought which may or may not be something.

Hapgood Of course – tell us your thought.

Merryweather Well, I was thinking about it and something wasn't quite right. The Russian delivered to the changing room and he came straight out again . . .

Hapgood Yes?

Merryweather He didn't have time for a swim or anything.

Hapgood Uh-huh.

Merryweather Well, this is the thing – I was thinking about it and I'm pretty sure his towel was dry when I followed him in but it was wet when I followed him out . . . I was wondering if anybody had noticed that. (*Pause.*) Well, it was just a thought I thought I'd leave with you.

Hapgood It's a good thought, Merryweather, worth thinking about. Thank you.

Merryweather Fine. Any way I can help.

Hapgood Actually, there's a job you can do for me.

Merryweather Good – of course –

Hapgood It's down the A30 past Staines.

Merryweather Right. A meet?

Hapgood A sort of meet. Just past Virginia Water you take a right, the A329 to Bracknell, a couple of miles along there's a prep school, St Christopher's.

From the Lillywhites' bag she produces a pair of brand new rugby boots and gives them to Merryweather.

Get there at exactly one fifty. You'll find a lot of small boys charging around outside. Stop the first boy you see and say, 'Do you know Hapgood?'

Merryweather 'Do you know Hapgood?'

Hapgood The boy will say, 'Yes, sir.' There's an outside chance he'll say, 'I am Hapgood, sir,' but probably not. Give him this, and say, 'I have a message from Mother.'

Merryweather 'Do you know Hapgood? I have a message from Mother.' Is this the message?

Hapgood No, the message is, 'The garage key is on Roger's hutch.'

Merryweather 'The garage key is on Roger's hutch.'

Maggs comes in with the cups. He goes to add them to the tray.

Hapgood St Christopher's – the Bracknell road – one fifty.

Merryweather Right. 'The garage key is on Roger's hutch.'

Hapgood Thank you very much, Merryweather.

She has helped him out of the door. Maggs is following Merryweather out.

(*To Maggs*) Pawn to rook four, and tell him to put his queen back.

Maggs (*continuing out*) Pawn to rook four.

Maggs closes the door behind him. Pause.

Wates It's Ridley.

Blair Mm.

Wates I'm sorry. (*He is commiserating, not apologizing.*) You'll have to turn over everything he ever touched.

Hapgood We're already doing that.

Wates (*surprised, wrong-footed*) Since when?

Hapgood Since yesterday. Paul's been here all night. (*She flicks her thumb along Blair's jaw bone, a technical gesture.*) You look awful.

That's Wates wrong-footed twice.

(*To Wates*) Do you remember Ganchev, our Bulgarian? – Paul and I think that's one which needs looking at, did he tell you?

That's three times. He is suddenly really angry.

Wates You guys!

Hapgood Wates –

Wates My friends call me Ben!

Hapgood I don't care what your friends call you, I want to tell you something – I will not be tagged by your people in my own *town*! I took them all round Lilly-whites and I can number them off, don't think I can't, I've been followed by marching bands that did it better, and if they're not pulled by the time I go to lunch you're off the bus. Is that entirely clear?

Wates It's clear.

Hapgood Good. Did they tell you I popped into Fortnum's? (*From the little Fortnum's bag she takes a lemon, which is all the bag contains and adds it to the tea-tray.*) Where are we, Paul?

Blair passes her Wates's pink diagram.

Blair Where we are is that when the bleep died it was no longer in the briefcase, it was in the water, and Ridley was by the pool. We're no further than that. But it's really quite attractive: every month, Ridley helps to pack Kerner's briefcase. That's his job. Kerner's job is handing the briefcase over to the Russians.

Wates It's made in heaven.

Blair Yes. The opposition don't care which way Kerner is bent, either way he's a channel for Ridley. Yesterday it nearly came apart but only because of the leak in Moscow. Ridley had to remove the evidence.

Wates Why did he remove your films?

Blair (*smoothly*) Obviously because he put *in* a roll of film and they all look the same.

Wates And the bleep?

Blair Oh, you know, pass-the-parcel . . . did you ever play that? The object is not to be the one holding the parcel when the music stops. Ridley drowned the signal when . . . someone else was holding the . . .

Wates (*deflecting*) Yes, all right. (*Pause.*) And he did all that without opening the briefcase?

Blair Ah, yes. That's the bit we're still working on.

Wates I'd say you have a problem.

Blair We have a hypothesis.

Wates A *hypothesis*?

Blair Mmm. Actually, it's Mr Kerner's hypothesis.

Blair and Hapgood are complicitly wary of Wates, not secretive but slightly embarrassed, expecting his derision.

Wates And is this *hypothesis* a hypothesis you can share?

Hapgood It's twins.

Wates It's twins?

Hapgood Two Ridleys.

Long pause. Blair and Hapgood watch him nervously.

Wates (*evenly*) Yeah that would do it.

Hapgood and Blair relax.

Hapgood Thank you, Ben. Well, should I be mother?

SCENE FIVE

An indoor shooting range. But we don't really know that yet. We see Ridley, downstage in the only lit area, ready to shoot, holding his gun towards the dark upstage. Ridley shoots six times. His shots are aimed at six illuminated targets which make their sudden and successive appearances. Some of the targets are 'blue' and some (most) are 'green'. (Or, cut-out figures, of villains and civilians, with some changes to the dialogue.)

No targets are showing when we see Ridley. He starts shooting when the first target appears.

Ridley's six targets come up as four greens, then a blue, then a green. He hits the first two, misses the third and fourth, hits the fifth, which is the blue, and the sixth. Ridley's conversation is with an amplified voice. Ridley doesn't have to raise his voice to reply, but his voice echoes.

Voice Stop shooting. Two misses, three greens and you killed a blue. Reload.

Ridley Reloading.

Voice On your go, and remember blue is our side.

Ridley Yes, sir.

Hapgood enters quietly, walking behind Ridley's back.

Voice Mr Ridley, on your go.

Ridley Go.

The first target is blue. Ridley lets it live. The next five are all green, rapid. Ridley hits four, misses the fifth, and hardly has time to curse before the target is knocked out by a sixth shot, from Hapgood's gun.

Voice Wait a minute – wait a minute –

Hapgood comes into Ridley's light, putting a small automatic into her handbag.

Hapgood Hey, Ridley.

Ridley Mother.

Voice Is that you, Mrs Hapgood?

Hapgood (*cheerful*) Hello, Mac. How've you been?

Voice Ma'am, you're breaking the rules.

Hapgood I know, I'm hopeless. Will you give us the shop for a while?

Voice Do you want the mike?

Hapgood No, no need.

Voice I'll be in the back.

Hapgood Thank you.

We lose the echo.

(*To Ridley*) I have to talk to you.

Ridley Funny place to choose.

Hapgood I'm not sure that I want to be seen with you, Ridley.

Ridley considers this. He considers her. He has his gun in his hand. He puts the gun away behind him, into his waistband under his jacket next to his spine. He takes out a packet of cigarettes, puts one in his mouth, puts the packet away, and feels for the lighter.

Don't light it.

Ridley takes the cigarette out of his mouth and holds it unlit.

Ridley What's the problem?

Hapgood The problem is, someone's playing dirty and we're favourite.

Ridley (*quite pleased*) You and me? What have we done?

Hapgood The story is we're bent. We've been using Kerner to pass real secrets. Yesterday it went wrong for us and we had to steal them back during the meet. You passed the briefcase to me and I emptied it.

Ridley If this is Wates why doesn't he go for the obvious? The stuff was never in there.

Hapgood Wates tracked it to the pool, he had a finder on the bleep. It stayed alive till the briefcase got to me.

Ridley laughs.

Ridley I think I see. You cracked the transponder in your teeth.

Hapgood I was in the shower. It doesn't work in water.

Ridley likes that even better.

Ridley And what about the Geiger? Weren't you clean?

Hapgood No. When I opened the briefcase to see if we had a result . . . How do you like it so far?

Ridley (*delighted*) It's beautiful. I'm beginning to think you did it. I don't see that you'd need me.

Hapgood Well, there are a couple of other things. Wates has been digging up the back garden and he thinks he's found some bones he can make bodies out of.

Ridley Like what?

Hapgood Like Athens.

Ridley Ah, Athens. We *met* in Athens. Oh, Mother . . . Athens was the best time of my life.

Hapgood Was it? We had an operation that blew up in our faces.

Ridley What's that to Wates?

Hapgood Well, that girl in Athens, the night she was busted, she said you were there, outside.

Ridley That was rubbish. I was with you.

Hapgood I know.

Ridley In a parked car in Piraeus waiting for our Russian who never turned up, we were pretending to be lovers.

Hapgood Don't leer, it suits you.

Ridley What else?

Hapgood Ganchev.

Ridley Good heavens. What a team.

Hapgood I tell you, Ridley, I'm sick of being your alibi. I can't blame Wates for wondering about us.

Ridley Did Wates talk to you?

Hapgood No.

Ridley He talked to Paul Blair? Blair wouldn't be impressed. It's all circular. It can't be me without you, it can't be you without me, so it's both of us. Whatever happened to neither? Did Blair listen?

Hapgood He listened but he thinks he knows better.

Ridley Trust, you see.

Hapgood No, he thinks it's Kerner.

Ridley Yes, that makes sense.

Hapgood Why?

Ridley Every double is a risk – Blair would have to consider it.

Hapgood Well, I hope he's wrong.

Ridley That's a funny thing to say, Mother.

Hapgood (*with passion*) *Kerner is my joe!* I turned him. If he's bent, something must have turned him back again – recently, a few months . . .

Ridley What would that be?

Hapgood (*shrugs*) *Toska po rodine.*

Ridley What's that?

Hapgood Homesickness, but squared. You have to be Russian.

Ridley That could be. Did he leave a family?

Hapgood Why?

Ridley When I processed him after the meet I found a photograph, fingernail size, cut out with scissors, like

538

from a team photo. It was hidden in the lining of his wallet, an amateur job picture of a boy in a football shirt.

Hapgood (*looks at him steadily*) What did you do with it?

Ridley I put it back, Mother. Do I have to keep calling you Mother? You can call me Ernest. (*Pause.*) Call me Ridley.

Hapgood You're all right, Ridley. The firm will miss you.

Ridley Say again?

Hapgood You're suspended. So am I. Wates took his story upstairs. Paul Blair is running my operations. Do you think I got you here for fun?

Ridley God almighty. What do we do now?

Hapgood You do what Blair tells you. In my office, seven o'clock, and you're there to listen, don't talk out of turn. By the way, we're not telling the Americans.

Ridley Trust me. (*then a flat challenge*) Why don't you, as a matter of fact?

Hapgood You're not safe, Ridley. You're cocky and I like prudence, you're street smart and this is a boardgame. In Paris you bounced around like Tigger, you thought it was cowboys and Indians. In Athens you killed a man and it was the best time of your life, you thought it was sexy. You're not my type. You're my alibi and I'm yours. Trust doesn't come into it.

Ridley Well, go and fuck yourself, Hapgood, (*He now takes his lighter out and lights his cigarette with deliberate, insolent defiance.*) since we're on suspension. You come on like you're running your joes from the senior common room and butter wouldn't melt in your pants but you operate like a circular saw, and you pulled me to watch your back because when this is a street business I'm your bloody type all right, and in Athens if you could have got your bodice up past your brain you would have screwed me and liked it. (*He starts to leave.*)

Hapgood Ridley.

He stops.

Safety.

Ridley I didn't reload.

Hapgood You saved on the blue.

Ridley That's true. (*He takes his gun from the holster, checks it and puts it back.*) This is all right.

Hapgood What is?

Ridley I like it when it's you and me.

Ridley leaves.
Kerner enters, coming towards her out of the dark and into the light. She sees him and is not surprised. She takes her radio out of her bag.

Hapgood (*to radio*) Is he clear?

Radio Green.

Hapgood I'm here to be told. (*She puts the radio back into her bag. To Kerner*) Do you mean there's another one like him?

Kerner It's a hypothesis.

Hapgood So where's the other one?

Kerner Maybe that was the other one.

540

Hapgood Joseph! (*Their manner is as of intimate friends.*) Did you look at Wates's diagram?

Kerner (*nods*) Positional geometry. Leibnitz. I'll tell you about him.

Hapgood No, don't.

Kerner You're right, it's marginal. I'll tell you about Leonhard Euler. Were you ever in Kaliningrad?

Hapgood No, I'm afraid not.

Kerner I was born in Kaliningrad. So was Immanuel Kant, as a matter of fact. There is quite a nice statue of him. Of course, it was not Kaliningrad then, it was Konigsberg, seat of the Archdukes of Prussia. President Truman gave Konigsberg to Stalin. My parents were not consulted and I missed being German by a few months. Well, in Immanuel Kant's Konigsberg there were seven bridges. The river Pregel, now Pregolya, divides around an island and then divides again, imagine nutcrackers with one bridge across each of the handles and one across the hinge and four bridges on to the island which would be the walnut if you were cracking walnuts. An ancient amusement of the people of Konigsberg was to try to cross all seven bridges without crossing any of them twice. It looked possible but nobody had solved it. Now, when Kant was ten years old . . . what do you think?

Hapgood Did he really? What a charming story.

Kerner The little Kant had no idea either. No, when Kant was ten years old, the Swiss mathematician Leonhard Euler took up the problem of the seven bridges and he presented his solution in the form of a general principle. Of course, Euler didn't waste his time walking around Konigsberg, he only needed the geometry. (*He* *now produces Wates's diagram on pink paper.*) When I looked at Wates's diagram I saw that Euler had already done the proof. It was the bridges of Konigsberg, only simpler.

Hapgood What did Euler prove?

Kerner It can't be done, you need two walkers.

Pause.

Hapgood Good old Euler.

Kerner You like it?

Hapgood (*nods*) It makes sense of those twin Russians trailing their coats around the pool. Last year the Swedes got themselves a KGB defector and the famous twins turned up in his debriefing with a solid London connection. If two Ridleys are for real they must have felt the draught. Those two jokers at the meet were brought in as decoys. Reflectors. I never believed in the twins till then. I know about reflectors.

Kerner Has this place been dusted?

Hapgood Dusted?

Kerner We can talk?

Hapgood (*amused*) Oh, yes. We can talk. (*She regards him steadily.*) *Now* he's careful.

Kerner The photograph? I'm ashamed.

Hapgood (*sudden force*) No, I am. Oh, fiddle!

Kerner I mean, 'an amateur job'.

Hapgood Oh, Joseph.

Kerner Yes, I'm one of your Joes. How is the little one?

Hapgood He's all right. He's fine. Stop sending him chocolates, they're bad for his teeth and not good for his hamster. Dusted is fingerprints, you know. Microphones is swept. Where do you pick up these things?

Kerner Spy stories. I like them. Well, they're different, you know. Not from each other naturally. I read in hope but they all surprise in the same way. Ridley is not very nice: he'll turn out to be all right. Blair will be the traitor: the one you liked. This is how the author says, 'You see! Life is not like books, alas!' They're all like that. I don't mind. I love the language.

Hapgood (*the language lover*) I'm awfully glad.

Kerner Safe house, sleeper, cover, joe . . . I love it. When I have learned the language I will write my own book. The traitor will be the one you don't like very much, it will be a scandal. Also I will reveal him at the beginning. I don't understand this mania for surprises. If the author knows, it's rude not to tell. In science this is understood: what is interesting is to know what is happening. When I write an experiment I do not wish you to be *surprised*, it is not a *joke*. This is why a science paper is a beautiful thing: first, here is what we will find; now here is how we find it; here is the first puzzle, here is the answer, now we can move on. This is polite. We don't save up all the puzzles to make a triumph for the author.

Hapgood (*insisting*) *Joseph* – twins. Who's in charge and is he sane?

Kerner His name was Konstantin Belov, and, yes, he was sane, though in my opinion absurd.

Hapgood More.

Kerner He is not in charge now. The twins are his legacy.

Hapgood You knew him?

Kerner Sure. His training was particle physics, before he got into State Security. One day Konstantin Belov jumped out of his bathtub and shouted 'Eureka!' Maybe he was asleep in the bath. The particle world is the dream world of the intelligence officer. An electron can be here or there at the same moment. You can choose. It can go from here to there without going in between; it can pass through two doors at the same time, or from one door to another by a path which is there for all to see until someone looks, and then the act of looking has made it take a different path. Its movements cannot be anticipated because it has no reasons. It defeats surveillance because when you know what it's doing you can't be certain where it is, and when you know where it is you can't be certain what it's doing: Heisenberg's uncertainty principle; and this is not because you're not looking carefully enough, it is because there is *no such thing* as an electron with a definite position and a definite momentum; you fix one, you lose the other, and it's all done without tricks, it's the real world, it is awake.

Hapgood Joseph, please explain to me about the twins.

Kerner I just did but you missed it.

Pause.

Hapgood It's crazy.

Kerner (*unmoved*) Oh, yes . . . but compared to the electron it is banal . . . Yelizaveta, when things get very small they get truly crazy, and you don't know how small things can be, you think you know but you don't know. I could put an atom into your hand for every second since the world began and you would have to squint to see the dot of atoms in your palm. So now make a fist, and if your fist is as big as the nucleus of one atom then the atom is as big as St Paul's, and if it happens to be a hydrogen atom then it has a single electron flitting about like a moth in the empty cathedral, now by the dome, now by the altar . . . Every atom is a cathedral. I cannot stand the pictures of atoms they put in schoolbooks, like a little solar system: Bohr's atom. Forget it. You can't make a picture of what Bohr proposed, an electron does not go round like a planet, it is like a moth which was there a moment ago, it gains or loses a quantum of energy and it jumps, and at the moment of quantum jump it is like *two* moths, one to be here and one to stop being there; an electron is like twins, each one unique, a unique twin.

Hapgood Its own alibi.

Kerner It upset Einstein very much, you know, all that damned uncertainty, it spoiled his idea of God, which I tell you frankly is the only idea of Einstein's I never understood. He couldn't believe in a God who threw dice. He should have come to me, I would have told him, 'Listen, Albert, He threw *you* – look around, He never stops.' What is a hamster, by the way? No, tell me in a minute, I want to tell you something first. There is a straight ladder from the atom to the grain of sand, and the only real mystery in physics is the missing rung. Below it, particle physics; above it, classical physics; but in between, metaphysics. All the mystery in life turns out to be this same mystery, the join between things which are distinct and yet continuous, body and mind, free will and causality, living cells and life itself; the moment before the foetus. Who needed God when everything worked like billiard balls? What were you going to say?

Hapgood It's like a fat rabbit with no ears.

Kerner Oh yes. You mean a *khomyak*.

Hapgood Yes, a *khomyak* called Roger. (*Pause.*) Joseph, after this thing with Ridley you're blown, you know, your career will be over.

Kerner Except as a scientist, you mean.

Hapgood Yes, that's what I mean, I won't need you any more, I mean I'll need you again – oh, sugar! – you *know* what I mean – do you want to marry me? I think I'd like to be married. Well, don't look like that.

Kerner What is this? – because of a photograph in my wallet? It is not even necessary, I never look at it.

Hapgood Won't you want to meet him now?

Kerner Oh, yes. 'This is Joe.' 'Hello, young man.'

Hapgood (*defiantly*) Well, I'm going to tell him, whether you marry me or not.

Kerner I'm not charmed by this. If I loved you it was so long ago I had to tell you in Russian and you kept the tape running. It was not a safe house for love. The spy was falling in love with the case-officer, you could hear it on the playback. One day you switched off the hidden microphone and got pregnant.

Hapgood That's uncalled for. I loved you.

Kerner You interrogated me. Weeks, months, every day. I was your thought, your objective . . . If love was like that it would not even be healthy.

Hapgood (*stubbornly*) I loved you, Joseph.

Kerner You fell into your own honeypot –

Hapgood (*flares*) That's a damned lie! You unspeakable *cad!*

Kerner – and *now* you think you'd like to be married, and tell Joe he has a father after all, not dead after all, only a secret, we are all in the secret service! – no, I don't think so. And suppose I decided to return.

That brings her up short.

Hapgood Where? Why would you do that?

Kerner Toska po rodine.

Hapgood You mustn't say that to me, Joseph. Please don't say it.

Kerner You would not tell.

Hapgood I might. Take it back.

Kerner comforts her.

Kerner Milaya moya, rodnaya moya . . . it's all right. I am your Joe.

She suffers his embrace, then softens into it.

Cad is good. I like cad.

Hapgood Honeypot . . .

Kerner Is that wrong?

Hapgood Honey*trap*. And anyway that's something else. You and your books.

Kerner I thought you would marry Paul.

Wrong. Hapgood stiffens, separates herself.

Hapgood I'll see you tonight. And let Paul do the talking. Keep your end of it as simple as you can.

Kerner Worry about yourself. I will be magnificent.

Act Two

Hapgood's office, evening. Blair sits in Hapgood's place.
Hapgood sits to one side. Ridley sits to the other side.
They are waiting. When Ridley gets bored with this he
opens his mouth to say something.

Blair (*mildly*) Shut up, Ridley.

The door opens and Maggs comes in with a potted
plant, with card attached, and delivers it to Hapgood.
She opens the little envelope and looks at the florist's
card, replaces the card and puts the envelope back
where it started on the potted plant. Meanwhile
Maggs receives a nod from Blair and leaves the room,
returning immediately to let Kerner into the room.
Maggs retires again closing the door.

(*Greeting Kerner*) Joseph!

Kerner Hello, Paul.

Blair Sit here, won't you?

Kerner (*turns to Hapgood*) So. Something special.

Hapgood ignores his glance. After a slight pause,
Kerner takes the chair down-table opposite Blair.

Blair This is a friendly interview. That's a technical term.
It means it is not a hostile interview, which is also a
technical term. I'll define them if you wish. (*Pause.*) Well,
I won't protract this.

From a dossier he produces about half a dozen
five-by-eight black and white photographs; pages from
a typewritten document.

548

Have a look at these, would you?

He pushes them down the table to Kerner who spreads them face up in front of him.

I'm afraid they're not very good – photographs of photographs – but you can probably see what they are.

Kerner Of course.

Blair One of your regular reports on the anti-matter programme you're running with the Centre for Nuclear Research in Geneva, April/May; copies to the main contractors, the Livermore Research Laboratory in California, through the SDI office in the Pentagon, travelling by embassy courier from Grosvenor Square; and copies to the Defence Liaison Committee, also by hand; both lots under the control of this office, where indeed the copies are made; a very limited circulation, fifteen copies in all, nine American and six British. In fact, however, these photographs are of a British copy. The white patches are the erasure of the circulation number printed on to each page *ab origine*. Washington adds an American circulation prefix, missing from these pages but not erased. All clear so far?

Kerner Where did the photos come from?

Blair Moscow. They were received in Washington two days ago from an American agent in place, not an *American*, of course; 'in place' means –

Kerner Please, I am not illiterate.

Blair The six British copies have a read-and-return distribution of eleven. That includes the Minister, the Liaison Committee and the Prime Minister's box. It doesn't include your lab, or this office where our copy is kept on file with the turnkeys.

Kerner May I ask a question?

Blair Yes, do.

Kerner Why are you sitting in Mrs Hapgood's chair?

Blair That is a very fair question. The answer is that Mrs Hapgood isn't here. Mr Ridley isn't here either. They are on paid leave, which is why they can't be with us this evening, and which is why this is a friendly interview.

Kerner (*laughs*) Oh, Paul, have you broken the rules at last? – turned by a pair of pretty eyelashes?

Hapgood Behave yourself, damn you!

Blair (*intervenes calmingly*) Please . . . As you know, there is a regular traffic of monitored information going to the Soviets from this office, organized and prepared by Mrs Hapgood and Mr Ridley, and delivered to you for delivery to your Russian control. In other words a channel already exists. As a precautionary measure, Mrs Hapgood and Mr Ridley have been relieved of their duties. In the same spirit of caution rather than insinuation, your research programme will have to be interrupted for a while, in the national interest. Notice of your own suspension will reach you by messenger at eight o'clock in the morning.

Kerner Paul, listen – you don't know how many people get their hands on this . . . my lab – the Whitehall secretariat, the turnkeys, the Minister's wife, his mistress – who knows? – also it could be an American Embassy copy before it receives the Washington prefix. There's probably fifty, sixty people, the channel means nothing.

Blair The pages were photographed on some kind of table-top, I expect a little hurriedly as is often the way in these affairs. The last page – photograph number six – is not well framed. You can see how it happens: the pages were pinned together at top left and turned over one by one, and the five turned pages have twisted the sixth page a little askew. The frame has caught the edge of a further document lying underneath.

He reaches into his dossier again and produces another photograph which he slides down the table.

This is the enlargement. It is in fact a set of angular distributions of neutron production on a uranium target in a cyclotron, whatever that may be and I don't want you to tell me. The important point is that taking the two documents together, we are talking about something which has a circulation of three, which is why I thought I'd bring you together for a chat, just between ourselves for a moment.

He includes Hapgood and Ridley who stay expressionless.

I'm sorry it's awkward for you and Mrs Hapgood but these things have to be faced.

Kerner (*indicating Ridley*) What about him? Isn't it awkward for him?

Blair Yes, but not in isolation. For reasons I can go into if you wish. Ridley – Mr Ridley – and Mrs Hapgood are tied together on this one, for better or worse. (*Pause.*) Well, I'll explain, then.

Kerner No, it is not necessary. (*He pushes the photographs back towards Blair.*) Not hurried, only careless.

Hapgood (*just conversation*) Joseph, don't do this. I don't need it. Tell the truth.

Kerner The truth is what Paul knows it is.

Hapgood (*to Blair*) He's lying to you because he thinks it's me.

Blair waits. Hapgood starts to lose control of her tone.

Oh, wake up, Paul! Why would he? (*to Kerner*) Why would you? Why would you give away your work?

Kerner Because it's mine to give. Whose did you think it was? Yours? Who are you? You and Blair? Dog-catchers. And now you think I am your dog – be careful the dog didn't catch you.

Hapgood Don't give me that! (*to Blair*) He's straight, you know damn well he's straight – he's my joe!

Kerner (*laughs, not kindly*) Pride. And your certainty is also amusing – you think you have seen to the bottom of things, but there is no bottom. I cannot see it, and you think you are cleverer than me?

Hapgood (*heatedly*) He's a physics freak and a maverick, the Russians picked him for this because he had a good defector profile and he didn't fool us, he fooled them, he despises the Soviets, he'd never play ball and he has no reason to. *He has no reason* – give me his reason.

Kerner They found out about Joe.

Pause. Hapgood poleaxed, as it were. Blair stays level.

Sorry.

Blair How?

Kerner I don't know.

Blair When?

Kerner More than a year. They came to me and said, 'Well, so you have a child with your British case-officer.

OK – congratulations, we were stupid, but now it is time to mend the damage. For the sake of the boy.'

Blair What did they mean by that?

Kerner What do *you* think, Paul? I didn't ask. (*to Hapgood*) I had to, Lilya.

Hapgood Joseph. All you had to do was tell me.

Kerner That is naive. (*to Blair*) Not just the normal reports. You should know this.

Blair What else?

Kerner My programme.

Blair This trap business?

Kerner They had the trap, they had the laser optics for handling the particles. They couldn't put it together – nobody could put it together because when you cool it to near-absolute zero –

Blair Joseph – get to it.

Kerner Everything was halted, it was like needing two trains to arrive together on the same line without destroying each other.

Blair So it couldn't be done?

Kerner Oh, yes. Like many things which are very difficult it turned out to be not so difficult if you have the right thought. These things are not, after all, trains, they travel at nearly the speed of light, and they are very small, so they can do things which are truly crazy. I was fortunate to have the right thought, and now it was possible to make an experiment with my thought. I worked out the programme for this.

Blair Did they know that?

Kerner No, we are speaking at last summer. June. But last month was the Geneva test and my programme was good. It could not be contained, of course; a good result is the gossip of the scientific world, and it was the end of the dance for me and my Soviet control. They said I had lied, broken the bargain, they said it was an ultimatum now, or they would take my son, and they absolutely would have taken him.

Blair So you gave it to them.

Kerner Of course.

Hapgood Paul –

Blair I know. Let me. (*to Kerner*) But the only meet you've had since your Geneva test was yesterday.

Kerner I mean yesterday. At the pool.

Blair At the pool? How did you deliver?

Kerner On disc.

Blair But that was a chickenfeed disc – we cleared the printout.

Kerner No, it was on the boot-tracks.

Blair Explain that.

Kerner The normal readout was the chickenfeed. There was a key-code for the hidden files.

   Hapgood stands up.

Blair (*to Hapgood*) Stay calm. (*He presses the intercom.*) Maggs – come in.

Kerner What is the matter?

   Maggs enters from his office.

Blair (*calmly*) Oh, Maggs . . . get Mrs Hapgood's son to the phone, would you? – headmaster, matron, anybody, but fast.

Hapgood unfreezes.

Hapgood I'll call the payphone, his dorm hasn't gone up.

Kerner It's all right – they don't want him now –

Blair Go, Maggs!

Maggs But Joe isn't there, sir . . . Merryweather came back. Joe wasn't in school – he had permission . . . well, Mrs Hapgood sent for him to be picked up, the driver had a letter –

Blair Merryweather?

Maggs He came back at about half past three. (*to Hapgood*) I'm sorry . . . I didn't know you'd be out – it's in your box –

Hapgood *Oh, Christ*, Maggs.

Blair (*to Maggs*) Go and check.

Maggs goes out. Hapgood has found Merryweather's message in her in-tray. It is in a sealed envelope which she opens.

Kerner But I gave them everything –

Blair I'm afraid not –

Kerner Yes I did – I delivered –

Blair Stop talking, Joseph – we intercepted your delivery, they never got your disc.

Kerner You blowed it! You bloody fool!

Ridley seems to be out of it. He approaches the desk and picks up the photoframe and looks at it for a moment.

Ridley (*to himself*) God Almighty.

Blair goes to the door and opens it.

Blair (*shouts*) Maggs!

Hapgood (*calmly enough*) He isn't there, Paul. (*She has been looking at the contents of Merryweather's message.*)

Kerner (*to Hapgood*) They won't hurt him, they'll want to trade.

Blair I know that but we can't trade. (*to Hapgood*) He's not harmed, he's in a safe house with babysitters – you *know* that. They'll find a way to talk to you but it won't even come to that – it's a local initiative and a stupid one, it's going to be stopped from the Moscow end, I promise you, the diplomatic route and no nonsense –

Kerner (*loud*) Don't do that – they can't admit to a thing like this.

Blair You're out of it now –

Kerner You will put them in a corner –

Blair Then they can crawl out of it –

Hapgood For God's sake shut up!

It has become a row.

Ridley Why don't we just give it to them? What does it matter? Wait for the call and make the trade. If it comes tonight make it tonight, a kid like that, he should be in bed anyway, we can all get some sleep.

Look, what are we talking about? Are we talking about a list of agents in place? Are we talking about blowing the work names? The cover jobs in the Moscow Embassy? Any of those and all right, the boy maybe has to take his chances. But what has Kerner got? (*derisively*) The solution to the anti-particle trap! Since when was the anti-particle trap a problem?

For a moment Blair wavers. Then –

Blair Shut up, Ridley. (*to Hapgood*) I'll take that disc.

Ridley Don't give it to him.

Blair Ridley, you're out of line.

Ridley (*loses his temper*) Don't tell me I'm out of line, I know about this and you don't know fuck, all you know is to talk Greek. Kerner is supposed to be the one with the brains and he doesn't have enough to know he's pimping fantasies for people with none. There's nothing on that disc except physics and it will stay physics till little Hapgood is a merchant banker. *There is no gadget here. It has no use.* It's the instructions for one go on a billion dollar train set, and that's all it is. Strategic Defense, my arse.

(*To Kerner*) Listen, you tell them the first time I say something which isn't true and I'll stop. Livermore thinks it can make an X-ray laser to knock out a ballistic missile and Kerner's bit of this is a new kind of percussion cap for the bullet: when the bullet is a laser you need a percussion cap like an H-bomb, one bomb per bullet, naturally it destroys the gun as well as the target but what the hell, all right, you trigger the bomb and the X-rays will lase for you, and if you can do it by putting matter together with anti-matter you get a nice clean bang, no fallout, and Kerner gets the Peace Prize. Leave aside that all the particle accelerators on earth produce no more anti-matter in a year than will make a bang like twenty pounds of dynamite. Leave aside that to make the system work up there in the sky you need about fifty million lines of information code and at NASA they can't handle half a million without launch delays and the Russians probably wouldn't wait. Leave everything aside and there's still the problem that Kerner's bullet can't shoot inside the earth's atmosphere. The gun in the sky is no good for anything except ICBMs coming up through the ceiling, and you've got five minutes because after that your target has turned into eighteen warheads hidden in a hundred decoys and a million bits of tinfoil – and *that's* only until the Russians work out the fast-burn booster which will give you a fighting window of sixty seconds. I mean, this is the military application of Kerner's physics if you're looking ten years ahead, minimum. It's a joke. I'd trade it for my cat if I had a cat.

(*To Blair*) And you'll blanket this operation and play ransom games with the little bugger – for what? Do you think you won't screw it up?

Blair (*to Hapgood as though it's just the two of them*) There isn't a *choice*. I'm running this and I'm not giving you a choice. You have to trust me.

Pause. Hapgood opens a drawer in her desk, takes out the electronic 'key', opens the safe, removes a disc-box, closes the safe, gives the box to Blair.

(*Going, to Kerner*) You're with me.

Kerner Lilya . . .

Hapgood Do everything Paul says.

Kerner follows Blair out, leaving the door open. Hapgood sits quietly, looking at nothing. Ridley doesn't quite know what to do with himself.

Ridley Sorry. (*He gets up and moves towards the door.*)

Hapgood Ridley, close the door.

Ridley closes the door.

I gave him the dummy.

Ridley What?

Hapgood I gave him the dummy disc from your briefcase.

Ridley Christ almighty.

Hapgood If you don't like it you'd better say.

Ridley Like it or not we can't do it, we'll never be clear.

Hapgood We're already in front. They made contact – Blair missed it.

Ridley How?

Hapgood (*taking the card from the potted plant*) Interflora. 'Mum. – I'll phone tomorrow, two o'clock.' I thought – it's not Mother's Day.

Ridley Listen – tell Blair. It's no good without him – he'll have the watchers outside your flat before you get home, you'll be babysat like the Queen of England, nothing will reach you, there'll be a tap on your phone and on every line into this building.

Hapgood Except this one (*the red one*). It's the one Joe will tell them, he knows the trip-code. I've always broken the rules.

Ridley And what then? You won't be able to go to the bathroom, let alone a meet.

Hapgood I know all of that.

Ridley That's if Blair isn't sitting here when the call comes in, he'll go where you go.

Hapgood I won't be here. You'll be here.

Ridley Jesus, I can't answer it. It has to be you.

Hapgood It will be me.

Ridley You can't be in two places at once.

Hapgood (*suddenly out of patience*) I'm not busking, Ridley, I know how to do this, so is it you and me or not?

559

Pause. Ridley nods.

I'll need two or three hours. Have you got a radio?

Ridley Not with me.

Hapgood takes her radio out of her bag and gives it to him.

Hapgood I'll reach you on it: don't try to talk to me on anything else. Don't go home, go to a hotel.

Ridley Mother, I know what to do. (*He goes to leave.*) Will you be all right?

Hapgood (*nods*) Stay close.

Ridley It's all right, I'm with you.

But she spoils it for him.

Hapgood That thing's got a two-mile range, stay close.

Ridley nods and goes, closing the door.
Hapgood waits. She opens a desk drawer and takes out another radio. She lays the radio on the desk and waits again. The radio must have a blink-light; perhaps we can see it. Hapgood picks it up.

(*To radio*) Is he clear?

Radio Green.

Hapgood (*to radio*) I'm here to be told.

She puts the radio back on the desk. She starts dialling on the red telephone. Maggs enters, wearing a topcoat.

Maggs Good night, Mrs Hapgood.

Hapgood Good night, Maggs. Thank you.

Maggs I won't ask.

Hapgood That's right, Maggs. By the way, I won't be in tomorrow.

Maggs I'll hold the fort. (*He leaves closing the door.*)

Hapgood (*into phone, brightly*) Hello! Who's that? Sandilands! Can you tell Hapgood it's his mother? Wait a minute, aren't you the one who sells boots? . . . no, no, it's all right – perfectly all right, in fact quite reasonable, I thought, you can't get much for a pound nowadays . . . Two *pounds?* But surely . . .? Oh, a pound *each* – well, fair enough, yes, I can see that . . . Yes, darling, I'll hold on for him –

> *In the middle of all that Blair has quietly entered the room and is collecting the contents of his dossier, sorting things out, putting them away.*

(*Mutters*) Merchant banker . . .?

Blair You know, you're going to get into such trouble one day . . . *I mean, that's the Downing Street one-to-one red line* – what are they supposed to think when they pick it up and it's *busy?*

Hapgood Oh God, so it is. (*huffily*) It's a perfectly natural mistake, Joe uses it far more than they do.

Blair That's my point. (*grumbling*) You use the security link with Ottawa to play chess, you arrive in Vienna after dog-legging through Amsterdam on a false passport and then proceed to send postcards home as if you're on bloody holiday, you use an intelligence officer on government time to dispatch football boots around the country . . . For someone who's so safe you're incredibly, I don't know, there's a little anarchist inside you, I wish you wouldn't . . .

Hapgood Don't be cross, I'm tired.

(*Into phone*) Oh – thank you, Sandilands – I'll hang on, Paul . . .

Blair Mm?

Hapgood I know this isn't necessary and don't start getting cross again, I –

Blair (*somehow irritated, apparently*) It's all right, it's done –

Hapgood You don't know what I –

Blair Yes, yes, watchers at the school till this thing is over, and Cotton has joined the ground-staff, marking out the rugger pitches, do him good, he was looking a bit pasty.

Hapgood I absolutely refuse to live without you, do you understand that?

Blair Of course.
    You know, it's going to be tricky doing the swap without a boy to swap.

Hapgood Well, we'll just have to do the best we can, won't we?

Blair Of course.

Hapgood (*into phone*) Oh, hello, Joe! Are you all right, darling?

Kerner enters with a bottle of vodka and three cups.

Kerner Magnificent.

Blair Thank you.

Kerner No, me. You were terrible. I never believed a word of it.

Hapgood (*into phone*) No, it was just to tell you not to phone tomorrow in case you were going to. I'm away.

Blair (*to Kerner*) Not even the photographs?

Hapgood (*into phone*) Oh, good.

Kerner The photographs I liked.

Blair Yes?

Hapgood (*into phone*) *In* the hutch? Well, I was nearly right.

> *Meanwhile Kerner has poured three tots of vodka into the cups.*

Thank you, Joseph.

> *Kerner and Blair toast each other and knock back the vodka.*

(*Into phone*) Well, you're daft – do they fit?

Blair (*to Kerner*) Come on, then.

> *Blair puts his cup down and leaves the room. Kerner closes the door after him and remains in the room.*

Hapgood (*into phone*) That's all right . . . when is Saturday? The day after tomorrow . . . well, probably, I might. Home or away?

> *Kerner gently takes the phone from her and listens to the phone for a few moments and then gives it back to her, and leaves the room.*

(*Into phone*) Yes, I'm here. Yes, all right. Well, let me know on Saturday morning.

Yes, Joe, I'm here to be told.

> *She puts the phone down.*

SCENE TWO

*Now we are in a new place. The first and obvious thing
about it is that it is a photographer's studio. The second
thing is that it is also where somebody lives; the room
is skimpily furnished as a living room. There is a front
door and also another closeable door leading to the
other rooms in what is evidently the photographer's flat.
There is a telephone.*

*It is mid-morning. The room is empty. The doorbell
rings. Hapgood comes flying out from the other door.
We haven't seen her like this. She is as different from
her other self as the flat is different from her office; the
office being rather cleaner, tidier and better organized.
Hapgood opens the front door, and it's Ridley. Ridley
has been shopping: glossy Bond Street carrier bags.
He stares at her.*

Ridley Mrs Newton?

Hapgood (*casually*) Oh, shit.

Ridley I'm Ernest.

Hapgood Well, you're not what I want, so keep your
clothes on.

Stupid bugger! Not you, darling, come in anyway. (*She
is already heading for the telephone.*) What did they do?
Pick you from the catalogue? I'll try and sort it out –
charge them for half a day if it looks like their fault – it
won't be the first time – (*now into the phone*) It's Celia, I
want Fred.

Would you mind not wandering around.

*Her last remark needs explaining. Ridley has dropped
his parcels and is now, frankly, casing the joint. He is
not taking a lot of notice of her. He moves around*

*coolly as if he owns the place, and in due course he
leaves the room, disappearing through the 'kitchen
door'.*

(*Into phone*) Hello, darling, you're losing your grip –
I said a Roman soldier, not an Italian waiter, and also
he looks queer to me . . . Don't tell me what I mean,
you're gay, he's queer, he's got a queer look about him,
he won't sell bamboo shoots to a fucking panda, never
mind boxer shorts . . . Well, I'll look at his body and
let you know – Fred? – Have you gone? – No, the phone
clicked – (*She looks around and finds that the room
is empty.*) Hey – ? What's his name? (*She calls out.*)
Victor!

Ridley wanders back into the room.

Ridley (*casual*) Hang up.

Hapgood What do you think you're doing? (*into phone*)
Is he a regular? Well, I don't fancy him –

*That's as far as the phone call gets because Ridley, still
maintaining a sort of thoughtful cruise, disconnects
the call.*

Now listen –

He looks at her. She goes from fear to relief.

You're Betty's friend. God, I am sorry, darling, I'm Celia,
don't be offended, being rude about the models is the
house style, it saves a lot of nonsense about being paid
for the reshoot. And anyway you do look like an Italian
waiter. What does Betty want? – I don't owe her any
favours, she never does me any, I mean there must be
lots of photographic work going in the spy racket. She
says I won't keep my mouth shut – can you believe it?
Can you smell burning? – Oh, sod!

She leaves the room in a hurry. Ridley has been looking at her like somebody looking at a picture in a gallery. He reaches into his jacket and produces his radio.

Ridley (*on radio*) Mother.

Hapgood (*on radio*) Ridley.

Ridley You're out of your fucking mind.

Hapgood (*on radio*) What's the matter?

Ridley She may be your twin but there the resemblance ends. She's a pot-head, it reeks, she's growing the stuff in the window-box, she won't stop talking, she picks her nose, she looks like shit, I mean it doesn't *begin* . . .

Hapgood (*on radio*) Where is she?

Ridley In the kitchen burning things . . .

Hapgood (*on radio*) I'm signing off.

Ridley No, listen –

But evidently she has cut him off. He puts his radio away and goes to pick up his shopping. He puts it on the sofa, perhaps, and anyway starts unloading the carrier bags. They are full of clothes in tissue paper. There's also a shoe box and other stuff. It all adds up to one outfit, suitable for the office.

While he is doing this Hapgood bangs her way back into the room (she probably wouldn't have bothered to close the door so a door on a spring might be useful).

She is nibbling the unburned portion of a croissant, which rapidly gets as far as the wastepaper basket.

Hapgood And you made me warm my croissant to a frazzle. What have you got there?

Ridley Clothes, shoes, make-up . . . Is there a bathroom?

Hapgood No, we pee in the sink. Can you try to show a little charm?

Ridley Your sister said do what he tells you.

Hapgood So what?

Ridley Run a bath.

Hapgood Why?

Ridley You look as if you need one.

Hapgood Now just a minute –

Ridley And wash your hair.

Hapgood *Just a minute.* I'm not going to a party, I've got a busy morning.

Ridley Victor isn't coming. It's ten twenty and we're leaving here at one fifteen, just under three hours. I'll explain as you go.

Hapgood Will you indeed. (*She picks up the phone again and starts dialling.*)

Ridley Who are you calling?

Hapgood I want to talk to Betty.

Without hurrying much, because she is still dialling, Ridley yanks the phone cord which comes away from the wall bringing fragments of plastic and bits of skirting-board with it.

Ridley You don't talk to Betty, you don't talk to anybody, in fact you don't talk so much in general, and you don't swear at all, get used to it, please.

Hapgood You bloody gangster, that telephone is my livelihood!

Ridley Is that right? You'll have to fall back on photography.

> *She swings at him. He catches her wrist. With his other hand he takes a wad of bank notes out of one pocket.*

That's two thousand pounds. (*He lets go of her wrist and takes a similar wad out of another pocket.*) So's this. That's now, this is later.

Hapgood What is it for?

Ridley It's for looking nice and not talking dirty, and answering a telephone. After that, we'll see.

Hapgood Why?

Ridley I'll tell you when it's time.

Hapgood Then why would I do it?

Ridley For the money, your sister said. I want to know about you and your sister, sibling bribery is a new one on me.

Hapgood Well, you can go and –

Ridley Every time you swear I'm taking £50 out of this bundle. You'll get what's left.

Hapgood – fuck yourself.

> *Ridley separates a £50 note from the bundle of money (which is perhaps secured by a rubberband), and puts the remainder back into his pocket.*

That's theft.

Ridley No, it's arson. (*Because his hand has come out of his pocket with his cigarette lighter with which he sets fire to the note.*)

Hapgood You're all nutters. I knew it then. Is Betty in trouble?

Ridley When?

Hapgood If she's in trouble, I don't mind helping.

Ridley You knew it when?

Hapgood Whenever – all those years ago when we did the interviews.

Ridley Tell me about that.

Hapgood I failed the attitude test. Betty was exactly their cup of tea so they kept her anyway.

Ridley Anyway?

Hapgood They were seeing twins – it was a phase. Nutters is not the word.

Ridley laughs.

Ask Betty, they had a reason, she'll know what it was. Well, that cheered you up.

Ridley Yes. Will you have a bath and talk nice and do what I tell you?

Hapgood Is it her money?

Ridley Not exactly.

Hapgood I wouldn't take it if it was hers.

Ridley Fine. It's ten twenty-five.

Hapgood What did you say your name was?

Ridley Ernest. Do you want me to scrub your back?

Hapgood No, thank you.

Ridley Take the clothes. They're for you to put on.

She gathers them up to take them out.

Hapgood They're not really me.

Ridley That's right.

Hapgood leaves the room. Ridley stays where he is.
The next time he moves, he's somebody else.

INTER-SCENE

So we lose the last set without losing Ridley. When the
set has gone, Ridley is in some other place . . . which
may be a railway station, or alternatively a place where
boats come in, or an airport; whatever the design will
take, really. The main thing is that he is a man arriving
somewhere. He carries a suitcase. He is a different
Ridley.
It's like a quantum jump.
And now we lose him. Perhaps he walks out. Perhaps
the scene change has been continuous and he is now
erased by its completion.

SCENE THREE

Blair and Kerner are at the zoo. Blair has the 'pink
diagram'.

Blair I must confess I always thought that one Ridley
was enough and occasionally surplus to an ideal
arrangement of the universe. Now we've got one in
Kensington and one who could be anywhere. I imagine
he doesn't hang around, he'd come in and out as required.
Could be on a British passport, more likely not. This is,
of course, assuming that he exists. Does this (*the diagram*)
prove twins?

Kerner No. An invisible man is also a correct solution.

Blair You chaps.

Kerner Mathematics does not take pictures of the world, it's only a way of making sense. Twins, waves, black holes – we make bets on what makes best sense. In Athens, in Paris and at the Pool, two Ridleys satisfy the conditions. He was his own alibi. So we're betting on twins. But we need to be lucky also, and today is Friday; is it the thirteenth?

Blair You chaps don't believe in that.

Kerner Oh, we chaps! Niels Bohr lived in a house with a horseshoe on the wall. When people cried, for God's sake Niels, surely *you* don't believe a horseshoe brings you luck!, he said, no, of course not, but I'm told it works even if you don't believe it.

Blair continues to look grave.

What is the matter, Paul?

Blair Those photographs. Think of Ridley sitting there. He's been sending film to Moscow and now here are these prints, spread out on the table, courtesy of the Washington pouch. Awkward moment for him. And yet, suddenly he's in the clear. Kerner owns up. Well, we can't have Ridley sitting there wondering why you're owning up to his pictures. Ridley knew this wasn't his batch, because he photographed his pages flat, separately; they weren't pinned together by the corners and turned over. And those figures peeping out underneath, the whatsit production in the cyclone-whatever, they were nothing to do with him.

Kerner I assumed naturally they were not Ridley's pictures.

Blair Did you? I wish you'd said so. I wish you'd said, 'Paul where did you get that photo?' . . . because you see, those cycleclip numbers were pulled together from different sets, the way somebody might do it at the Moscow end, and it really upsets me, Joseph, that you weren't . . . I don't know . . . surprised.

Kerner Cyclotron, Paul. It's a sensible word. Cycleclip is bizarre by comparison. (*Pause.*) Poor Paul. Everybody is a suspect. (*reminded*) Explain something to me. I forgot to ask Elizabeth. Prime suspect: it's in nearly all the books. I don't understand. A prime is a number which won't divide nicely, and all the suspects are prime. It's the last thing to expect with a suspect. You must look for *squares*. The product of twin roots. Four, nine, sixteen . . . what is the square root of sixteen?

Blair Is this a trick question?

Kerner For you, probably.

Blair Four, then.

Kerner Correct. But also minus four. Two correct answers. Positive and negative. (*Pause.*) I'm not going to help you, you know. Yes – no, either – or . . . You have been too long in the spy business, you think everybody has no secret or one big secret, they are what they seem or they are the opposite. You look at me and think: *Which is he?* Plus or minus? If only you could figure it out like looking into me to find my root. And then you still wouldn't know. We're all doubles. Even you. Your cover is Bachelor of Arts first class, with an amusing incomprehension of the sciences, but you insist on laboratory standards for reality, while I insist on its artfulness. So it is with us all, we're not so one-or-the-other. The one who puts on the clothes in the morning is the working majority, but at night – perhaps in the

572

moment before unconsciousness – we meet our sleeper –
the priest is visited by the doubter, the Marxist sees the
civilizing force of the bourgeoise, the captain of industry
admits the justice of common ownership.

Blair And you – what do you admit?

Kerner My estrangement.

Blair I'm sorry.

Kerner I'm thinking of going home, perhaps you know.

Blair No, I didn't.

Kerner Ah, well.

Blair It may be tricky for you.

Kerner Do you mean leaving or arriving?

Blair That's roughly what I'm asking *you*?

Kerner Of course. Dog or dog-catcher. I forget. It's true
that when the KGB came to me in Kaliningrad I had
already thought of coming West, but to be honest the
system I hated was the vacuum tube logic system. We
were using computers which you had in museums.
I wasn't seeking asylum, I was seeking an IBM 195.

Blair No. They put you up to it and Elizabeth turned
you. You were her joe.

Kerner Yes, I was. There is something terrible about
love. It uses up all one's moral judgement. Afterwards it
is like returning to a system of values, or at least to the
attempt.

Blair (*angrily*) Yes, values. It's not all bloody computers,
is it?

Kerner No. The West is morally superior, in my opinion.
It is unjust and corrupt like the East, of course, but here

it means the system has failed; at home it means the system is working. But the system can change.

Blair No, it can't. Come on, Joseph, *you know them* – Budapest in '56 – Prague in '68 – Poland in '81 – we've been there! – and it's not going to be different in East Berlin in '89. They can't afford to lose.

Kerner (*shrugs*) It's not my job to change it. My friend Georgi has offered to arrange things if I want to go.

Blair Why are you telling me?

Kerner I declined his offer.

Blair I'm glad, Joseph.

Kerner I prefer British Airways.

Pause.

Blair You should have accepted.

Kerner (*angrily*) Oh, yes! – You don't want to look, and then you'll get spy pattern.

Blair I like to know what's what.

Kerner Of course! Yes – no, either – or.

Blair That's right. You're this or you're that, and you know which. Prophecy is a pastime I can't afford, I've got one of my people working the inside lane on false papers and if she's been set up I'll feed you to the crocodiles.

Kerner One of your *people*? Oh, Paul. *You* would betray her before I would. My mamushka.

Blair Good. Good, Joseph. (*He seems pleased by the way that went.*) Now. Is the sister thing going to work?

Kerner Oh, yes. I was afraid of it, but with Mr Ridley it will be all right. (*He starts to leave, pause.*) I never saw

Elizabeth sleeping. Interrogation hours, you know. She said, 'I want to *sleep* with you.' But she never did. And when I learned to read English books I realized that she never said it, either. (*He walks away.*)

SCENE FOUR

Hapgood's office. It's empty.
   The door is opened with a key from the outside.
Ridley enters the office.

Ridley (*addressing Hapgood outside*) Move.

Hapgood enters behind him. She is wearing the clothes which he brought to the flat.
   Ridley closes the door. Hapgood looks around.
   Ridley has a bag, perhaps a sports holdall.

Sit there.

Ridley does everything smoothly and quickly. He riffles through a stack of printed documents (technical magazines perhaps) on the desk and extracts a sealed envelope, which he tears open. It contains a small key and a scribble.

Hapgood What if somebody comes in?

Ridley It's your office, for God's sake. (*He gives her the key.*) Middle drawer.

Hapgood uses the key to open the middle drawer of the desk.

Remote key.

Hapgood This?

She shows him the electronic key for the safe. Ridley takes it. He consults the scribble, programmes the key,

575

opens the safe. From the safe he takes a disc-box – a new one, i.e. a sealed once-only box of the same type. He closes the safe. He puts the disc-box into his bag, together with the torn envelope and the scribble. During this:

Are you going to tell me what I'm doing here?

Ridley Sure. Any phone that rings, don't pick it up. I'll pick it up.

He picks up the red telephone, looks at its underneath, puts it down again; from the bag he takes a simple 'eavesdrop' connection, a single ear-piece ready to be wired up into a telephone receiver; and a screwdriver.
 At that moment, the door opens and Maggs walks in, with a file, much as yesterday.

Maggs Good afternoon Mrs Hapgood, you came in after all. Do you want to see the decrypts?

Hapgood looks at Ridley.

Ridley Hello, Maggs . . . aren't you supposed to be having lunch?

Maggs Yes, sir.

Ridley Well, piss off then. Go to the pub.

Maggs I was in the pub. (*to Hapgood*) I got the desk to bleep me if you came in – just the top one, really, it's green-routed and Sydney's been on twice this morning.

Hapgood Has he?

Maggs Sydney – they only want a yes or no.

Ridley Let them wait.

Hapgood No, I can do that.

Ridley Are you sure, Mother?

Hapgood What's the matter with you today, Ridley? (*She takes the 'top one' from Maggs and peruses it with interest.*) Mm . . .

Ridley Perhaps you'd like me to . . .

Hapgood Fascinating.

Maggs Just a yes or no.

Hapgood Yes! Definitely yes! (*She passes the paper smartly back to Maggs.*) Thank you, Maggs. I'll do the rest later.

Maggs McPherson came in if you want it.

Hapgood Really?

Ridley It's five minutes to two, Mother.

Hapgood I want to know about McPherson.

Maggs Bishop to queen two.

Pause.

Hapgood Right.

Ridley *Mother.*

The red phone rings. Maggs lifts it up.

Maggs (*to phone*) Mrs Hapgood's office . . . just a moment. (*He gives the phone to Hapgood and leaves.*)

Ridley Shit!

Hapgood What do I do?

Ridley Talk!

Ridley has two desperate concerns: to wire up his 'eavesdrop' and to prompt Hapgood. But it's hopeless, a mess.

Hapgood (*to phone*) Hello . . . yes, it's her, it's me . . .

Ridley *'I want to talk to Joe'* . . . *'I want to talk to Joe!'*

Hapgood (*covering the phone*) I can't hear! (*into phone*) Yes . . . Eleven thirty . . . (*to Ridley*) Someone wants a meeting.

Ridley Where? Keep them talking, ask for Joe . . .

Hapgood Yes . . . Where? . . . Right . . .

Ridley is nowhere near ready when she puts the phone down.

Ridley I'll kill you for this! – Eleven thirty where? *Where?*

Hapgood is still contemplating the phone warily.

Hapgood Ten Downing Street.

Ridley *What?* Oh, Jesus!

Hapgood Was that it?

Ridley No. I thought they were early.

Hapgood Who's Joe?

Ridley ignores her, he works on the red phone.

Listen, I can't do this if you don't tell me what I'm doing.

Ridley I'll tell you when it's time to tell you. God almighty . . . I ought to slap you bow-legged.

Hapgood You don't mean Betty's Joe, do you? Ernie?

Ridley Ridley.

Hapgood Ridley. What's the silly cow been up to?

Ridley Don't you like her?

Hapgood Of course I like her, she's my sister.

Ridley completes his work, and pauses to consider her.
He's unsettled, somehow thrown by seeing her in this
office, in these clothes . . . She is so obviously
Hapgood.

Ridley Mrs Newton. What happened to *him*? You're
divorced?

Hapgood I'll say. Bastard owes me thousands. Actually
it was Mr Newton who did for Betty and me. She said
he'd go bad, warned me off, sister to sister. So I crossed
her off my list and married him. Then he went bad. So
of course I never forgave her.
  Do you mean she plays chess without a board?

Ridley Looks like it.

Hapgood That sounds like her.

Ridley She's something.

Hapgood Showing off, I meant.

Ridley Why aren't you close?

Hapgood Well, she was always the scholarship girl and
I was the delinquent. Having the kid was good for her,
she always thought the delinquents had the bastards and
the scholarship girls had the wedding. It shook up her
view of the world, slightly. Do you mind if I light up?

Ridley She doesn't smoke.

Hapgood It's all right, it's not a real cigarette.

She puts a home-made cigarette in her mouth; Ridley
snatches it away and keeps it.

Ridley For God's sake, don't you know where you are?

Hapgood So what do we do now?

Ridley *(looking at his watch)* We wait. *(He leans over to reach the buttons on Hapgood's desk.)* When I do this, *(He snaps his fingers.)* you say, 'No calls, Maggs, no interruptions.' *(He snaps his fingers.)*

Hapgood No calls, Maggs, no interruptions.

Maggs's Voice Yes, ma'am.

Satisfied for the moment, but nervy, Ridley paces.

Hapgood He probably thinks . . .

Ridley Yeh, nice thought.

Hapgood Speak for yourself.

Ridley I was.

Hapgood Don't fancy your fuckin' chances.

Pacing, Ridley, as though absentmindedly, takes the bundle of money out of his pocket, detaches a £50 note and sets fire to it with his lighter. He carries on pacing, she carries on looking at him.

Sit down, for God's sake.

Ridley sits at the table.

Ten of hearts.

Ridley What about it?

Hapgood Ten of hearts – now you.

Ridley sighs.

Ridley King of hearts.

Hapgood Two of clubs.

Ridley Well, what are we playing?

Hapgood Go on.

Ridley Ace of spades.

Hapgood Seven of diamonds.

Ridley Haven't you got any spades?

Hapgood Play your cards.

Ridley Six of hearts.

Hapgood Two of hearts.

Ridley This is stupid. Nine of clubs.

Hapgood Jack of clubs.

Ridley Jack of spades.

Hapgood Snap!! Bad luck . . .

Ridley jumps irritatedly to his feet, and then the red phone rings.

Ridley *Leave it!*
Listen – Betty's Joe has been kidnapped – this is the people who took him.

He takes her left hand, calmly, lays it palm-down on the desk, and using his own hand as a blade he chops her hand across the knuckles, with coolly judged force, enough to make her cry out with pain.

You want to talk to Joe – where's Joe, where's Joe?

He lifts the red phone now and puts it into her right hand, meanwhile putting the extra earpiece in his ear. Hapgood is whimpering and disoriented.

Hapgood (*into phone*) Hello, where's Joe, I want to talk to Joe – I – Yes – yes – yes –
Yes. I heard – can I talk to –

Ridley relaxes. He takes the phone from her gently and replaces it. The phone call has taken perhaps

*fifteen seconds. Hapgood springs away from the desk,
from him, crying, comforting her injured hand.*

Ridley You were very good!

Hapgood You bloody maniac!

*Ridley is disconnecting his eavesdrop, replacing
everything into his bag.*

Where's Betty? – is it true about Joe?

Ridley Yes, it's true. But we'll get him back. Eight hours
to kill.

*Ridley retrieves her cigarette from his pocket, lights it
and puts it in her mouth.
    Hapgood draws on the cigarette, still shocked,
trembling, settling down.*

You were fine. We can go now. Me first. Count twelve
and I'll see you outside. (*He picks up his bag. Carefully
he takes away her cigarette, takes a drag himself, and
keeps the cigarette. He opens the door.*) Welcome to the
firm.

*Ridley leaves. Left alone, Hapgood relaxes, although
her hand is still painful. Maggs enters, anxious.*

Maggs Is everything all right, Mrs Hapgood?

Hapgood Yes, Maggs – everything's fine. (*She heads
through the open door.*) Queen to king one.

Maggs (*following her out*) Queen to king one.

SCENE FIVE

*A cheap hotel room. It is evening; dark. Perhaps a neon
sign outside. Hapgood, fully dressed, has gone to sleep
on the bed. Ridley stands watching her. Perhaps he is*

changing into the clothes which he will wear in the next scene. Ridley takes out his radio.

Ridley (*to radio*) Mother.

No answer.

(*To radio*) Mother.

No answer.

(*Louder to radio*) Mother – where the hell are you!

Hapgood, on the bed, has stirred awake.

Hapgood How much longer?

Ridley A couple of hours. (*He puts his radio away and takes his gun out of his holster and checks it.*)

Hapgood Ernest . . . I hardly dare ask you this, but is your mother in the secret service too?

Ridley ignores that. He puts his gun back into the holster.

What's that for, Ernie?

Ridley It's for killing people. It's a gun.

Hapgood Do you kill people, Ernie?

Ridley You'll be the second.

Hapgood I don't like this.

Ridley Me neither. Somebody's lying to somebody. They're lying to her or she's lying to me.

Hapgood Would she lie to you, Ernie?

Ridley Telling lies is Betty's habit, sweetheart – lies, fraud, entrapment, blackmail, sometimes people die, so Betty can know something which the opposition thinks she doesn't know, most of which doesn't matter a fuck, and that's just the half they didn't *plant* on her – so she's lucky if she comes out better than even, that's the edge she's in it for, and if she's thinking now it wasn't worth one sleepless night for her little prep-school boy, good for her, she had it coming.

Hapgood Maybe she did.

Ridley She should have given him a daddy instead of getting her buzz out of running joes to please an old bastard who . . . (*A thought strikes him, strikes him as funny.*) who's been running *her* for years!

Hapgood What do you mean, Ernest?

Ridley Your sister carries a torch. When it came to a choice she traded in a daddy for a joe who would have been blown overnight if he was known to be the father.

Hapgood *Talk English!*

Ridley I'll get her kid back for her but it's only personal. If she's set me up I'll kill her.

Hapgood You're potty about her, Ernest. I'm disappointed in you. You don't know if you're carrying a torch for her or a gun, no wonder you're confused. You're out on a limb for a boy she put there, while she was making the world safe for him to talk properly in and play the game. What a pal, I should have a friend like you.

Ridley It's not her fault. Do you think you cracked it taking snaps of fancy junk? She's all right. Anyway, I like kids, and you never know, now and again someone is telling the truth.

Hapgood You're all right, Ernest. You're just not her type.

Ridley Yeh, she says I'm not safe. Too damned right I'm not. If I was safe I wouldn't be in a whore's hotel with somebody's auntie waiting for a meet that smells like a dead cat.

Hapgood Where would you be?

Ridley Anywhere I like, with a solid gold box for a ticket.

Hapgood You can walk away, Ernie, it's only skirt.

Ridley Shut up.

Hapgood (*cranking up*) You'd better be sure, she plays without a board. You haven't got a prayer.

Ridley *Shut up!*

Hapgood If you think she's lying, walk away. If you think bringing back her son will make you her *type*, walk away. You won't get in the money, women like her don't pay out – take my advice and open the box.

Ridley (*grabbing her*) *Who the hell are you?*

Hapgood I'm your dreamgirl, Ernie – Hapgood without the brains or the taste.

She is without resistance, and he takes, without the niceties; his kiss looks as if it might draw blood.

SCENE SIX

The pool. Night. Empty. A towel hangs over the door of Cubicle One (any cubicle).
It is dark. Ridley (Two) enters from the lobby carrying a large torch. He looks around with the help of the torch. He moves upstage. We see only the torch now. The torch-beam comes back towards us. Ridley (One) walks into the beam. He has come from the showers (depending on the layout). He carries the sports bag. He approaches the

torch. The two men embrace briefly. Our Ridley remains: The one with the torch retires. (The torch, of course, changed hands upstage – here and subsequently we only clearly see, and only hear, the actor who plays Ridley.)

Ridley now opens his holdall, takes out a disc-box and posts it under the door with the towel on it. He removes the towel and enters Cubicle Two. He hangs the towel over that door.

Hapgood enters from the lobby. She pauses. Timid.

Hapgood Ernest . . .?

Ridley with the torch, reveals himself.

Ridley It's OK. Call the boy.

Hapgood hesitates.

Call the boy.

Hapgood Joe . . .

Joe (*out of sight*) Mummy . . .?

He appears from upstage in the cubicle area. Hapgood moves to where she can see him.

Hapgood Hello, darling. It's all right.

Ridley Stay there, Joe.

Joe halts.

Do it.

Hapgood opens her bag, takes the disc-box from it, and posts it under the door of Cubicle Two (where the towel hangs). She pulls the towel down and tosses it over the door into the cubicle. She comes back to Joe and takes his hand.

Hapgood Off we go.

Hapgood takes Joe out through the lobby doors, followed by Ridley.

When they have gone Ridley (Two) comes out of Cubicle Two, holding the towel and the disc which Hapgood had posted. He takes the towel to Cubicle One, where it had originally hung, and tosses it over the door. The door of the cubicle opens. Wates is inside. Wates has a gun.

Wates (*just conversation*) Hey, Ridley. Here's what you do. You walk, you don't talk.

Wates walks Ridley upstage into the dark cubicle area. Pause. Blair comes from upstage and approaches Cubicle One. He takes from the cubicle the disc which had been posted there. Blair moves out towards the lobby but before he gets there Ridley comes in. Ridley is amused.

Blair (*greeting*) Ridley.

Ridley laughs.

Ridley It never smelled Russian, not for a minute. It smelled of private profit. No wonder the kidnap was so clean. Uncle Paul. What a breeze.

Blair Except . . . surely . . .

Ridley Except the boy will tell. I'm thinking.

Blair I should.

Ridley There was no kidnap.

Blair Better.

Ridley There was never any kidnap. You and Hapgood.

Blair Much better.

Ridley You and Hapgood. Make it look right, make a mug of me and the sister, and afterwards both of you back in place like china dogs on the mantelpiece.

Blair Now you've lost me. Something about a sister.

Ridley The sister is perfect. I know about this. She's here and she's not here.

Blair I keep thinking you said sister.

Hapgood has now come in quietly from the lobby.

Surely you know Mrs Hapgood?

Ridley I know her sister better. (*to Hapgood*) Don't I?

She gives nothing away.

Give me a minute, I'm slow.

A radio talks, softly, briefly. It is in Hapgood's hand. She raises it to her mouth.

Hapgood Mother.

The radio mutters and stops. She puts the radio in her bag.

Ridley Listen, be yourself. These people are not for you, in the end they get it all wrong, the garbage cans are gaping for them. Him most. He's had enough out of you and you're getting nothing back, he's dry and you're the juice. We can walk out of here, Auntie.

Hapgood You should have opened the box.

Ridley I could have walked away with it any time and let the boy take his chances. This way you got both, my treat.

Hapgood There was nothing in there except a bleep.

Pause.

Ridley Well, now I don't know which one you are. One of them fucks and one of them –

Hapgood Don't, Ridley –

> *Ridley is going to kill her, as promised. Everything goes into slow motion, beginning with and including the sound of Hapgood's gun, lasting probably five seconds. Ridley has got as far as taking his gun out when Hapgood shoots him.*
>
> *Meanwhile, Wates is leaning into view, upstage, slightly late, gun in hand. Strobe lighting.*
>
> *Blair doesn't move.*
>
> *Meanwhile the cubicles are disappearing, and we are to find ourselves outside rather than inside the lobby doors. If the doors themselves remain the sign 'Men' is no longer reversed.*
>
> *Ridley (i.e. his body) is erased along with the cubicles and becomes a body on a stretcher, the face covered by a blanket. The gunshot and the strobe extend through this scene change. At the end of the change we are left with Hapgood, Blair and Wates, the stretcher with stretcher bearers, and the Ridley Twin, handcuffed, under arrest being led away. Ridley, passing the stretcher, manages to look at the face under the blanket. He cries out indistinctly and is led away (by Merryweather).*
>
> *There is the flashing blue light of an ambulance offstage. All this happens swiftly, continuously from the gunshot.*

Blair (*to Wates angrily*) Where were *you*?

Wates I was second, he was third. (*to Hapgood*) Oh, you *mother*.

Blair (*to Wates*) I want that ambulance out of here.

Wates No rush.

Hapgood Ben –? It was the shoulder.

Wates No, ma'am.

Hapgood It was the shoulder.

Wates I'm sorry. It's not like targets.

Pause. Hapgood moves a few paces towards where the stretcher left and then comes back to Wates.

Hapgood Ben, thank you for your co-operation.

They shake hands.

Wates You bet. (*He leaves.*)

Blair Come on, Elizabeth, Joe's waiting.

Hapgood We said we'd do it without Joe.

Blair It had to look right.

Hapgood You lied to me.

Blair Without the boy it wouldn't have looked right.

Hapgood I was willing to risk it.

Blair I wasn't.

Hapgood I'll never forgive you for that, never ever.

Blair I know that. I knew that.

Hapgood And what am I supposed to tell him?

Blair Tell him it's a secret. Small boys understand that.

Hapgood What do you know about small boys?

Blair Well, I was one.

Hapgood Paul –

Blair No, no, you'll get over it.

Hapgood No.

Blair What about your network?

Hapgood *What network?!* Ridley's blown it inside out! Christ, Paul, I must have been buying nothing but lies and chickenfeed since Joe was in his pram!

Blair One has to pick oneself up and carry on. We can't afford to lose. It's them or us, isn't it?

Hapgood What is? What exactly? The game has moved on. Read the signs. It's over.

Blair Try telling that to the opposition.

Hapgood Oh, the KGB! The opposition! Paul we're just keeping each other in business, we should send each other Christmas cards – oh, f-f-fuck it, Paul!

So that's that.
Blair turns away, hesitates and leaves. The next time Hapgood moves she is standing by the rugby pitch.

SCENE SEVEN

Hapgood stands on the touchline. She isn't looking at much.
Kerner is standing some way behind her, wearing an overcoat.
Some rugby sounds.
Kerner comes down to join her.
Hapgood sees him.

Hapgood Joseph . . . You came to say hello?

Kerner On the contrary. (*He looks front, a bit puzzled. Gamely*) Interesting.

Hapgood It hasn't started yet. They're just practising.

Kerner Oh yes, which one is he?

Hapgood (*pointing*) New rugby boots. I'm awfully glad to see you.

Kerner (*spotting him*) Oh, yes.

Hapgood He'll come over when they take their track-suits off. I tried to find you this morning.

Kerner I was buying my ticket. Also a suitcase.

Hapgood I heard you've been sending your luggage on ahead for months. Does Paul know why?

Kerner (*shrugs*) Paul thinks I was a triple, but I was definitely not, I was past that, quadruple at least, maybe quintuple.

Hapgood They found out about Joe, didn't they? They turned you back again. You made up the truth.

Kerner It is nothing to worry, you know.

Hapgood I'm not worried. I'm out of it now. This is him.

> *Joe runs in, wearing his tracksuit, which he takes off now. His rugger kit is clean. The new boots.*

Joe Hello, Mum.

Hapgood Good luck, darling. This is Mr Kerner – Joseph. Another Joe.

Joe Hello, sir.

Kerner Hello. How are you?

Joe All rights'a, thankyous'a. (*to Hapgood*) Will you be here after?

Hapgood Yes, see you later.

She has the tracksuit. Perhaps the top half goes round her neck. Joe runs off. Pause.

Kerner Very nice. Very English. (*Pause.*) Of course, he *is* half English, one forgets that. Well . . . good.

Hapgood Do you want to stay for tea? They lay it on for parents.

Kerner Better not, I think.

Hapgood Oh, Joe.

She breaks down. He holds her, awkwardly.

Prosty, Josef. [I'm sorry, Joseph.]

Kerner *Da nyet – vyet u menya byl vybar, Lilichka.* [No, no. I had a choice too, Lilychka.]

Hapgood *Nyet tagda u tibya nye bylo vybora* – [You had no choice then.]

Kerner *Da – mu ya pashol . . . ya napishu kagda dayedu . . .* [Yes, I'd better go. I'll write when I get there.] (*He kisses her and starts to leave.*)

Hapgood How can you go? *How can you?*

She turns away. The game starts. Referee's whistle, the kick.
  After a few moments Hapgood collects herself and takes notice of the rugby.
  When the game starts Kerner's interest is snagged. He stops and looks at the game.

Come on St Christopher's – We can win this one! Get those tackles in! (*She turns round and finds that Kerner is still there. She turns back to the game and comes alive.*) Shove! – heel! – well heeled! – well out! – move it! – *move it,* Hapgood! – that's good – that's better!